414546

D1327801

BRITAIN'S IMPERIAL ADMINISTRATORS, 1858–1966

THE COMMEMORATIVE PLAQUES IN WESTMINSTER ABBEY

The Indian Civil Service

1858–1947
HERE ARE COMMEMORATED
THE CIVIL SERVICES
OF THE CROWN IN INDIA
LET THEM NOT BE FORGOTTEN
FOR THEY SERVED INDIA WELL

What doth the Lord require of thee
But to do justly and to love mercy

This Memorial Tablet was Unveiled by Her Majesty The Queen
6 March 1958

The Colonial Service

TO ALL THOSE WHO SERVED THE CROWN
IN THE COLONIAL TERRITORIES

Whosoever will be chief among you
Let him be your servant

This Memorial was Unveiled by Her Majesty Queen Elizabeth II
23 March 1966

The Sudan Civil Service

1898–1955
TO COMMEMORATE THE WORK OF MEN AND WOMEN OF OUR RACE
WHO LABOURED TO SERVE THE PEOPLE OF THE SUDAN

This Tablet was Erected 1960 Nisi Dominus frustra

(by courtesy of the Dean and Chapter)

Britain's Imperial Administrators, 1858–1966

Anthony Kirk-Greene

Emeritus Fellow
St Antony's College
Oxford

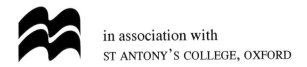

in association with
ST ANTONY'S COLLEGE, OXFORD

First published in Great Britain 2000 by
MACMILLAN PRESS LTD
Houndmills, Basingstoke, Hampshire RG21 6XS and London
Companies and representatives throughout the world

A catalogue record for this book is available from the British Library.

ISBN 0–333–73297–9

First published in the United States of America 2000 by
ST. MARTIN'S PRESS, INC.,
Scholarly and Reference Division,
175 Fifth Avenue, New York, N.Y. 10010

ISBN 0–312–22555–5

Library of Congress Cataloging-in-Publication Data
Kirk-Greene, A. H. M. (Hamilton Millard)
Britain's imperial administrators, 1858–1966 / Anthony Kirk-Greene.
p.   cm. — (St. Antony's series)
Includes bibliographical references and index.
ISBN 0–312–22555–5
1. Great Britain—Colonies—Administration—History.   2. Colonial
administrators—Great Britain—History.   I. Title.   II. Series: St.
Antony's series.
JV1060.K565   1999
321'.08—dc21
                                              99–15264
                                                  CIP

This book is printed on paper suitable for recycling and made from fully managed and
sustained forest sources.

10   9   8   7   6   5   4   3   2   1
09   08   07   06   05   04   03   02   01   00

Printed and bound in Great Britain by
Antony Rowe Ltd, Chippenham, Wiltshire

BLACKW

13·10·00

Contents

List of Tables

Acknowledgements

This book represents one of two complementary studies of the generic District Officer, the symbol of colonial authority and the personification of imperial government. Both are designed for post-imperial readers who, in contrast to their parents' generation, have never encountered a serving imperial administrator in their life, and for whom a career which annually attracted hundreds of British graduates in search of Crown Service overseas has not been an option for the past half-century. This first volume, primarily an institutional history of the formation and function of the District Officer, draws on the official and secondary literature and the published memoirs on Britain's three overseas civil services, the Indian Civil Service, the Colonial Administrative Service, and the Sudan Political Service, each of which came to a close forty to fifty years ago. Such an analytical account will serve as a necessary background to the second volume, a collective portrait of the District Officer in Africa (where three-quarters of the Colonial Service worked), which will principally draw on personal experience and private papers. The first paints the scene; the second depicts the actors. The motivation of both volumes is to respond to the challenge posed, publicly, in Jack Simmons' inaugural lecture at the University of Leicester all of fifty years ago, 'The thing that interests me most of all in the history of the British Empire [is] the lives of the men who made it'; and, privately, in fellow imperial historian Reginald Coupland's virtually contemporaneous assertion that 'Personality is the really interesting thing in history.' In the interpretation of both these prescriptions, as in the construction of both volumes, it is the study of the generic District Officer of imperial administration that stands at the centre.

For the generous opportunities to research into and reflect on the generic DO I have a list of acknowledgements almost as long as the time I have been involved with the topic. At one end, for the final period of research and writing up I am deeply grateful to the Leverhulme Trust for their award of an enabling Emeritus Fellowship. At the other end, in temporal terms, I have drawn on my own career of four wartime years in the Indian Army and ten years as a District Officer in Northern Nigeria, a learning experience indispensable to this project and unrepeatable today. In the middle, as it were, from 1957 until my retirement in 1992, there was first the privilege of designing and directing the pioneer training course for potential Nigerian District Officers at the Institute of Administration at Zaria, soon incorporated into the Ahmadu Bello University; and then, from 1967, the stimulation of working with colleagues in Commonwealth History at the University of Oxford and the extensive support of my work given by the Warden and Fellows of St Antony's College. There were, too, rewarding insights and knowledge gained from my good fortune in having been Research Officer for the oral history programme of the Oxford

Colonial Records Project in 1967–73 and then from 1980 to 1984 the Director of its archive retrieval and collection successor, the Oxford Development Records Project. In between, there have been regular visits to a dozen ex-colonial territories; conferences and seminars and symposia with fellow imperial historians in America, Canada, Australia and Europe; and over forty years of invoking skilled guidance from long-suffering librarians, above all the staffs of Rhodes House Library and Queen Elizabeth House at Oxford, the Hoover Institution at Stanford, the Centre for South Asian Studies at Cambridge, the Sudan Archive at Durham; and, in London, the former Colonial Office Library and Records, the India Office Library and Records (now moving to the new British Library buildings), the Foreign and Commonwealth Office Library, the Royal Commonwealth Society (since moved to Cambridge), the Institute of Commonwealth Studies and the Public Record Office, Kew.

Four expressions of personal gratitude remain to be recorded: to Margaret Matheson and Marie Ruiz, for their secretarial support; to Andrew Fairweather Tall and Richard Lofthouse, my research assistants; to Shehu Othman and Anne Rafique for their editorial assistance; and to my wife, Helen, who – quite literally – has enabled the whole writing of this book.

St Antony's College   Anthony Kirk-Greene
Oxford

List of Abbreviations

ADC	Aide-de-Camp; Assistant District Commissioner
ADO	Assistant District Officer
AEF	Afrique Equatoriale Française
AOF	Afrique Occidentale Française
BEA	British East Africa
BMA	British Military Administration
BSA	British South Africa Company
BWA	British West Africa
BWI	British West Indies
CA	Crown Agents (for the Colonies); Central Africa
CAC	Corps d'Administrateurs Coloniaux
CAS	Colonial Administrative Service
CBE	Commander of the Order of the British Empire
CMG	Companion of St Michael and St George
CO	Colonial Office
CRO	Commonwealth Relations Office
CS	Colonial Service
CSAB	Colonial Service Appointments Board
CSC	Civil Service Commission
CVO	Commander of the Royal Victorian Order
DC	District Commissioner; Deputy Commissioner
DO	District Officer
DSP	District Superintendent of Police
DTC	Department of Technical Co-operation
EICo	East India Company
FCO	Foreign and Colonial Office
FEA	French Equatorial Africa
FO	Foreign Office
FMS	Federal Malay States
FWA	French West Africa
GBE	Knight Grand Cross Order of the British Empire
GCB	Knight Grand Cross of the Bath
GCMG	Knight Grand Cross of St Michael and St George
GCVO	Knight Grand Cross of the Royal Victorian Order
GH	Government House
GO	General Order(s)
GOC	General Officer Commanding
HCT	High Commission Territory

HE	His Excellency
HH	His Honour
HMC	Head Masters Conference
HMG	Her (His) Majesty's Government
HMOCS	Her Majesty's Overseas Civil Service
IBEACo	Imperial British East Africa Company
ICS	Indian Civil Service
IO	India Office
IOLR	India Office Library and Records
IPS	Indian Political Service
ISC	Imperial Service College
KBE	Knight Commander Order of the British Empire
KCB	Knight Commander of the Bath
KCIE	Knight Commander of the Indian Empire
KCMG	Knight Commander of St Michael and St George
KCSI	Knight Commander of the Star of India
KCVO	Knight Commander of the Royal Victorian Order
KG	Knight of the Order of the Garter
KP	Knight of the Order of St Patrick
KT	Knight of the Order of the Thistle
LSC	Lump Sum Compensation
LVO	Lieutenant Royal Victorian Order
MAS	Malayan Administrative Service
MBE	Member of the Order of the British Empire
MCS	Malayan Civil Service
MVO	Member of the Royal Victorian Order
NA	Native Administration; Native Authority
NR	Northern Rhodesia
OAG	Officer Administering the Government
OBE	Officer of the Order of the British Empire
OCAP	Oxford Colonial Archives Project
OCRP	Oxford Colonial Records Project
ODA	Overseas Development Administration
ODRP	Oxford Development Records Project
OETA	Occupied Enemy Territory Administration
PC	Provincial Commissioner; Privy Councillor
PRO	Public Record Office
PS	Private Secretary
PSC	Public Service Commission
PSV	Private Secretary to the Viceroy
PUS	Permanent Under Secretary
RNCo	Royal Niger Company
SAD	Sudan Archive, Durham

SCS	Sudan Civil Service
SDF	Sudan Defence Force
SDO	Senior District Officer
SLA/B	Special List A/B
SoS	Secretary of State
SPS	Sudan Political Service
TAS	Tropical African Service
TCD	Trinity College, Dublin
USC	United Services College

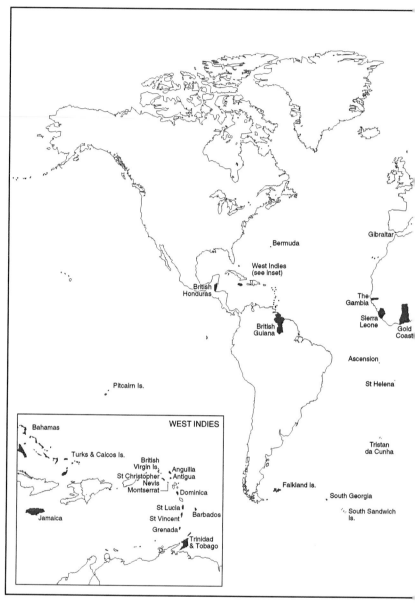

- Bermuda
- Gibraltar
- West Indies (see inset)
- British Honduras
- The Gambia
- Sierra Leone
- Gold Coast
- British Guiana
- Ascension
- St Helena
- Pitcairn Is.
- Tristan da Cunha
- Falkland Is.
- South Georgia
- South Sandwich Is.

WEST INDIES

- Bahamas
- Turks & Caicos Is.
- British Virgin Is.
- Anguilla
- St Christopher
- Antigua
- Nevis
- Montserrat
- Dominica
- St Lucia
- St Vincent
- Barbados
- Grenada
- Jamaica
- Trinidad & Tobago

Britain's depende

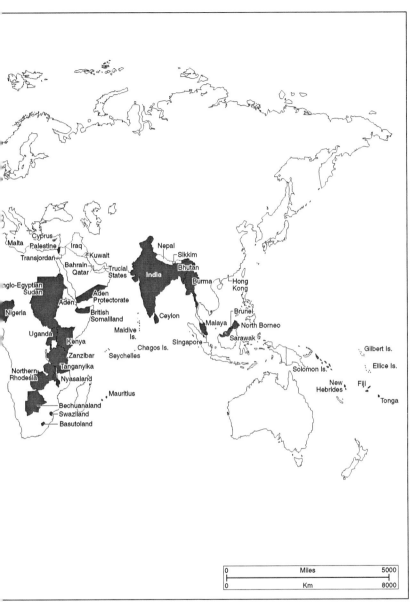

Malta
Cyprus
Palestine
Transjordan
Iraq
Kuwait
Bahrain
Qatar
Trucial
States
Nepal
Sikkim
Bhutan
India
Burma
Hong
Kong
Anglo-Egyptian
Sudan
Aden
Protectorate
Aden
Nigeria
British
Somaliland
Ceylon
Maldive
Is.
Brunei
Malaya
North Borneo
Uganda
Kenya
Zanzibar
Tanganyika
Chagos Is.
Seychelles
Singapore
Sarawak
Gilbert Is.
Ellice Is.
Northern
Rhodesia
Nyasaland
Solomon Is.
New
Hebrides
Fiji
Mauritius
Bechuanaland
Swaziland
Basutoland
Tonga

0	Miles	5000
0	Km	8000

...ritories, *c.* 1939

Introduction

This book presents a comparative synoptic history of the administrative branches of Britain's three principal overseas civil services during the imperial century of c.1860–1960. These were the Indian Civil Service (ICS), 1858–1947; the Sudan Political Service (SPS), 1899–1955; and the Colonial Service, whose literally inceptive and terminal dates remain open to definitional debate within the proven time-span of 1837–1997.[1] The focus is on the administrators, not on the officers of the professional agricultural, engineering, forestry, medical etc. departments of the overseas governments.

In its concentration on Britain's imperial administrators, the central figure anatomized here is not the pre-eminent proconsul in Government House but the generic District Officer (DO) in the field. Irrespective of whether he was locally known as the Collector or the District Commissioner or the Government Agent, the office of DO carried an empire-wide connotation. As the field representative of the colonial government, the proverbial man-on-the-imperial-spot, the DO was at once the symbol and the executive agent of Britain's imperial administrations. Who he was, how he was selected and trained, what his work was, and what became of him when he was overtaken in mid-career by the transfer of power to the newly independent countries, is at the heart of this study. Thus it deals with two linked tranches of British history, abroad the imperial and at home the social. In both cases the period is that of the past: the possibility of a career in a Crown civil service overseas for British graduates is no more.

While the ICS has been subjected to intense academic scrutiny since its disbandment fifty years ago and has generated an extensive deconstructional literature of its own, the same volume of analytical attention has not yet been directed at the smaller SPS nor, basically because of its size and spread, to the less homogeneous CAS. This is the first book-length attempt to look at the three Services together and to consider their appeal, in their common context of Britain's overseas administrative services, as an attractive and respected career choice for several thousands of British graduates during the first half of the twentieth century. All three Services shared the quintessential office of DO/DC, the situation and the very symbol of British civil administration overseas, and all three administrations were predominantly staffed by British officers, often reflecting shared background, education, training and motivation.

Part I sets the historical background. In Chapter 1, the societal milieu from which the potential DO emerged is analysed, with attention given to the heavy socializing influences of the public school and its impact on the formation of a reservoir of putative imperial administrators invested with the requisite mindset, character and ethos. Chapter 2 looks at the expanding British empire, with its conspicuous climax at the close of the nineteenth century, and the consequent problem of how to govern it both bureaucratically in the metropolitan structure and administratively in the overseas possessions. While the three major civil services established for the latter purpose form the centrepiece of Part II, the prior Chapter 3 complementarily considers some of the smaller cadres of British administrators, both Crown and anterior Chartered Company staffs, which operated in the emergent empire. Among these were the Indian Political Service, the Egyptian Civil Service and HM Consular Service. There were, too, the up-country administrators in trading firms like the Honourable East India Company, the Imperial British East Africa Company, the Royal Niger Company and the British North Borneo Company, each of which was to provide the basis of the new administration, along with a number of officials, when the Crown came to take over from Company rule.

Part II is devoted to a detailed examination of the ICS, the CAS and the SPS, individually in Chapters 4, 5 and 6. In each case, an account of the historical evolution of the Service is accompanied by data on the social and educational provenance of its officers, their recruitment and training, and by illustrations of the nature of the work of the generic DO, often derived from their own records as a supplement to the official and observer sources. To prevent the inescapable similarities in what Rudyard Kipling called 'The Day's Work' of the generic DO from degenerating into repetition, the focus of the research into each of the Services has been partly adjusted. In broad terms, in Chapter 4 emphasis is placed on the vast variety of work undertaken by the ICS in what was truly an empire within an empire; in Chapter 5, it is the defining milestones in the creation, changing shape and dissolution of the empire-wide CAS which earn major treatment; and for the SPS in Chapter 6, where the DO cadre was smaller and compact, fuller consideration is paid to the career trajectories of individuals. Throughout, detailed attention has been given to the intricacies and peculiarities of each Service's preferred system of selection and training as part of the inculcation of its own ethos. Although space prevents a comparative examination of the composition and training of the generic DO in other European Colonial Services, a brief look at the formation of the French *commandant de cercle* at the end of Chapter 5 throws further light on his British counterpart in the CAS. This core Part concludes in Chapter 7 with a fresh direction of research and analysis into the who's who of imperial administration, this time at the topmost level of Viceroy, Governor-General and Colonial Governor. These were ranks which, while not always filled from within the Service, nevertheless centrally impacted on the work and career – and often the ambition – of the generic DO.

Part III winds down the history of the ICS, CAS and SPS as each is overtaken by the transfer of power. Chapter 8 considers the impact of the constitutional planning for imperial withdrawal on the localization of the hitherto predominantly British civil services as India (1947) and the Sudan (1956) achieved independence and the Colonial Office closed its doors in 1966. In Chapter 9 the reverse face of localization is considered, the schemes for compensation to overseas civil servants for premature loss of career and the directions in which now surplus imperial administrators turned in their search for another job, along with the national pressures for some sort of successor Commonwealth Civil Service.

The final chapter complements the thrust of the opening one. If Chapter 1 examines who these elite corps of overseas administrators were and what sort of influences conditioned their decision to aspire to a career in imperial administration, as a prelude to analysing in Part II how they were selected and trained and what their work consisted of as a DO, then Chapter 10 reflects on how they managed to carry out their duties, what attributes they needed to display and deploy, and what resources, personal as well as institutional, they could call on in the game of what was, in the final analysis, one of 'White Man's Bluff'. Such a discussion leads into the closing reflections on the image of the DO, in the mind and memory of the ruled as well as of the rulers, and a comment on some of the wider themes and topics in imperial service overseas which, in another and larger context, post-imperial scholars have yet fully to explore. The chapter concludes by speculating on what the loss of a respected and much sought after career in Crown service overseas might mean to the post-imperial generations of job-seeking graduates whose grandfathers' profession has become today as *passé* as that of the not-so-long-ago Odeon organist or of Robert Louis Stevenson's more distant yet still recognized Leerie the Lamplighter.[2] Here the novelist Rumer Godden may in the event be nearer the mark with her prophecy that in what was once the Empire the DO would only feature in tales told to the children, than the Viceroy Lord Wavell's equally genuine belief that the British would be remembered not by the institutions they created 'but by the ideal they left behind of what a DO should be'.[3]

Part I
Environment

1 Anatomizing the Making of the Generic District Officer

It is impossible to read the literature on Britain's overseas administrative services without encountering the qualifying term 'elite': an elite Service, a *corps d'élite*, an administrative elite.[1] If the study of Britain's Home Civil Service has, since the Trevelyan-Northcote Report of 1854, focused on access to merit through open competition, that on her overseas civil services has emphasized their elite properties. In all three overseas administrative Services under scrutiny here, it is the concept of careful admission through scrupulous choice into a select service which recurs, culminating in Philip Mason's image of 'picked men, picked from picked men'.[2]

The prominence of this element of elitism is even more conspicuous in the post-imperial literature. Here sociology has replaced institutions as the principal thrust of historical enquiry: now it is a matter of the players rather than the game as the focus of analysis of Britain's imperial administration. It is not hard to link this growth of interest in the concept of an administrative elite with the Socialist ambience of post-war Britain, with its class-conscious undertones critical of a minority making decisions for the majority.[3] That post-war fascination with the bureaucratic elite in Britain was to coincide, in studies of the emergent Third World, with a growing concern over the formation of what were called the 'educated elite' (i.e., Western-educated) and the threatening absence in the putative independent democracies of the bulwark of a middle class or Weberian status groups as well as of an adequate bureaucratic infrastructure.[4]

In the event, the intellectual concern with the bureaucratic elite was just as much a revival of interest in British society as a new direction of the post-war era. Among its historians G. M. Trevelyan had found no difficulty in extending his social history of England across six centuries, from Chaucer to Queen Victoria (albeit without either class or elites featuring in the index), and F. M. L. Thompson subsequently required three volumes to handle the social history of Britain for only two centuries.[5] But now it was the turn of the sociologists to practise their discipline. To heal the rift between observation and enquiry which had emerged at the turn of the century, history now became more social and social scientists learned to be more historical. The works of leading social scientists of an earlier age were revisited, writers like Montesquieu, Tocqueville, Saint-Simon, Weber, Pareto and of course Marx, all social historians as much as sociologists. The influential work of the 1930s by Cole – in its turn, as with the sociology of the 1960s, generated by a social rethinking, post-national crisis, in this case the General Strike and the Great Depression – was reinvoked for the study of class.[6] Now, however, the focus was not so much on class *per se* – Marwick's 'All-Absorbing Topic'[7] – as on class within class. Mosca's identification of an organizing and directing 'Ruling Class' and R. H. Tawney's 'Acquisitive Society' could be narrowed into something even more exclusive, with just the hint of sinisterism relished by the egalitarian urge of the 1960s, *à la* Hugh Thomas's promotion of the concept of the 'Establishment', C. Wright Mills' influential repackaging of the 'Power Elite' and Michael Young's oligarchic label of the 'Meritocracy'.[8]

Elite *pur sang* was now considered too wide a term to be a valid sociological tool in the study of organized social life, and so the 1960s brought the introduction of specialized elites, each associated with the social order and all mutually linked, together stimulating interest because of their powerful – but, meaningfully, not always public – activity as primary moulders and movers of society. Many of these elites within an elite were located within the bureaucracy, where, besides an ardent revisitation of Max Weber's influential construction of a rational bureaucracy by those responsible for training new civil services for the independent states,[9] labels like mandarins, prefectoral elite, competitive elite, business elite, strategic elite, governing elite and the whole milieu of so-called 'Corridors of Power' enriched the vocabulary and appeal of elite theory. Thanks to the subsequent TV caricature of Sir Humphrey Appleby, stereotype Whitehall mandarin *par excellence*, the process went on to rejoice a later generation now intent on the demystification of, and no longer their regular incorporation into, the higher Home Civil Service elite.

Despite the fact that by the time the new sociology was in its stride the Indian Civil Service, the Colonial Administrative Service and the Sudan Political Service were no longer extant models of elite formation and behaviour, the contemporary interest in the Whitehall elite[10] went into historical reverse gear and began to be applied, retrospectively and rewardingly, to the study of the former civil services of empire. In particular, attention was turned to such underlying elements of elite formation within Britain's overseas civil services as the procedures of selection and recruitment (sociology's 'replacement') and of 'attraction' (those rewards calculated both to motivate and maintain competition for the Service). First the Indian Civil Service, and later the Sudan Political Service, presented themselves as prime candidates for 'elite' enquiry.[11] Intellectually, the focus comfortably and revealingly extended from the corridors of Whitehall to the verandahs of Delhi and Khartoum.

Promoters of elite theory commonly endorse the argument advanced by T. B. Bottomore in an early discussion of the new sociology, namely that the primary characteristics of such a group are that it is 'small, well-defined, homogeneous (as a result of training and the practice of occupation), and cohesive'.[12] Rupert Wilkinson's associated study of governing elites importantly took as its definition 'a distinctive group holding high status in its community and knit together by a strong group feeling, ethos and style'.[13] The thesis of the present study is that the imperial administrations featured in it reflect a clear correspondence with these two sets of definitional characteristics. The reducing level of tangible class differentiation in the accepted English social sense and the occasional ascription of caste (e.g., in the ICS's colloquial label of 'The Heaven

Born')[14] to those overseas administrative elites do not undermine the validity and relevance of the Bottomore or Wilkinson constructs. Caste precludes social mobility; and the very definition of 'open competition' in place of patronage for posts in the ICS and the Colonial Service's Eastern Cadetships made it clear that caste was outlawed. Similarly, because of the intrinsic connection of class with birth, the fact that the imperial civil services admitted – as the evidence consistently demonstrates – into their ranks young graduates whose fathers were at the time incontrovertibly classified as 'working class', meant that they could not be judged to be inflexibly class-bound.

The argument underlying this study is that where class as a factor could be said to have come into the ICS, CAS and SPS, it was as a secondary, not a primary construct. Furthermore, where such a wrinkle did exist it could be ironed out in the nurtured formation of the potential imperial administrator, above all in the public school. Unlike the contemporary professions of the army (in particular the cavalry regiments and the Guards) and diplomacy, the ability to consider a career in the new imperial civil services of the late nineteenth and early twentieth centuries was not premised on the *sine qua non* of having private means.[15] In those new civil services the element of class became not that of family, the primary context of English class, but of class formation, of elitist moulding: not of birth but of nurturing – and the very term involves a high degree of express engineering and deliberate elite formation. That socialization process, of topping up or of calculated conversion where necessary, was, the argument continues here, carried out in the public – and growingly the grammar – schools and, actively but less pressingly, in the universities. The new public schools of the Victorian age, whose emergence and evolution were from the beginning intimately linked with empire, were ready to challenge the assumed monopoly of the classic Clarendon Schools[16] in the art of the making of the English gentleman and in the task of playing a major part in staffing the Empire. That integration quickened after the middle of the century when the new imperialism allegedly became invested 'with a mysticism akin to that which shrouded the concept of the English Gentleman'.[17] Eton and Harrow might have the head start of pupils already being of gentle birth, but from the 1860s in no way would the nine Clarendon Schools be the only ones committed to and succeeding in turning out young gentlemen. In Asa Briggs's judgement on the emergent Victorian middle class, 'the new institutional morality was based on the old code of the gentleman'.[18] By proudly offering, in bold prospectus as well as through growing repute, a gentleman's education, a school had no need to draw a distinction between on the one hand teaching a gentleman and on the other tuition in how to become one. In terms of their end product, if not necessarily of their primary material, all schools saw themselves as what have been described as 'factories for gentlemen'.[19]

The fluid social composition of the new bourgeoisie or professional elite of Victorian Britain eschewed patronage and outflanked 'family' in both public appointments and public schools. Open competitive examinations took care of the first; the new public schools looked after the second. Who needed Eton or

Harrow to staff the expanding Crown services overseas, civil and military, when in the almost unbelievable space of a mere twenty-five years, from 1841 to 1865, the new professional families and those of what were called 'the new industrial and mercantile' classes could rely on finding the same deliberate inculcation of character, loyalty, hierarchical respect, service and self-discipline for their sons, all the elements of 'godliness and good learning' and Christian manliness of which Rugby and Winchester were so justifiably proud? All were now on offer at the new foundations of Cheltenham, Marlborough, Rossall, Radley, Glenalmond, Lancing, Bradfield, St John's Leatherhead, Epsom, Wellington, Clifton, Haileybury, Malvern and Fettes. In turn each was fed by scores of fresh preparatory schools jointly committed to the role of Cradles of Empire.[20] Every one of these new public schools, along with yet later foundations, quickly joined the Clarendon Schools in providing the catchment area from which the new imperial civil services, generally via the universities but occasionally directly from school, were throughout the hundred years of their existence to draw so deeply and so rewardingly. In his study of the late Victorian public schools Mangan, following Bertrand Russell, argues that three sets of values became enmeshed: imperial Darwinism, institutional Darwinism, and the gentleman's education. He maintains that 'headmasters were intoxicated with the grandeur and nobility of the gubernatorial exercise'.[21] Paul Rich's concern with imperial freemasonry has taken the study of the public school influence into another dimension from that conventionally understood by the link between public school and empire, but his fundamental thesis occupies common ground: Britain's imperial administrators drew heavily on the socialization of their school environment and experience.[22] By the beginning of the First World War Old Wellingtonians and Old Marlburians behaved and felt as pukka as the Wykehamist and Etonian gentlemen, and by the beginning of the Second World War the dominant public-cum-grammar school product had been collapsed into a single, undiscriminating and unmistakable sahib.[23]

In general, however, the intimacy between a public school education and preparation for imperial service was unambiguous. As Peter Parker puts it:

> The more ennobling features ascribed to imperialism were already dominant within the schools. The subordination of self to the community, personal striving for the common weal, the upholding of traditions and loyalty to the community, all acted as training for the administration of Empire.[24]

Nor was the public-school virtual obligation to live away from home for months at a time ('Town House' pupils were consistently looked down on by boarders as not being quite pukka; the hybrid concept of 'weekly boarders' was as yet unknown) anything but an advantage in the imperial life to come, of long separation from family and an ever-ready ability to rough it and fend for oneself. 'One is licked into shape', comments the hero of a classic public school novel, 'for the big things, diplomacy, politics, the Services.'[25]

With the abundance of group terms persuasively coined for interpreting the sociology of imperial administrators, it could be otiose to create a fresh group identity beyond what is invented in this study as 'the generic DO'. However repackaged, it remains undeniable that in analysing the correspondence and coherence of Britain's cadres of imperial administrators, one is dealing above all with a cohort of men conditioned by their education (not so much learning as socialization) and taught to adopt shared values and respect a common code. The resonances of the public school system are strong in elite theory. Wilkinson's image of a 'prefectoral elite' and its exercise of 'gentlemanly power'[26] have most recently been echoed in Cain and Hopkins' portrait of gentleman capitalists as part and parcel of the 'gentlemanly order' behind the Empire.[27] Venturing beyond the Square Mile, they maintain that if the ICS was 'the most impressive illustration of gentlemanly imperialism in its formal guise', the Colonial Service, especially in Africa, represented the highest stage of the phenomenon because it arrived last on the scene and survived longer.[28] Still within the orbit of the public school of (and for) gentlemen as the dominant influence in the formation of the generic DO, Mangan has placed emphasis on 'the games ethic', concluding that the games field was supremely well served by the obligations and opportunities of empire.[29] It is a thesis raised by another observer of imperial administration to the level of the possible identification of an 'athletocracy' of overseas administrators,[30] hedged, however, with the necessary caveat that many a first-class DO was a butterfingers to the bone when it came to college cricket and could not – nor wished to – tell a googly from a goalkick. In cloistered contrast, Clive Dewey's biographical excursus into the ICS has led him to the imagery of 'force-fed mandarins'.[31] In his post-imperial lookback, J. Morris generously – for he himself was among them in 1953 – admitted the imperial administrators to membership of the elite 'Everesters':

> they were sahibs ... and as such they were figures of Empire, a type becoming more remote, more misty, a little more risible as the decades draw on, but still recognizable as a category of Briton.[32]

After World War I a noticeable shift emerges, away from the conventional 'squirearchy' of the Shires portrait of the social background of Britain's overseas administrators to their family location among the new urban gentry of Southern England. Tidrick, in her search for the force behind the imperial administrators, widens the assumptions to include virtually the full range of human motives being at work in Empire service, and unconsciously comes close to the thrust of one of the questions posed in the final chapter here when she asserts that what was distinctively English about the imperial enterprise was 'not people's motives for going where they did but what they believed themselves to be doing when they got there'.[33] Ronald Hyam allows of no limitations at all on the human motives at work, finding emotional repression and sexual opportunity among the most vigorous dynamics of Britain's imperial administrators.[34] Hyam, too, has added a novel dimension to elite theory by including imperial administrators as conspicuous members of what he categorizes as the new, upper-middle and professional class of the circumcised. For this 'club', he quotes the contemporary emergence of circumcision as 'part of the whole corpus of phenomena and bundle of enthusiasms' prevalent at the turn of the century, calculating that by the 1930s two-thirds of public schoolboys were circumcised, against a mere ten per cent of 'working class' males.[35]

Above all, it is David Potter's prosopographical analysis of the ICS cadres which has generated an elite vocabulary most closely applicable to the wider context of all of Britain's overseas civil service cadres examined here. For Potter, the pan-Crown civil service convention of accepting a limited number of entrants, at regular intervals, and offering them (and only them) a clear career structure to the top and eventually towards handsome salaries constitutes 'the height of elitist administration'.[36] It is, however, his emphasis on the norms and values of what he calls 'the gentlemanly mode',[37] along with his recourse to Goldthorpe's concept of a 'service class',[38] which are echoed and endorsed by what is here interpreted as an homogenizing elite formation, prominently in public school and partly in university. Throughout, a running emphasis is also accorded to the 'status' of a career in a Crown civil service overseas, a choice at once respectable to family and friends, attractive to a good proportion of the undergraduate population of Britain's universities, and satisfying to them in its requirements, responsibilities and lifestyle.

Previous as well as current interpretations of the composition of the administrative elite tend to have underestimated the 'career' factor, in particular the cachet of a Crown service career. This may be because service under the Crown carries a markedly lower appeal and less allure among undergraduates than it did before the Second World War. By concentrating on the component parts of the service, historians may have ignored the totality of its attraction as a career – so much more than a job, the primary economic goal of the 1980s and beyond – for those many hundreds of Lord Cromer's envisioned 'active young men, endowed with good health, high character and fair abilities … the flower of those who are turned out from our schools and colleges'.[39] By pointing to the career factor, of a life of public service under the Crown, overseas, invested with rank, respectability, responsibility and reward, all set within a regulated pattern of advancement and identifiable benefits, the institutional make-up of the generic DO is taken an important stage beyond his hitherto personal elitism.

It is also possible, by analysing not so much the fact as the formation of that elitism, to construct a serviceable input-output model of the making of the generic DO. Regardless of his familial or social provenance, the argument runs here that once he enters the post-Arnold world of public – and progressively of grammar – school into which he was likely to have been propelled from a middle-class – often *nouveau* and upwardly mobile – family of professional parents, he becomes socialized and homogenized in accordance with the prevailing code of expected behaviour, at once accepted internally and admired externally. This code, at times articulated into a creed, was premised on the deliberately nurtured attributes ('virtues') of character, leadership, determination, discipline – including of self – service and fair play. 'A certain routine is necessary in education', mused a latter-day Secretary of State for the Colonies, himself a Wykehamist, 'to inculcate steadfastness and thoroughness, to teach us to surmount difficulties.'[40] And where, as could sometimes be the case, family life had not already fostered a sense of comfortable self-confidence, the public school system could be relied on to instil the habit of ready authority which was frequently looked on as its hallmark and ultimately the trait of the imperial administrator. The message was abundantly clear in the moralistic mottos chosen by the new public schools together with the precepts of their predecessors: *virtute studio ludo* and *labor omnia vincit* alongside *orando laborando* and Manners Maketh Man. Many of these were, of course, attributes already subsumed under the strong religious tone of a Victorian public school education, but the pro-active evangelizing zealot was likely to find a warmer welcome in a mission society than among his colleagues in the Provincial Administration. Some of the code was replicated in the contemporary social conventions of the university – more flexible than the traditions and taboos of public school conduct – and in turn could further help to influence the choice of career. Over if not above all brooded the spirit of sport, a behavioural educator second to none.[41]

Together these influences canalized into the creation of an *esprit de corps* and an ethos, reflecting exactly the kind of attributes that those subsequently responsible for recruitment (university appointments boards, talent-scouting dons, college tutors and housemasters called on for a reference, Civil Service Commissioners and members of the CO interviewing boards) believed to be desiderata in the potential DO and to guarantee the success of the imperial administrator. And when the choice of career turned out to be an imperial civil service, such was the continuity of the code that the prefect and the graduate now transformed into administrative cadet would experience a strong, even reassuring, sense of *déjà vu*. The passage from probationer to DO was a familiar one, similar to the progress from new boy to prefect a dozen years earlier. The public schools did not educate in vain: yesterday's prefects made tomorrow's good DOs. Their unwritten motto of *empire oblige* was generously subscribed to and imperial administration could often reflect 'the prefectorial system writ large'.[42]

In mores and motivation, then, the generic DO often practised and manifested what he had learnt at his school as constituting the signals of accepted success and the criteria by which he could expect to be judged when he moved into the world beyond the playing fields. Leadership brought respect as well as early responsibility, an aura of authority, and the dual discipline of self as well as of the Other. All were statuses that he enjoyed, so it was natural that he should turn his mind to a career where he could once again indulge in and earn them – for Morris, the DO's 'pleasure of authority and the chance of doing good'.[43] Up to at least the 1960s, the assiduous cult of the amateur, displaying modesty and decorum in triumph and resolute unemotion in adversity, was also an imperial virtue, sometimes learned at home, always inculcated at school, strongly encouraged at the university, and directly transferred into the Service.

A sense of fair play was inherent in a successful prefect and DO alike, however much Morris's modifier of 'more just than kind'[44] is in order. So, too, was a strong sense of service. Had the prefect-turned-probationer ever heard of the motto, the imperial maxim of *dominer pour servir* neatly fitted the bill and was measurably nearer the mark than the American George Santayana's over-cloying and over-quoted image of the generic British DO as 'a sweet, just, boyish master, unknown since the heroic days of Greece'.[45] Loyalty and never letting the side down were the foundation of institutional life, from school through college to Service. Among the numerous examples of verse in imitation of Henry Newbolt's now devalued *Vitaï Lampada* or *Clifton Chapel*, both of them on a one-time par with that national anthem *manqué* 'Land of Hope and Glory', was one which must have caused many a member of the final selection board, like the young interviewee himself, to have swallowed hard as he succumbed to the public-school-cum-Empire adrenalin and mystique of Donald Hughes'

> The greatest glory of our land
> Whose crimson covers half the maps
> Is in the field where the wicket stands
> And the game is played by DECENT CHAPS.[46]

Without embarking on yet another treatise or anthology of the numerous definitions of what a gentleman is (or is not)[47] we may conclude that to be thought of as a gentleman was in itself an attribute. It is not surprising that, for generations of ICS officers and other imperial administrators reared on the classics and seldom at a loss to conjure up a Latin tag or Greek comparison to clinch an argument, Plato's Guardians should, even before Philip Mason's inspired incorporation of them into the literature of imperial rule, have come to their mind as an analogue, brought up as they were from childhood 'to imitate whatever is proper to their profession and to model themselves on brave, sober, religious and honourable men'.[48] In summary, the public schools not only instilled in a boy the qualities required by that imperial class which the expanding empire needed but also taught him the art of imperial administration: 'he learned, in short, to rule.'[49] At the Colonial Office, the pivotal judgement of Sir Ralph Furse, long-time Director of Recruitment, on the public schools is no less terse and to the point: 'We could not have run the show without them.'[50] The public schools constituted a powerful training ground for the generic DO.[51] In his faith in the prefect-cum-captain of the XI as constituting the *beau idéal* of DO material, Furse likely had Kipling's definition in mind:

> It's not wealth or rank or state
> But 'get up and go' which makes men great.

Allusion has been made in the preceding pages to the influential inculcation at school of a profound sense of loyalty, so essential when the schoolboy and undergraduate went on to become a subaltern or civilian cadet. However, one important gloss on this quality needs to be made, and in the context of the imperial civil services of Part II the earlier the better in this study. While it remains true that Britain's overseas administrators were recruited by the British government and received letters of appointment signed by the Secretary of State for India or for the Colonies, once *en poste* the officer's loyalty, by his own inclination as well as *de facto*, lay not to Westminster but unequivocally and unswervingly to the government in Delhi or Lagos or Kuala Lumpur, etc. For the generic DO anything else was unthinkable. In the case of the SPS, of course, they were *de jure* the servants of the government of the Anglo-Egyptian Condominium administration, never of HMG. It is this instinctive convention of automatic, total and even unconscious loyalty to the government of the periphery and not that of the centre which generates a second comment on the loyalty of imperial administrators. American students of empire in particular find it hard to grasp that this loyalty was totally compartmentalized from any instigated patriotism and that any imperative of a 'Rule Britannia' triumphalism or flag-wagging mission rarely formed a central role in the training of Britain's imperial administrators.

Extra-murally, the institution's (school or university) psychological and intellectual encouragement of imperial service was, up to 1939, often reinforced by the physical influences of family and friends. The choice of a career was frequently governed by a strong tradition of Crown service. It was not long before what the CO recruitment branch files excitedly marked 'S/F' (Son of Father) became a conditioning reality in each Service. Second and even third generation men (unto the fifth or sixth are recorded in the case of India)[52] followed their forebears' footsteps, while the father of a young undergraduate who was not himself in a Crown service overseas could be relied on to know an ex-ICS man at the Club or a retired colonial administrator further up the avenue in leafy Cheltenham or sedate Tunbridge Wells.[53] Nor, still in the boundaries of the family as a force of imperial motivation, must the home-reading influence of Rudyard Kipling, G. A. Henty, Rider Haggard and Edgar Wallace, and subsequently the *Boy's Own Paper* and the cinema, be dismissed: the evidence of retrospective memoir and oral history is too strong for denial.[54] As Martin Green explained the phenomenon in his aptly titled literary excursus, *Dreams of Adventure, Deeds of Empire*:

> The adventure tales that formed the light reading of Englishmen for two hundred years and more after Robinson Crusoe were the energizing myth of imperialism ... collectively, the story England told herself as it went to sleep at night, and in the form of its dreams....[55]

More prosaically, A. V. Arthur, one of the rare overseas administrators to have had a career in both the ICS and the SPS, has related how

> in my second year at Cambridge, in 1935, I saw the film 'Sanders of the River' ... [it] enthralled me and I decided *there and then* that this was the life for me [italics added].[56]

In considering the social profile of the imperial administrators, the label of 'middle class' has been as inseparable from their background as the term 'elite' from their Services. Leaving aside the incumbents of Government House, just a few of whom came directly from or ended up in the House of Lords (cf. Chapter 7), very few imperial administrators were drawn from the nobility or aristocracy. The DO who was a Baronet or the Honourable So-and-So was more likely to have been of the nineteenth century than of the post-First World War years. Tidrick is right in her judgement on the Colonial Service to talk about 'the deceptively aristocratic appearance possessed by that generally very middle-class enterprise' and to assert how these new middle classes, 'in appropriating to themselves hitherto supposedly aristocratic qualities, assured their fitness for political power'.[57] There were some DOs who came from the landed gentry, especially, before c.1920, second or younger sons for whom the Crown civil services overseas could now be added to the army, the church, law and diplomacy as an acceptable profession. But the concept of an imperial administration rooted in the rural gentry arguably owes more to the occasional squirearchical air of the up-country DO in action or to the influence of the colonial novel than to the exactitude of ancestry.[58]

Nevertheless, in the Palestine Service and in the Middle East in general James Morris recognized many scions of the rural gentry, fulfilled and feeling 'at ease and at home with Arab gentlemen ... the meeting of equals'.[59] More and more the overseas civil services became a sought-after career for sons of the emergent professional and industrial classes of Victorian Britain, doctors and solicitors and bank managers, together with the growing numbers of post-patronage civil servants themselves, both here and abroad. 'We were', noted a typical member of the typical inter-war intakes, 'mostly the younger sons of the professional middle-class.'[60] By 1914, as Cain and Hopkins argue, aristocratic power was in unequivocal decline, and power and prestige progressively devolved upon the new gentlemanly class arising from the service sector.[61] Here were the middle class, a category varying with chronology and sometimes the class of the observer (E. M. Forster thought of the ICS as an upgraded middle class), on which the Crown civil services overseas were to depend so heavily and to appeal so emphatically as career began to replace occupation and professionalism was substituted for patronage among the post-Northcote/Trevelyan graduates.[62] Among Jowett's arguments to convince his Chancellor, William Gladstone, why Oxford should gear itself towards securing a preponderance of appointments in the new Indian administration was his belief that 'it would give an answer to the dreary question which a College Tutor so often hears – "What line of life should I choose, with no calling to take orders and no taste for the Bar and no connexions to put me forward in life?"' [63]

Always, of course, there were exceptions to prove the social rule, able young graduates from non-public school and lower-class backgrounds. Mangan calculates that perhaps 5 per cent of the SPS could be classified as of non-public school origin, while Potter's estimate of 7 per cent of the ICS before 1914 and as high as 16 per cent of the post-war intakes as non-public school still leaves overall some 80 per cent respectively drawn from public schools in England, Scotland and Ireland.[64] What bound each Service together, it is argued in the present study, was not initial class but the shared socialization of public or grammar school and university. This resulted in the common acceptance of the codes and ethos nurtured there as an intimate prelude to the *esprit de corps* of their Service which they went on acceptedly to adopt and promote. It is this fusion of homogenizing public school foreground with, where extant, the bonus of family background, which is advanced here and which allows Cain and Hopkins to claim that the men who shaped imperial destinies were neither Olympian figures removed from material concerns nor representatives of the industrial bourgeoisie: 'Their conception of national interest rose above party and class ... a view of the world sufficiently spacious to encompass other allegiances,' a view based on well-ordered, if largely unspoken, priorities.[65]

Provenance, of course, can be regional and religious as well as social or occupational. The three overseas civil services considered here were British, not English. Even when the large majority came from English public schools, many of them were Ulstermen and Welshmen; and from the 1920s many again were from the Dominions, not excluding Ireland. Above all, the Scots stood out: Scotland and empire have long been as integrally associated as haggis and whisky. Statistics have been calculated principally for the ICS, though in the SPS we knew that overall as many as 8 per cent attended Scottish public schools while other Scots went to school south of the border.[66] In India, Scots accounted for 13 per cent (and the Irish 5 per cent) of the Europeans on the ICS books in 1939. In the case of the CAS, the ban on access to biodata records means no such detailed analysis of regional provenance has yet been undertaken, but what evidence is available points, Scots apart, to an expanding Home Counties provenance at the expense of any North country core. Given the nature of public school reputation and location, as eminent in the North and the Midlands as in the South or West, and the readiness up to 1939 of parents to send their children to boarding school hundreds of miles away from home untrammelled in their choice of good school by extended half-term exeats, the public school attended is no indicator of regional birth and upbringing. It does, of course, bear ready resonances for other kinds of interpretative data. Potter makes the same regional point in another way when he asserts that if you met an ICS officer in India between the wars who did not have a Scottish or Irish accent, you could bet your last rupee, especially if he were an older man, that he had been to an English public school.[67]

Less attention has conventionally been paid in British establishment and Service prosopography, as in British public life generally, to religion or political party affiliation than in many other countries, e.g. USA or France. While it is possible to establish among colonial governors that, for example, under ten per cent were Catholics or Jews,[68] and it is easy to identify the partisan allegiance of nearly all the Viceroys, such information is neither generally available in the case of the generic DO nor was it of much concern or interest within the respective Services. If the classification (but not, of course, the argument) of race as a factor did not arise earlier outside the special case of India (see Chapter 4), this is because administrative officers were *ipso facto* European, that is to say overwhelmingly British. Leaving aside the unique possibilities of a biracial structure in the ICS dating back to the 1860s and the progressive case of the British West Indies where local graduates were appointed as DOs before World War II,[69] the CAS and SPS remained emphatically and all but exclusively British in their DO posts right down to the 1940s.

In the formation of Britain's imperial administrative elite, with the critical years being, as argued here, those of its socialization and values-inculcation at school, there is irony in the fact that out of Britain's over one hundred public schools which regularly sent pupils into the imperial civil services in the century under scrutiny, only two incorporated this prominent role into their name. They were the atypical United Services College, of *Stalky & Co.* fame but not one of the HM Conference schools, and the Haileybury/Imperial Service College, which had its origin as the *ad hoc* East India Company training school for Writers. Even after its transformation into a 'straight' public school, Haileybury liked to stress that its Modern Side, advertised as having only a limited number of places available, was specially designed to prepare boys for the public Services, civil and military.[70] Its record in staffing the ICS and SPS continued to remain at the higher end. The USC's contribution to the SPS was precisely one (0.25 per cent) in over fifty years. For the rest, their contribution to the provision of Britain's imperial administrators was perhaps too sterling to need any imperial advertisement in their name or prospectus. Nor within Britain's public schools was there any Imperial Service class to balance the near-ubiquitous Army class. The function of the proudly named Colonial College at Hollesey Bay in Suffolk (1887–1903) was to turn out handy colonists, part of the 300 000 'gentle emigrants' who left Britain for the empire between 1880 and 1914, not for the training of colonial civil servants.[71]

Nor, for all their influence and importance in the process, did the universities specifically incorporate preparation for the imperial civil services into their curriculum. Their mission was educating, not training. And when, from the mid-1880s in the case of the ICS and the mid-1920s for the CAS, Oxford, Cambridge, Trinity College Dublin and later London, agreed to provide teaching resources for probationers, the programmes and the lecturers were overwhelmingly academic and the curriculum – to the subsequent chagrin of many cadets and of their seniors at the receiving end – far from vocational. A proposal made in 1874 that a single College might be established at Cambridge or Oxford (where Max Mueller suggested a concentration at All Souls) got nowhere.[72] During a whole century of imperial administration, Britain never created anything like an Empire Staff College for its overseas civil servants. It was France and not Britain which established a separate, professional, elite Ecole Coloniale. Nothing came of the strong plea by Marshal of the Royal Air Force Viscount Trenchard in 1942 to set up a Colonial Staff College, under a 'galvanizing personality' as Commandant [*sic*].[73] Up to the end of empire the British believed, as with the predecessor civil services of Rome and China, that an education in the humanities would be an advantage to their overseas administrators in the exercise of the art (never the science) of imperial administration.

What therefore emerges from this disinclination to concentrate on training imperial administrators at either school or university, while at the same time these continued to make a sizeable contribution in shaping and supplying potential DOs, is the unusual spread of the educational catchment area. Just occasionally the old boy network experienced a spasm of prominence: Rugby (or Wellington) and the Punjab had their moments of neo-legendary popularity, and Winchester steadfastly contributed 50 per cent more than any other public school to the staffing of the SPS. No school excelled Marlborough and Wellington in the number of old boys joining the Colonial Service. Otherwise, it was any of several dozen old school ties that DOs might sport, with markedly fewer from Eton, Harrow and St Paul's after the First World War. In the list drawn up for the Colonial Office recruitment division in 1942, a total of 659 successful candidates for the CAS in the decade 1931–41 came from 230 different public and grammar schools. Only 13 of these registered double figures.[74] Perhaps surprisingly in the event, the rainfall of overseas civil service recruitment from the public schools turns out to have been characterized by numerous and widespread drops, not by single heavy downpours.

At the turn of the century there were 370 schools recognized as public in accordance with Honey's handy, off-the-cuff criterion of schools where members would have accepted each other as members of the public schools community.[75] This was a total twice as generous as membership of the rigid Head Masters' Conference (HMC). In the present study, the public and grammar schools have on purpose been hyphenated into a single independent sector, for, as Ogilvie has pointed out, from the 1920s grammar schools consciously tended and tried to model themselves on the public schools in their search for acceptance into the envied HMC.[76] In the inter-war ICS, for instance, Bradford Grammar School had as many old boys as either Eton or St Paul's; Manchester Grammar School contributed on a par with Oundle and Tonbridge; and St Olave's Grammar School outnumbered Westminster, Shrewsbury and Malvern. In the SPS, Cardiff High and Leeds Grammar School produced as many DCs as Aldenham, Dover, Merchiston or St Lawrence Ramsgate. While in all – and the figure tells all – over 80 per cent of the British component of the ICS between the wars came from public schools, Potter's analysis of the 795 officers reveals that these came from as many as 225 schools.[77] This averages out at 3.5 per school. No less strikingly, the 182 recruited between 1914 and 1941 were drawn from 141 different public schools. In the whole of the inter-war period, only seven public schools produced more than ten ICS men each.[78] Indeed, the 'new' public schools, symbolized in the emergence of the dozen or so founded between 1840 and 1865 which were still conspicuously in business a hundred years later, had made a significant impact on the staffing of the overseas civil services by the end of the century. Between 1896, the year in which the examination for the Home, Indian and Colonial (then meaning the Eastern Cadetships of Ceylon, Hong Kong and the Straits Settlements) Services was combined into a single competition, and 1911, when the Royal Commission on the Public Services in India compiled its detailed report on the educational background of the new administrative elite, the 1337 successful candidates for all three civil services (ICS, 'Colonial' and Home) were drawn from over 150 public schools in Britain. A further 114 successful applicants came from 'other' 'Public' schools, mostly 'Secondary', in Britain, with as many as 64 of them providing no more than three apiece over the fifteen years.[79] Once again, while it is the public school factor which dominates, it is its spread, not its concentration, which impresses.

Turning to the SPS, its approximately 400 officers listed in the official register covering the fifty-three years of the Service's recruitment of Britons were drawn from over one hundred schools. If seven of these produced more than ten each (30 came from Winchester, 20 apiece from Eton, Rugby and Marlborough), seventy of them still produced one or two each.[80] No such statistics yet exist for the CAS, but there is nothing to suggest any narrower school basis of recruitment. On the contrary, the indications are that the net was cast wider yet up through the 1950s and into the 1960s, with more grammar-school entrants yet with the public schools (markedly more of the lesser than the major) continuing to provide perhaps up to two-thirds, and with the state schools now beginning to make a contribution.

Yet once in the Service, networking was rarely a hangover from school, nor was it significantly influenced by university: basically it became a feature of the Service ethos itself. The occasions on which the 'old boy' network did manifest itself were for the most part in social gatherings, cutting across the civil service boundaries to include military officers from the garrison or cantonment, the few ex-public school commercial directors or agents (the 'box-wallahs', taipans, even 'counter-jumpers' of the East), and any other old boys, perhaps bankers or solicitors, who might be around. The Government of India's annual exodus to Simla was often the excuse for Old Boys' dinners – one which Dufferin graced with his viceregal presence was for Old Etonians, who sat down 16 to table.[81] The reunion dinner of the Hong Kong branch of the Oxford and Cambridge Club was said to be frequently punctured with dated references to 'the Other Place'. But where networking was concerned, the real reunions were not the Old Boys or alumni ones; they were the Service ones, like the ICS dinners held every cold-season in Presidency and provincial capitals, or the Corona Club and the 'Fallen Angels' one at Henley-on-Thames held each summer respectively for CAS and SPS officers on leave.

If it was the public (and grammar) school which could mould or build on a disposition for imperial service, often in harness with family experience and circles, it was frequently the university which clinched the career decision. The influences at work were varied. They included earnest discussions with fellow students or with tutors about what to do after graduating; an enthusiastic letter from a friend a year or two ahead in College and now a cadet in Nyasaland or en route for Hong Kong; an exciting talk with a young SPS officer revisiting his old College on leave, part nostalgically, part talent-spotting; perhaps a counselling session with a member of the University Appointments Board, who could well have been a DO himself. 'It all started', records one DO-to-be, at the

University, 'when an Oxford friend joined the Colonial Service and infected me with his enthusiasm for the opportunities which it seemed to offer, doing a useful job with a wide range of responsibilities concerned with people and their needs.'[82] Even professorial lectures on European expansion might produce a practical dividend, though just as frequently it seems to have been seeing '*Sanders of the River*' at the Regent or '*Four Feathers*' at the Rex which did the trick.

When it comes to the university, however, the distribution of the recruitment statistics differed markedly from those relating to schools of entry. The landmark Royal Commission on the recruitment of Class I (Home), ICS probationers and Eastern Cadets quoted above recorded only eight universities in Britain, other than Oxford or Cambridge, as having provided successful candidates over the fifteen-year period from 1896 to 1911, against twenty times that number of schools. There were, of course, far fewer universities in Britain, even by 1939 barely a quarter of the 96 that exist today, so that it is much easier to ascribe the individual contribution to recruitment. There was, too, the status of Oxford and Cambridge, an influence shared with Trinity College Dublin and London as each went on to play a calculated and public role in the post-graduate teaching of probationers for Britain's expanding civil services. The statistics are eloquent. In the official record for the period 1896–1911 of the successful candidates for the combined CSC competition, which included the Home Civil Service as well as the Indian Civil Service and the Eastern Cadetships, 247 of the graduates came from Oxford, 142 from Cambridge, 23 from TCD, 17 from Edinburgh and 14 from the Royal (subsequently National) University of Ireland. Of the remainder, seven were from Glasgow, six from Aberdeen, five from London, two from Manchester and one from Leeds. Within the Oxbridge group, 22 had previously studied at other universities, including 10 at Indian universities. In all, only nine had no university education.[83] Extending this data, in the ninety years of its existence three-quarters of the ICS came from Oxford and Cambridge. In the case of the SPS, Oxford and Cambridge accounted for seventy per cent of its graduate DCs. Of the rest, 6 per cent were graduates of the RMC Sandhurst, 2 per cent from TCD, and 3.5 per cent came from the four senior Scottish universities.[84] As for the CAS, the Oxbridge monopoly between the wars was striking, providing 79 out of the 83 university administrative cadets in 1927 and 84:88 in 1928. In 1937, a typical year, 80 per cent of the 157 entrants into the CAS had been to Oxbridge.[85] Yet in considering the relative influence of public school and university in the making of the generic DO, it is salutary to recall the significance of Potter's post-imperial prioritization in the high noon of the imperial administrator, that 'the best identification of an English gentleman was someone who had been to a public school: having been to Oxford or Cambridge also helped'.[86] For both Services – and the fact triggers many deriving questions if not all the answers – the lead of Oxford over Cambridge was substantial.[87]

Treading angel-like on dangerous ground, the present study implies that in the formation of the generic DO of Britain's three major overseas administrative services, from new boy Mark I (first term at public school) to new boy Mark II (first tour cadet), there is both faith and fact to conclude that there existed a pervasive model of imperial leadership whose ideal, the English gentleman, could if necessary be made as well as born, fashioned and standard-ized above all at school and to a lesser degree at university, so that by the time he was incorporated into the ethos of the Service few could tell – and fewer still would wish or need to – the difference. The empire-moulding milieu in which the potential DO was reared, that of 'tradition' sometimes unconscious, some-times blatant and on occasion aggressively gung-ho, was influentially in the background when it was not in the foreground. What is more, it was character-ized by continuity, throughout his formative years from five to twenty-five, and by deconcentration: over two hundred schools and a score of universities all took part in the process of finding and forming the putative DO. He in his turn was not slow to respond to the moulding.

While this study is primarily a historical presentation, with its focus on who the imperial administrators were and what their work was, it cannot overlook the context of the sociological debate on the fashioning and nature of a ruling elite. Its research has benefited from and borrowed from such compelling con-cepts as Bottomore's cohesiveness of an administrative elite, Goldthorpe's image of a service class, and Mason's influential label of Platonic guardians trained to rule according to their own understanding of the Good and the Beautiful; from Potter's norms and values of the gentlemanly mode, Wilkinson's easy exercise of gentlemanly power and Raven's postulate that rule and administration were the special provinces of the gentleman; and even from Ranger's deflationary formulation of neo-tradition which, invaluable overseas Service commodity that it was, required regular renewing in order to sustain its hold and continuity.[88] Together these and other contributory insights have played an influential part in underpinning the basic thesis promoted here, that the generic DO was a clear example of the homogenizing public school code and culture duly translated into the ethos and the *esprit de corps* of Britain's imperial administrative elite.

2 An Empire to be Administered: the Metropolitan Organization

THE TERRITORIAL EVOLUTION OF THE MODERN BRITISH EMPIRE

On the eve of the Second World War – as it turned out, in itself an event destined to become an imperial turning-point of unforeseeable magnitude – the British Empire comprised almost twelve million square miles. That was over a quarter of the world's inhabited land mass, eighty times the size of Great Britain. Modestly, the Colonial Office, with authority over thirty-five countries, took care to point out that this impressive statistic did not include those territories which Britain or one or other of its Dominions was administering on behalf of the League of Nations.[1] More modestly still, the Colonial Office maintained a category of Miscellaneous Islands. 'Various islands and rocks throughout the world are British territory', ran the definition, but, it was conceded, 'many of these have no permanent inhabitants'.[2] Nor, of course, did it include the million or so square miles and 9m inhabitants of the joint condominium of the Anglo-Egyptian Sudan. Some of these possessions were islands with sizeable offshore jurisdiction, and the substantial Tanganyika Territory had 20 000 of its 360 000 square miles classified as water. The post-First World War acquisitions of League of Nations mandates added a further 10 per cent to the Colonial Empire. To put this into some sort of ready-to-recognize imperial perspective, 7.5 m square miles comprised the four self-governing Dominions of Canada, South Africa, Australia and New Zealand, while India accounted for another 1.8 m square miles, so the Colonial Empire, in so far as the direct responsibility of the British government exercised through the Colonial and not any of the separate Dominions, India or Foreign Offices was at issue, amounted to nearly 2 m square miles, carrying a population of approximately 50 million. Add to this the 35 million living in the Dominions and the 400 million in India, and the Empire could claim a quarter of the world's population. In comparison, the Roman Empire held jurisdiction over 120 m people in an area of 2.5 m square miles.

If 1939 was, in territorial terms, the zenith of the British Colonial Empire, that 'very varied agglomeration'[3] of 50 m souls under fifty distinct administrations, its accumulation had in no way been a matter of steady incrementalism. Territory had been lost as well as gained over the previous two centuries, most conspicuously with the secession of the thirteen American colonies and their declaration of independence in 1776, but also with the relinquishment of British authority in such lower-profile possessions as, for example, Surinam in 1815, the Ionian Islands in 1864, Heligoland in 1890, Weihaiwei in 1930 and Transjordan in 1946. Other possessions, like the Falkland Islands and Tobago, came and went and came back in the roundabout of imperial control between, in these two cases, Spain, Holland, France and Britain. Within a mere decade, too, of this defining baseline of 1939, India and Burma, Ceylon and Palestine, were no longer in the British Empire. Yet a mere generation earlier, the Empire had received a substantial – and, as it turned out, the ultimate – injection of territorial capital: on the conclusion of the Great War, parts of the extensive overseas possessions of Germany and parts of the Ottoman Empire were placed under British administration through mandates from the League of Nations, the most notable additions being Tanganyika and Palestine. To understand the complexity and the changing size and shape of the Empire which Britain administered, it is helpful to understand the fluctuating gains and losses among its possessions over the two hundred and fifty years before the Empire reached its territorial peak in 1939.

After the Treaty of Utrecht (1713) Britain was left in possession of the New England States; Newfoundland, where attempts at colonial settlement dated back to 1583, New Brunswick and Nova Scotia; a group of islands in the Caribbean – arguably Britain's first jewel in the crown – among them such well-known colonies as Jamaica, Barbados and the Bahamas; the Bermudas, Gibraltar, and St. Helena, occupied by the East India Company after the Dutch had abandoned it in 1651; and what were really no more than slave-trading stations along the West African Coast, like the Gambia and the Gold Coast. Aside from the New England States and the expanding commercial activity of the East India Company, further territorial expansion came about with the major European wars of the second half of the eighteenth century. The Treaty of Paris (1763) added to the British Empire the rest of Canada and more islands in the West Indies. Then by the Treaty of Amiens (1802), Ceylon and Trinidad were ceded by the Netherlands and Spain respectively.

But it was in the nineteenth century that Britain was to acquire most of her colonial possessions. The ending of the Napoleonic wars brought her, under the two Treaties of Paris (1814 and 1815), the Cape, Malta, Mauritius and the Seychelles, and more territory in the Caribbean, including Guiana and Tobago. By 1816 the Colonial Department could officially describe its function as 'Transacting the business of all His Majesty's Colonies in North and South America and the West Indies, the settlements on the Coast of Africa, the Cape of Good Hope, the Isle of France [Mauritius], Ceylon and New South Wales'.[4] But if that was a sonorous enough roll-call of imperial territory, to list all the colonial acquisitions associated with the reign of Queen Victoria would be like reading a gazetteer of the world.[5] In the future Dominions, there was now British Columbia and the Canadian Northwest; in the Pacific, Australia, New Zealand, Tasmania and British New Guinea; and in Africa, Natal, Zululand, the Transkei, Rhodesia, Basutoland and Bechuanaland. As part of what was subsequently to be recognized as the Colonial Empire, Hong Kong, Fiji, Lagos and much of the Gold Coast were ceded, and from Penang and Singapore Britain progressively extended its authority over the Malay peninsula, with the Straits Settlements separating from British India to become a Crown Colony in 1867. Civil administration was established in the Falkland Islands in 1843. To resort to a latter-day Colonial Office vocabulary, Hong Kong was 'secured by cession' in 1842, Cyprus was 'acquired by agreement' in 1878 and an extension of British Kowloon was 'obtained on lease' in 1898.

The last decades of the century were characterized by Europe's expansion into Tropical Africa, culminating in calls made at the Berlin Conference of 1884–5 for a measure of rationalization through agreed (however imperfect) 'spheres of influence' and designated areas of 'effective occupation' as Britain, France, Germany and Portugal competed for some sort of delimitation and definition of the territories which they had competitively acquired.[6] By the turn of the century Britain had succeeded in establishing recognition of its presence in those territories which soon became known as, in West Africa, the Protectorates of Sierra Leone, of Northern and Southern Nigeria, and the Northern Territories of the Gold Coast; in East Africa, Uganda, Kenya, Zanzibar and British Somaliland; and in Central Africa the Protectorate of Nyasaland. In South Africa, the Transvaal and the Orange Free State were annexed. By 1900, Britain had added to its Empire over a million square miles in Africa. By then, too, in the Pacific a number of the Solomon Islands were transferred to Britain and Tonga came into the British sphere of interest. As for India, when Queen Victoria celebrated her diamond jubilee with lavish imperial pomp and circumstance in 1897, Britain was already approaching its 150th year of authority there.

The ending of the First World War brought a further – and general – accretion to Britain's imperial possessions. Iraq, Palestine and Transjordan were added to her Middle East responsibilities under the League of Nations system of mandates; the whole of German East Africa, other than the north-west corner which was assigned to Belgium, went to Britain, along with portions of Togoland and the Kamerun in German West Africa. Further south, German South West Africa was entrusted to the Union of South Africa. Elsewhere, the mandate for German New Guinea was assigned to Australia and that for Samoa to New Zealand. The island of Nauru, all eight square miles of it, was to be governed by an administrator appointed from Australia and approved by Britain and New Zealand. The Colonial Empire had acquired a further half a million square miles under the new mandatory system.

The dismantling of this enormous empire, so many times the size of its mother country, took a far shorter time than that required for its spasmodic construction over four centuries. Following the shock loss of the Thirteen Colonies in 1782, the next group to sever the imperial bonds were the Dominions, who in the 1920s sought to terminate their subservience to the Colonial Office and bring about the logical conclusion to the implications of responsible government set forth in the historic Durham Report of 1838,[7] outlined in 1907, confirmed in 1926 and culminating in the 1931 Statute of

Westminster. They established the pattern of leaving the Empire but remaining in the Commonwealth, a model observed by every British colonial territory on achieving independence other than Burma, Palestine and Somaliland, with moments of leaving (and sometimes rejoining) indulged in by Ireland (1949), South Africa (1961), Pakistan (1972), Fiji (1987) and, for Nigeria, suspension (1995). Neither the Anglo-Egyptian Sudan nor the constitutionally comparable Anglo-French New Hebrides were, of course, ever members of the Commonwealth.

The pace of imperial withdrawal quickened with the independence of India and Pakistan in 1947, and Burma, Ceylon and Palestine in 1948, followed by regional peaks like Africa in the 1960s and the Pacific in the 1970s. The basis of Britain's decolonization was in nearly every instance that of mutual agreement, a negotiated timetable, and an orderly demission of authority and transfer of power. Only occasionally was withdrawal accompanied by armed rebellion from within (for example, Ireland, Palestine, Aden, Cyprus, Kenya), generally amounting to a delaying factor in granting independence rather than a war of colonial independence leading to a new direction of imperial relationship. Unlike the French experience of decolonization in Indochina and Algeria, or Portugal in her African empire in the 1960s and 1970s,[8] retreat occasioned by military aggression had not been part of the British experience since the mid-1970s. The occupation of Malaya and Hong Kong during the Second World War was temporary, however permanent its message was in retrospect, and the Argentinian invasion of the Falkland Islands in 1982 was repulsed in a full-scale defensive war. The UDI of Southern Rhodesia in 1965 and the handing over of Hong Kong in 1997 were both *sui generis*, one a constitutional showdown and the other a diplomatic negotiation. Today, with no more Dominions Office since 1947, no more Colonial Office since 1966 and no more Commonwealth Relations Office since 1968, all that is left are the remnant 'Dependent Territories', as the new Foreign and Commonwealth Office preferred to describe them.[9] By the mid-1990s these numbered barely a dozen: St. Helena with its own 'Dependencies' of Ascension and Tristan da Cunha, Bermuda, Gibraltar, Hong Kong, the Cayman Islands, the Falkland Islands, Anguilla, and the Turks and Caicos Islands, along with the British Antarctic Territory, the British Indian Ocean Territory, and South Georgia and the South Sandwich Islands, none of the last three dependencies having any resident British administrative staff.[10] Hong Kong was handed back to China in 1997. Table 2.1 presents a statistical summary of the British Empire in its terminal stage, in relation to the three overseas civil services whose personnel and work provide the focus of this book.

THE ORGANIZATION OF THE BRITISH EMPIRE, 1660–1968

Formal empires, once they have been acquired – whether by annexation, treaty or mandate – have to be administered. The only exception to this principle in

Table 2.1   Terminal Empire

	Area (sq. m)	Population (million)
India (1947)	1 808 679	400 000 000
Sudan (1947)	968 000	9 000 000
Colonial Territories (1952)	1 965 000	77 500 000
Africa	1 584 977	61 626 000
Eastern	130 056	10 076 000
Atlantic and Indian Ocean	122 207	1 469 500
West Indies	98 908	3 422 000
Pacific	24 880	547 000
Mediterranean	3 696	845 000

Source: Adapted from C. Jeffries, *The Colonial Office*, 1956, Appendix 1.

the British Empire was what the Colonial Office used resolutely, right to the end, to define as 'Miscellaneous Islands', which, though British territory, had no permanent inhabitants to administer. One of the last of these acquisitions was Rockall, an uninhabited island lying in the Atlantic Ocean 200 miles to the west of the Outer Hebrides, which was annexed by Britain in 1955. To have administrators *in situ*, with all the position and paraphernalia of – whatever the exact title down the ages and across the oceans – *vice-rois* and their executive agents to whom the imperial authority was devolved in varying measures, is one of the features which distinguish the practice of formal empire from the concept of informal empire. The latter flourishes on commercial relationships, can survive on personal influence, and calls for no executive imperial representation, whereas in the case of the former manifestation of empire the presence of Crown representatives and administrative personnel is *de rigueur*. Such local structures, of officials whose duty it is to carry out the policy of the imperial power, in turn presuppose a level of responsible organization in the metropole. In the case of the British Empire, these institutions ranged, over the centuries, from non-governmental Boards through Directors of Chartered Trading Companies to full-blown Government Departments and Ministries under a Secretary of State. Britain's experience of responsibility for administering an empire at the metropolitan end has, like the Empire itself, expanded and evolved over three hundred years of the exercise of some level of governmental control.

Colonial affairs, which in the seventeenth century largely meant concern with the settlement of British emigrants and their descendants in North America and the West Indies, were first brought together in London in 1666. Starting with a Committee of the Privy Council appointed 'for the Plantaçons', by the end of the year it had transformed into a Council of Foreign Plantations, responsible for the central administration of what were eventually to develop into the colonies. The diarist John Evelyn was made a member of this Council in 1671, noting his satisfaction with the award of an annual salary of £500 'to encourage me'.[11] A year later, in 1672, this Council was amalgamated with the Council for Trade, adopting the hybrid name of the Council of Trade and Plantations. It proved an ineffectual body and was quickly abolished. For the next twenty years the Privy Council itself took charge of colonial affairs. However, it was reconstituted in 1695, and for almost a hundred years it was the Council for Trade and Plantations which was responsible for the oversight of the increasing number of colonial possessions which Britain began to acquire through the successive Treaties of Utrecht (1713) and of Paris (1763). Additionally, the growing affairs of India were brought into its jurisdiction in 1748, until they were transferred to a separate Board of Control in 1784, properly known as the Commissioners for the Affairs of India.

Although the office of Secretary of State has been traced back to the reign of Henry III, colonial affairs did not justify such elevated attention until 1768. His office, the third principal Secretaryship of State to be created (a second had been established in 1708 to deal exclusively with the affairs of Scotland), was known as the Secretary of State for the American or Colonial Department. It was an office which was to last, with changes in its jurisdiction and title but not its primary responsibility for the affairs of the colonies, for two centuries, almost to the year (1768–1966). However, following the loss of the American colonies, the new Department was abolished in 1782. Once again it was the Privy Council which was drafted in to cope with colonial affairs. At the same time the responsibilities of the two principal Secretaries of State were restructured into 'Home' and 'Foreign' offices: it was, however, on the Home Department that Colonial affairs were devolved, the section being known as the Plantations Branch. These arrangements were but temporary, and in 1784 a Committee for Trade and Foreign Plantations was appointed, taking over the responsibilities of the Home Office's Plantation Branch.

After these vicissitudes, responsibility for colonial affairs in London settled down to sixty years of constancy, though in the event they were to remain combined with the portfolio for War from 1794 until 1854. The war with France led to the appointment in 1794 of Mr Dundas (later Lord Melville) as Secretary for War. The erstwhile Committee for Trade and Foreign Plantations relinquished its concern with colonial matters and continued with the work which eventually led it to be known as the Board of Trade. Nominally, responsibility for War was now combined with that for the Colonies, though the bureaucratic amalgamation of the two Departments did not take place until 1801, when Lord Hobart assumed charge of the unified portfolio of the War and Colonial Department. Once the French wars were concluded, the Earl of Bathurst's principal concern, as Secretary of State, reverted to colonial matters, including their defence. Each of his two departmental Under-Secretaries of State received a salary of £2000, against his £6000. The Colonial Office staff in 1831 totalled some thirty persons, two-thirds of them clerks, the remainder including a librarian, a précis writer, a housekeeper, and two office porters.[12] Allowing for a generous interpretation of

the term 'colony' in the first half of the nineteenth century, the number of possessions for which the CO was responsible ranged from 29 in 1806 to 34 in 1828. For
administrative purposes they were grouped geographically into North America,
West Indies, Mediterranean and Africa, and Eastern divisions; and, for business,
into 'legislative colonies', consisting of the remnants of the old settler empire in
North America and the West Indies, and the 'non-legislative' colonies such as
New South Wales and all the colonies recently taken from the continental
powers, like Trinidad, Mauritius, Ceylon and the Cape of Good Hope.[13]

The urgency of the Crimean War called for the appointment of a Minister
with sole responsibility for the war, and in 1854 a separate Secretary of State for
the Colonies was created. While the Colonies had thus enjoyed a measure
of separate control since 1768, full independence under their own Secretary of
State did not come until 'Colonial and War' were split and a fourth Secretary
of State was established.[14] Yet, as Blakeley has argued, regardless of the variety
of titles dreamed up for Colonial affairs throughout the two centuries since the
inauguration of a Council of Foreign Plantations in 1660, 'the basic function of
this office remained the administration of the overseas dependencies with as
little trouble and expense to the home government as possible'.[15]

The ministerial vicissitudes of the allocation of responsibility for colonial
affairs in the ensuing century were far less than they had been between 1660
and 1854. A major change did not take place for seventy years. In 1925, following the report of an internal committee (Scott) on the higher establishment of
the Colonial Office, a new Secretaryship of State for Dominion Affairs was
created in order to take over from the Colonial Office the burgeoning business
relating to the consciously self-governing Dominions.[16] In fact, the two offices
continued to be held by the same Minister, notably by Leo Amery, the only MP
ever to have headed (at different periods of course) the three imperial offices of
Secretary of State for Colonial Affairs, 1924–9, for Dominion Affairs, 1925–9,
and for India, 1940–5. There were further periods when the two posts were
again temporarily combined, for instance when Malcolm Macdonald at the
Colonial Office took over the Dominions Office as well on the sudden death of
Lord Stanley in November 1938. The joint establishment of the two Offices,
Colonial and Dominions, persisted–though with separate but equal Permanent
Under-Secretaries – until 1947, when the latter was restyled the Commonwealth
Relations Office.

The India Office was closed down at the independence of India and Pakistan
in 1947, the last (and only twelfth in ninety years) Permanent Under-Secretary
being, albeit for less than a year, Sir Archibald Carter. In 1962, matters once
again moved nearer than further apart, when Duncan Sandys assumed the
duties of Secretary of State for the expanding Commonwealth Relations portfolio while still holding the shrinking Colonial Office one.

The shape of things to come was already apparent in 1960. Nigeria now followed Ghana and Malaya into independence, pace-setters for the rest of the
colonial empire. In 1961 the Department of Technical Co-operation (DTC) was
converted into a new Department of State with its own Minister, charged with

overseeing the provision of technical assistance hitherto undertaken by the three Ministries of the CO, the FO and the CRO. Sir Saville Garner, head of the Diplomatic Service and the last Permanent Under-Secretary of the Commonwealth Relations Office 1965–8, had no doubt that the emergence of the DTC had a major impact on the evolving relations between the CO and the CRO. For the first time since 1925 'there was now an organizational link, and some of the affairs of independent and dependent territories were handled in the same unit'.[17] In 1964, this department was abolished to make way for yet another new, post-colonial Department of State, the Ministry of Overseas Development (MOD). As the colonial years receded, so too did the obligations of aid differ and dwindle, and in 1975 the Ministry was downgraded to an Administration within the Foreign Office, the Overseas Development Administration (ODA).

The culmination, however, was dramatic and abrupt, going beyond the imperial timetabling speculated on by the Plowden Committee on Representational Services Overseas[18] in its consideration of a single unified Service resulting from the eventual amalgamation of the Ministries involved (cf. Chapter 5). The Colonial Office was closed down in 1966, consequent on the establishment of a Commonwealth Office integrating the rump of the Colonial Office as a Dependent Territories Division into the new Ministry: its name artfully combined the historical initials of the Colonial Office with the thrust of the Commonwealth Relations Office. By 1968 the integrated and renamed Foreign and Commonwealth Office (FCO) remained the sole legatee of the remnant parts of the one-time British Empire.

Such an overview of the institutions created and abolished between 1660, the year of the establishment of the Council of Foreign Plantations, and 1970, when overseas development was switched from an autonomous Ministry to a department and the remaining colonial territories had been downgraded to a department of Dependent Territories, both within the FCO, has gone beyond the scope of the present study with its focus (Part II) on the history of the three principal overseas Civil Services, the Indian Civil Service (1858–1947), the Colonial Administrative Service (*c.*1895–1966) and the Sudan Political Service (1899–1955). Each had, in the century under scrutiny, its own Office to which it was responsible, though, as we shall see, in no case did that Office comprise membership of the same Administrative Service which implemented its London-derived and sanctioned services overseas. It is to the metropolitan organization and structure for the control of each of these administrative Services that we now turn before embarking on how they were recruited, trained and operated in the field.

THE INDIA OFFICE

The Act of 1858, whereby responsibility for the administration of India passed from the East India Company to the Crown (the Charter Act of 1833 had simply called on the Company to wind up its commercial affairs) necessitated a total restructuring of the scheme of government. At the apex now was a new Ministry in Whitehall, with the post of an extra Secretary of State attached, additional to and quite separate from the two Secretaries of State responsible for Foreign and, since 1854, for Colonial affairs. This, then, was the decade in which the metropolitan administration of the British Empire assumed a new look and required new machinery. The anterior Honourable East India Company, whose own civil service had long regarded themselves as servants of the Queen[19] and in 1842 had come yet closer to the conventional status of a Crown Civil Service when the ranks of its executive servants were altered from Senior Merchant, Factor and Writer to civil servants of the first, second and third class, is considered in Chapter 3.

As a Chartered Company, its Governor-General had been responsible on the one hand to a Court of Directors, answerable in turn to the Court of Proprietors or the shareholders, and on the other, through the Board of Control, to the Crown and to Parliament. Now a Secretary of State would replace these intermediary bodies, aided by a Council appointed by him to 'conduct' business correspondence in Great Britain – a brief that could be but an uncomfortably short step from the formulation of Indian policy, especially when coupled with its authority to exercise a financial veto. In their – if not always in the Secretary of State's – favour was the fact that this small body of men, ranging from ten to fifteen in all between 1883 and 1909, were all 'Old Indians', in keeping with the intention of the 1858 Act to furnish the new India Office with a reservoir of advice derived from first-hand experience of India. In 1874, however, such appointments for life were abolished in favour of an appointment for ten years, revised again in 1907 to seven years with the possibility of a five-year extension. The Council of India Act of 1907, predecessor of the Morley-Minto reforms of 1909, saw the appointment of the first two Indians to the Council (and in 1909 the first such appointment to the Viceroy's Executive Council), afforced by a third Indian member during the war. By the 1919 Government of India Act supreme authority in India was vested in the Governor-General in Council – an office which had been restyled Viceroy when in 1858 he became the personal representative of the Sovereign – subject to the control of the Secretary of State. Executive orders of the Government of India were issued under the collective authority of the Governor-General in Council.[20]

The fact that the India Office has been so commonly looked on as the 'Home Government of Britain's largest and most complex overseas possession',[21] an imperial government in miniature, is reinforced by the fact that not until the end of World War I was its powerful permanent staff, with an establishment nearly five times that of the Colonial Office at the end of the century, brought under the control of H. M. Treasury in the same way as the rest of the Home Civil Service. That unique institution, the Council of India, provided the India Office with, in the opinion of one Indianist historian, 'a certain Indian ethos that set its 'paper empire' apart from the departments of state dealing with peoples elsewhere'[22] and often exhibited, as Donovan Williams argues, a more incisive grasp of the realities of the local Indian scene than that evinced by either the Colonial Office or the Foreign Office.[23] In the hands of such an arch-civil servant as the gifted Arthur Godley, who held the headship of the India Office for the astonishing period of twenty-six years (1883–1909) and declined the Permanent Under-Secretaryship of the Foreign, War or Colonial Offices, Asquith's description of Godley as 'the real Governor of India under a succession of Viceroys'[24] (for which appointment he himself had been shortlisted by the Cabinet) was an apt and acceptable *bon mot*. Godley's 'reign', as it were, at the India Office more or less coincided with the critical extinction in the 1880s of the hangover structure, spirit and culture of the defunct East India Company exuded by many of the inherited personalities (Williams' 'tyranny of the past'[25]). It also coincided with the readier communications with and control over the Government of India by Whitehall enabled from the 1870s by the opening of the Suez Canal and, above all, by the completion of the telegraphic link between London and Calcutta. By then, too, in the graphic chronology of Kaminsky, the Council of India was no longer made up of those who had themselves figured in the conquest and consolidation of the Raj: the new members 'had not personally experienced the trauma of the Sepoy Mutiny and did not debate in despatches as their predecessors had done the reasons for the near collapse of British rule in India'.[26] Sixty years later, a parallel quickening and tightening in imperial affairs was repeated in the Colonial Office when, thanks (though not always literally so in the Government Houses) to the advent of air travel, colonial governors could be called home for consultation within a matter of hours or an official from the Colonial Office, on occasion the Secretary of State himself, could be in Blantyre or Belize the next day. In the India Office of the 1890s as in the Colonial Office of the 1950s, the exercise of enhanced control and personal communication was the next best diplomatic device to subverting the ground-rule taboo of open intervention by Whitehall in the execution of imperial government by its chosen men on the spot.

Both because of the role of the unique Council of India on the conduct of Indian affairs in the metropolis and because of its mythology which in the 1860s and 1870s constructed a negative image of reactionary obstructionism, now and then carried to the point of rubber-stamp passivity or a sheer deficiency in reputation and intellect,[27] the composition and function of this institution call for a short comment in this context of the India Office as the Home Ministry of the Indian Civil Service examined in Chapter 4. Putting to one side the original fifteen members appointed in September 1858, eleven of whom had been directors of the East India Company (among the rest was one man of outsize stature, Sir John Lawrence, who six years later became Viceroy), the one thing the Court's membership was never short on, even after the departure of the old Indian hands, was the attribute – often loudly lamented by governing bodies when it is not on offer – of first-hand experience. Men of the calibre of Lumsden, Lyall and Strachey, all appointed in the 'new age' of the 1880s, were household names in India. That position of personal experience was reinforced by the unusual provision that members of the Council could not be removed by either the Secretary of State or the Prime Minister. *En revanche*, the former was entitled to overrule the Council if he saw fit – as he did spectacularly, in the drafting of the Cantonment Bill in 1890. But he could never escape the knowledge that the original intention of the 1858 legislation had been to set up a system of checks and balances over the Secretary of State himself, shared between the Crown, Parliament and India. Like Africa a century later, India was not the kind of issue on which an able and ambitious politician would want to pin his career.[28] For personal reasons, the Queen became less involved, and it was the Council of India which dominated the India Office staff still feeling their way in a new Department of State.

Yet for all the accusations of foot-dragging, irresponsibility and lack of imagination levelled by Secretaries of State, Viceroys (notably Elgin and Curzon) and Indian nationalists down the years, there can be no denial that the Council of India enjoyed three valuable attributes: they knew from first-hand what they were talking about, they offered a degree of continuity in the fly-by-night appointment of a political Secretary of State, and they were to a considerable extent insulated from the pressures of politics, home as well as Indian. There is evidence that the good intentions of the Council of India may have been better appreciated by the civil servants of the India Office than by any of the other parties with which it came, sometimes bruisingly, into contact. Sir Arthur Godley, now elevated to the House of Lords as Lord Kilbracken and, admittedly, speaking five years after his retirement from the hurly-burly of life at the India Office, described the Councillors' knowledge of Indian affairs as 'priceless', and strongly deprecated any proposal to diminish its influence. His metaphor was compelling: 'A captain of the ship may be an excellent navigator, but for local knowledge he depends, nay he is compelled by law to depend, upon a pilot.'[29]

Kaminsky makes the point, central to this study, that the officials at the India Office were very different from those in the Colonial or Foreign Office. Here was a body of civil servants who had 'an identifiable empire to which they could attach their loyalties',[30] going well beyond the common Whitehall motivation of wishing to enhance the status of one's own Office. For all the internal grumbling about the conservative conduct of the Council for India, the India Office appears to have shared with them an underlying belief that its ultimate function was to sustain British rule in India, even when trimming its sails to the demanding winds of Indian nationalists. Demission was arguably less a policy in the India Office before 1940 than decolonization was in the Colonial Office before 1950. If self-government for India had been promised in 1917, over the ensuing quarter of a century the India Office still seems to have been preoccupied with the maintenance and performance of the Raj. Significantly, for instance over the issue of such a detail as the age limits for acceptance into the Indian Civil Service, the policy-advising Council comprised many ex-members of that Service. Their strong internal linkage continued until the Home Civil Service and the ICS were both brought under a common Civil Service Commission. In contrast, the Colonial Office was never expected to initiate policy; its constitutional role was to discuss matters referred to it by the Secretary of State. Overall, the India Office was more intimately involved with the Indian Empire than the Colonial Office was with its colonial empire.

In terms of internal administrative structures, the India Office had no need to suffer the headaches endured by the Colonial Office in its distribution of business between subject and overlapping geographical departments: economic and establishments, defence and legal, all were pan-Indian matters and did not have to be re-thought out in terms of the differing Pacific, Atlantic or Indian Oceans, etc. Even the latter-day addition of a Reforms Office in the India Office, with all its attendant problems in the 1930s, did not have the spread of context required by the Colonial Office's latter-day Constitutional Planning department of the 1960s. Ten years before independence, the India Office was straightforwardly structured into one Administrative Division, with half a dozen Secretaries responsible to the Permanent Under-Secretary through (since 1921) a Deputy Secretary for such matters as finance, military, political, economic and establishments. These in turn were supported by some thirty-five Principals and Assistant Principals. Servicing the Administrative Division were a small Executive Division and a large Clerical Division, staffed by over two hundred members of the clerical grade. There was a separate India Audit Office, a score of Miscellaneous Appointments, including an Assistant Government Director of Indian Railway Corporations, an Administrative Officer for Currency Duties and another for statistical quotations, and the important Library and Records staff.

Two other structures furnished the dominant establishments, difference between the operation of the India Office and the Colonial Office. One, as we have seen, was the existence – and a highly prominent and positive one, too – of the advisory Council for India, with its group of influential Members under its own Vice-President, all nominated, to quote the official wording, to advise 'The Secretary of State for India in Council'. The Council in London was serviced by its own Clerk of the Council, of Assistant Secretary rank, and his assistant and two Resident Clerks, all seconded from the Home Civil Service. The Colonial Office never had any organization to set beside this. Another difference was the coexistence in London of an Indian Trade Commissioner and an Office of the High Commissioner for India. This was organized into departments, each with a substantial staff, e.g. a department for Indian students in the UK. These had their own hostel, at 21 Cromwell Road. Once again, this was a Colonial Empire phenomenon which did not come on the scene until the last few years before territorial independence,[31] whereas the first Indian High Commissioner to London was appointed in 1920. Further light, perhaps in terms of British politics rather than Empire affairs, might be shed on the underlying differences of these two Departments of State by comparing the length of time successive Secretaries of State and succeeding Permanent Under-Secretaries of State held office. For India, there were four Secretaries of State between 1866 and 1868, and as many as three changes in 1885–6, but against this Sir Charles Wood held the office for seven years and E. S. Montagu for five, while the Earl of Kimberley was appointed on three occasions (1882, 1886 and 1892). A long period in office was a distinct characteristic of the Permanent Under-Secretary, with only eight civil servants holding the post between 1860 and 1930. The Colonial Office, which started off with five appointments as Secretary of State in its first eighteen months, records Joseph Chamberlain in office for eight years and several, like Leo Amery and Alan Lennox-Boyd, for five. As for Permanent Under-Secretary, the Colonial Office too observed the principle of continuity, with just two appointments between 1860 and 1892 and a total of only nineteen different holders of the office between 1825 and 1966.

A final point of connection – separation might be more accurate – between the two Empire Departments of State was the vivid lack of interchange with their overseas civil services which existed right up to the end. Reciprocity was not the order of the day. This was true, too, at the seniormost level. Hardly any colonial civil servant was appointed to a governorship in India, as Sir George Bowers, with twenty years of colonial governorship of Queensland, New Zealand, Victoria and Mauritius behind him, lamented when he unsuccessfully applied for the governorship of Madras in 1881.[32] A few ICS officers moved laterally to governorships outside the continent, such as Bartle Frere and John Maffey, and a few others made an earlier career transfer out of the ICS and climbed the Colonial Service ladder to the top, among them Bernard Bourdillon and Evelyn Baring. Others turned down a colonial governorship after India, like Sir Alfred Lyall who was offered both the Cape and New Zealand. Lord Metcalfe remains unique, having been successively Governor-General of India (1835), Governor of Jamaica (1839) and Governor-General of Canada (1843).

Whereas few if any studies of the Colonial Service could be properly written without considerable attention being paid to the role of the Colonial Office in the recruitment and management of the Colonial Service, many of the one-time standard works on the Indian Civil Service, like those by O'Malley (1931) and Blunt (1937), manage to conclude their analyses without so much as an entry in the index to the India Office.[33] A welcome exception to this brusque exclusion is Philip Mason's study, not so much of the Service as of the 'characters' among the men who made up the Service, first the Founders and then the Guardians.[34] His incorporation of the India Office, though still slighter than *mutatis mutandis* the Colonial Office would be in any comparable study, contains a memorable passage:

> The influence of the India Office was different. Of course the India Office was not really at all like the picture of it framed by most officers in India, a place of cobwebbed and shady corridors, where life stirred only drowsily, like a hedgehog awakened from winter sleep, where the *élan vital* had given up all hope and men thought only in terms of files, reminders and reasons for inaction... But that the consideration of legal forms and constitutional precedent, the elaborate enumeration of possible dangers, took a high place among the

functions which the India Office carried out, its warmest defenders would agree. It put forward in fact the kind of views which it is proper for a solicitor to put; but it was also in control, and a business managed entirely by solicitors is likely to proceed with caution.[35]

THE COLONIAL OFFICE

An outline of the evolution of the metropolitan arrangements for its colonial affairs has already been given up to 1854, the year in which the Colonial Office emerged under its own, sole Secretary of State. A Parliamentary Secretaryship, to share the dual responsibility assigned to the Secretary of State for the Colonial and War Departments, had been established in 1830: it was held in 1835 by Sir George Grey, who in 1854 became the first Secretary of State for the Colonies. With the accelerating expansion of Empire in the second half of the nineteenth century there went *pari passu* a staff increase at the top of the Colonial Office. The top civil service post of Permanent Under-Secretary of State was shared between only three officials for the first thirty-five years of its existence (1825–59): the inadequate Robert Hay, 'obtuse but bold',[36] Sir James Stephen, ranked by a leading pre-war historian of the Colonial Office among its three greatest P.U.Ss.[37] (this despite the sneering sobriquets of Mr Over-Secretary and Mr Mother-Country[38]), who went on to become a professor at Oxford; and the highly intellectual Herman Merivale, who came from a professorship at Oxford and went on to become head of the India Office. Even before the Colonial Office's separation from the Department of War, the upper hierarchy responsible for colonial affairs was expanded by the creation of an Assistant Under-Secretaryship, and by the end of the century business had so increased that the number of staff in this senior grade had been raised to four. Although the Assistant Under-Secretaries were reduced to two in 1911, they doubled again when the affairs of the Middle East were added to the Colonial Office in 1921. Ten years later a Deputy Under-Secretary was added to the establishment, and the outbreak of war brought in an extra Assistant Under-Secretary in 1940 to take charge of the critical Economic Division. When at the end of the war the Empire entered a new – and ultimate – phase, on the Ministerial side the team was reinforced by the addition of a new post, that of Minister of State for Colonial Affairs. Only five politicians ever held it.

The most internally dramatic of the pre-World War II changes in the organization of the Colonial Office, however, came in 1925, seventy years after its own independence. On the eve of the constitutionally radical 'Balfour formula' announced at the milestone Imperial Conference of 1926, a new post of Secretary of State for Dominion Affairs was created to take charge of business relating to the five self-governing Dominions (then also including the Irish Free State, constituted in 1922), the new self-governing colony of Southern Rhodesia, and the three South African [*sic*] Protectorates of Basutoland, Bechuanaland and Swaziland. These three High Commission Territories did not come under Colonial Office jurisdiction for staffing purposes until 1961. In the event, the same Minister held both posts until 1930, when J. H. Thomas became the first separate Secretary of State for the Dominions. In 1935, and again in 1938, the dual office was again briefly held by one person, Malcolm Macdonald. Under the 1935 organization, responsibility for the whole business of the Imperial Conference was transferred to the new Dominions Office. This had been set up at the fifth Colonial Conference, held in 1907 (the inaugural one took place in 1887), when the Colonial Office was reconstituted into three Divisions: Dominions, Crown Colonies, and General. Nevertheless, a common Colonial Office establishment had remained in place, with staff below the rank of Assistant Under-Secretary being fully interchangeable between the three Divisions. The 1925 joint organization continued until 1947, when the Colonial/Dominions Office administrations were separated. The remnant India Office was absorbed into the Dominions Office, and together they formed the new Commonwealth Relations Office. Further mergers took place in 1966, when the Colonial Office and the CRO staff came together to form the Commonwealth Office, and again in 1968, when this dual character Office amalgamated with the Foreign Office to become the Foreign and Commonwealth Office.

Housed at first in No.14 Downing Street, in 1876 it moved into the new block of buildings at No.12 designed in Renaissance instead of Gothic style by Sir Gilbert Scott. During the war members of the expanded Colonial Office staff were scattered ('out-housed', in the local Office vernacular) in Queen Anne's Gate, Victoria Street, and in Palace Chambers. In 1946 the CO moved to Great Smith Street, occupying Sanctuary Building and Church House. The rapid dissolution of the Colonial Empire put paid to the grandiose post-war Colonial Office planned for Parliament Square, on the site of the old Westminster Hospital and the former Stationery Office, at an initial cost of over £3 million and within a building period firmly calculated at two and a half years. Work on the foundations was actually started but was suspended in 1952, first as an economy measure and then in late 1954 in response to a stay requested personally by Churchill who had his own vision (in the event, unfulfilled) of a grand design for the whole of Parliament Square. Finally, the project was abandoned in the mid-1950s as being totally out of keeping with the political atmosphere and needs of the time.[39]

The purpose of this section on the Colonial Office is not to record the history of its evolution, on which a number of thorough accounts exist,[40] but to present it in outline as the background to the staff and work of the Colonial Administrative Service examined in Chapter 5. The most influential aspects of development within the Colonial Office relating to this are three: the internal allocation of business; staffing; and the role of the Colonial Office in the selection and training of colonial civil servants before they were taken on the strength of their respective territorial governments. The fact that the Colonial Office staff numbered 125 all told in 1909 at the half-way stage in its hundred and twelve year history as a single Ministry of the Crown, having risen from

60 in 1880 and reaching 220 in 1924, and stood at 640 officials of all grades in its final year of 1966 (the staff had peaked at over 1200 in the hyperactive mid-1950s) is, however revealing and meaningful as part of a study of one of the major Ministries of state responsible for the direction of imperial affairs in the century from 1860 to 1960, of less importance to the present study than an analysis of who the Colonial Office staff were and, in particular here, of their relationship with the Colonial Service.

Taking first the division of business at the two selected dates of 1910, by which time the gains of the new imperialism of the late Victorian era had been incorporated into the Colonial Office machinery, and 1966, when the CO came to an end, the principal shift in the Office's structure is manifested in the refinement of the simple geographical distribution of business in the Crown Colonies Division, renamed after the First World War the Colonies and Protectorates Division. This dealt with colonial affairs in a set of regional departments: West India, the Far East, West Africa, East Africa and the Mediterranean. Nigeria had its own department, not because of any territorial importance but in order to handle the business of the planned amalgamation of the separate Northern and Southern Protectorates in 1914 and subsequently to take care of the additional responsibility devolved on Nigeria and the Colonial Office by the award of a League of Nations mandate for part of the Cameroons at the end of the First World War. In the same period, a Middle East Department was added to the CO's geographical structure in 1921 and a Tanganyika Department was set up, dealing not only with the new mandated territory (1924) but also with the geographical hotchpotch of Somaliland, Nyasaland and the new (1924) Northern Rhodesia. The other half of the Colonial Office business, the General Department, was inevitably called on to raise its jurisdiction above territorial and regional boundaries, although the doyen of experienced insiders, and unequivocally the most entertaining of its chroniclers, Sir Cosmo Parkinson, declared that such incidents did not trespass far beyond the mundane matters of what he dismissed as 'office establishment' rather than the high ground of policy.[41] A former Permanent Under-Secretary (1916–21), G. V. Fiddes, was even more forthright in his description of the General Department as that 'into which are swept up a host of miscellaneous matters which could not be conveniently dealt with in any one geographical department'.[42] The geographical departments, on the other hand, dealt with everything that concerned their designated territories, specialist, technical and personnel matters as well as political and administrative.

The only specialist adviser in the Colonial Office before 1926 was the Legal Adviser, though to an extent one could equate the responsibility of the Inspectors-General of the West African Frontier Force and of the King's African Rifles with that of military advisers. In technical work, too, the bulk of the advice and of the execution was in the hands of the Crown Agents for the Colonies. Staffed since 1909 by CO officials, comparable to regular civil servants but recognized as servants of the Crown and not as a department of the Crown, the office dates back to 1833. Its function was, as the commercial and financial agents in Britain for all the colonial governments, to provide professional advice to the geographical departments on public works, engineering and railway construction. They also looked after the recruitment of professional and technical staff for colonial appointments.[43] On other professional matters, the Colonial Office progressively liaised with Home Departments like the Boards of Trade, Education, Agriculture and Fisheries. The Second Division, as the non-Administrative grade was for a long time called, staffed the Colonial Office Library and Records, the Accounts and the Printing Departments, as well as the Copying Department, the only section of the Colonial Office which then employed women other than cleaners. Its typists were, like the senior staff, all meticulously listed by name in the annual *Colonial Office List*, duly designated 'Miss' right up to 1966 with hardly a 'Mrs' among them.

The First World War brought fundamental administrative reform to the Colonial Office in its wake. What a long-time Colonial Office official like Sir Charles Jeffries acknowledges as the pre-war 'convenience' of the geographical departmental structure, whereby each maintained its own coherent set of files and correspondence dealing with single territories as a self-contained entity and where 'experience, precedent and common sense prevailed',[44] was quickly found to be inadequate for the post-war extension and complexity of Empire. Two powerful imperial influences were also in play in the 1920s. Lugard's frank thesis of a reciprocal mandate, 'that Europe is in Africa for the mutual benefit of her own industrial classes and of the native races in their progress to a higher plane',[45] with its echoes of Joseph Chamberlain's vision a quarter of a century earlier of developing new territory as 'trustees for civilization, for the commerce of the world',[46] coincided with the League of Nations' call for accountability by its administering authorities. In their stewardship of the mandate, they were charged to observe 'the well-being and development of peoples not yet able to stand by themselves form a sacred Trust of Civilization'.[47]

Accordingly between 1925 and 1935 the Colonial Office set about the foundation of a series of Subject Departments, directed at and able to deal comprehensively with matters affecting colonial territories as a whole. In addition, its advisory services were expanded, notably through the appointment of a number of official Advisers to the Secretary of State in the professional fields. In 1921 a Commercial Adviser was appointed, followed by a Chief Medical Adviser in 1926. This was followed in 1929 by an Agricultural Adviser, with a Labour Adviser in 1938 and Advisers on Animal Health and on Education in 1940. Although an Advisory Committee on Education had been in existence for many years, an Adviser was not appointed until 1941. A further half-dozen Advisers' posts were created after the war.[48] The Inspectors-General of the Colonial armies in West (WAFF) and East (KAR) Africa were combined in 1931 into a single Inspector-General of African Colonial Forces. They did not survive the war. A Police Adviser was appointed in 1948, the title being changed to Inspector-General of Colonial Police in 1950.

Thus by 1948 the Secretary of State could profit from the counsel of no less than fifty professional Advisers, Specialists and their Deputies, including six

Consulting Physicians and a Colonial Attaché resident at the British Embassy in Washington DC. Additionally, he could call on over two dozen Advisory Committees. While most of the Advisers brought with them Colonial Service experience, a few in this period came in from service in India or the Sudan. Still the spread of reform within the Colonial Office continued. Patronage now gave way to personnel management in the Colonial Office, particularly from 1930 in the method of making appointments to the Colonial Service. In 1932 came the unification of the Colonial Services from territorial Services when a single Service was initiated (see Chapter 5). In 1934 a bipartite General Division was formed, comprising an economic as well as a general department. A Social Services Department was opened in 1938, widened a year later to handle the new policy of Colonial Development. Finally, with war unambiguously in the offing from 1938, a Defence Department was added.

After 1945, the Geographical Departments that had existed in the Colonies and Protectorates Division and in the Middle East Division before the creation of the Dominions Office in 1925 (hitherto itself a separate Division within the Colonial Office) and their subject departments were reordered to reflect the new priorities and realities of empire now that Ceylon and Palestine had left it. They were complemented by further Subject Departments ('these upstarts' in the idiom of one senior official)[49] like Communications, Public Relations, Research and Welfare, with a whole new Division for Economic and Financial Affairs. By 1954/5 the Colonial Office was organized into 30 Departments, nine of them geographical but the bulk of them incorporated into three Divisions, Economic (seven Departments), Colonial Service (four, known simply as Departments A, B, C and D) and Legal. Among the remaining Departments were Establishment and Organization, International Relations, Social Service, Students, and Library. This multiple 'Arrangement of Business in the Colonial Office', as the structure was termed internally, was supplemented by a whole range of official Associations, Institutes and Committees linked with colonial affairs, more than fifty all told. No wonder that Sir Cosmo Parkinson, with thirty-five years service in the Colonial Office, under twenty Secretaries of State and eight Permanent Under-Secretaries, was struck, on his retirement in 1945 by the incredible contrast in the volume of work handled by the Colonial Office, with 90 000 colonial despatches and letters registered in 1909 against 300 000 in 1939 – before any of the wartime crises had erupted in the Empire. A century before he had joined the Colonial Office, the number of despatches sent had been 902 from and to 35 colonial administrations.[50] Like most modern institutions in the pre-computer age, empire and bureaucracy went hand in hand.

So much for the routine business of managing a post-war Colonial Office. But time was not standing still, least of all in the Empire. The Colonial Office kept ahead of the changes associated with the fresh policy of decolonization, and though there is some doubt about sustained contact between the Colonial Office and the India Office on the precedents and details of handling the transfer of power,[51] colonial governments could not complain of a lack of information and guidance from within the Colonial Office itself. It added a

Constitutional Planning Unit to the Subject Departments, an Information Department and a Parliamentary Liaison Unit, as well as an African Studies Branch. Institutions like the Commonwealth Parliamentary Association, the Royal Institute of Public Administration, the Local Government Advisory Panel, the Inter-University Council for Higher Education and the British Council were all more than willing to play their part in helping the Colonial Office over the transformation of empire and the training of local civil servants.

It remains to examine who those Colonial Office officials were who provided the immediate point of contact with the thirty-eight colonial governors and their 18 000 Colonial Service officers *en poste* in 1957, when decolonization started in Africa, that dominant constituent part of the Colonial Empire. What must be borne in mind is that the CO and the CS were two fundamentally different Services, in recruitment, conditions, performance and rewards – in brief, in terms of a career.

The Colonial Office was essentially part of the Home Civil Service. What few officers from the Colonial Service it employed between the wars and in the period 1946–66 were short-term appointments, on secondment from territorial governments (known as 'beachcombers') or else re-employed retired officers (commonly known as 'retreads'). For all the periodic investigations into the pros and cons of a merger between the Colonial Office and the Colonial Service to form a single unified Service with interchangeable postings on the model of the Foreign Service, such a scheme was never introduced. Entry into the Colonial Office, which, as one of the first Departments of State to come under the scrutiny of Trevelyan and Northcote in 1853 soon introduced its own supplementary examination and system of interview,[52] from the 1860s began to earn a reputation for intellectual quality among applicants for the First Division of the Home Civil Service from the universities.[53] Allowing for the status of Sir Henry Taylor, author of *The Statesman* (1836), as one of the intellectual giants appointed (1824) to the Colonial Office in the pre-examination era of patronage, the fact that early examination success into the Colonial Office included men of the calibre of C. P. Lucas and R. L. Antrobus, and scholars such as A. S. Keith[54] and H. E. Egerton, indicates the attention exercised on young university men by a career in the Colonial Office – Pugh's 'brilliant generation' of CO officers in the second half of the century.[55] As Sir Andrew Cohen[56] testified, to work in the CO was an ambition and a recognition that was, despite Baillie Hamilton's lugubrious description of the Office in the 1860s as 'a sleepy and humorous office ... where there seemed no enthusiasm, no *esprit de corps*, and no encouragement for individual exertion',[57] to last down the years. For many it was Parkinson's reaching 'the haven of their choice'.[58] From 1877 entry to the Colonial Office, which since 1856 had operated on a system of individual examination following nomination, was through the competitive Home Civil Service examination and in 1896 this was combined into a joint Home, ICS and Eastern Cadetship Service entrance examination. It was believed that a clerkship in the Colonial Office was as a stepping stone not only to senior levels within the office but likely high office in the colonies themselves.[59]

At the topmost level there was an intermittent fusion of the Colonial Office and Colonial Service staff, with a handful of colonial governorships being offered to the former. Examples from the 1940s, well after the Colonial Service had pressed on the Secretary of State the argument that with its enhanced professionalization the option of appointing military officers, MPs and Home Civil Servants was no longer necessary and should become the exception rather than the rule, include governors like Sir Edward Gent to Malaya (1946) and Sir Gerald Creasy to the Gold Coast (1948); and from an earlier period Sir Augustus Hemming (1898) and Sir Sydney Olivier (1907), both to Jamaica. The record in this interchange context belongs to Sir Edward Stubbs who, following thirteen years in the Colonial Office, went to Ceylon as Colonial Secretary in 1915 and then moved on to four successive governorships, ending up with that of Ceylon in 1933–7. As Lord Carnarvon had observed way back in 1874, he felt it to be 'of advantage when some at least of our Governors are men who have been well trained in our Office and are familiar with its traditions and practice'.[60] Inevitably, perhaps, there was often a core of Colonial Service complaint that the outsider was not a success – Sir Gerald Creasy in the Gold Coast and, with the debate equally vigorous from both viewpoints, the reformist Sir Andrew Cohen in Uganda (1952–7), were two hotly argued instances within the Service.

The 'abduction' of talent in reverse at this topmost level was very rare. In the twentieth century very few colonial governors moved up to the post of Permanent Under-Secretary at the Colonial Office, notable being Sir Samuel Wilson in 1925 and Sir John Macpherson in 1956, with Sir John Maffey from the Sudan in 1933. Uniquely, Sir John Anderson sandwiched the top post in the Colonial Office (1911–16) between two colonial governorships, the Straits Settlements (1904) and Ceylon (1916). Among outsiders coming in to head the Colonial Office, Sir James Masterton-Smith was transferred from the Ministry of Labour in 1921 and Sir Francis Hopwood had come across from the Board of Trade in 1907. Both were already Permanent Secretaries. None was as unusual a move as the nomination of Sir George Gater of the London County Council to head the Colonial Office in 1940, for four months only and then being reappointed in 1942, when he served a full five-year term.[61] Shortly before and during the First World War, a succession of colonial governors were tried out in the Colonial Office in the rank of Assistant Under-Secretary – Sir Henry Moore (1937), Sir Alan Burns (1939), Sir William Battershill (1941–5) – but the experiment was then discontinued.

A palpably higher degree of interchange, though never amounting to a firm quota of posts at either end, was the so-called 'beachcombing' arrangement. This derived from the Warren Fisher reforms of 1930 (see Chapter 5) relating to the system of Colonial Service appointments to posts in the Colonial Office. The proposal was that, in order that the Whitehall-based Colonial Office staff should learn something about conditions in the territories which they were responsible for servicing and generally administering, there should be an opportunity for as many as possible of the new Assistant Principals to spend, after a few years in the Colonial Office, one tour of service in the colonies. In a way this was an extension of Chamberlain's arrangement at the turn of the century to second three Colonial Office clerks to Milner's staff at the Cape,[62] with at least an ulterior motive of supplying the Office with some much-needed practical experience of the government of the colonies. Now some Assistant Principals were seconded as Private Secretary to the Governor, others worked as 'real' Assistant District Officers. One of the first cases was that of John Martin, later Deputy Permanent Under-Secretary at the Colonial Office (1956–63). Having entered the Dominions Office in 1927, he was seconded to the Malayan Civil Service from 1931 to 1934, and so enjoyed the field experience that he seriously thought of putting in for a transfer (in the event, a very rare occurrence). On the eve of decolonization the Colonial Office speeded up beachcombing, loaning six officers to the colonies in 1952 and a further seven in 1963.[63] On grounds of health, one or two Colonial Service men did transfer to the permanent staff of the Colonial Office, like A. D. Garson who started as a cadet in Nigeria in 1928, was seconded to the Colonial Office in 1933 as an early beachcomber, and stayed there for the rest of an influential career in its Colonial Service Division.

One variant of beachcombing, not intended at the time, was for a newly appointed Colonial Service cadet, raring to put his university training course behind him and get on with the real job of field administration, to be loaned to – 'kidnapped by' was the vocabulary used at the deprived Government House end – the Colonial Office for a year, because of 'pressure of business in the CO', before being sent out to the territory to which he had been posted. These 'abductions' were a forte of Sir Ralph Furse, the persuasive personality officially in charge of recruitment from 1930 to 1948 and unofficially from 1924 as Private Secretary (Appointments) to the Secretary of State. As the career of P. Renison showed, such a hiccup in his posting did no harm to his rise in the Colonial Service.

But the equally important aims and emphasis of the 'beachcombing' arrangement was to give Colonial Service officers a chance to work in the Colonial Office, usually at Principal level, and learn what life was like at the other end. It was a principle that while in the Office, their own territory was never on their schedule: no governor would welcome a directive signed by one of his junior officers on behalf of the Secretary of State. This taboo can also be understood by the Colonial Office's practice of minuting. From the 1850s on a convention existed in the Colonial Office that minutes, and often drafts for policy memoranda, should always originate from below: in Fiddes' experienced gloss, 'the result is that from the day of his entrance into the Office, its youngest member into whose hands a paper may come in the first instance is at liberty to expound his views thereon to an extent limited only by his sense of the fitness of things'.[64] The reader of CO files cannot help being impressed by the candour with which comparatively junior officers might minute upwards on the views expressed by distinguished colonial governors in their despatches addressed to the Secretary of State, in a manner quite out of keeping with the protocol observed within the governor's own secretariat.

At a more senior level, an excellent way for the fortunate Colonial Office officials to gain first-hand experience of 'the other side of the world' was when they were assigned to accompany the Minister or Parliamentary Secretary on an official tour (the Hon. W. G. A. Ormsby-Gore, later Lord Harlech, was an assiduous tourer in the 1920s) or else as secretary of a Royal Commission or Colonial Office commission of inquiry. The imaginative Malcolm Macdonald, when Secretary of State in 1938, went so far as to envisage a kind of sabbatical year in the colonial territories for officials who had put in ten years at the Office.[65] Unlike the French, no serious thought seems to have been given to the creation of a Whitehall-based Colonial Inspectorate. Yet in 1954 alone, members of the Colonial Office staff, from the Permanent Under-Secretary down to Principals, managed to make over fifty visits to more than 120 overseas territories.[66] This, too, was the period when the hard-pressed Colonial Office introduced one more refinement of the interchange principle of beachcombing. They took on their staff a number of recently retired Service officers, from among former Governors and Chief Secretaries such as Sir Bernard Reilly and Sir Gerald Whiteley, and from long-scale officers who had reached the rank of Provincial Commissioner or even only Senior District Officer, e.g. R. S. Hudson, P. A. Tegetmeier and C. J. J. T. Barton. In 1957, for example, the Colonial Office was employing 17 re-engaged officers in the rank of Temporary Principal, more than half of them ex-Colonial Service, as well as another six serving officers on secondment. Perhaps as a portent of what lay just round the corner, in 1966 the Colonial Office staff was diluted with an injection of eight appointments on loan from the Diplomatic Service.[67]

The associated Dominions (from 1947 Commonwealth Relations) Office and Overseas Development Administration (earlier Department of Technical Co-operation, 1961–4, and then Ministry of Overseas Development, 1965–70) staffs do not feature in this study other than passingly in Chapter 5 and, momentarily in Chapter 10, as recipients of redundant Colonial Office and Colonial Service personnel following independence and the closing of the CO. Although after 1928 an obligation to serve as agents of the Dominions Office abroad if required became, as in the Foreign Office, part of the conditions of service, their recruitment continued to lie squarely, like the Colonial Office but unlike the Colonial Service, in the hands of the Civil Service Commission with its responsibility for the Home Civil Service. Treasury housekeeping and Civil Service doctrines kept a check on any tendency to Dominions Office separate-ness in the years from 1925 to 1947 while they were ostensibly a single Department of State with two Ministers. They occupied the same building in Downing Street; they shared many administrative services, including the Library, Accounts and Legal Advisers; and the Dominions Office staff were interchangeable with those of the Colonial Office (but not of the Colonial Service). For all that, despite the frequent use of the term of 'the Commonwealth Service', the DO/CRO staff remained unequivocally part of the Home Civil Service until the creation of the new Diplomatic Service in 1965. Fundamentally, the Dominions Office/Commonwealth Relations Office was a home-based Office, never an overseas civil service. The comparative conclusion of one of the most articulate heads of the Commonwealth Office is instructive:

> Broadly speaking, the functions of the India Office and the Colonial Office were administrative and regulatory: those of the Dominions Office and Foreign Office diplomatic and political... Correspondence between the I.O. and the C.O. and their agents abroad tended to be direct but impersonal, with the minimum of explanation of reasons and no flourishes; the I.O. style could be peremptory and that of the C.O. brusque.[68]

In summary, what is critical in this study is to grasp that the Colonial Office and the Colonial Service were, despite their nomenclature and in the face of common sense, two separate institutions. At the heart of the divide was the fact that the two Services were differently recruited and offered very different kinds of career. It is an open question whether that late nineteenth-century split, between the Colonial Office officials being recruited through competitive examination and the Colonial Service officers (with the exception of the single-figure annual admission into the Eastern Cadetships) being recruited by patronage up to 1932 and thereafter by references and interviews but never exams, and the consequent sense, however rarely voiced, of intellectual superiority over those 'serving in the colonies', ever dissipated within the Colonial Office. One historian of the Colonial Office has argued that the Office remained 'handicapped' by the organization of its Colonial Service, and that with few exceptions in the nineteenth century its clerks regarded the Office's servants in the colonies as 'ignorant, untrustworthy, quarrelsome and indiscreet'.[69] Nor was this sense of superiority confined to junior officials. One Permanent Under-Secretary himself expressed the view that the governors of most crown colonies were 'very inferior persons'.[70] In particular, that stormy petrel Sir John Pope Hennessy, who held no less than six colonial governorships in the 1870s and 1880s, was written off by the Colonial Office as 'vain, unscrupulous, wanting in sound judgement and common sense, and prone to quarrel with his subordinates'.[71] Even the political class in the Colonial Office had little good to say of their colonial civil servants. For Sydney Olivier, along with Sidney Webb one of the 'most famous drop-outs'[72] from the Colonial Office, the Colonial Service was nothing short of a 'wasteland of talent', and its Permanent Under-Secretary, G. V. Fiddes, 'a rabid, narrow-minded judge'.[73] Webb went on to become Secretary of State for the Colonies (as Lord Passfield) and Olivier Colonial Secretary and then Governor of Jamaica and Secretary of State for India; both were elevated to the House of Lords. The Earl of Kimberley wondered whether anyone could be 'more difficult to deal with than a wrong-headed Indian or Colonial judge'.[74] In riposte, those in the colonies could impatiently dismiss the home officials as uninformed meddlers, and Sir Frederick Lugard, no admirer of the Colonial Office, declared the PUS Fiddes to be the rudest man he had ever met.[75] Such polarity and antipathy between the centre and the periphery, which in the military generally reflects the mutually dismissive attitude of field commanders towards the general staff despite the fact that both belong to a single Service, was exacerbated in the context of the colonial empire, with its separate methods of recruitment and appointment.

Even when, in the 1930s and the 1940s, the derision gap narrowed and mutual perceptions mellowed, the perceived difference in selection and hence quality was never quite forgotten even though it might no longer be the nineteenth century first response to colonial crisis and problems. However thankful most Colonial Service officers were that they had chosen to escape a life of what they believed to be humdrum and routine in Whitehall, however relieved most Colonial Office staff would be that they did not have to put up with the discomfort and limitations of a life in the colonies throughout their career, and however strenuously and sincerely both might aver that they would not wish to exchange their respective professions for any other job, by the 1950s the esteem of the new generation of ex-service men in both Crown Services matured in their improving evaluation of each other's institution. The closing of the gap in communication as well as in the difference in career formation in demobilizing Britain played its part. Cross-experience, though officially promoted through beachcombing as an antidote to inter-service rivalry since 1930 and supplemented by a certain amount of overseas visiting (but never inspections) on the part of Colonial Office personnel, particularly once air travel became a regular means of transportation, brought the two branches of imperial administration together far more frequently in the era of decolonization than it ever had at the height of empire. The series of constitutional conferences held at Lancaster House and Church House or in Lagos and Nairobi, inseparable from an orderly transfer of power, and the annual Summer Schools on Colonial Administration held at Cambridge from 1947 onwards and at Oxford just before the war meant that there was now a far greater awareness and appreciation of what each was doing than had ever been practised or possible before. A healthy pre-war determination by junior Colonial Service men on leave never to set foot in the Colonial Office again once the final Selection Board had been held, for fear of being seen to toady or of experiencing disdain, could now be replaced by surprised pleasure not only at the courtesy of the reception but also at the depth of knowledge about the problems of the area displayed by the Colonial Office staff. By 1950 Sanctuary Building and Church House had moved a long way from the Downing Street atmosphere of 'aloofness' said to characterize the Colonial Office of 1925, where, according to R. B. Pugh, 'the culture of London seemed so polished that it was hard to treat with proper seriousness the aspirations of Toronto and Auckland, Lagos or Belize'.[76]

In the final analysis, however, and in the 1950s as much as in the 1890s, for all the frequently shared attributes of class, school and university (and Pall Mall clubs), and from 1945 often of common experience in the armed forces, there remained an inherent, if now unspoken, career division between 'us' and 'them'. This was the polarized principles of recruitment, the competitive examination against the interview and personal record. Muted as it was by the 1950s, it emerged unmistakably in the 1960s when the Foreign Office and the Commonwealth Relations Office closed ranks and barred the prematurely retired Overseas Civil Service officers (and earlier those from the Indian Civil Service and the Sudan Political Service) from any direct transfer into the Home Civil Service recruited Departments. An inter-departmental stand-off was now taking place in Whitehall and a bitter end-of-empire rivalry between the Colonial Office and the Commonwealth Relations Office, once joined in dissoluble wedlock, now surfaced as the former shed its imperial responsibilities and the latter picked them up, amid allegations of the 'fear' of the one and the 'disdain' of the other.[77] Nobody could have fought harder for the Colonial Service than did the Colonial Office;[78] yet with both institutions equally a-dying, any hope of victory over the restructured Foreign and Commonwealth Office for the re-employment of CAS staff cut short in mid-career through no fault of their own was as remote as, a century earlier, had been the likelihood of retaining the historic principle of patronage in Britain's new-look Home Civil Service.

THE FOREIGN OFFICE

A modern Foreign Office official might well be horrified to come across an entry to his Home Ministry in a study of Britain's colonial and overseas civil services. While Her Majesty's Diplomatic Service, as what are today labelled 'UK-based Foreign Office employees' with the built-in intimation of the primacy of mobility,[79] serve abroad in diplomatic and consular posts, and indeed are contractually obliged to do so in contrast to their 'home-based' Foreign Office colleagues for whom a posting abroad is not part of their terms of service, the practice has been to intersperse full tours of duty in a British mission with full tours of duty back in the Foreign Office in London. This is the reverse of the career pattern of the literally 'overseas' civil services studied here, for whom successive tours of service abroad were the norm and a spell *en poste* in London was very much the exception, if it ever took place at all. Furthermore, despite the clear title of 'Foreign' as the opposite of 'Home' Civil Service, it was not until the Second World War, following the merger of the Diplomatic Service and the Foreign Office and the implementation of the recommendations for the incorporation of the Consular and the Commercial Diplomatic Services in 1943,[80] that a unified Foreign Service can be said to have emerged as distinct from the Home Civil Service.

Even then, the conventional antithesis of 'Home' and 'Foreign' was in no way so clear-cut when it came to Britain's Crown Services: while for Britain's imperial civil services it meant service in a dependent country, for the Foreign Service it meant being accredited to an independent country. In the broadest of geographical terms, this dual structure of imperial Britain's relations with the outside world meant that from *c.*1900 until the emergence of the Third World in *c.*1950 most of the Foreign Service posts were in Europe and the Americas, leaving the bulk of Britain's interests in Africa and Asia in the hands of its overseas civil services. The Consular Service (see Chapter 3) breached this generalization, the recognition of the autonomous status of the Dominions took the process a stage further, and after 1968 a top-ranking Foreign Service officer might be posted as Ambassador to a 'foreign' country or as High Commissioner in a Commonwealth country – or successively to both – the difference being not one of status but simply of nomenclature. Even the apparent groundrule that Foreign Office officials were never posted to any parts of the British Empire could be breached in the final years of dependence, for instance when members of their staff were sent to Khartoum (not a Commonwealth country capital) to open what would shortly become the first British Embassy or again to Lagos to help the Nigerians set up their own Foreign Service. Since the creation of a Foreign and Commonwealth Office in 1968, too, the FCO appoints and services the [colonial] Governors, Commissioners or Administrators of Britain's Dependent Territories. Some of these, particularly in the Caribbean, have been former members of Her Majesty's Overseas Civil Service, as the Colonial Service was restructured and redefined in 1954 (see Chapter 5), such as Rex Hunt's appointment to the Falkland Islands in 1982, while others have been drawn from the regular Diplomatic Service cadre, like Sir David Wilson's appointment to Hong Kong in 1987. In retrospect, Sir Charles Johnston's secondment from the Foreign Office to the Colonial Office as Governor of Aden in 1960 contained more seeds of an evolving practice than was thought likely within the Colonial Service at the time.[81]

Yet there are two further reasons for bringing the Foreign Office into this study over and above their post-end-of-empire responsibility for the remnant colonial (restyled Dependent) territories since 1968. One, in chronological terms, reaches back to the beginning of Britain's nineteenth-century empire, especially in Africa. Much of British East Africa, which in due course became known as Kenya and Uganda, and that area of British Central Africa which was subsequently called Nyasaland, were at first placed under the control of the Foreign, not the Colonial, Office; and their governors were appointed by the Foreign Office, with the title of Commissioner. The first four Consuls-General or Commissioners in charge of Kenya, from 1896 to 1906, were drawn from the Foreign Office, among them Sir Arthur Hardinge and Sir Charles Eliot, who ended up respectively as ambassador to Madrid and to Tokyo. In Uganda, from 1894 to 1903, the Commissioners, among them the diplomat Sir Gerald Portal, were answerable to the Foreign Office. In Nyasaland, where Sir Harry Johnston was Commissioner from 1891 to 1897, Foreign Office administration continued till 1907. A similar situation existed in what became Nigeria, with the Foreign Office appointing the Commissioner of the Oil Rivers, and then from 1891 of the Niger Coast Protectorate up to 1900. The experience of Zanzibar as a Foreign Office responsibility was longer still, and it was not until 1913, after more than seventy years of consular administration, that the last Consul-General handed over to a nominee of the Colonial Office.[82] At the same time, one could take the 'colonial' story back beyond the turn of the century specifics to the whole 'consular' heyday of Africa in the nineteenth century, with the appointment by the Foreign Office of a series of 'African' consuls.[83] Some were successful, others merely spectacular, but all made their name. Besides those mentioned above, they involved Colonel Hanmer Warrington, HM Consul in Tripoli from 1814 to 1846; David Livingstone in Central Africa, Richard Burton in Lagos, Harry Johnston in Nyasaland and Roger Casement in the Bights of Biafra and Benin, all of them among the kaleidoscope of 'characters' who served as Victorian Foreign Office consuls in places which became Edwardian Colonial Office territories. With the Consular Service (see Chapter 3) up to 1914 divided into sections for China, Japan, Siam and the Levant as well as General (under which Africa was subsumed), it is arguable that in a number of circumstances the subsequent British colonial presence is historically insepara- ble from the anterior consular one. Yet, for the purposes of this study, the so- called 'Barbary Consuls' were primarily individuals – or families, like the remarkable Warringtons in Tripoli and Drummond Hays in Morocco – not basically imperial services.

It is on the next score that the Foreign Office earns a firm place in this study of Britain's overseas civil services. This is the case of the administration of the Sudan. While, logically enough albeit lacking any integration, the Indian Civil Service (Chapter 4) 'came under' the India Office and the Colonial Service (Chapter 5) 'came under' the Colonial Office, the Sudan Political Service (Chapter 6) remained the exclusive, if remote, responsibility of the Foreign Office. Such an exceptional British arrangement derived from international history.

In 1885 General Gordon was murdered in Khartoum and the Turco-Egyptian government and their British advisers were driven out of the Sudan by the Mahdist rebellion. Following its reconquest by Kitchener in 1898 Lord Cromer, the British Consul-General and Agent in Cairo, took a leading part in devising and drafting the 1899 Anglo-Egyptian Agreement, whereby the British and the Egyptians were designated as 'co-domini'.[84] The concept of a Condominium was a unique invention by the British Foreign Office, applied only in the case of the Anglo-Egyptian Sudan (1899–1956) and the Anglo-French Hebrides (1906–80). Egypt had historically been a Foreign Office concern, that of Her Britannic Majesty's Government, and was never a colonial responsibility despite the *prima facie* anomaly of its designation as a British Protectorate in 1914. Her senior representative in Cairo was thus titled a High Commissioner and not, until 1952, an Ambassador. In 1899, the new machinery for the administration of the Anglo-Egyptian Sudan became the responsibility of the Foreign Office. There it stayed, throughout the life of the Condominium. Correspondence was between the Governor-General and the Foreign Secretary. Within the Office, the Sudan and its Political Service were in the portfolio of the Egyptian Department, which also included Libya, Liberia and Africa (General), and in the mid-1930s was under an official of Counsellor rank who had just returned to London from a spell as acting High Commissioner in Cairo. A separate Abyssinian Department also existed, responsible for the two adjoining non-British Somalilands and Eritrea.

Such a relationship brought both advantages and disadvantages to the Sudan Political Service in ways unknown to its sister Indian Civil and Colonial

Administrative Services. To many at the Palace in Khartoum and its Secretariat, it was a relief to be led on such a light rein from Whitehall. To others, especially as the transfer of power gathered speed, the Sudan lost out by (unlike the Colonial Service) having no precedents for comparison, no lessons to learn from, and none of its own personnel to bring in with first-hand experience of other ways in other territories. The Whitehall touch was remarkably light. One cynical view was that the only time the Foreign Office made its presence felt was when it appointed one of its diplomats to the post of governor-general (Sir Robert Howe, 1947–55) as well as his successor in the final year before independence, Sir Knox Helm, who had come in through the Levant Service. A marginally more charitable ascription is the recognition that it was a British ambassador in Khartoum who made a generous public tribute to the Sudan Political Service in a book on its history – thirty years after it had been wound up.[85]

Overall, while no study of and few memoirs from former members of either of the other two Services could contemplate constructing the record without paying at least a degree of attention to the name and role of the 'parent' Ministry, in the case of the Sudan Political Service the Foreign Office presence can often be removed to the background, even beyond the periphery. For example, there is no reference at all to the Foreign Office in the index of such a standard retrospective history of the Service as that carefully compiled by one of its senior officers (Henderson) in 1987, or in that of such well-informed memoirs as those by G. W. Bell, R. Davies or J. S. R. Duncan, or even the well-researched volume in the *Nations of the Modern World* series (see Bibliography). And, lest such rejection be interpreted as an in-Service point of pride, the index to Daly's authoritative, one thousand-page history of the Condominium which was completed only in 1991, remains devoid of any recognition of the existence of the Foreign Office among the 2500 entries in its index. In many ways, the Foreign Office just did not obtrude on, or was not perceived to be important in, the daily life and work of the Sudan Political Service.

Here was a lacuna, conscious or not, which is not generally reflected in the Service literature until the Bevin–Sidky Pasha Protocol of 1946. Then the Foreign Office's attitude towards Cairo began to generate a sense of suspicion among the British administrators that the Sudan was being sacrificed on the altar of appeasement with Egypt, leaning towards a policy of wider unity of the Nile Valley rather than endorsing the promotion of a policy of 'the Sudan for the Sudanese' which the Service felt would best serve the interests of the people of that country. The FO position was, as the Civil Secretary noted in his journal, interpreted by the Sudan Political Service as a move 'to sell the Sudan to Egypt'.[86] Between their twin loyalties, to the Foreign Office as their masters and to the Sudanese as their trustees, there was no hesitation over which had priority: His Majesty's Government had sold the pass. It came, as its top official bluntly charged, as a great shock to the members of the Sudan Political Service. Bitterly, the head of the Service wrote these machinations off as 'a typical Foreign Office production', with the grave implication of immoral behaviour.[87]

THE OVERSEAS CIVIL SERVICES: A NOTE ON PERIODIZATION

This summary analysis of the development of the Empire and the structures evolved in the metropole for its oversight and management furnishes the necessary background to the scrutiny of the three corps of administrators charged with the execution of policy in the overseas territories which comprises Part II. While it is their recruitment, work and ethos that provide the core of this book, with an envoi on the effect of the transfer of power on their latter-day predicament as 'administration' metamorphosed into 'politics' on a par with the Whitehall which many had shunned as dull in their undergraduate days of career options, this background chapter on the home organization of empire and its civil services needs to clarify one final matter: each Service's chronology within the umbrella pattern of Britain's overseas civil services.

Although the time-span adopted here is essentially the hundred years between the inauguration of the Indian Civil Service in 1858 and the closing down of the Colonial Office in 1966 – what may be looked on as the golden age of Britain's imperial administrators – those dates do not signify the cut-off dates of the three Civil Services. What they do encompass is the period, of almost a complete century, when these three major civil services offered a full, fulfilling, and frequently prestigious career, attracting generations of public school and university men in search of responsibility, recognition and reward abroad in a civilian rather than a military capacity. It remains to settle on the determining dates of the existence of these overseas civil services before we consider their specific characteristics. In each instance, there is room for debate on the exact chronology.

In the case of the Indian Civil Service (ICS), while it became a Crown Service in 1858 following the débâcle of the Mutiny under the administration of the East India Company, it cannot be looked on as a totally new civil service. Not only had the Company's civil servants tended to consider themselves servants of the Crown, all the more so after 1833 when the Charter had been revised to oblige them to run down their trading activities and concentrate on public administration. There was also a marked measure of continuity in the locality and scope of their work which the ICS inherited, including the functions of secretaries to the Presidency governors, executive posts and judicial posts, down to the very nomenclature of the administrative hierarchy. Indeed, the continuity can be taken further: if the Company's civil administration in 1842 totalled 836 posts, the ICS strength in 1939 was still no more than 1299 posts. At the other end, although the ICS unarguably terminated when independence came in 1947 and the subcontinent was split into India and Pakistan, most of the serving 'Indian' officers of the ICS transferred to one of the two 'family' successor Services, the Indian Administrative Service (IAS) or the Civil Service of Pakistan (CSP), taking with them, like the Indian Army, vigorous traditions as well as three centuries of administrative service history. For our purpose, too, just as the independent administrative services of India and Pakistan started in 1947 not in a vacuum but with a legacy of administrative experience and ethos, so this study of the ICS, though starting in its foundation year of 1858, acknowledges the shaping contribution of its predecessor East India Company's civil service. Thackeray's portrait of the Collector of Boggley Wallah in the 1830s[88] represents as clear a declaration as any of the lineal descent of the ICS, from Joe Sedley to John Beames and H. M. Kisch and, *mutatis mutandis*, all the recognizable way to Philip Mason and R. V. Vernède in the 1930s (see Bibliography).

The periodization of the Colonial Service is a matter of far greater complexity, in its ending as in its beginning. This is not surprising, given the tortuous and erratically cumulative net growth (for there were losses of territory too, and not only in North America) of Britain's colonial responsibilities, from the initial governorships of places like Virginia, Newfoundland and Bermuda in the early 1600s down to the fact that, despite the transfer of Hong Kong in 1997, almost four hundred years on, a dozen dependent territories remain in the care of the Secretary of State of the Foreign and Commonwealth Office at the beginning of the twenty-first century.

Although a set of official guidelines for Public Officers was drawn up in 1837 and continued into the 1960s under the rubric of *Colonial Regulations*, there was officially no such institution as the Colonial Administrative Service until 1932. Administration of many of the earliest colonial possessions lay in the charge of naval or military officers, sometimes known as Superintendents or Agents. To revert to the satirical pen of William Thackeray, it was a Colonel Rawdon Crawley, 'a distinguished Waterloo officer', who was appointed by the Colonial Office to the governorship of Coventry Island; significantly, for it was in 1847 that the novel was first published, in monthly parts, there is a direct reference to Crawley's appointment to the Colonial Service.[89] Sir Charles Jeffries, a leading Colonial Office historian, observes that the machinations involving poor Colonel Crawley's exile to a distant colonial governorship more or less reflect 'the popular idea of the Colonial Service' for much of the nineteenth century.[90] But by the 1870s Sir Drummond Wolff, who had started his career in the Foreign Office, was ready to claim among his credentials for a post at Tehran that he had had experience in the Colonial Service, a reference to his time in the Ionian Islands.[91] With the acquisition from the 1890s of large tracts of Africa, territorial services for their administration began to mushroom in the first half of the century, and when Joseph Chamberlain took over the Colonial Office in 1895 he was able to set up a committee to look into the future of what he was ready to recognize as *the* Colonial Service. The claim by another committee in 1929[92] that the Service could look back on a century of existence is both pardonable and understandable in legal terms, but in practice Heussler is nearer the mark when he describes the Colonial Service as Britain's 'organizational response' to the expanded governmental responsibilities derived from her overseas acquisitions in the last two decades of the nineteenth century and defines it as a phenomenon of the twentieth century.[93] Yet even the Chamberlain minute on the Colonial Service was not fully accurate. Officers still joined a territorial Service (the Nyasaland Administrative Service, the

Northern or the Southern Nigeria Service, the Gold Coast Administration, etc.). At the same time, the older Eastern Cadetships, staffing Ceylon, the Straits Settlements, and Hong Kong as they were transferred from the Indian administration to the Colonial Office during the nineteenth century, operated on their own, with different rules for entry and separate conditions of service from the rest of the notional Colonial Service. They opted, too, for a style of organization closer to the Indian model than the colonies of settlement style predominant in the Colonial Office, 'charged with responsibility for carrying on the various departments of government, including the judiciary'.[94] They even evolved a degree of unity among themselves, though not of unification, and from 1882 allowed candidates in the common entrance examination to express a preference for one of the three colonies.

But if the legal myth of a single corps, H. M. Colonial Service, was not literally realized until 1932, when the first of its unified branches, the Colonial Administrative Service (CAS), took over from the dissolved territorial Services, such a narrow interpretation would be misleading. It would not only ignore a century of history and half a century of professionalizing cadres of administrators. It would also reduce the lifespan of the Colonial Administrative Service to a mere thirty years, for in 1954 the Colonial Service was abolished and replaced by Her Majesty's Overseas Civil Service (HMOCS). It is for this reason that, while observing the valid dates of 1837 for the first known set of Colonial Service Regulations and of 1932 for the first manifestation of the unification of all the territorial Services approved in 1930, the defining date applied to this study is 1895. It was in that year, within six months of assuming office, that Joseph Chamberlain, widely looked upon as the father of the modern Colonial Service, called for research and a report on how colonial appointments were made, especially in the dependent territories: in the settlement colonies, those with responsible government, the majority of the appointments were made locally by the Governor, his own nomination alone requiring the approval of the Secretary of State. Chamberlain's aim was to distinguish which appointments might properly come under the heading of 'the Colonial Service', for he was of the opinion that the Service was 'lamentably weak, both at home and abroad'.[95] It is the milestone, and unpublished, Selborne Report, commissioned in 1895 and considered in detail in Chapter 5, which constitutes the appropriate beginning of the search for a single Colonial Service to replace, or at least to associate the individual territorial administrative Services, as a complement to the entity of the Indian Civil Service. Its appositeness for selection as the opening year of this study of the Colonial Administrative Service is reinforced by the fact, that among the searching questions put to the Selborne Committee for resolution, was one which invited it to consider whether the Colonial Service should be merged with the Indian Civil Service into some kind of a single imperial administrative service or whether it should be allowed to develop its own identity.

But if 1895 can stand as a viable and acceptable date for the beginning (but not necessarily the origin) of the modern Colonial Service, ambiguity still envelops any terminal date. Unlike the coterminous events of Indian

independence and the dissolution of the Indian Civil Service in 1947, no integral coincidence can exist for such a multi-territorial institution as the Colonial
Administrative Service. That the Colonial Office closed in 1966 had little
bearing on the continuing work of the Colonial Service's successor Overseas
Civil Service (1954), other than that departmental concern for its members
passed from a Secretary of State for the Colonies (up to 1966) to a Secretary of
State for Commonwealth Affairs (1966–8) to the Secretary of State for Foreign
and Commonwealth Affairs (1968–). He became 'responsible for transfers, promotions and discipline of members of HMOCS serving in Dependent
Territories and appointments of senior officers such as Governors, Senior
Administrative, Judicial and Legal Officers',[96] having shed his previous post-
imperial responsibility for compensation schemes and pensions payable by
former colonial governments by transferring it from the FCO's Dependent
Territories unit to the Overseas Development Administration. The fact is that,
granted the official metamorphosis of the Colonial Service into the Overseas
Civil Service in 1954 (and in some respects the change was cosmetic, arguably
more noticeable in nomenclature and image than in function and responsibility
in those territories in, for example, the Pacific and Indian Ocean, which did not
become self-governing until the 1970s and 1980s), HMOCS was, forty years on,
still in existence. It was the handover of government in Hong Kong in 1997 that
signified the final closure of the Overseas Civil Service, leaving those with a
penchant for anniversaries to be able to point to precisely 160 years, 1837–1997,
of the documented existence of a Crown civil service operating in Britain's
dependent territories. The ending of HM Colonial Service and HMOCS was
officially commemorated in Westminster Abbey in May 1999.

The Sudan Political Service is the easiest of Britain's three major overseas
civil services to which to give a coherent calendar shape. Yet it, too, is not
entirely innocent of definitional ambiguity in its beginning, and even less so in
its terminal date. The starting point, 1899, was the year when Cromer in Cairo
and Kitchener in Khartoum put together a skeleton administration to run the
newly reconquered Sudan. In its formative years, all three of the Inspectors
(*mufettishin*) appointed, the lineal forebears of the generic Sudan District
Commissioner, were military officers seconded from the Egyptian Army.[97] They
were responsible to a British provincial governor (*mudir*), who was at the same
time the military commandant of the area. A similar pattern of appointments
ensued in 1900, with the next cohort of field administrators all drawn directly on
secondment from the Egyptian Army. Nor were these mere fly-by-night attachments. All were to remain in the Sudan Civil Service until they retired –
anytime, as it turned out, between 1913 and 1923. It was only in 1901 that the
inaugural cadre of civilians, together with a further intake of military officers,
were recruited as Assistant District Commissioners in the Sudan Civil Service.
Nevertheless, both the Service and its chroniclers have been content to date its
foundation year as 1899.

The ending of the Service, known everywhere but seemingly without official
pronouncement as the Sudan Political Service from the 1920s,[98] is cloaked in yet

deeper ambiguity. Those who maintain that 1956 is the correct date have much history on their side: this was the year in which the Sudan achieved independence. Yet that was on January 1st, and if January 1st was the first day of a sovereign Sudan – Flag Day as it was called – then, so runs another argument, since the Governor-General's office closed officially for the last time at 2pm on 31 December,[99] the Sudan Political Service technically ended in 1955. Indeed, perhaps because the timing of independence for the Sudan was so last-minute and hastily arranged, the protocol and ceremony of Flag Day, with a military band, 101-gun salute, and the lowering of the old and the raising of the new flag to tumultuous cheers, did not in the event take place in Khartoum until that first day of independence. This was contrary to the convention throughout the decolonizing British Empire, of midnight on the night before – the typical media headline of 'Freedom at Midnight'.[100] The terminal year of 1955 is also advanced by no less a scholar and Service historian than Sir Harold MacMichael, who declared that 'the British Political Service had by 1955 ceased to exist'.[101] Others have argued that because of the rapid rundown of the Sudan Political Service in accordance with the 1953 plan for the accelerated Sudanization of the Administration, the Service virtually came to an end in 1954. 'The Political Service is nearly all gone now', wrote Robertson, head of the Service, in a private letter dated 10 November 1954, 'and all will have left by Christmas'.[102] G. W. Bell, himself one of the last to leave, confirms that 'very few' British administrators continued to serve beyond the end of 1954.[103] Yet others have fixed on the date of 1953, following on the recruitment of the last three men into the Sudan Political Service in late 1952; and therefore maybe, in the name of logic, 1952 itself. In Chapter 6, the preferred dates of 1899–1955 follow the terminal date adopted in the plaque to the work of the British in the Sudan in Westminster Abbey.

Finally, there remains the question of a small irritant which disrupts the presentation of the major overseas civil services studied in this book in either of the shorthand forms of 'Crown Civil Services' or corps of 'imperial administrators'. Clearly the SPS was not a Crown service; for all its Foreign Office responsibility, it served the Anglo-Egyptian government. Not even the ICS bore, as did the Colonial Service and its follow-on Overseas Civil Service, the 'by appointment' title of 'Her Majesty's Colonial Service'. But the use of 'imperial' in relation to the three corps of administrators, while unexceptionable in the case of the ICS and the CAS, can be challenged by the SPS on the literal grounds of the Sudan never having been part of the Empire. In the post-independence era, when scholarship has taken up the wider study of Britain's overseas civil services, some members of the former Sudan Political Service have voiced their rejection of the use of the terms 'imperial' and 'colonial' in association with their role in the administration of the Anglo-Egyptian Sudan. Others accept the term 'imperial administrator' to describe the nature of their work as a DC but eschew 'imperial' when it comes to their Service. A similar discomfort has been expressed by some members of the latter-day H. M. Overseas Civil Service at bracketing it with the pre-1954 Colonial Service, even though both Services operated only in colonial territories. For all the understandable SPS sensitivity, younger post-independence scholars like Martin Daly entertain no inhibition about titling one of the volumes of his magisterial history of the Condominium 'Imperial' Sudan. Accordingly, while we have retained the neatness of the common and identifying denominator of 'imperial administrators' in this study of the ICS, CAS and SPS, in the text we have in general restricted the use of 'imperial' to the generic DOs and preferred the group form of 'overseas civil services' when referring to all three Services.

Before turning in Part II to an anatomy of these three major overseas civil services, Chapter 3 takes into account some of their influential predecessor Services and Britain's other, smaller administrative services overseas.

3 On Company and Other Crown Service Overseas

Part II examines the recruitment, composition, structure and work of the Administrative (in some instances and at some periods called Political) branches of Britain's three principal overseas civil services: in the Indian Empire, in the Colonial Empire, and in the Condominium of the Anglo-Egyptian Sudan. In the century covered by this study, these were the imperial civil services which regularly offered a life-time career in government administration overseas to hundreds of young Britons educated predominantly in British public schools and graduating pre-eminently from British universities. No exact figure has been put on the total of Britons who chose this kind of career abroad, but an idea of the scale can be gathered from the following statistics for the twentieth century alone. Between 1919 and 1939 almost 1700 appointments were made to the Colonial Administrative Service, with a further 1500 between 1945 and 1950 and over a hundred in each of 1953 and 1957.[1] The Indian Civil Service, with 950 posts held by Europeans in 1899, was still appointing an average of 30 British probationers a year in its years of declining attraction, 1925–35, following on 500 British appointments between 1904 and 1913 and a further 130 in the reconstruction years 1919–21.[2] The Sudan Political Service had a total cadre in its existence of approximately 500 posts, every one held by Britons. All this was for the Administrative Services alone, without taking into account any of the professional men and women who sought an appointment in the Empire, averaging between 1919 and 1957 a further five hundred a year into the Colonial Service alone. In 1995, a whole generation – and more – beyond the end of recruitment into the imperial civil services on permanent and pensionable terms, there were still 27 000 former overseas civil servants and their dependents drawing a Service pension.[3] Here then, growingly in the second half of the nineteenth century and substantially in the first half of the twentieth, was a sizeable career goal for hundreds upon hundreds of British graduates – in an age when the number of universities in Britain was barely a fifth of what it is today.

Yet it must be stressed that these three Services were not the only opportunities open to British graduates in search of a non-military career in government administration abroad. In terms of the career and work prospects, and of the socio-educational catchment area which those Services trawled, others too call for a brief consideration here. What is more, in several instances a biological link obtains between some of them and the Crown civil services featured in Part II. This might be lateral as in the case of the Indian Political Service or lineal as in the case of the Chartered Companies, a common instrument of territorial expansion in India, Africa and South-East Asia, whose field administrators

57

often transferred into the new territorial Administrative Services. Others again, like the long-time Consular Service and the short-lived Egyptian Civil Service, earn inclusion on the grounds that they not only attracted a similar – and often the same – kind of young Briton but they also operated in many kindred socio-geographical areas of the world, on government service in regions like North Africa, South-East Asia and the Persian Gulf. If the Diplomatic Service is not included here, it is not solely because of its distinguishing career pattern of regular interchange between an abroad and home posting, but also because up to the end of our period in the mid-1960s the Foreign Office domain (outside the context of its Consular Service department) was, in terms of embassies and legations, predominantly in Europe, the Americas, and the Far and Middle East. That was not the location of formal Empire and its civil services. The FO was in the business of representing, not of governing and administering.

ON CHARTERED COMPANY SERVICE

There are three reasons for making more than a passing reference to the administrative staff of some of the prominent Chartered Companies which flourished in the nineteenth century and, in the case of the East India Company and of several smaller Royal trading companies, during the preceding centuries. One is that they could offer a life akin – and in the case of the East India Company, very similar – to what was to become a career in Britain's overseas civil services. Secondly, in many instances they constituted the direct predecessor administration of areas where the Crown went on to assume authority. Lastly, that moment of handover from Company to Crown was often accompanied, to the advantage of the new imperial government, by the transfer of a number of seasoned administrators into the new imperial civil service. Some, notably in turn-of-the-century Tropical Africa, like E. J. Berkeley and F. E. J. Jackson in Uganda, W. Wallace in Nigeria and R. T. Coryndon in Kenya, went on to hold top ranks in the Colonial Service; Sir Frederick Lugard himself came into the Colonial Service at the age of forty-two as High Commissioner of Northern Nigeria after eight years of serving four different Chartered Companies in the field.

India

In many respects, the nearest of kin to the imperial civil services in Part II among the Chartered Companies was the Honourable East India Company. This is not only because a whole quarter of a century before its rule was handed over to the Crown, the Company, having already lost its monopoly in 1813, was instructed to wind up its commercial activities and restrict itself to administrative functions. Shortly afterwards, its agents, previously known as Factors, were renamed Collectors, the title widely adopted by the successor Indian Civil Service on its establishment in 1858. They had since the middle of the

eighteenth century begun to adopt the title of 'civil servants' and already tended
to look on themselves as servants of the Crown. Since then it is noticeable how
no historian of the ICS has failed to acknowledge the resonances in the administrative legacy, in structure and function, as India's government passed from
Company to Crown. The Crown took over from the Company one privilege profoundly cherished by members of the new ICS, the fact that theirs had, since
1765, been a Covenanted Service.[4] Those who have seen in the choice of the initials, CO, emerging from the merger of the old Colonial Office and the former
Dominions Office into the new Commonwealth Office in 1966 as a happy
attempt to blend change and continuity may also have discerned a similar diplomatic recognition by the initials of the Crown's new Indian Civil Service in 1858
(ICS) being the same as those used in the abbreviation of Honourable East
India Company's Service (HEICS).

Philip Mason, the leading historian of the ICS, does not hesitate in unequivocally attributing the 'beginnings' of the ICS to the year 1769, when Harry
Verelst set about reaffirming and extending to the whole of Bengal and Bihar
that supervisory system by British officials which the Company had in 1761 tentatively introduced in Chittagong and other ceded districts of Calcutta. The
instructions to the Company's supervisor were to be echoed in District Officer's
guides and manuals not only in British India but throughout much of the
Empire for almost two hundred years to come:

> Amongst the chief effects which are hoped for from your residence in that
> province ... are to convince the Ryot [the peasant] that you will stand
> between him and the hand of oppression; that you will be his refuge and the
> redresser of his wrongs ... that honest and direct applications to you will
> never fail producing speedy and equitable decisions; that, after supplying the
> legal due of government, he may be secure in the enjoyment of the remain-
> der; and finally to teach him a veneration and affection for the humane
> axioms of our government. Versed as you are in the language, depend on
> none where you yourself can possibly hear and determine. Let access to you
> be easy and be careful of the conduct of your dependents.[5]

The shortened form of 'East India Company' did not come into usage until
1833, the charter having been granted in 1600 to 'The Governor and Company
of Merchants of London trading in the East Indies'.[6] Although the Company
was for its first century and a half essentially a Merchant Service, it introduced
in 1675 a regular schedule and gradation of posts for its staff. On appointment,
Apprentices were required to serve for seven years before securing preferment
to the rank of Writer. Most of them had come in from Christ's Hospital, which
provided a distinctive commercial education. For appointment to Writer there
were no age limits before 1784, when Burke's India Act fixed the entry age at
not less than fifteen and not more than eighteen, later revised to twenty-two.
For a long time the sole qualification had been, quite literally, good penman-
ship, a knowledge of commercial accounting not being introduced until 1682. A
Writer served a covenanted term of five years before he could advance to the

post of Factor, or of Agent where larger factories existed. Above that, a Company servant could rise to the rank of Merchant or Senior Merchant. Yet merchants though they primarily were, in the three principal settlements of Calcutta, Madras and Bombay where the Company had acquired territorial rights, its staff were at the same time engaged in municipal administration and judicial functions in the institutions it had established. In terms of remuneration, an inadequate salary was offset by the opportunity to trade on one's own account, an arrangement at first opposed but in the end conceded by the Company as an integral element in conditions of service. This lasted until the Covenant was introduced in 1765.

It is generally accepted that Clive's assumption of the *diwani* or financial administration of Bengal in 1765 marked the watershed between the Company's concern with trade and with administration. The use of the term 'civil servants' now became commonplace. Under Warren Hastings' governorship of Bengal in the 1770s, reinforced by the direction of Cornwallis' administration in the 1780s, the Company's merchant service visibly and progressively began to assume the role and many of the features and characteristics of an imperial civil service. By reorganizing the revenue system and redesigning the judicial system, Hastings laid the foundations of a civil service which Cornwallis was to build into a recognizable bureaucracy. From now on a creeping transformation was taking place. In 1813 the Company had its trading monopoly cancelled, and in 1833 it ceased to be a commercial body, retaining its administrative and political powers in trust for the Crown. A decade before the Mutiny the Company carried 836 British officers on its books, 776 of them serving in India itself.[7] Its three Presidencies were divided into more than 150 Divisions and Residencies, with judicial and executive posts. These were held by Merchants, Factors and Writers, the whole cadre being restyled into 1st, 2nd and 3rd class civil servants in 1842.

This is not the place to recapitulate either the rise or fall of the East India Company. Its claims to being a palpable predecessor to the Indian Civil Service have been presented. One more piece of evidence in the linkage of the two Services, Company and Crown, remains. It was an aspect, too, of such Company–Crown transfers that was to feature prominently in Africa at the turn of the century. This was the number of Chartered Company servants who applied and were accepted for transfer into the new Crown civil service. Many feature in the pantheon of 'the British in India', names like Elphinstone, Malcolm, Metcalfe and Wellesley.

Africa

The case of the other Chartered Companies has a different impact on the successor Crown civil services. Whereas in the East India Company history, the most conspicuous and continuing link was the strong legacy of the system of administration inherited, for many of the Chartered Companies whose domain the Crown took over the dominant link lay in the number of experienced field administrators who secured a transfer to Crown service. It is only the directly antecedent Companies, those whose personnel were able to transfer into the successor Colonial Administrative Service, which are considered here. They, in turn, often had their own commercial forebears – the trading posts along the West Coast of Africa experienced no fewer than six commercial administrations between 1632 and 1821, when the Crown assumed direct control for the settlements along the Gold Coast.

In West Africa, several experienced Agents from Sir George Taubman Goldie's 1886 Royal Niger Company staff were taken into the Colonial Administrative Service in what was shortly to become Nigeria. Some of them had served the Company in the Niger hinterland for more than ten years. Furthermore, Sir Frederick Lugard, with his own experience of the quality of some of the Agents he had worked with in both the important British East Africa Company in Uganda and the African Lakes Company in Nyasaland, could quickly tell the good from the mediocre. He persuaded the Colonial Office to let him attract the best among the Royal Niger Company's Agents by offering them enhanced salaries. Thus, while the transfers from Company to Crown were not many in 1900, unlike the case of East Africa those that were sought and accepted were among the best of Goldie's men. These included W. (later Sir William) Wallace, who acted as High Commissioner for a while, and, among the Residents, J. A. Burdon, later Governor of British Honduras, A. H. Festing, and W. P. Hewby, who was still remembered in the north-east province of Bornu fifty years later.

In East Africa, the Imperial British East Africa Company (1888) had its origins in Sir William Mackinnon's British Steam Navigation Company, with interests in Zanzibar. Like its counterpart on the West Coast, the IBEA also strengthened the provincial cadres of the new Crown administration of British East Africa (in due course Kenya and Uganda), with a number of able administrators, such as John Ainsworth, the early model of 'a conscientious and caring District Commissioner',[8] and Frank Hall, one of the rare graduates in the service of the IBEA. Another successful transfer was C. W. Hobley, who in fact was not a trading agent but the Company's geologist. He went on to serve as a District Commissioner in Uganda and Kenya and spent a further twenty-five years in the Colonial Service beyond his Company days. Altogether Hardinge, the Foreign Office's first Commissioner in what would one day be Kenya, took over a substantial proportion of Company staff. With them they brought experience to the spread of the new and still rudimentary form of Crown government. Ten had been at the trading stations along the coast as far north as Kismayu. Most were, however, from what Mungeam calls 'the rough and ready school of the Company',[9] stationed in Zanzibar or on the mainland. A few had had experience elsewhere in Africa, in South Africa or the Congo, but for the most part the Company had recruited its agents directly in Britain, thereby earning the contemporary contempt of 'Mackinnon's raw young Scots'. Few had enjoyed much formal education, though none was quite as innocent of it as James Martin, the exotic Maltese sailmaker, illiterate but an accomplished manager of men in both Company and Crown Service. Among those in charge of the critical stations along the route up into Uganda were J. Ainsworth and C. R. W. Lane at Machakos, F. Hall and E. J. H. Russell at Kikuyu, and D. Wilson in the Taita Hills between. Another five officers came across from the Company into the central administration in Mombasa.[10]

Uganda was a smaller affair. F. J. Jackson had been in charge of a major Company caravan in Uganda in 1889, a country of which, after transferring to the Protectorate Service in 1894, he became Governor under the Colonial Office in 1911. W. Grant also stayed on in Uganda after the dissolution of the IBEA Company, becoming the first District Commissioner of Busoga. Among the top managers (Administrators), only E. J. L. Berkeley, who had held the post for a year in 1891–2, and J. R. W. Piggott (1892–5), came across to the Crown service respectively as the Foreign Office's first Commissioner for Uganda and Sub-Commissioner for Mombasa in 1895.

The 'rough and ready school' from which many of the Company agents came is indicated above. An educated background was not among their qualifications. Some of the most damning comments on the calibre of transferred officers came in the confidential report compiled in 1909 for the Colonial Office by the new Governor, Sir Percy Girouard.[11] Admittedly, he was out to impress the CO by his new-broom briskness. 'No one', he wrote, 'can quite guess the administrative chaos of this place.' In particular, he complained that, whereas Lugard in Nigeria had in 1900 been allowed to offer salaries that would induce the best men to move across from the Royal Niger Company, in East Africa the Crown had simply taken them over, with the result that the government had been saddled with incompetent officers. Within the Colonial Office the suspicion soon grew that Girouard was going too fast or had already gone too far, especially when he started to cast aspersions, some on the competence and others on the morals or social background of officers who had already served the Protectorate Government for the past ten years without any adverse comment.

Cecil Rhodes' British South Africa Company (1889) was the last of these substantial inputs from Company to Crown service in Africa. It was not until 1924 that the British Government took over the administration of the Rhodesias. Even then, the BSA Police were an active force right up to Zimbabwe's independence in 1980. In the case of the BSA, the Crown virtually took over the Company's officials lock, stock and barrel and incorporated them into the Colonial Service of the new Northern Rhodesia.[12] Named Commissioners or Collectors and Assistant Collectors, their Divisional work was, in a way comparable to the lineal descent from the East India Company to the Indian Civil Service, very much along the lines adopted by the Crown when it took over Northern Rhodesia. The Company's two Rhodesias had been amalgamated in 1911 as the single unit of Northern Rhodesia, and then taken over by the Crown in 1924. But 1924 was not 1894. By now, the Colonial Service was held in high repute, all the more so as the attractions of a career in the Indian Civil Service were currently dimming, and it could offer to the former BSA officials the prospect of a full career in Africa. In a man like Roger Coryndon, who had been Cecil Rhodes' Private Secretary, then the BSA Company's representative in Barotseland and then Administrator of North-West Rhodesia in 1900–7, the Colonial Service had one of the ablest, for he went on to become Governor of Uganda and of Kenya. Neighbouring Nyasaland had also started off as an area of Company rule, under the British Central Africa Company and the African Lakes Company, becoming a Protectorate under the Foreign Office in 1889 before being taken over by the Colonial Office in 1907. Like Girouard in Kenya, H. H. Johnston felt that the officers he had inherited, ex-Company and ex-Indian Army, were 'a motley crowd', and quickly set about recruiting a better class of educated Britons as Assistant Collectors.[13] However, one of the original administrators, R. E. Codrington, was to go on to become Deputy Administrator of North-East Rhodesia, and R. S. Rattray became a well-known official in the Gold Coast.

South-East Asia

While the African element of the changeover from Company to Crown rule closed with the cession of the Rhodesias by the BSA Company to the British government in 1924, two other non-Crown civil services, both in South-East Asia, continued to recruit British officials through to the end of the First World War and so offer an overseas career similar to that available to young British undergraduates in the Colonial Administrative Service.[14] These were the North Borneo Company, the last of Britain's Chartered Companies, and the Brooke family's 'Rajahdom' of Sarawak.

Following the cession by the Sultan of Brunei of part of his territory to a British syndicate under Sir Alfred Dent, the British North Borneo (Chartered) Company acquired rights over the territory in 1882. In 1888 the British government declared a formal protectorate over North Borneo, at the same time agreeing that the Company would continue to administer it. The British appointed consular officers and took care of foreign relations, but left all the internal administration to the Company other than the nomination of the governor, which had to be approved by the Secretary of State for the Colonies. Most of the governors appointed between 1888 and 1942, when the Japanese occupied Borneo, were drawn from the Malayan Civil Service. The Company, under its Court of Directors, divided the area into two Residencies, East Coast and West Coast, and established its own Civil Service of North Borneo. On the eve of the Second World War, this carried a full, Colonial Service-style, central administration of Secretaries and Heads of Departments, together with two Residents, four District Officers, six Assistant DOs and nine Cadets.[15] Nearly all of the senior officers had started their career as Cadets in the Chartered Company's North Borneo Civil Service. One of the last links with the days of the Company administration was J. Macartney, who on coming down from Oxford in 1936 went straight into the Company's administration as a DO and, after suffering internment during the Japanese occupation, saw the government's transfer to the Crown in 1946 and its independence in 1963.[16] After the war, North Borneo did not revert to Company administration but was made a Crown colony, along with the attached island of Labuan, which had already been annexed to the Straits Settlements since 1907. North Borneo now became part of the Colonial Empire and was so staffed. It remained thus until its independence in 1963 as Sabah within the Federation of Malaysia.

In 1841, the Sultan of Brunei ceded another part of his territory, Sarawak, this time to an individual and not a company. For over a hundred years it was the Brooke (James) family which 'possessed' Sarawak, though in 1888 it was brought under British protection and between 1942 and 1945 was occupied by the Japanese. At the end of the war the third Rajah Brooke (Charles Vyner), who had succeeded his father H. H. Sir Charles Brooke in 1917, passed his rights to the British government and Sarawak became a Crown Colony administered by the Colonial Service until it gained independence in 1963. Only four colonial governors were ever appointed, one of them (D. S. Stewart) being assassinated soon after he assumed office in 1948. The Rajah's civil establishment was large, with nearly one hundred British staff, of whom three were designated Residents, 26 Administrative Officers, and ten Cadets. Many who entered the Sarawak Service came from the West country, where the Brookes had originated. Until a graduate entry developed in the 1930s, most were eighteen year olds with few qualifications and no appropriate training.[17] In the eyes of most, Sarawak had the edge over North Borneo in respect of its administration; in the latter commercial considerations consistently came first, in the former the policy of all three Rajahs had been to develop the country.

Though not a Chartered Company, the unique Brunei set-up is germane to this study of British career civil servants overseas. Brunei, whose Sultans had ceded both North Borneo and Sarawak to foreigners, accepted the status of a British protectorate in 1888 and, from 1906, agreed to the appointment of a British Resident 'to advise and assist in the administration of the State'.[18] Constitutionally, he was responsible to the Governor of Sarawak as High Commissioner for Brunei. An Assistant Resident was added in 1931, and a further post followed in 1950. However, the four administrative districts were in the charge of Malay, not British, District Officers. Most of the State heads of departments were held by officers on secondment from the Sarawak establishment, while the Resident always came from the Malayan Civil Service.

The British North Borneo Company was the last of a long line of Chartered Companies to administer an area of the British Empire. Their contribution, in structure and style and sometimes, at the moment of transfer from Company to Crown, in staff, should not be overlooked in any history of Britain's civil services overseas.

THE EGYPTIAN CIVIL SERVICE

Even if the Egyptian Civil Service did not offer its young British entry the kind of career in district administration which was at once the hallmark and the allure of a cadet's apprenticeship years in the Indian Civil, Colonial Administrative and Sudan Political Services, in its Ministry opportunities it was a powerful magnet for those endowed with intellect, ambition, and often good family connections, who sought a responsible, well-paid and pleasant appointment overseas. This career opportunity – it was rarely a full career Service – came about as a result of a Foreign Office mission by Lord Dufferin, then ambassador at Constantinople, to enquire into local feelings in the aftermath of Britain's occupation of 1882. This had ostensibly been to restore Turkey's authority after the revolt led by an Egyptian colonel, Ahmed Arabi. In the local consul's report on his soundings among the Egyptians (he had contacted 'representatives of the *ulama*, the gentry, the mercantile classes, and tradespeople: to have descended lower in the social scale would have been neither profitable nor advisable'), Dufferin was gratified to read that, despite a certain dissatisfaction at 'the rare employment of native Egyptians in the higher grades of public service', there nevertheless existed a 'unanimous and earnest wish' for Englishmen to be associated with Egyptian functionaries at all levels of the administration.[19] This was subsequently – and even more acceptably – qualified to read that the only current objection to foreign employees was that they constituted 'a mixture of all nationalities' instead of exclusively the preferred English. Between 1883 and 1886 some two hundred foreign appointments were made to the Egyptian Civil Service each year, mostly but by no means exclusively of Britons, with a consequent large reduction in the hitherto annual intake of several hundred staff (again a number of them British) that had been the pattern of the past twenty years. By 1886 there were 299 British (some of them Maltese) officials in Egypt. As Cromer, who was then Consul-General in Cairo, described it in 1887:

> The Army, the Financial Department and the Public Works Department are mainly in European hands ... [here] a considerable number of French, Italian, Austrian, German and Greek subordinates are employed. The principal places are, however, held by Englishmen, and the administrative systems of these Departments distinctly bear the mark of English influence.[20]

The Departments of Justice and of Public Instruction still remained largely in Egyptian hands. Twelve years later, the number had risen to 455, and at the end of the Protectorate (1914–22) the Milner Commission found that Egyptians held less than a quarter of the higher posts in the Egyptian Civil Service while the proportion of British officials in such posts had risen to 59 per cent.[21] But with the declaration of independence in 1922, nationalist demands for Egyptianization of the civil service met no further brake. By 1927 the number of British officials employed was small, remaining steady at about 575 through to 1939 (mostly in Education) after touching a peak of approximately 1600 in 1919. There were still over 400 British officials in Egyptian government service in 1945.

What was the structure of the Service and what was the role of its British officials? The title of Britain's chief representative in Egypt was, right up till when the country was redefined as a British Protectorate in 1914 and a British High Commissioner was nominated, that of Consul-General and British Agent. This reflects the strong commercial origin of the British presence in the country, a presence represented and reinforced by the operations of the Levant Company and the East Indian Company there in the nineteenth century. The Consul-General was based in Cairo, with a Vice-Consul resident in Alexandria. The completion of the Suez Canal in 1869 confirmed Britain in its determination that it could not either allow another European power to control this commercial jugular vein to India or stand by and watch the Egyptian government being choked by the pressure of its problems. So, following Lord Dufferin's assessment of the Egyptian problem, Sir Evelyn Baring (later Lord Cromer) was summoned from India, where he had been Private Secretary to the Viceroy, his cousin Lord Northbrook, to assume the new post of Consul-General and British Agent in Cairo. Through his dramatic overhaul and tight control of Egypt's finances, Cromer virtually ruled Egypt from 1883 to 1907: not for nothing was the nickname 'Over-Baring' quickly coined for such a prince among proconsuls. With him he brought a party of Anglo-Indian (as the terminology then went) aides to help him reorganize and revive the Egyptian finances. As one observer has tartly put it, the number of British officials coming to Egypt seemed to grow in keeping with the size of the country's debts.[22] Ten years later there was still no Egyptian Ministry that did not have a powerful British adviser and his team of British officials. By the time the French withdrew from Egypt under the terms of the Anglo-French Entente of 1904, leaving Britain in sole *de facto* control of the Egyptian government, the total of British advisers had swamped that number of thirty-nine which Cromer had looked on in 1891 as 'the backbone of the Egyptian Civil Administration'.[23] They now numbered about one thousand, almost ten per cent of Egypt's civil service.[24]

These British officials included finance and customs experts, land settlement and irrigation specialists, and members of the police and judiciary. Many brought with them experience of Indian administration. Their contribution to the reconstruction of Egypt was substantial, for instance that of Sir Archibald Colvin as Commissioner of the *Caisse de la Dette Publique* in succession to Cromer[25] or, among irrigation engineers, C. Scott-Moncrieff, who undertook clearing the canals and rebuilding the lifeline Nile barrages, and W. Willcocks, who built the Aswan dam. Thomas Russell was instrumental in suppressing the hashish trade, and Sir John Scott set about reforming the notorious court system. The army was transformed under a British Commander-in-Chief, or *Sirdar*, another manifestation – and often less loved – of the British presence; among the holders of the post was Kitchener, from 1890 to 1899. All this was done in the name not of Britain but of (in this case) the Egyptian Government and the Egyptian Civil Service. It was from the romantic idealism of Wilfred Scawen Blunt that there emerged the description of the British occupation as 'The Veiled Protectorate'. When Cromer left in 1907, he took with him the belief that Egypt could never survive without foreign guidance in civil and military affairs. It was a misplaced pessimism disastrously echoed at Suez almost exactly fifty years later. His successor, 'the Overshadowed Proconsul' Sir Eldon Gorst,[26] despite his replacement of a number of British with Egyptian officials in the administration and of the autocratic Kitchener, could hardly be said to have demonstrated any suggestion that, a quarter of a century after it had been called in to steer the Egyptian ship out of trouble, Britain was not still at the helm in Cairo.

The Egyptian Civil Service was not a full-blown imperial administration within the tradition of the overseas civil services examined in this book. Furthermore, its role was conspicuously an advisory one, not one of official overrule. In terms of Service ethos-building, too, it lacked the glamour and the image of the generic DO at work 'in the bush': Egypt was scarcely the cultural and undeveloped wilderness conventionally associated with the typical imperial administrator's job. Yet scores of British officials found in it a rewarding life if not a real career.[27] Within the Oxbridge graduate world, it was a prized position. Consequently, for the most part their first-hand testimony tends to differ in two ways from that recorded by their peers in the Crown civil services discussed in Part II. They observe from a central, Ministry standpoint, rarely as a junior in the field and never as one of the generic District Officers; and they write more as individuals and less as members of a Service who face and climb the same career ladder. The British were mostly Advisers not executive agents, and Ministry not Provincial ones at that. The Provinces did have their British officials, but they were there in an advisory, not an administrative capacity. Unusually, C. S. Jarvis held the post of Governor of the Sinai Peninsula for thirteen years (1923–36). To an extent, the system was a dual or diarchal one, with overseeing and directing officials operating in tandem with a local executive administration, yet quite different in attitude and action from the structures and practice of colonial administrations, even those committed to the code of indirect rule. Government by advisers may turn out not to be government at all.

It was one of Cromer's achievements to have inaugurated a properly constituted and reasonably effective civil service through which to administer the country, something which, either as an Egyptian or European one, did not exist up to 1882. Yet even at that time the debate was vigorous whether, as Colvin maintained, a small European leavening was critical to keeping the Egyptian government machinery working, or whether the Egyptians would be so incensed by this alien and interfering presence that any extra efficiency would quickly dissipate.[28] The Police were the first to alter the nature of the pre-Cromer bureaucracy by going beyond the practice of short-term, mid-seniority secondment of officers (long used in the Egyptian Army too) and appointing a group of young Britishers as first-time police cadets. The Public Works Department followed suit, recruiting pupil or junior engineers from Britain to oversee contracts for the barrage construction. Yet another department which turned to Britain for young men looking for a post abroad was the Department of Public Instruction. Overall, it was arguably Sir Eldon Gorst, from his pivotal position of Adviser at the Finance Ministry, who formalized the creation of what might be called the Anglo-Egyptian Civil Service, by setting up a recruitment agency and selection board in England to offer university graduates direct appointments to posts within the Ministries in Cairo or Alexandria. While Cromer had been in the British Agency, the right sort of nineteenth century patronage went a long way. By the time Gorst came to succeed him, in 1907, as His Britannic Majesty's Representative, he had come (or been brought round) to a policy seen as virtually that of 'Egypt for the Egyptians – and no English need apply'.

For all this, an Egyptian Civil Service there undoubtedly was. Ronald Storrs, who ended up in the Colonial Service as governor of Northern Rhodesia and then of Cyprus, provides a revealing source about those it recruited. In 1903, having gained 'a reasonably good First', he was asked by his father what he proposed to do. He replied: 'Something that involved no more examinations.' The immediate bonus was a return to Cambridge, for a year of 'savouring rather than studying Arabic'.[29] There were four of them in all destined for Egypt, one assigned to the Ministry of Finance in Cairo and the rest to the Ministry of the Interior in Alexandria. At that time, A. M. Innes was Under-Secretary and H. N. Bowden-Smith was Private Secretary to the Financial Secretary, Sir Vincent Corbett. The legendary Harry Boyle, who had taken up an Egyptian appointment in 1885, was now the Oriental Secretary, and in course of time Storrs, having started off as Private Secretary to the Financial Secretary, succeeded Boyle. Boyle, like Storrs but unlike Coles and Russell *infra*, did not spend the whole of his career in Egypt. He served in Cairo from 1883 to 1909, most famously in the post of Oriental Secretary. But he failed in his bid to transfer into the Levant Service, where good use could have been made of his knowledge of the Middle East. Instead he ended up as Consul-General in Berlin, until the coming of World War I. In 1921 he decided to indulge in a sentimental journey back to Egypt, spiritually his native soil, on a six-week Foreign Office mission to General Allenby, the new High Commissioner in Cairo. Allenby's Chief Secretary, R. H. Greg, described the mission as 'singular and difficult', and for most of the time Boyle had to disguise himself as an ordinary tourist.[30]

Among other leading Egyptian Civil Servants were C. E. Coles, Sir Thomas Wentworth Russell and Lord Edward Cecil. Like Storrs, each has left a memorable account of his time in the Service. Coles Pasha, who was one of Cromer's Anglo-Indian importations, ended up as Inspector-General of Prisons. He had served ten years in the Indian Police when in 1883 he was offered a temporary appointment in Egypt on a five-year contract, together with four other officers all from the Government of Bombay. His superior in the Ministry of Interior as Under-Secretary was C. Lloyd, who had succeeded the well-known General Valentine Baker. On arrival he found that, tellingly, half his 1000-strong police force in Alexandria were Europeans, a fact which had precipitated an xenophobic riot in the city the year before. Identifying many of these as 'undesirables', he disarmed the undisciplined Swiss company, 'who talked very big about their republic', and marched them down to the harbour for immediate repatriation.[31] Coles attributed the hostility he encountered in Alexandria (*'le plus brutal des anglais'*) to his being an Indian official and hence one who might introduce methods of administration deemed in the Ministry to be unsuitable for the

Egyptian situation. Despite this and his self-conceded faults of temperament, his work in the Egyptian Civil Service prospered and within fifteen years (his short-term contract had soon been revised) he reached the post of Inspector-General of Prisons, occupying it until 1913.

Russell Pasha spent almost fifty years in the Egyptian Civil Service, during which he rose all the way from sub-inspector to, in 1917, Commandant of the Cairo Police. Remarkably, he was to serve in that position for another twenty-nine years, earning the confidence of no less than 32 Egyptian administrations. His final post, to which he was appointed in 1929, was as the internationally respected Director of the Egyptian Central Narcotics Intelligence Bureau. When he retired in 1946, Russell was the last in the line, from Valentine Baker in the 1880s, of British officers recruited to strengthening the Egyptian Police Force.[32] He owed his recruitment to his cousin P. Mackell, who had been seconded from the Egyptian Army as Adviser to the Minister of the Interior. 'I found', Russell commented, recalling his last year at Cambridge, 'his stories and accounts of life and work in Egypt most attractive,'[33] a comment which reveals that, for all its limitations as an untested career, the Service had already caught on in the universities as a new dimension to the range of government service overseas.

Lord Edward Cecil, later darling of the Beefsteak Club, served in the Egyptian Ministry of Finance for almost twenty years from 1912 as Financial Adviser. At the time even his shorthand clerk was an English official, Mr Tomkins. He records how, as Cromer's Indian and 'painfully influential' pooh-poohing subordinates retired, the new breed of Anglo-Egyptian officials won their case for annual leave.[34] As the only Englishman to be present at meetings of the Council of Egyptian Ministers, Cecil was looked on as the most powerful British official in the Egyptian Civil Service.

Such men, though perhaps more uniformly celebrated (and eminently literate) than the commonality of the Egyptian Civil Service, are representative of the calibre of many of the junior British officials brought in, first under Cromer's talent-spotting patronage and then under Gorst's wider-looking Board of Selection, to replace a hundred years of predominantly French influence by high-profile officials like Sir Arthur Chitty, appointed Post-Master General of Egypt in 1876, and Baron de Kusel, who became the powerful Controller-General of Customs and was, despite his name, very much an Englishman.[35] As elsewhere in the formal British Empire, British officials may not have totally succeeded in creating the uncorrupt and efficient local Civil Service *à l'anglaise* that they felt they should rather than they thought they could (one recalls the despairing, racist text on and illustrations of Egyptian officials in the writing of a well-known middle-ranking member of the Service).[36] But of one thing there can be no doubt: they enthusiastically created their own British society in Cairo.[37] This crystallized in such institutions as the sumptuous Gezira Sporting Club, where the British and Egyptian ruling classes met, though the cosmopolitan nature of the internationally celebrated Shepheard's Hotel was not enough to save it from being burnt down and looted in the anti-British riots of 1952. In contrast, the Turf Club was as exclusive as many a British club, from Pall Mall to Hong Kong. The most prestigious, elite and exclusive institution to belong to was, of course, the British Agency. For all that, as Hopwood observes, the British civil servants disembarking at Port Said could not escape the superior glare of the real sahibs and memsahibs sailing on to India.[38]

The Egyptian Civil Service is inseparable from Lord Cromer. He it was who set it up, recruited it, and tirelessly ensured its success. In a secret memo to the Foreign Office in 1921, his former Oriental Secretary Boyle enclosed a note on what he called 'The Cromer Myth', writing glowingly of that Golden Age.[39] For others, however, 'the Lord' has remained 'the perfect imperial administrator',[40] a prince of proconsuls. His was a style of 'Over-Baring' aloofness which communicated and commended itself to his compatriots and wore off on his Civil Service. He embodied his own Service. In hindsight, Cromer may have unwittingly – or was it indifferently? – done more to stimulate Egyptian nationalism than he did to reform Egyptian officialdom. Modern analysts of the successor public services to those established under imperial control ask, in the Egyptian case, why the British did not do for the Egyptian bureaucracy what they did – and what Cromer knew from his own experience they did – in India. The answer they come up with is that not only were the British in Egypt for a far shorter time and in a less secure position, but that British influence never penetrated Egyptian rural society to the same extent that it did in India.[41] At the top, of course, Cromer's personality and philosophy were not inclined to any power sharing, least of all with a subject race of which he could speak so contemptuously.

Finally, three points can be made in the comparative context of Britain's overseas civil services. First, one senses a lack of mutual respect between the ICS and the Egyptian Civil Service:

> We in Egypt profess to despise Anglo-Indians as people who are out of touch with Europe and essentially provincial, whilst they, on the other hand, talk with contempt of our size and village politics. One method of showing this lofty hostility is to pretend not to understand anything about the other's country or language.[42]

Secondly, the point has been emphasized that, for a number of reasons, the Egyptian Civil Service was arguably less of a career, less of a Service. With its international social life and evidence of an early 'tourist trade', Egypt offered a quality of life unknown to any generic District Officer *en poste*. Finally, much can be deduced from the observation of Coles Pasha, one of its longest-serving members and one who came to Egypt after a substantial apprenticeship in the Indian Services:

> There is one thing about the Anglo-Egyptian Civil Service peculiar to Egypt which, I think, does not help a man to become a successful administrator. I refer to the system of inspection without any actual charge. Young fellows in the service spend the first ten years of their life, if not more, wandering about the Provinces inspecting and reporting on the work of others, though they

themselves have never been through the mill. The inspectors may give advice but not orders, and the official advised is not bound to obey, the system of government being that all orders to a Mudir shall come from the Minister, and to the Mamur el Merkaz (local administrator) from the Mudir. In practice, no doubt, an inspector with any strength of character gets his orders carried out without awaiting the official instructions from either Minister or Mudir; but he does so at his own risk, and, unless the matter be very urgent, official instructions are usually awaited.[43]

THE INDIAN POLITICAL SERVICE

If a career in the Consular Service (below) appealed to those in quest of single-handed experience in far-off places all over the globe, and in the case of the Levant Service those who may have been inspired by a Doughty or later a Lawrence, the Indian Political Service (IPS) was able to attract young men likely nurtured in the novels of G. A. Henty and A. E .W. Mason or in the deeds of Kim and fascinated by the stratagems of the Great Game. For the writ of the IPS ran wide in much of that land of British living legend, the North-West Frontier, as well as in the domesticated ambience of royal courts and the diplomatic art of official advice and indirect rule.

In contrast to its cousin Service, the Indian Civil, the Indian Political Service was not a Secretary of State's Service. It comprised officers seconded, in the proportion of 70:30, from the Indian Army and the ICS. A third, smaller component was drawn, in the words of one of the Service's leading historians, 'for special reasons' from the Indian Police.[44] Allowing for leave, there were seldom more than 100–120 officers on duty at a time in the External Affairs and Political Departments which jointly made up the IPS. Because the IPS was not open through direct recruitment like the majority of Crown Services, its members carried with them their own Service pension rules, Army officers having to retire by the age of 55 and ICS officers at the end of 35 years of service. They were, as Chenevix Trench emphasizes in his obituary portrait, every inch a Viceroy's Service.[45]

The Indian Political Service traces its history back to 1783, when the Government of India, still a Company and not yet a Crown administration, established a Foreign and Political Department. In due course it ranked as a senior department in the Secretariat, along with Finance, Home, Railway, Legislative, etc., and was established as a separate Service in 1939. Essentially, the work of a Political officer took one of three forms: service in India's 563 Princely States, that area of the subcontinent which was not constitutionally part of what was called British India and which comprised two-fifths of the country in size and a little less than one-fifth in population, hence sometimes labelled as Indian India; service on the Frontier, by which was understood that explosive, exciting and exacting region situated north-west of the Punjab roughly between Afghanistan and Kashmir; or service in foreign countries, outside the geographical confines of India but within the government of the Indian Empire, such as the Persian Gulf or along the Himalayan Frontier. In 1947, the total strength of the IPS was about one hundred and fifty, a rise of twenty officers above the figure for 1939.

Under their own Department in the Delhi Secretariat, the Foreign and Political Department of the Government of India, sometimes referred to as 'the Foreign Office', they enjoyed by the 1930s the leadership of two Secretaries instead of the standard singleton, one the Foreign Secretary and the other the Political Secretary. These were supported by a strong Secretariat of Joint Secretaries, Deputy Secretaries, and an Under-Secretary. The Political Secretary's office dated from 1914, when the third echelon of the IPS was created to take charge of the affairs of the Indian States. A further change took place as a consequence of the Lee Commission report, when in 1925 the civilian and military Politicals were placed on a common salary scale, that of the ICS being adopted. In the same period, further tidying up was effected by the incorporation into the IPS of the 28 officers who were still serving in the growingly anomalous Bombay Political Department.[46] The 1935 Government of India Act introduced a new post at the top: that of Political Adviser to the Crown Representative, i.e. the Viceroy. Of the twenty permanent Heads of Department who carried the title of Foreign Secretary between 1867 and 1947, only two were military Politicals, and every Political Secretary (1914–47) was drawn from the ICS. The IPS was divided into First Class Residents, who, like Chief Commissioners, were addressed as His Honour: and Second Class Residents and officers on the long or time scale in the State, who together were known as Political Agents.

Uniquely in the context of the imperial services studied in this book, all recruitment for the IPS was on secondment. Basically, ICS officers could apply once they had passed their departmental exams, had not completed five years in the Service, and were unmarried. For the Indian Army, the conditions were the same, save that the time limit was one of age: twenty-four. To introduce those joining from the Indian Army to the art of the Government of India's bureaucracy, they were required to spend eighteen months on attachment to a district, frequently in the United Provinces, for training in revenue and judicial work, at the end of which they sat a modified form of the ICS departmental examination.[47] No military experience was required of those accepted from the ICS. All IPS officers were then on probation for three years, during which they were not allowed, on pain of being returned to one's regiment or province, to get married. 'Subalterns of the Poona Horse', dictated the Commanding Officer to an aspirant IPS candidate, Walter Magor, 'are expected to spend their money on polo ponies, not on wives.'[48]

The precise formula for the staffing of the IPS has been called 'a statistician's joy'.[49] It allowed the recruitment of two members from the ICS every year, subject to a reduction by one in every fifth year, and four – or five – officers from the Indian Army, in alternate years. While applications exceeded vacancies, many a Provincial Governor or Commanding Officer declined to part with his best officers, and there were frequent cases when the authority of the Viceroy was invoked by the Foreign and Political Department. A commonplace write-down was to categorize Politicals as being made up half of soldiers who did not like the thought of fighting and half of civilians averse to hard work, 'with nothing to do but shoot tigers and suck up to a lot of degenerate Rajahs'.[50] Once Indianization of the IPS got into its post-Lee stride, the ICS/IA hold over recruitment was loosened by the recruitment of a number of Muslim members, mostly somewhat older men, from the Provincial Civil Service for service on the Frontier. Hogben, who offers a series of reasons to explain the Politicals' reluctance to admit Indians to their ranks (among them their romantic but conservative sense of paternalism which made them slow to accept anything as fundamental as a change of colleagues), concludes somewhat lukewarmly that the record was 'not one of the brighter pages in the history of an otherwise often humane and interesting group of men'.[51] Few Indian officers served in the States.

While proof of exceptional linguistic ability constituted a plus mark in a candidate, it was widely sensed that for acceptance into the IPS, to quote the informed opinion of one of them, 'the claim which above all weighed was relationship to a member or a retired member of the Service'.[52] Certain Provinces and certain regiments, too, tended to provide a high proportion of Politicals: the Punjab and the UP, and the Central India Horse. An in-service application was followed by no formal examination, the critical stage being an interview with the Foreign and the Political Secretaries. At that interview the candidate was invited to express a choice for Service in the States, on the Frontier, or in a 'consulate' abroad. The interview concluded with a less-than-looked-forward-to luncheon with the Viceroy *en famille*.[53] Curzon had argued for a simple formula of 2:1 admissions from the ICS and the IA, on the ground that ICS men were better suited than military officers for the kind of work required in the Princely States. Although this proportion was not accepted, and indeed was virtually inverted, military Politicals, who were in the majority, did tend to be given the Frontier postings and those in the consulates. As a minute by Sir Harcourt Butler, one-time Foreign Secretary and later Governor of Burma, once famously put it: 'We want lean and keen men on the Frontier, and fat and good-natured men in the States.'[54] There was a suggestion in the late 1920s that the cadre of Political Officers who were dealing with the sensitive Princely States, whose attitude towards the Indianization of the Public Services was uniformly hostile other than that of the Maharaja of Gwalior, should no longer be recruited from the traditional services of the ICS and the IA, but be sought from a separate cadre recruited directly from England. Another modification proposed was to alter the joining age so as to allow the recruitment of older officers who had served so effectively in the Frontier Scouts and become fluent in Pushtu. None of these ideas took ground save for a handful of appointments on long contract, and the 70:30 formula and the method of recruitment survived right up to the end.

Each of the three branches of the work of an officer in the Indian Political Service was strikingly different. Though once a Political, always a Political

(R.T.U., return to one's original Service [unit], was rare), most Politicals were able to have experience of more than one specialization and some worked in all branches. Politicals assigned to the States generally started their life in the heavily-apprenticeship post of Personal Assistant to the Resident ('A.D.C. cum-makee-learn').[55] The work of a Resident or Agent in an Indian State (the title of Residency was the preferred usage in single-state jurisdictions such as Hyderabad, Mysore, Kashmir, Gwalior, Baroda) at times came close to being an enhanced diplomatic version of the classic Resident's role in Sultanate Malaya or in the Emirates of Northern Nigeria, where advice and guidance proffered to the traditional royal ruler supplanted the more direct administrative role of his opposite number, the Chief Commissioner, in those IPS jurisdictions like Baluchistan and Coorg where the principle of indirect rule was not the order of the day. 'The Resident did not administer,' states Mason, 'he was in the State to guide, to advise, to suggest ... he needed rare qualities: he must not let leisure degenerate into idleness nor forbearance into indifference ...'[56] An intimate knowledge of pedigree, protocol and precedence ranked high in the attributes needed and impeccably learned by the Resident, whether in complex Rajputana and powerful Hyderabad or in the smaller Gujarat and Deccan States. He had to know what was done and what had to be done, both before and after the death of a ruler. The attention paid to matters of protocol like titles of address and of reference, the correct number of salutes all the way from 21 guns for the five most senior Ruling Princes down in steps of two to nine for the thirty ranking ones (Trench's 'little hill Rajahs')[57] and none at all for Banka Pahari among the Central Indian States, lend credence to the argument of a positive diplomatic element in Agency work.

Just how tightrope the Political's betwixt-and-between position was, both fish and fowl yet wholly neither, was adroitly caught in the report of the 1929 States Committee. 'It calls', they conceded, 'for great qualities of character, tact, sympathy, patience and good manners. He has to identify himself with the interests of both the paramount power and the princes and the people of the States, and yet he must not interfere in the internal administration.'[58] Among them, the plum post was Resident at Hyderabad, with that of Agent to the Governor-General in Rajputana coming a close second. For all the diplomatic practice of cultured good manners and the unquestioned official priority of advice over authority as the mainspring of the relationship, few Rulers would have queried the tell-all judgement put forward by the Diwan of Bikanir, the fellow-travelling K. M. Panikkar: 'The whisper of the Residency is the thunder of the State, and there is no matter in which the Resident does not feel qualified to give advice.'[59] As time went on, and in the particular case of longer postings in the States without a move vertically or horizontally, the Resident's functions could well become less Foreign and more Political. The guidance given in his *Manual of Instructions* that 'he should leave well alone: the best work of a Political Officer is very often what has been left undone'[60] was not a lesson lightly learned. There was perhaps more than humour in the Service dictum that Indians preferred their Maharaja with all his faults (and these could be as many as the States themselves) to the Collector with his virtues (and they, too, were numerous). Among the many features that characterized the Indian States and set them markedly apart from British India, their vast variety was conspicuous, whether it was in size, sophistication or the preoccupations of their Rulers. Mason's brief verdict says all: 'There was much to be done in some States, very little in others.'[61]

All these were factors that the young ICS officer who had at least a hankering after the perceived glamour of life as a Political needed to wonder about and weigh as his initial five years in the Service approached its conclusion and the time came to make up his mind whether, for likely the rest of his career, to remain in the Executive branch, where the emphasis was on general administration or land revenue, or else go for one of the specialist alternatives like the Secretariat, Judiciary or the Political. It is to Philip Mason one again turns for the most compelling of Service-perceived comparisons:

> The political officer was inclined to look at his colleague, the district officer in British India, with a touch of patronage, as a dull dog and perhaps not entirely a social equal. The district officer gazed back with a spice of envy at a life usually more pleasant and picturesque than his own, but with a certain grim pity, too, for one who had – as it seemed to him – deliberately chosen less work and a less arduous responsibility. The political officer was perhaps less inclined to talk shop than his colleague in British India; it would be fair to picture him as usually more amiable and agreeable, more often witty and an excellent companion. But there certainly were some political appointments in which it would have been eccentric to work after lunch; there were many political officers who had never dealt with a riot. If there was more consciousness among them of all the coloured diversity of India, of the poetic reality of a past living in the present, there was perhaps less awareness of the political reality of a future clamorous for recognition. It was, in short, more common among political officers than in the administrative service to find a tendency to complacency with things as they were, a certain cynicism as to political progress.[62]

For all Mason's Province rather than Political undertones, some of the most inspirational Service memoirs have come from the pens of Political officers holding the post of Resident or Agent to the Governor-General. The memoirs from Politicals who attained the peak of their career in some of 'the wonderland' States like Sir Conrad Corfield, Sir Malcolm Darling (who was tutor and guardian and eventually Private Secretary to, as it were, E. M. Forster's Rajah of Dewas), Sir Kenneth Fitze, Sir Arthur Lothian, Sir Humphrey Trevelyan and Sir Edward Wakefield are unsurpassed for the insight into their responsibilities and the rewards of work in the States (see Bibliography).

The Frontier districts and agencies, where Political Officers operated as Deputy Commissioners (DC), represented a very different – some would say almost antithetical – style of life and work from that obtaining in the States. Centred on but not confined to the North-West Frontier Province, this unit of government was created in 1901 with six Districts in the plains and another six Agencies in the hills. Each was under a DC, who also had a portion of designated Tribal Territory under his charge. There is general endorsement of the view that, whether the Political's service origins lay in the ICS or in the Indian Army, the same definable kind of person was attracted by and found his way to the Frontier. With such neo-romantic names, recognized even in England and certainly later in Hollywood, as Khyber and Waziristan, predominantly peopled by Pathans and Mahsuds, and intermittently pacified by irregular levies and regular units with titles like the Khyber Rifle Frontier Scouts and the Corps of Guides complete with their own rich shorthand of Piffers and *lashkars*, Gilgit and D.I.K., *jirgas* and *gashts*, here was one – *the* one? – area of Empire known to every inter-war adult filmgoer and British schoolboy aspirant to a post in imperial service, thanks to the mind-captivating talents of Rudyard Kipling and Alexander Korda. In such a life, whether in the administration of the NWF Province or in relations with the Tribal Territories, personal courage was invariably added to the twin attributes of every Political, called on to act as both diplomat and intelligence officer. In the IPS, as in the Indian Civil, Colonial Administrative and Sudan Political Services, the *sine qua non* in the potential officer's make-up was that elusively undefinable but readily recognizable quality of 'character'. If the States officers in the Political Service had their literary giants to tell their tale, so did the Frontier officers, with valuable contributions from, for instance, Sir Olaf Caroe, Sir Basil Gould and Sir Fraser Noble. Among the Frontier officers, too, were men whose stature grew from generation to generation and was passed down in memory more than memoir, men like J. Abbott and R. Sandeman and F. Mackeson in the nineteenth century, A. Parsons and G. Roos-Keppel in the early years of the twentieth century, and G. Cunningham and O. Caroe in the final decade of the IPS, along with many others immortalized in Frontier legend and lore.

It was the Foreign section of the Indian Political Service which offered the greatest spread of postings. These ranged from what was known as the Settlement of Aden, from its days of inclusion within the Bombay Presidency and through its constitution as a separate province in 1932 under a Chief Commissioner and Resident until it was handed over to the Colonial Office in 1937, and the Persian Gulf, with consuls in places like Muscat, Bahrain and Kuwait; to the Himalayan Frontier agencies like Gilgit; and, in the north, Tibet, Sikkim and Assam, and in the south, Pondicherry and Goa, those two areas of India governed by foreign powers other than Britain. In the Gulf States, of the 65 IPS officers who served there between 1957 and 1967, 37 came in from the Indian Army, 11 from the ICS and 17 from the Indian Police or on unformalized secondment.[63]

The formation and work of the Indian Political Service has not always received its due in histories of the ICS.[64] Sometimes it is virtually ignored on account of its not being a Secretary of State Service or of not being a career Service *ab initio*. Sometimes it is dismissed as no more than one of the Departments of the central Secretariat. Yet others leave it aside as no more than the diplomatic corps of the Government of India. It has not been until the 1970s and 1980s, long years after its demise in 1943, that the Indian Political Service has begun to find the memorialists it deserves and thus allow students of Britain's imperial civil services to grasp the range of its achievements and begin to understand why it attracted so many from the ICS, the Indian Army and the Indian Police to its ranks. The IPS was yet another opportunity for the young Briton to serve his country abroad in a civil capacity.

Not every Viceroy entertained such a high opinion of the Political Service as Curzon did: in his forward policy he had felt that he was very much its head.[65] In 1939 Linlithgow referred to the medievalism of the IPS and 'its large proportion of somewhat second rate men'.[66] Earlier Minto had shown a more perceptive understanding of the constant counter-pulls of loyalty and service in their 'dual capacity as the mouthpieces of government and also as the interpreters of the sentiments and aspirations of the state'.[67] To an extent, the IPS's long and distinguished past may have been overshadowed by perceptions of their last act of all. How far did their loyalty to the States betray 'their' Princes when the devil-and-the-deep-blue-sea moment of decision faced the Rulers on whether, come independence, to join the all-India Federation or go it alone? How far were they, not surprisingly often 'emotionally involved in the survival of the States',[68] guilty of misjudgement in encouraging the Chamber of Princes to stand firm on the lapse of Paramountcy? Trench's own valediction accuses Mountbatten of gross betrayal of trust, of Viceregal dishonesty and deceit in his final dealings with Rajput princes and Pathan tribesmen. More charitably, though not necessarily more accurately, is E. M. Forster's comment on how Indian bureaucracy periodically seemed to lose its imagination and its way. Being impeccably right and absolutely wrong has its place in the continuing controversy on the Last Act. Historians continue to debate the conundrum and criticize or defend those who attempted to solve it on the strength of their own convictions and conscience.

Leaving aside the two principal IPS historians cited in this section, Creagh Coen and Chenevix Trench, few would cavil, whether in the then of the Indian Empire or the now of retrospective interpretation, with the generous epitaph constructed by the pre-eminent social historian of them all, Philip Mason: '[they were] a body of picked men, picked from picked men.'[69] There can be few neater expressions of that much-written-about sociological concept of 'an elite corps'.

THE CONSULAR SERVICE

The British Consular Service was an independent Crown Service until its incorporation in 1943 into a restructured Foreign Service, itself fashioned out of an amalgamation of the Diplomatic Service and the Foreign Office in 1919. The Consular Service's territory was principally Europe and the Americas, along with Asia and parts of Africa, the focus continents of Part II. Though its emergence as a Service can be traced back to 1825, identifiable consuls were *en poste* before that. Its sense of a measure of 'below-stairs' inferiority *vis-à-vis* the Diplomatic Service, in status, society and salary, in uniform and even Clubs, was an acknowledged fact of Crown Service life as well as a ready perception in the public mind. Down at the Vice-Consul level, there was not only a subtle difference between a British Vice-Consul and His Majesty's Vice-Consul, who held a Royal Commission, but also, less subtly, between a salaried and an unsalaried (or honorary) one. Not for nothing has one of its most recent historians dubbed it 'The Cinderella Service'.[70]

From the bonding together of Britain's merchant adventurers, 'trading in alien and occasionally hostile cities',[71] the practice grew up of their electing from among their number a magistrate. The title of Consul was adopted by these Factories, and the years from 1485 to 1648 are well described in Platt's choice of 'The Age of the Mercantile Consuls'. After 1649 consuls became public servants, and state officials took over from merchant consulates. Canning's Consular Act of 1825 converted these individual state services into a single Crown Service of full-time, salaried and pensionable officials. By 1858 there were some three hundred British Consuls, many of them, however, not appointed until they were in their thirties and forties. This was, of course, still the era of patronage, and an appointment to the Consular Service lay in the gift of the Secretary of State for Foreign Affairs. It was not until 1903, considerably later than most of the Crown civil services other than the Colonial Service, that His Majesty's Consular Service instituted regulations for a system of recruitment, promotion and transfer. But for a good many years still to come the Consular Department within the Foreign Office was staffed not by Consuls but by FO clerks, who had no experience of the work of consular officials.

The North African posts, collectively known as the Barbary Consulates, had been under the Colonial Office until their transfer to the Foreign Office in 1836. Along with the Moroccan Consulates, their work was heavily political and judicial, a far cry from the quasi-diplomatic consulates in the lesser European states which could often be regular missions in all but name. Elsewhere in nineteenth century Africa, the Lagos Consulate flourished from 1851 to 1861, and the Oil Rivers and Niger Coast Protectorates came on the scene in the 1890s. They did not survive once the Crown assumed control of the new Colony and Protectorate of Nigeria. The consulate in Zanzibar, on the other hand, remained active from 1840 to 1913 and after 1873 was upgraded to a consul-generalship.

The Consular Service was divided into five departments: General, China, Japan, Siam and Levant. The seaport consuls, who in the Victorian age frequently doubled as marine superintendents, were now mostly subsumed under the General department. Two specialist branches, the Far Eastern Service and the Levant Service, had been in place since the nineteenth century. Invested with judicial powers and pastoral responsibilities, their work went beyond the routine role of seaport consuls acting as little more than a registrar of ships and seamen sailing under the British flag. In the particular case of the Levant Consuls, their work went further still and assumed something of the role of political officers. This was an expectation among the Siam consular cadre, too. The Chinese Consular Service, to which were subsequently added the consular staff in Japan and Siam, came into separate existence in 1843. It recruited young men in the age bracket of 18 to 24, for whom mastering the language was the imperative in the formation of the cadre known as student interpreters. The top echelons of the Consular Service allowed for three grades of Consul-General but among subordinate consuls below the rank of Vice-Consul there was no classification. Promotion was slow, leading to long-timers calling it the 'death' Service. Often Vice-Consuls, who were graded, waited till they were in their forties before receiving promotion; two of the group of only 17 vice-consuls promoted in the period 1918 to 1928 were over fifty years old.

Within the British Consular Services, it is perhaps the Chinese and Levant Services which could claim the most relevant comparison with the Crown civil services featured in Part II. The Siam Service was generally considered to be a bit of a backwater, and once the Japan Service lost its extraterritorial responsibilities it also lost its semi-political role and became so routine as to be looked on as having degenerated into an indistinguishability from the General Service.[72]

It was Britain's enjoyment of extraterritorial rights in China, which lasted the whole century from 1843 to 1943, that had led to the creation of the China Consular Service. At one time or another they were responsible for staffing almost fifty consulates. Their meticulous chronicler P. D. Coates has calculated that over the hundred years a total of 307 officers served in the Foreign Office's China establishment, the last entrant being appointed in 1934. In comparative terms with the overseas Services studied in Part II, this is lower even than the Sudan Political Service, with its total of approximately 500 in 55 years. The fact that the China Service numbered approximately 60 in 1900 and 80 in 1927 does indicate that even though some of these posts were held by clerical officers (sent out from the home establishment to the dismay of the Legation Minister, Sir Miles Lampson,[73] who was all for reviving the ex-public schoolboy intake for the posts of student interpreter), continuity *en poste*, with all the attaching value of experience and language, remained a feature of the Service.

Before the competitive examination was introduced for this branch of the Consular Service in 1861, the family origins of its officials were anticipatedly diverse. Thereafter it began to reflect more and more the offspring of the rising middle class. Many of the new consuls enjoyed a family connection with China or the East, and it is possible to discern by the end of the century the emergence of family connections as sons of Chinese consular officials were admitted into the China Service, with a sprinkling of sons of Indian Civil or Colonial Service officers among them. By now, too, the turn-of-the-century Civil Service debate was on in the Foreign Office. Very well, granted the argument that the Consular Service needed a 'better' type of entrant, what did this mean and how did one achieve it? Was it public-school men (glossed by Coates as 'an expression evidently [then] used as a synonym for a gentleman')?[74] Was it university graduates, regardless of whether they might not all be gentlemen? Or men who, though probably coming from a somewhat lower social class, had the advantage of actually knowing something about trade and commerce in their own or their home life? Once the examination principle was introduced, a process of limited rather than open competition allowed the gentility factor to be introduced by means of the kind of references sought and through an interview before a Foreign Office selection board. From 1910 candidates for the China, Japan and Siam Consular Services were required to sit the same examination as those for the Diplomatic, Home and Indian Civil Services and the Eastern Cadetships. According to Coates, in 1926, and again in 1934, Whitehall took the view that the China Service, the one-time *corps d'élite* within the Consular Service, really was scraping the bottom of the barrel.[75] Nevertheless, in the same way as the Levant Service generated a number of outstanding Oriental Secretaries, so did the China Service produce a number of first-class men in its prize post of Chinese Secretary. It was, too, a Service which could realize Allen's observation how 'to young Britons born in the early years of this century the East was a mysterious and exotic place'.[76]

Following the loss of its extraterritorial rights in 1943, a few consulates were opened in 1946 by former China Service officials, now belonging to an integrated Foreign Service. But these did not last beyond 1949, when the Communists drove Chiang Kai-shek out of the Chinese mainland to Formosa. The Service's leading chronicler expresses its epitaph like this:

> So ended the tightly knit Service, whose members had been proud of its separate identity and of their specialist functions and skills, and had been bound together by a strong *esprit de corps*. Despite a not inconsiderable proportion of failures and a scattering of black sheep, the majority of the Service had been united, too, by an unwritten and nearly always unspoken code of personal conduct, the pillars of which were devotion to duty, integrity over money, and a sense of personal honour.[77]

The new Levant Consular Service got off to a better start than Palmerston's scheme in the 1840s for training interpreter attachés, nominated by the Vice-Chancellors of the Universities of Oxford and Cambridge, at Constantinople in a bid to rid the embassy of foreign dragomans, notably the ubiquitous Pisani family. Inheriting the consular establishments of the Levant Company after its affairs were wound up in 1825, when many of the Company staff transferred to the new Crown Service, in the 1870s the Levant establishment comprised two Consuls-General and eleven vice-consuls and consuls.[78] By 1890 twenty-six natural-born British officials had joined it, in a positive move to replace the local Levantine elements whose probity was questionable and was looked on as damaging to the reputation of the British consulates.

Linguistic skill became the dominant factor in recruitment. At first the language was taught in Constantinople, but from 1894 instruction was made available at Cambridge (the Oxford scheme proved unsatisfactory), where the Levant interpreters came under the same supervisory Board as the ICS probationers.[79] Such was the intensity of the language training, both at Cambridge and then in the early years abroad, that Platt is of the opinion that if they survived all this, the Levant consuls were 'as fully trained as any British public servant overseas'.[80] Besides the requirement of being examined in no less than six languages, Latin and French being compulsory for all applicants, there were three further requirements that shocked at least one of the five successful candidates – and subsequently one of the stars of the Levant Service – in the 1906 examination:

> I had to swear an affidavit that I was not married (there was nothing in the regulations to prevent my getting married the next day if I wished); there was a medical examination ...; and I had to produce a guarantee of £500 that I would not resign from the Service within five years from the date of appointment.[81]

Before the First World War, of course, it was Turkish that lay at the centre of the work of the Levant Consular Service, and in that Ottoman era a posting to Constantinople, accredited to the Sultan's Court, was regarded as the plum of the Service. It was the war which was to project Arabic to centre-stage, with Britain, in the Lawrence aftermath, establishing a Legation in Jedda. Eccentrics like H. St J. Philby were very much in the adventurous consular mould of men like Doughty and Burton. Others, like H. Dickson, who started as a District Officer in Southern Iraq in 1918 before moving to Bahrain as political officer, became Arabists *pur sang*. Others again, like John Young and Cecil Hope-Gill, kept popping up here and there all over the Middle East between the wars.[82] Importantly for the Colonial Administrative Service, some of the Mandatory Service assembled to administer the captured Palestine as the Occupied Enemy Territory Administration (OETA) were drawn from both the Egyptian Civil and the Levant Consular Services, forming the founding cadre of the Colonial Office's new Palestine Administrative Service.[83] Partly for this reason, pressure grew in the Foreign Office to merge the now less-stretched Levant Service into the General Consular Service: a small Service could too often mean a stagnant career pattern. There were periods, as with Persia in the 1930s, when specialization within the Service threatened to become bloated: no less than 29 consular posts in a single country.[84] The rank of student interpreter was the first to be abolished, but dissatisfaction over promotion prospects continued until amalgamation was approved in 1934. In 1936 the Levant Consular Service came to an end.

It was in the Levant Service above all that the echoes of colonial service are at their loudest. A comment made by an experienced Levant Service officer is very much to the point:

> Every consul in the [Middle] East bears a more or less political character, and is duly engaged in the conduct of negotiations with the native authorities which require all the tact and intimate knowledge of men that are supposed to be essential qualifications of the trained diplomatist.[85]

Consular courts, keeping the peace, exhortations to social improvement and administrative reform, a ready eye for corruption among dragomans and cavasses, and petitioners crying out 'Sahib! Save us from the Turks ... we are British subjects and the Consul-General is our only protection'[86] are as much part of the pre-1939 Colonial Service as they were familiar to members of the Levant Consular Service.

The Consular Service was never large. In the mid-1930s, in the wake of the decision to combine all new entrants to the Consular Service under the heading of an 'Amalgamated Service' from 1934 (1935 for the China branch alone), there were on the FO establishment 3 Inspectors-General of Consulates, 25 Consuls-General (only one of whom had been awarded a knighthood), 86 salaried and 40 Vice-Consuls, along with nearly 400 unsalaried Consuls and vice-consuls, all in the General Service.[87] The Levant Service still had 13 Consuls-General and 80 Consuls and Vice-Consuls of its own, with the China, Japan and Siam Services each being smaller. Ten years after the Foreign Service integration reforms of 1943 the Consular Service numbered 306, most of them classified as Branch B officers. By 1968, this had fallen to a total of 276 Consuls-General, Consuls and Vice-Consuls. By then, with consular posts but no more Consular Service, the Consular Department was one of sixty Departments in the Foreign Office, responsible for over 150 Consular Districts, half of them now held in the rank of Consul-General, in nearly 100 countries.

In what was arguably its heyday, up to the 1930s, with thirty-odd posts in the Far Eastern Service and nearly forty in the Levant Service, the Consular Service had offered young Britons in pursuit of government employment abroad a huge variety of postings which, though not matched by comparable rewards on the promotional ladder, was unavailable to those who joined a single territory Crown civil service. The fact that, back in 1898, there were over fifty applications for the seven vacancies in the China Service illustrates that the small Consular Service, too, was ranked along with the large Indian Civil and evolving Colonial Administrative Services by Oxbridge graduates as an attractive overseas career in a Crown civil service.[88] Twenty years on, competition was equally strong: S. Cunyngham-Browne passed high, only to be told that there was a three-year waiting list.[89] If complaints of inferiority and mediocrity, 'the imprint of the second best', originated largely from within the Service – above all when its members compared themselves to their not-so-distant cousins in the Diplomatic Service – nevertheless the Consular Service, and in particular the Levant and the China Services, exercised a genuine allure for graduate potential recruits. On balance, it probably deserved far better candidates than those summarily justified in the lukewarm recommendation of one of its members, who described his Levant Service as 'a good service for a boy without much brains, without much ambition, and with a moderate private income'.[90]

When that luminary of the Levant Consular Service, Sir Reader Bullard, was reflecting in 1903 on what career he might aspire to, he came across a crammer's Civil Service prospectus which mentioned that what was known as the Levant Consular Service staffed posts in the Ottoman Empire, Persia, Russia and Ethiopia, besides offering two years at Cambridge University at government expense. 'Could anything be more attractive?', he asked himself, to a

young man aged nineteen at the beginning of the twentieth century.[91] Bullard ended his career as H. M. Ambassador in Tehran.

THE OETA AND BMA

There are three further, but far smaller, instances of Britain's imperial civil services in action which, though transitory and essentially constructed on secondment, deserve notice in the context of this chapter.

The first is the Iraq Civil Service, assembled in Iraq towards the end of World War I when Great Britain was awarded a mandate by the League of Nations for parts of the former and now vanquished Ottoman Empire. The area of Mesopotamia had come under British control early in the war, and from 1920 the office of the High Commissioner in Iraq was created. This lasted till 1932, when the mandate was terminated and Iraq became independent. The most famous of the four High Commissioners was Sir Percy Cox from the Indian Political Service, who was Civil Commissioner from 1914 to 1917 and High Commissioner 1920–23.[92] At the same time, His Britannic Majesty became the Mandatory for the neighbouring Transjordan, where in 1921 a Resident was appointed, H. St. J. Philby. In 1928 the High Commissioner for Palestine became *ex officio* High Commissioner for Transjordan. Only two Residents held the office from 1921 to 1946, when Transjordan emerged as the independent kingdom of Jordan. They were supported by an Assistant Resident (the post was at one time held by H. M. Foot) and a small British staff of Advisers and Directors and the Commandant of the Arab Legion. In both these Middle East administrations the Colonial Service nucleus of the high-profile mandated territory of Palestine (1920–48) is to be found.

But in its beginning the putative Iraq Civil Service was better known as the Occupied Enemy Territory Administration (OETA). Its civil side was scarcely a bureaucracy to be proud of. 'We were inefficient, ill-educated', ran the judgement of one of its more senior officers drafted in from Egypt in 1917 as Military Governor of Jerusalem, Ronald Storrs,[93] even though OETA's Chief Political Officer was of the calibre of the remarkable General Clayton, 'one of the best known figures in the Near East … never in the way and never out of the way'.[94] Lamenting Britain's failure to appoint to OETA some 'Colonial or Chief Secretary – perhaps from Ceylon – familiar for a quarter of a century with the broad principles and technical minutiae of administration',[95] Storrs, who went on to act as Chief Secretary pending the arrival of Sir William Deedes, drew a grim portrait of what his OETA was composed of:

> There were a few professional soldiers. Apart from these our administrative and technical staff, necessarily drawn from military material available on the spot, included a cashier from a Bank in Rangoon, an actor-manager, two assistants from Thos. Cook, a picture-dealer, an Army coach, a clown, a land valuer, a bo'sun from the Niger, a Glasgow distiller, an organist, an

Alexandria cotton-broker, an architect (not in the Public Works but in the Secretariat), a Junior Service London Postal Official (not in the Post Office but as Controller of Labour), a taxi-driver from Egypt, two school-masters and a missionary.[96]

Furthermore, while most spoke Arabic, having come from Egypt, none knew Hebrew. It is not surprising that the Foreign Office soon commissioned the intrepid Gertrude Bell to conduct an inquiry into the civil administration of Mesopotamia.[97]

In Africa the assumption of civilian administration in Tanganyika was not the same as that carried out in the former enemy territories in the Middle East. Civil administration, set up in 1917, frequently drew its officers from the Colonial Service in neighbouring British possessions, among them H. C. Byatt, C. Dundas and P. E. Mitchell, all future colonial governors. Unlike OETA, they were not given military rank.

If the OETA that emerged in the Middle East after the First World War was the model of a modern imperial administration, its related BMA (British Military Administration) which was set up in occupied enemy territory towards the end of the Second World War was a very different affair.[98] Especially relevant in the context of this book is the OETA (as it was first called) established in Eritrea in February 1941, along with its expanding administration of the African territories from which the Italians were ousted in the months that followed: Ethiopia, Eritrea and Somaliland in the east, Tripolitania, Cyrenaica and Libya in the north, and Madagascar to the south. As a comparison with OETA's First World War experience in the Middle East, as well as for the purpose of this chapter, it is the personnel who made up the BMA in Africa that call for mention here. The Chief Political Officer appointed in 1941 was Sir Philip Mitchell, the Colonial Service Governor of Uganda and now gazetted in the temporary rank of Major-General as Political Adviser to General Wavell.[99] The Deputy CPO for Ethiopia (the title was subsequently changed to Military Administrator) was Maurice Lush, of the Sudan Political Service, formerly Governor of Northern Province, and now seconded in the rank of Brigadier.[100] His deputies were drawn from the Tanganyika Service (Lt-Col. Dallas) and the Sudan (R. F. E. Laidlaw). Lush established nine Political Missions in Ethiopia. The Emperor's personal Political Adviser was Brigadier D. A. Sandford.[101] For the delicate Madagascar mission, L. E. Grafftey-Smith of the Levant Consular Service was detached from the British Embassy in Cairo to assist Lush. Interestingly, in its day the BMA in Africa thought of establishing a combined corps of political and military officers along the lines of the Indian Political Service, and one of its officers, G. T. Fisher, was posted to take over from Brigadier Chater as Military Governor of Somaliland in 1943. Above all, in the context of this book, in the lower echelons the BMA employed a number of District Commissioners from the Colonial and especially the Sudan Political Services. A few, too, could point to this experience when they subsequently applied to join these Services.

Part II
Governance

4 The Indian Civil Service, 1858–1947

INTRODUCTION

In the eyes of those Britons who, in the age of Empire, were to an extent aware of – and, more relevantly, were actors in – imperial administration, and in the minds of most young men who had already set their sights on a career in administration overseas, the Indian Civil Service enjoyed pre-eminence in the ranking order. 'The Civil Service of Pakistan is the successor in Pakistan of the Indian Civil Service', proclaimed an official recruiting pamphlet in Karachi a few years after independence, 'which was the most distinguished Civil Service in the world.'[1] Half a century later, in advertising a retrospective memoir on the Sudan Political Service, the publisher found no difficulty in situating the topic for a possibly disoriented post-imperial readership by the reminder that the SPS 'was of a renown comparable with that of the Indian Civil Service'.[2] In between, too, Indian members of the former ICS have not hesitated in their claim that the District Officer was hand-picked for the most prized of all Britain's imperial civil services.[3] Nor, expectedly, have the former British members of the ICS, recording their memoirs of what by definition must be among the last of first-hand accounts, been slow to praise.[4] In the intervening fifty years, as research has deepened into who Britain's once-upon-a-time imperial administrators were and why they opted for that kind of overseas career, the evidence has hardened that among these aspirant Crown career graduates – and often their families – there existed in the opening decades of the twentieth century, unofficially yet palpably perceived, a preferred hierarchy in the status of Britain's overseas civil services. The existence of that ranking is aptly condensed in the common graduate response of the time, still recalled in memoir, that 'I didn't think I stood a chance for the ICS, so I applied for the Sudan Political' or 'I wrote down the Colonial Service as my second choice – and got in'. Uniqueness may be unquantifiable, but in elitism gradations can comfortably coexist.

Yet acclaim, like glamour, has its fashions. The Indian Civil Service has been no stranger to the revisionism which has marked the post-imperial age, in this case the study not only of the ideology of imperial rule but in particular of the performance of the imperial rulers. Here, however, the argument of a policy of overt racial discrimination which reduced the Sudan Political and Colonial Administrative to exclusively British ('European') Services right up to the final decade of alien overrule in most colonial territories (see Chapter 9) and to the very end in the Anglo-Egyptian Sudan (see Chapter 6) is necessarily softened, though not entirely muted, in the study of the ICS. While the first African was not admitted into the Provincial Administration of the Gold Coast (the so-called 'model' colony in Africa) until 1942, fifteen years before independence, the first Indian gained entry into the Indian Civil Service in 1867 and by 1932, the same period of fifteen years before independence, Indians already comprised about a quarter of the ICS. This is a fundamental difference in the evolutionary composition of Britain's overseas civil services.

Nevertheless, while Indian scholars have understandably looked for elements of racial rejection within a racially unified civil service, British and American scholars have often been no less hostile in their post-imperial analysis, seemingly intent on questioning and undermining the assumption of superiority that the ICS was believed to hold in British esteem, however limited the area of public awareness may have been. Contemporary research has shown, for instance, that the ICS was characterized by discontent and demoralization after the First World War;[5] that such was the drop in its career prospects, progressively from 1915 onwards and acceleratedly from the mid-1920s, that the ICS was faced with a critical shortage of satisfactory recruits from Britain;[6] that the 'Steel Frame' of ICS administration had begun to buckle even before the First World War;[7] that from an even earlier period its popularity among British graduates had declined alarmingly;[8] and that for the last twenty to forty years of its existence, i.e. two 'Service' generations, a combination of civil violence, including the assassination of ICS officials (both attempted and successful) and the enforced acceleration of Indianization and constitutional change, had confronted the District Officer in India with a chilling shrinkage in his authority and status, and together punctured the balloon of the ICS as young Britons' premier career choice of Crown service overseas.[9]

For all that – and it is a lot – British recruitment for the ICS did not dry up. The quality of the cadres who joined after the defining Government of India Act of 1935, which put real substance on the declaration of eventual self-government made in 1917, was still looked on as superior.[10] This is despite the fact that following the cool impact of that Act on career prospects in British universities, when the number taking the examination in London collapsed from 13 in 1934 to five in 1935, the India Office decided to adopt for 1936 the practice of accepting candidates on the strength of their honours degree, without further examination. Improved conditions of service in the Colonial Administrative Service from 1930, and particularly after the enhancement of their training arrangements through a postgraduate year at Oxford and Cambridge, succeeded in generating a greater interest in its career prospects. Yet all things being equal, inter-war graduates determined on a career in overseas administration placed the ICS above the SPS or CAS. For graduates aiming for a government career overseas between 1900 and 1920, and still to a considerable extent up to 1939, any reason not to 'have a shot at the ICS' as the university appointments boards counselled would probably be a personal (not a likely First?) or family (is India finished?) one in deciding which of the three Services ranked as *la crème de la crème*. Arnold Toynbee maintained that at Balliol College before 1914, 'any freshman who had no clear idea of what he wanted to do after he went down was put down for the ICS by the dons as a matter of routine'.[11]

Deconstruction of the romantic base of Empire has been part and parcel of its intellectual reassessment. While the elitist myth of an omnipotent and omnicompetent ICS may properly be questioned and reinterpreted, its contemporary mystique within the socio-educational class to which it had long appealed and from which it had persistently recruited is not something that can be concealed or spirited away. Nor, despite the sapping of post-imperial scholarship by certain tunnellers as they lay their mines under the ICS, is the Service's reputation for quality likely to be annihilated by such explosions: injured yes, destroyed no.

ORIGIN

The long-standing origins of the Indian Civil Service lay, as we saw in Chapter 3, in the Civil Service of the Honourable East India Company which, in 1772, superseded the primarily merchant service dating back to 1601. In 1833 the Company was called on to relinquish totally its trading responsibilities, and in 1842 its mercantile titles were replaced by the bureaucratic hierarchy of First, Second and Third Class Civil Servants. The extension of British rule from the three historic Presidencies of Bengal, Madras and Bombay at the end of the eighteenth century, and later into the Punjab and the North-West Frontier Provinces, depended largely on the military not only for its acquisition but also for its initial administration, a system of government neatly symbolized in the pre-Mutiny Punjab by the Lawrence brothers, Henry the Soldier and John the Civilian (later Viceroy).[12] The point made here is that at the time of the transfer from Company to Crown in 1858, there already existed under the Company a basic system of administration and the framework of a civil service which were inherited and adapted rather than abolished by the new ICS. This included the nomenclature of field administration, Commissioners and District Officers, which in turn was borrowed by the later Colonial Administrative and Sudan Political Services. Thus 1858, watershed as it was, was no earthquake in the fundamental structure of civil administration in India: that shock came more through the introduction of recruitment by means of competitive examination instead of nomination in 1853 than by way of the conversion from a Company to a Crown Civil Service in 1858.

Under the Company, each of the Presidencies had had its own civil service establishment. In the 1840s, the Company had 776 civilians stationed in the three Presidencies. Together these comprised ten Government Secretaries, 115 officials in the judiciary and 651 in the executive. These were distributed across 39 Residencies or Agencies and 60 Districts in the Bengal Presidency; six and 22 respectively in Madras; and 12 and 16 in Bombay.[13] Because any newly acquired territory was placed under the Presidency of Bengal, it was the Bengal civilians who had served most widely. When the Crown took over, there were 846 posts on the Company's civil establishment. The new Service was defined as the 'Covenanted Civil Service of India'. The practice of signing a covenant with one's employer dated back to Cornwallis's time, and from 1813 the title of an officer in the Covenanted Civil Service was reserved for graduates of the Company's training establishment, Haileybury College.[14] Under the Crown, before he was allowed to set sail for India each member had to sign a covenant with the Secretary of State setting out his terms of service. Officials recruited in India were enrolled in the uncovenanted service. This indenture, issued on behalf of the Secretary of State for India in Council, bound the Covenantor 'to serve as a member of the Civil Service of India in the Province known as XYZ during His Majesty's pleasure'. It went on to require his acceptance of a series of obligations and conditions, involving his 'genuine fidelity', obedience, keeping regular accounts, 'the preservation of chattels and realties', and 'not to divulge secrets'. He was also forbidden to 'accept corrupt presents or make corrupt bargains', to trade contrary to law or regulations, and 'to quit India without leaving and to satisfy all debts to His Majesty before departure'.[15] It was another twenty years, in 1878, before the Government decided that every Covenanted civil servant would be liable to assignment anywhere in India, and the title of 'Bombay [etc.] Civil Service' officially lapsed. Nevertheless, the habit of adding 'Madras Civil Service' or 'Punjab Civil Service' continued for some time.[16] In the Punjab the executive branch of the ICS, the Commissioners, Deputy and Assistant Commissioners, together with the judicial branch, adopted the title of officers in the Punjab Commission.

A common and accepted practice evolved, continuing through to the end, for members of the ICS to add the abbreviated suffix to their name as with honours and decorations, e.g. 'A. B. Brown, Esq., I.C.S.' or 'C. D. Green, Esq., C.I.E., I.C.S.' The form 'E. F. Gray, Esq., I.C.S. (rtd)' continued through the obituary notices of the 1990s. The practice was unique among the civil services reviewed here: there was never any 'C.A.S.' or 'S.P.S.', though at one time an irked Sir Hugh Clifford is said to have authorized his officers in the Malay Civil Service to even the score with the arrogant ICS by adding 'M.C.S.' after their name. A proposal put to the Aitchison Committee of 1886 that the form 'Covenanted Civil Service of India' should be replaced by 'Imperial Civil Service of India' was not adopted. The form 'All-India Service' came into fashion after 1912, but the 'Civil Service of India' as in the Covenant was gradually transformed into both popular and formal usage as the 'Indian Civil Service' and the abbreviation 'ICS' became standard practice. As a group, they were often referred to as 'Civilians', in contrast to the 'Military' cadres in India, recalling the Company's distinction between those trained for civilian work at its Fitzwilliam, later Haileybury, College and for its military wing at Addiscombe College.[17]

RECRUITMENT

By the standards of the Sudan Political Service and of individual territorial governments staffed by the Colonial Administrative Service, the ICS was a large service. But then British India, i.e. excluding the Princely States, was a large country: by any imperial standard, an empire within an Empire. As with the Colonial Administrative Service (not the wider Colonial Service) and the Sudan Political Service (not the larger Sudan Civil Service), the Executive and Secretariat posts, along with those in the judiciary, constituted those held by the Indian Civil Service (not the Indian Political Service). Ignoring the Listed Posts, that is to say those in the administration held by Indian and Anglo-Indian officials who had started their career in the Provincial Services and been promoted into the All-India cadres (no more than 85 in 1939), the strength of the ICS expanded very slowly, from 883 in 1869 to 1021 at the end of the century and 1142 by 1909. Part of the explanation lies in the fact that at its inauguration in 1858 it was not starting *ab initio* but was clearly taking over a going concern with many years of civil service structure and administration to its credit. The ICS reached a peak at the end of the First World War, when it numbered 1255. Declining to 1122 in 1929, on the eve of the Second World War it had climbed back to 1299, in the event its highest total ever.[18] Those who had been accepted for the 1939 intake were allowed to embark for India, even though war had by then broken out, but this was to prove the last regular intake. Twelve probationers were released from the army in response to the public advertisement issued in 1940, but it is generally accepted that 1941 saw the end of British recruitment into the ICS: it was the war and not yet independence that effectively put a stop on the ICS as an overseas career civil service for Britons. In 1944 officers serving in the Indian Army were invited to apply, and there is some evidence that a dozen or so were offered appointments.[19] Recruitment was officially reopened at the end of the war, and a number of applicants, undaunted by the inclusion of compensation terms for a probably foreclosed career, went through the Diplomatic Service 'country house' assessment. But those who were selected were informed in 1946 that the Secretary of State would be making no more appointments to the ICS.

Although vacancies were filled each year, ICS recruitment was characterized by fluctuations which seem to have had more to do with lack of suitable candidates than with lack of posts available.[20] From 1872 to 1877, some thirty appointments were made each year. Then came a run of eight fallow years (only 13 appointed in 1878), followed by a dramatic rise to an average of 48 all the way up to 1892, reaching 54 appointments in 1886. This rise continued, exceeding 60 each year from 1893 to 1898, to be once again followed by a decline, with the average for 1901–5 barely reaching 50. This is all part of the evidence arraigned above in support of the argument that the ICS never was the popular career it has been portrayed in Crown service lore. Arguably of greater determination in assessing the true state of the ICS's popularity as first choice among potential imperial civil service recruits would be to calculate the number of candidates competing for each available post. In his meticulous investigation of the pre-1910 figures, Spangenberg comes up with a median figure of 6 up to 1880, dropping to 4.5 in the 1890s and only 3.5 for the next 15 years: his range is from 10.3 in 1878 to a mere 1.9 in 1893.[21]

But a case can be made out that these variations do not reflect a lessening of interest in the ICS as a career so much as the mid-nineteenth century arguments over and alterations to what the ideal upper age limit for ICS entry should be, with its inevitable effect on the career expectations of the graduate intake. At one time the East India Company had accepted aspirant Writers aged anywhere between 15 and 22. Then, having established its own training College, it started to take in boys at 17 and, after two years at Haileybury, send them out to India when they were 19.[22] The emerging Civil Service Commission hoped, by reducing the maximum age from 23 to 22, to lure a graduate into the new ICS before he was seduced by 'the distinction he looks for at home'.[23] Six years later it was further reduced to 21, offering a two-year course in Indian subjects at the university, and in 1879 the upper age was lowered to 19, on the grounds that graduate recruitment not having achieved all that was expected from it at Oxford and Cambridge, it was time to go directly to the public schools and look for the best material there. Despite a trenchant attack from Benjamin Jowett, the formidable Master of Balliol College, Oxford, whose ambition was 'to inoculate the world with Balliol men' and who believed Oxford to be the finest – and sole – kindergarten for the ICS,[24] the upper age was not restored to 23 until 1892. Disorientingly, it was raised again in 1906 and, more understandably in the immediate aftermath of wartime conditions and needs, again in 1921. In summary, for the last fifty years or so of its existence, the age limits of entry into the ICS remained within the bracket of 21/22 as the minimum and 23/24 the maximum.[25]

Two interrelated factors should be taken into account in trying to grasp the juggling with the upper age limit. One was the complaint of Indian candidates. The Service had been open to them since 1853, but granted the complex, classics-oriented competitive examination and its inevitable emphasis on written English, the lower the cut-off age the higher the penalization of candidates not coming from British public schools. Secondly, and of paramount concern in the study of the ICS when set beside entry into its two sister Services, there was the whole phenomenon of the competitive examination. For once the universities rather than the Company's own College were the central recruiting ground, public examinations became the modifying force in determining the entrance age.

Not only did the competitive examination fundamentally distinguish recruitment into the ICS from that into the CAS or the SPS; it also preceded its introduction for entry into the British Home Civil and Diplomatic Services. The Company had laid down in 1833 that for every vacancy at its Haileybury College there should be a minimum of four nominations and that the place then be awarded through an examination. In 1854, following Lord Macaulay's enthusiastic endorsement of the value of an entrance examination for civil servants in India, Parliament took this a stage further by legislating that there should be no more appointments to the Company's civil service through patronage and that everyone should henceforth be selected by examination. The regulations implemented from 1855 were that candidates would now be required to show learning that was thorough rather than the Haileybury spread: 'knowledge of a wide surface but small depth was to be discounted.'[26] It was a tradition scrupulously continued by the new ICS. Only once did the British Government break with its tradition, established in the Company era even before the Crown took over, that entry into the ICS had to be through an open examination. This was when, in response to the negative impact of the constitutional concessions in the Government of India Act of 1935 on the collective undergraduate mind, the number of applicants sitting for the examination in London dropped by over 50 per cent. It was agreed to appoint on the quality of an applicant's honours degree without further examination. The result was startling: against five applicants in 1935, 208 opted for the new method and 56 took both. Seven were offered appointments.

In the historical terminology of the ICS as well as in the chronology, 1855 marked the bitter-sweet advent of 'The Competition Wallah'.[27] At first, this new breed, redolent of intellectual superiority and likely not on a par with men who might have more fire in their belly than thought in their mind, was a far from welcome arrival on the Indian scene. His seniors were, of course, mostly Haileybury men, and proud of it.[28] But when the Crown took over from the Company, the break, along with the 'natural wastage' of Haileybury men who opted for retirement from the Company service or were not offered a transfer to the new government service, may have helped to soften – without yet totally dissipating – the intensity of the instant rejection of the Competition Wallah. 'We want', pronounced one contemporary, 'neither priggish pedants nor polished dunces.'[29] In its acceptance of the gruelling competitive exam as the *bona fides* of its distinctive policy of seeking the best brains, the ICS was endorsing Macaulay's high-minded rhetoric in his defining Report of 1854 that for the civil service in India only 'the best, the most liberal, the most finished education' was good enough. Intellectualism, continuously assumed and consistently demonstrated, became the hallmark of the *beau idéal* ICS administrator, just as athleticism was widely interpreted as (and could often be shown to be) the badge of the SPS administrator.[30]

Given the prominence of the competitive examination in the ICS story and its absence in the recruitment of the CAS and the SPS, it will be helpful to consider its structure and role in some detail. While the other two Services attached importance to the final examination conducted internally by the universities at the end of the special training course organized from 1926, only the ICS combined the results of the examination for its probationers held at the end of their year's training at the university with those of the competitive examination held a year earlier, both conducted by the Civil Service Commission, to produce – and publish – a list of successful candidates … in public order of merit.[31]

An analysis of the results of the Civil Service Commission examination held in August 1932 provides a good picture of the calibre and the challenge of the competitiveness of the ICS as a Crown civil service career overseas. This was the final examination, reflecting both the CSC open exam of 1931 and the exams held at the end of the year's probationary course, still under the auspices of the CSC, in 1932. Thirty-two candidates passed, two 'failed to qualify' – both bearing English and not Indian names. Five academic subjects were compulsory: Indian History, Indian Penal Code, Code of Criminal Procedure, Indian Evidence Act, and an Indian language. The approved languages were Bengali, Burmese, Hindi, Marathi, Tamil, Telugu and Urdu. Riding was also obligatory. One optional subject had to be offered. Optional subjects included British History (all three takers in 1932 were Indian), Hindu, Buddhist and Mohammedan Law, Burmese History, Sanskrit and Persian. Indian History carried a total of 400 marks, with 600 for the language, 200 each for the other three compulsory subjects and for riding. Each optional subject had a 400 maximum mark. In each case except riding and the optional subject the pass mark stood at 50 per cent. There was no literal pass mark in riding, but candidates with under 100 marks were deemed to have 'shown a minimum proficiency'.

The candidates were listed in final order of merit, with combined examination marks set out in three columns showing the final examination, the open competition and the combined result. Taking here, as representative, the eventual two top and bottom passes, and the two (6 per cent) failures, the marks and final places awarded are shown in Table 4.1

Some of the marks call for comment. While Williams passed out first, he was placed only fourth in the final examination at the end of the probationers' course. There were only thirteen marks between the first two candidates. The bottom successful candidate scored 2124 marks overall, 777 marks below the top and 228 *below* the total marks of the higher of the two failed candidates. The highest mark scored in the open competition was 1276 (by the overall top candidate) and the highest in the final examination 1644, *above* that scored by the first two candidates overall. The lowest marks were 1063 and 825 respectively, with 1012 marks being the score of the last pass in the final exam. On individual papers, the highest and lowest marks awarded were: Indian Penal Code (200), 182 and several on 100; Indian History (400), 317 (an Indian candidate) and 200 (British); and Urdu (600), 495 and 300, both British candidates.

Table 4.1   ICS probationers final combined examination, 1932

Order of merit				Name	Marks awarded			
a	=	b	+	c		b	+	c	=	a
1		4		1	A. A. Williams	1625		1276		2901
2		3		3	E. G. S. Apedaile	1638		1250		2888
31		31		31	S. N. Russell	1203		1084		2287
32		32		26	E. F. Lydall	1012		1112		2124
Fail		Fail		21	[a European candidate]	1228		1124		2352
Fail		Fail		12	[ditto]	825		1170		1995

Key: a = Combined examinations; b = at final examination; c = at open competition.

Candidate 32, the bottom to pass, scored 10 out of 400 in his optional subject of Sanskrit. As for riding, the marks ranged from 142 to 38 out of 200. One of the candidates who scored under half marks in riding passed out overall in second place. In view of the close relationship between placing in the order of merit and the allocation of preferred Province, the bottom candidate in 1932 was not altogether surprisingly assigned to Assam.

In the 1938 CSC examination, the penultimate CSC one ever set for the ICS though nobody could have known it at the time, five of the 58 candidates (almost 10 per cent) failed to qualify at the end of the course. Once again, four of them scored a higher total mark on the final exam than some of those who gained admission; each registered a lower than pass mark on one subject. By now the three papers on Indian legal codes had been combined into a single Indian Law paper, still carrying 600 marks. Riding was still a formidable fence to clear: two candidates failed to qualify because of their low mark and a third was failed because he did not take the riding test. The top candidate, M. Zinkin, scored 1512 in the final exam, over 100 marks above the second in order of merit, A. C. Cowan on 1409. Three were in the 1200–1300 range and the score of five was between 1000 and 1100. The bottom candidate to be accepted earned 978 marks. The candidate at the bottom of the list, D. W. S. Ife, was young enough to resit the examination in 1939 – and this time succeeded.

The prior CSC open competition exam,[32] also held at Burlington House, took place in August, in time to notify successful candidates which university they would be going to for the probationers' course starting in October. There were compulsory papers in English, English essay, a language, elementary science, and the general awareness paper called 'Present Day Questions'. The range of optional subjects was extensive, aiming to cover the university discipline of all applicants. The written tests totalled 1600 marks, with a further 300 available from the interview – a not inconsiderable proportion in what was always looked on as an open, written competitive examination. However, the interview was in no way as determining as that for the CAS or SPS, nor was it anything like as rigorous as the written papers: in 1928, half the British applicants (but only five of the Indians) scored at least 240 marks in it. None managed to achieve 300. A serving ICS officer always sat on the interviewing panel. The number of vacancies to be filled was not announced until after the ranked list of results of the CSC open competition had been scrutinized by the India Office.

The CSC competitive examination was, of course, not designed for the ICS alone. Applicants for the Home Civil Service, the Diplomatic and Consular Services and (up to 1932) the Eastern Cadetships in the Colonial Service, sat the same examination. The marks required to be offered a post in the administrative grade of the Home Civil Service were higher than those necessary for entry into the ICS. Many British (but not Indian) candidates entered for more than one of the three concurrently examined Crown Services. For instance, in the CSC examination held in 1928, the last before the economic slump impacted on the UK job market, 121 British and 167 Indian candidates took the London examination. Among the former, 20 applied for the ICS only and

61 put in only for the Home Civil. Saumarez-Smith, who had set his sights on the Home Civil, took the exam in 1933 as a trial run since he was below the age for his first choice. When he succeeded in scoring enough marks for the ICS, he accepted the offer: employment was only just coming out of the recession.[33] Like Stanton Ife, Leslie Glass too took the ICS exam twice, with a crammer following his first failure after Schools. Even then, his name did not appear in *The Times* until all those above him had opted for their first choice of Service. 'Have you noticed', his father commented on reading the full book of everyone's marks, 'that at the end of the five compulsory papers you were top of all the Service? And that you dropped fifty places when it came to the subjects you were supposed to have studied at Oxford?'[34]

An outgrowth of the competitive examination was the emergence of the London 'crammers'. At first it tended to be the non-university men who had recourse to their progressively polished services, but soon university students also began to interrupt their own courses to spend time at the crammers. Sometimes this was for a year, sometimes just for the six weeks between taking Schools or the Tripos and sitting for the Civil Service examination at Burlington Gardens in August. Two of the best-known were Davies and Wren's in Powis Square, with the smaller Sturt's strategically located in Oxford.[35] In 1874, twenty years after the introduction of the Civil Service Commission examination, it was estimated that one-third of the successful candidates had attended a crammer.[36] In Victorian times it was reckoned that in the hands of a good crammer a probationer could in six weeks add 500 marks to his total.[37] Michael O'Dwyer did it, the other way round, as it were, passing the ICS exam from Wren's, spending his two years as an ICS probationer at Balliol College, and then staying on a third year to obtain his degree before sailing for India.[38] Mason implies that another well-known ICS officer eschewed any university teaching and spent his entire three years at a crammer.[39] There was a time when a candidate could offer all the subjects he liked, including Greek and Latin, French and German, Maths and Science, and of course English. But with the limitation imposed in 1906 by the Civil Service Commissioners on the number of subjects that could be offered at the examination, some of the point of cramming was lost. Cramming also encountered the criticism that it undermined the prestige of the ICS – learning by rote was what the *babu* did, not the *barra sahib*: '[This] is not the way in which the rulers of a nation should be prepared for their great duties, rulers who are to govern ... as much by the force of the impalpable qualities which make up the English gentleman as by mere ability and book-learning.'[40] For 'second thoughters', those who had not thought of the ICS in their final year at university, the crammer was a particular godsend: for instance, Francis Mudie, who graduated a Wrangler at Cambridge and spent three years teaching at Clifton and then Eton before he decided in 1914 to try his hand at the ICS.[41] It is perhaps surprising, given the combination of intellectual forcing house and bountiful enterprise that crammers were, that more research has not been undertaken on their staff, their teaching methods and their examination results. Mason is one of the few to award them a separate entry in his history of the

ICS. One is tempted to call for the addition to the educational data accumulated by the sociologists of the ICS the name of crammer attended as well as those of school and university.

In the absence of those data, the educational statistics of the ICS profile are telling enough. Of the first four intakes, the 73 entrants were drawn from 26 graduates from Oxford and 13 from Cambridge, with eight from other English universities, five from Scotland and no less than 17 from Irish ones – a proportion considered by the Civil Service Commissioners to be a dangerous omen.[42] By 1874, Oxbridge successes fell to under 10 per cent. However, over the whole lifetime of the ICS, there is no doubt which university proved to be the greatest provider (Table 4.2).[43]

Less attention has traditionally been paid by social historians of Britain's imperial administrators to what subjects they read at the university than to which university they attended. It was not, of course, until after the First World War that the range of subjects really expanded, with for example politics and economics, modern history and modern languages all beginning to establish themselves alongside the conventional classics as popular options in the Arts. The breakdown of, for instance, the 1928 results of the open competition show that, among the 32 passes from Oxbridge, two from Trinity College Dublin, and one each from Aberdeen and Manchester, almost half had still taken their BA in classics and a third in history.[44] Twelve had obtained a First and one, Penderel Moon, was a Fellow of All Souls. Interestingly, among the 15 successful Indian candidates, two had Firsts: both were in mathematics.

When it comes to schools representation, the picture is less positive. In the place of Oxbridge dominance, it is the spread that emerges as considerable, with Mason emphasizing that it was rare for any school to provide more than

Table 4.2   University provenance of the ICS, 1914–39

University	Entered ICS before 1914		Entered ICS after 1914	
	Number	*%*	**Number**	*%*
Oxford	244	47	214	41
Cambridge	150	29	180	35
Scottish university	68	13	40	8
Irish university	35	7	19	4
Other	20	4	46	9
None mentioned	4	1	17	3
Totals	521	100	516	100

Source: Potter, *India's Administrators*, table 7.

one or two successful candidates a year.[45] A later analysis has provided a wealth of school statistics.[46] According to Potter, among the 392 men who joined the ICS before the First World War, the public school origin was pronounced. For all the penny-packet spread, a select group of no more than fifteen public schools produced more than half of these, ranging from 26 from St Paul's and 18 each from Winchester and Clifton, through Charterhouse (16), Marlborough (15) and Rugby (14) in the middle, to Bradfield (8) and Haileybury (7). Between 1915 and 1941, over half the 222 probationers came from only 30 public (including three grammar) schools, with Rugby now leading the field on 20, followed by Winchester (15) and Wellington (14), and with Manchester Grammar as one of five schools recording four ICS successes each. Despite, then, the high profile of the older public schools in the Victorian period, newer ones and grammar schools soon seized the opportunity to make their contribution to the expanding imperial civil services and find worthy positions for their old boys.

The social make-up of the ICS, like its educational provenance, has elicited much scrutiny, not least because of the sobriquet of 'the Heaven Born', with its undertones of a Brahmin-like superior caste, destined to lead and rule. One misconception of the class dimension to the social myth of the ICS needs to be disposed of at the outset. For all its airs and, by post-imperial standards, well-appointed and superior lifestyle, the ICS was not an aristocratic Service. This was so even in the age of patronage. Here is a misapprehension from which few noble Viceroys, and certainly not a patrician like Curzon with his ready capacity to be appalled by the slightest hint of middle-class mediocrity,[47] ever suffered. Lord Lytton, too, had complained to the Secretary of State in 1876 that 'you must never forget that nineteen Civilians in twenty are the most commonplace and least dignified Englishmen'.[48] Members of the royal household who accompanied the Prince of Wales to India in 1921 were shocked at the social manners of ICS officials.[49] Several younger sons in the peerage and some sons of the landed gentry did find a career in the ICS, just as a few found their way into the Colonial Administrative Service: the English tradition of primogeniture meant that second and subsequent sons, particularly in the aristocracy, had to look elsewhere than their estates and the House of Lords for their career. For a long time it was the church, the army and diplomacy, but in the middle of the nineteenth century a new Crown Service opportunity arose, that of imperial administrator. It was, of course, not only in the family sense of 'the younger sons of the Manse' that India made its mark. It was also in the geographical one of Scots and Empire. Charles Allen points out that Scots, and to a lesser extent Ulstermen, had dominated the administration since the end of the eighteenth century and continued to provide nearly half the ICS well into the twentieth century.[50]

The data gathered by the Civil Service Commission on the 668 recruits into the ICS in its initial fifteen years (1860–74) is interesting not only by itself but also because it seems to establish something of a tripartite class pattern. While 10 per cent came from aristocratic families, 14 per cent came from what was then an acceptedly lower-class background. This left three-quarters of the ICS more or less where it was to be for the rest of its life, drawn from the professional families, the middle-class bourgeoisie whose emergence was inseparable from the new public schools of Victorian England.[51] Unambiguously upper-class abroad, they were for the most part unequivocally [upper] middle-class at home (Table 4.3).

The field widened, but did not alter much in direction, with the passing of time and the expansion of school and university educational opportunity over the century, but the social pattern of the ICS by 1870 was still easily recognizable in 1940. So, too, was the persistent presence of the unexpected leavening: sons of fathers who were an undertaker or an upholsterer, a draper or a druggist, a butcher or miller, together with a sprinkling among parental occupations of tailors, printers, storekeepers and railway workers. In the ICS's seventieth

Table 4.3   Social status of ICS recruits, 1860–74

			Number	*%*
I.	Aristocracy		67	10.0
	(Fathers were either peers or landed gentry)			
II.	Professional middle classes		506	76.0
	Occupation of fathers:			
	A.	Army officers (45); Navy officers (3);		
		Civil Service (16); Ambassador (1)	65	9.8
	B.	Clergymen: Church of England (115);		
		other ministers (39)	184	27.5
	C.	Indian Civil Service (47); Colonial		
		Civil Service (7), etc.	57	8.5
	D.	The legal profession	49	7.4
	E.	The medical profession	65	9.8
	F.	Merchants, industrialists, bankers	48	7.2
	G.	Educators	27	4.0
	H.	Architects and engineers	11	1.7
III.	Lower middle classes or lower classes		95	14.0
	A.	Accountants, agents, managers	20	3.0
	B.	Farmers, surveyors, millers, etc.	28	4.2
	C.	Printers, druggists, tailors,		
		undertakers, storekeepers, etc.	27	4.0
	D.	Clerks, stewards, railway workers	6	0.9
	E.	Not specified	14	2.1
Total			668	100

Source: Spangenberg, 'The Problem of Recruitment for the ICS', p. 343.

birthday intake, out of the 36 successful British applicants three were the sons of clergymen, two of missionaries, four of fathers (occupation of mother was not then an item recorded) in the teaching and three in the legal profession, and two each from medicine, Stock Exchange and the Home Civil Service. There were, too, the son of a clerk and son of a dairyman.[52] In the year before, ten out of the 36 came from parents in business and commerce, a high proportion when one recalls the continuing 'boxwallah' complex in British society in India. By the turn of the century, a further element was making its mark in the ICS: the sons of former Indian civil servants. In 1907, and again twenty years on, these totalled 10 per cent of intake, a figure which casts some doubt, as Ewing observes, on the validity of the comment made by the Secretary of the Cambridge University Appointments Board on the depth of post-Amritsar and post-Bengal undergraduate doubts and depression, that 'wild horses would not drag them into the ICS'.[53]

One social phenomenon is stronger in the ICS than in either of the other two Services. No prosopographer of the servants of the Raj in India (the ICS, IPS, Indian Army, Indian Police, etc.) can fail to be struck by the recurrence and network of 'Anglo-Indian' families, often reaching back to the Honourable Company and establishing a career influence of considerable intensity. When J. Cotton, son of an ICS officer, joined the IPS in 1934, he was the sixth generation in an unbroken male line to serve Crown and Company. Neither the coeval CAS nor the shorter-lived SPS can match that record, though at the topmost proconsular pinnacle the Bruce, Lambton, Grey and Baring families produced, within a hundred years, four Viceroys, three Governors-General, and three Secretaries of State for the Colonies.[54]

Overall J. S. Mill's description of the ICS as displaying Victorian middle-class character was never seriously overthrown.[55] Sir Penderel Moon, in his study of the last Viceroy but one, voiced the same opinion from inside the Service: it was the upper middle-class and not the aristocracy that was 'the mainstay of the British Raj and was largely responsible for its character'.[56] Yet that was only half the truth. There is much support for the Edwardian image of Plato's 'Guardians', promoted compellingly by another insider, the Service's leading historian Philip Mason, as a ruling class and hence willy-nilly a class apart. They were 'hard-working in a debilitating climate', concludes Dewey,

> incorruptible in a society riddled with bribery, celibate until middle age in a subcontinent which married at puberty. Above all, they were individuals. Yet they pretended to be men of action, to escape the stigma attached to clever-ness by the late-Victorian middle class … They quelled riots with a glare, silenced subordinates with a word, played games with manic determination … Whether they liked it or not, they were competition-wallahs chosen for their intellectual ability: mandarins unable to escape their condition.[57]

No less valid, and far more value-driven, is Potter's identification of the ICS, following the sociologists Goldthorpe and Renner, as collectively 'gentlemen of the service class'.[58] It is this aspect of identity, he argues, which generated norms and values in the ICS that had important administrative consequences.

It can be argued that, in contrast to the Colonial Administrative and Sudan Political Services' preference for admission by interview and references, the ICS's insistence on the principle of an open competitive examination enabled proven brain to take precedence over the claims of inherited breeding or of personality and poise. Rule-proving exceptions apart, the ICS was as conspicuously public school-based in its intake as were the SPS and the CAS. The social milieu of the ICS was well summed up in the important retrospect of one of its few members who retired early and joined the local business community in 1934, Sir Percival Griffiths:

> Most ICS people would have been the sons of moderately well-to-do people and would have come from the greater public schools. That gradually changed … and by the time that I went in possibly two-thirds came from the big public schools and the others came, as I myself came, from an ordinary grammar school and then gone on to university with scholarships. The Forest Service had very much the same background as the Indian Civil Service and the Police Service would nearly always be boys who had not gone on to universities, probably the same social class as the ICS but recruited straight from school. There were from time to time what we used to call domiciled Europeans who came into some of these services. They were very, very few in number. I think we must be honest and say that there was a feeling that they were not quite out of the top drawer.[59]

In any case, the optimistic philosophy ran, three years at the university followed by a further training year, particularly at Oxford and Cambridge, could be expected to rub away most of the rough edges and induce a touch – or at least an understanding – of social polish. After all, as well as acquiring that easy self-confidence and what A. P. Thornton has called 'the habit of authority'[60] which seemed to be naturally invested in public school boys and could quickly be acquired by the grammar school entry, what was education for if it did not lead to and enable upward mobility? And what else could a 'competition wallah' mean if it did not signal a mandarin in the making? And just in case, *pour ainsi dire*, the Civil Service Commissioners were always in the position of being able to award an influential mark on 'Interview' in their final assessment, with all that that could – or could not – mean. In the end, the strong ethos of the ICS could be relied on to instil that sense of gentlemanly *esprit de corps* of which Britain's imperial civil services were so proud. In the Indian case, it was a precept expressed right from the start, when in 1864 Sir George Trevelyan laid down in *Letters from a Competition Wallah* the fundamentals that

> the real education of a civil servant consists in the responsibility that devolves on him at an early age, which brings out whatever good there is in a man; the obligation to do nothing that can reflect dishonour on the service; the varied

and attractive character of his duties; and the example and precept of his superiors, who regard him rather as a younger brother than as a subordinate official.[61]

TRAINING

The post-graduate training course at one of the nominated universities (Oxford, Cambridge or London, with the Trinity College Dublin probationers course being discontinued in 1937) lasted for an academic year. Those candidates who had sat the qualifying examination in India – a method which was available from 1922 – were required to spend two years on the training course, reduced to one in 1937. A probationer's allowance was then £300 p.a., £350 for Indians. Indian history, law and legislation, and the language of the Presidency or Province to which the probationer had been assigned, were the principal subjects. Also compulsory, as we have seen, was riding, the scene – as it were – of many a probationer's fall. In the inter-war period, optional subjects involved a classical Oriental language and either Muslim or Hindu (or the Burmese equivalent) law. Language training was widely held to have been the most useful part of the course, but probationers frequently had a poor opinion of the relevance of the way in which Indian history was taught. 'No one in Oxford', writes one commentator, 'ever could stay awake through Verney Lovett's overprepared and sonorously delivered lectures'.[62] Cambridge assessments of the ICS year as an enjoyable and carefree time were in no way untypical.[63] As with the training course conducted for the Colonial Administrative Service and Sudan Political Service probationers, many of them found it undemanding, fulfilling Lord Hailey's candid acceptance of it as 'an interval of rest and relaxation after the strenuous years spent at University'.[64] Pre-dating a practice mooted for the Colonial Service in 1946, he speculated on whether a year's training *in situ* in India might not prove far more useful. In the event, the war did generate this very scheme, when in 1941 the probationers' course was held at Dehra Dun.

It was only at the end of the year's course and its culmination in the final examination that successful probationers were formally appointed to the ICS and signed their Covenant. Then, at last, it was a case of 'next stop Bombay' (or Calcutta or Madras), though there was still – if not quite yet appreciated by the probationer – the hurdle of that unforgettable journey up-country to one's first station to face up to. For V. G. Matthews, arriving in 1931 and posted to Assam,

it was a long haul, 2277 miles by train from Bombay... The Assam railway train creeps like a snail; you have to spend two nights and two days on the route from Calcutta. [65]

For all the weeks spent on the ICS course at the university, few probationers considered their training had really begun until they set foot on Indian soil. This was something more than the sense of relief common to all the overseas administrators featured in this book, that with the teaching now behind they could at last get down to doing. Even at Oxford some things could not be taught or learned despite Jowett's pre-emptive bid to secure the lion's share in staffing the ICS by building an Indian Institute as the centre for Indian studies, an initiative enhanced, in the view of its originator and ex-Haileybury graduate, Monier Williams, by the belief this would help revive among the ICS probationers that old *esprit de corps* which had been so evident and effective at Haileybury.[66]

The ICS was alone in its technique of a Settlement Camp for its new entry, something far more sophisticated and purpose-built than the pan-imperial practice of the new arrival being posted up-country under the watchful eye and helping hand of an experienced officer – a 'training' arrangement which depended entirely on how much time and trouble the senior was willing to devote to the junior. In the annual Settlement Camp, the central feature of the probationer's induction, he was clearly the understudy. Importantly, too, for future administrative harmony, it also involved officers from other departments. Settlement Camp lasted for three months, in the cool weather of December–March.[67] Under the supervisory care of the Settlement Officer and his staff, all the ICS and Imperial Police Service officers who had joined the Service that year were brought together. This was the perfect mechanism for them to get to know one another, for, given the ever-present possibility of communal rioting in India, their future was often tied up in a close magistrate and police relationship. While the District Officer was ultimately responsible for law and order, each district had its own District Superintendent of Police. In the United Provinces in 1925 one probationer reckoned that on his first tour he had 800 policemen to work with under their DSP.[68] All this led up to the final stage in the probationer's extended period of training, in England and India. This was sitting his departmental examinations in criminal law, revenue administration and the principal language of his Province. The departmental exams were governed by provincial, not central, regulations, and the language requirement could vary, e.g. in the United Provinces it included the prevalent vernacular (Hindustani) as well as calling for a knowledge of its two scripts, Persian and Nagri.[69] Then, and only then, would the long-time probationer see himself gazetted – allowing for differing provincial titles – as Assistant Magistrate, 2nd Class.

While the system evolved of linking the language learned to the Province of assignment, there were always a few rogue cases where the probationer did not learn the truth – the sometimes bitter truth – until the government *Gazette* was brought on board the P&O liner at Bombay. Even those who ended up, as it were, in the 'right' language-led Province did not know the station to which they had been assigned until they paid the required call on the Secretariat in the disembarkation port of Bombay, Madras or Calcutta.[70] Then by train inland to the headquarters of the Province, to learn which District one was posted to and to be introduced to senior officials there. A feature of the induction of all civilians right up to 1939 was the protocol attaching to leaving one's visiting card at all the right bungalows on the station and with all the right corners turned down – Secretaries, High Court judges, and other senior officials in the capital. Most probationers spent their first year as an Assistant Magistrate in the District Headquarters, under the caring eye of a senior DO. There he could not only find his feet and learn what a District Office was all about, but also, under mild supervision, undertake some district touring and try simple cases in the *kutcherry* or court-room. Importantly he could, too, start studying for the departmental examinations held each May and November. Among the study aids would be the gospel *ICS Manual*.[71]

In the whole corpus of personal memoir and oral history about one's induction into Service life, whether ICS or CAS or SPS, one feature is so recurrent that it is remarkable how it has been largely overlooked in the discourse on the apprenticeship of the overseas administrator. This is the effect, usually inspirational, occasionally injurious, but always influential, of the senior DO, etc., under whom one first served and from whom one learned, sometimes by design and sometimes by chance, what the job was and how (or how not) to set about it. Potter is right to draw attention, in his discussion of 'the shaping' of the young Political, that here is an influence which could be just as moulding as father's occupation and educational background when it came to explaining the behaviour of imperial administrators.[72]

STRUCTURE AND NOMENCLATURE

Regulations and terms of service were common to all British civil services, home and abroad, and in the case of the ICS, CAS and SPS could often be a factor in determining undergraduates in which of the Services they would seek a career. In the Indian case, one feature was peculiar to the ICS. This was the convention whereby the probationer who successfully passed his exams not only entered the ICS but simultaneously joined a Province (or Presidency) and there, unless and until he was transferred to the Government of India Secretariat in Delhi (earlier Calcutta) or was promoted to the governorship of another Province, he would remain, on the strength of 'his' Province's ICS cadre. Perhaps because of the sheer size of British India, approximately the same land mass as all the colonial possessions put together and several times the size of the largest territories such as the Sudan, Nigeria or Tanganyika, such a permanence of provincial 'home' was unique among those entering Britain's overseas civil services. Everywhere else one might expect to move, every tour or two, from province to province, though within the same colony until possibly promoted outside to another territory. The initial Colony was one's home, often right through to retirement. In India, it was the initial Province which remained one's home ... virtually for ever, as unlike the Colonial Service there were no other territories outside India (and subsequently, Burma) to move to. Not for the ICS officer the often peripatetic path of a rising career in the Colonial Administrative Service or the roller-coaster ride of the French system of regular cross-colony *rouage*.

This decisive arrangement took place between the passing of the Civil Service Commission examination and embarking on the year's training course at one of the four (later three) designated universities. Obviously the allocation of province governed the language the probationer would be learning on the course. In the case of British applicants, the provincial posting was handled by the India Office. The Government of India looked after the posting of its Indian probationers. At their time of applying, probationers were invited to express a preference for one Presidency or Province, just as those applying for the Colonial Service were allowed to name three preferred colonies. There the comparison ends: for while there was no guarantee that the CAS applicant who had opted for Malaya would not be assigned to Africa or maybe offered West Africa instead of the East Africa he had asked for, ICS probationers could increase the chance of obtaining the Province they wanted by passing out high in the final combined examination. Equally clearly, all postings, in India as elsewhere, were in the final analysis conditioned by vacancies: if the establishment of the United Provinces or Uganda was full but there was a post to be filled in Assam or Aden, then somebody would have to go to the administrations in less demand.[73]

For the ICS, apart from the strengthening of one's case by scoring a high place in the final CSC order of merit – a practice long recognized at Sandhurst in allocating its newly passed-out subalterns to regiments not necessarily of their choosing – a family connection with a Province could be an influential factor.[74] The Punjab, with its pride in the 'Punjab Tradition' of administration, a determined amalgam of positive action and *man bap* paternalism (the Lawrence code of the first article of faith being 'the man who is most ready to use force at the beginning will use least in the end'),[75] consistently emerged as the overwhelming number one choice of British probationers.[76] Between the wars at any rate, Bengal was counted among the least sought posts,[77] and neither Burma nor Assam ranked high.[78] In his detailed analysis of the 1928 intake, Beaglehole records that 50 per cent of the 56 British applicants put the Punjab as their first choice (only six got it) and 25 per cent as their second, with the United Provinces coming next with eight as first choice and 16 as second.[79] The choice of province was considerably widened by the creation of Sind and Orissa in 1936. The separation of Burma in 1937 did not close this choice for ICS probationers, though the ICS cadre there was now renamed the Burma Civil Service (Class I). Inevitably, such a system, for all its attraction and merit, carried the danger of how to ensure that the least favoured Provinces did not end up as, or at least feel that they were, the recipient of the bottom end of the annual ICS new entry. 'I had made Burma my first choice because it sounded romantic', one of the 1934 intake recalled. 'Although I was low on the list, I got my choice: Burma was not favoured by ambitious candidates.'[80]

Unexpectedly, perhaps, once in the ICS the young civilian encountered even less uniformity in the hierarchy of this single Crown Service than in the far wider-spread Colonial Service. A Secretariat under a Chief Secretary was standard, and each Presidency or Province was, according to its size and status, headed by a Governor, Lieutenant-Governor or Chief Commissioner. In most of the Provinces, the posts in the judiciary were filled from the ICS. Madras, however, divided its judicial branch into ICS and Provincial Civil Service postholders. On the administrative side, commonly known in the ICS as the executive, the typical and generic District Officer posts of the Colonial Empire and the Sudan were as varied as the multiple titles of Heads of Colleges at the University of Oxford (but not of Cambridge); in either case, 'history' was held to be sufficient explanation. For example, in Bengal the civilian would advance from Assistant Magistrate and Deputy Collector through Magistrate and Collector to Commissioner. In another Presidency, Madras, the promotional ladder went from Assistant Collectors and Magistrates through Sub-Collectors and Joint Magistrates to Collectors and District Magistrates. In Bombay, the remaining Presidency, the hierarchy was simplified into Assistant Collector, Collector and Commissioner. Among Provinces, such as the Punjab, Central Provinces, and again in Burma and Assam, the rank advanced simply from Assistant Commissioner through Deputy Commissioner to Commissioner, but in the United Provinces the progress was from Assistant Collector through Collector to Deputy Commissioner and Commissioner. Thus, despite the inclusive term of District Officer in the ICS literature, it was an office and not a rank. The pan-Empire initials of 'D. C.' stood in India for Deputy Commissioner and not the generic District Commissioner. Similarly, the ICS's 'S. D. O.' was a mere Sub-District Officer,[81] in no way to be set beside the Colonial Office's Senior District Officer. Overall, then, the chosen vocabulary of the fundamental District Officer of West Africa (and elsewhere within the Empire, notably in Malaya and the Pacific) and District Commissioner of East Africa and the Sudan is best translated in the ICS context by the Collector or Deputy Commissioner.[82]

Another Service feature distinguishing the ICS from its sister civil services was that at a certain, and still relatively junior, stage in his career the young civilian had to make up his mind on the direction in which he wished to see it develop. At the end of five or six years he would be invited (though his own wishes could be overridden in the wider interest of the Service) to decide whether he wanted to remain in the executive branch, the basic 'Collector' work, or be transferred to the judiciary. At the top of the former lay a Commissionership, membership of the Board of Revenue, or perhaps influence and high office in the Government of India Secretariat in Delhi, even a governorship. In the latter branch the status of the High Court beckoned. For some, too, now was the moment to opt for yet a third kind of career, a transfer to the multi-faceted life of the Indian Political Service (see Chapter 3). The complex career structure of the ICS is set out in Table 4.4.

Between the wars British India had more or less settled down in its administrative structure. There were some 250 'Districts' or subordinate administrative units within its twelve Provinces (in which Burma continued to feature after its formal establishment as a Crown Colony in 1937). Sind was added in 1936 and in the same year Orissa was separated from Bihar. To staff these at the appropriate level, as well as staffing the extensive Government of India Secretariat in Delhi, the ICS cadre was some 1300 strong. The IPS in the Princely states and the non-ICS (uncovenanted) Provincial Civil Service were separate entities. The provincial distribution of the ICS posts in 1939 is given in Table 4.5.

Table 4.4 ICS career structure

Years of service			
1–2	Assistant Collector/Assistant Commissioner under training		
2–10	Sub-Divisional Officer/Sub-Collector/Joint Magistrate. Under- or Deputy Secretary in a provincial secretariat.		
	Executive Branch	*Judicial Branch*	*Other Careers*
7–10 onwards	Collector/Deputy Commissioner and District Magistrate. Secretary or Joint Secretary in a provincial headquarters. A few other senior jobs at headquarters	Judicial training followed by appointment as Additional District and Sessions Judge and District and Sessions Judge.	Indian Political Service, Indian Posts and Telegraph Service, Imperial Customs Service, Indian Audit and Accounts Service.
		Selection Posts	
25 onwards	Chief Secretary, Commissioner, Member of Board of Revenue, Secretary to Governor.	Judge of Provincial High Court.	

Source: R. Hunt and J. Harrison, *The District Officer in India, 1930–1947*, 1980, 25.

Table 4.5　Provincial distribution of ICS posts, 1939

	Secretariat			Judicial			Executive & Miscellaneous			Totals		
	European	Indian	Total	European	Indian	Total	European	Indian	Total	European	Indian	Total
Government of India	49	21	70	–	–	–	59	5	64	108	26	134
Bengal	18	2	20	21	13	34	63	74	137	102	89	191
Madras	13	6	19	12	11	23	51	58	109	76	76	152
Bombay	5	6	11	7	10	17	46	36	82	58	52	110
Sind	4	1	5	2	3	5	5	9	14	11	12	24
United Provinces	5	9	14	17	12	29	75	64	139	97	85	182
Punjab	13	2	15	11	18	29	51	39	90	75	59	134
Bihar	5	5	10	12 }	7	19	40	28	68	57	40	97
Orissa	4	2	6				6	7	13	10	9	19
Central Provinces	5	6	11	8	1	10	24	27	51	37	35	72
Assam	6	1	7	2	2	3	20	10	30	28	12	40
North-West Frontier	4	0	4	0		2	4	0	4	8	2	10
Burma	16	6	22	17	5	22	59	27	86	92	38	130
High Commission	0	4	4	–	–	–	–	–	–	0	4	4
Totals	147	71	218	109	85	194	503	384	887	759	540	1299

Source: P. Mason, *The Men Who Ruled India*, vol. 2, 1954, 364–5.

CONDITIONS OF SERVICE

Given the runaway inflation in the value of the pound sterling since the end of the ICS in 1947 and the devaluation of the rupee in the earlier inter-war period, to express ICS salaries in money terms is far from meaningful fifty and more years later. It has been calculated that in mid-Victorian times, the young civilian's starting salary was twice that of the average clergyman – likely his father. As for provincial governors, with their substantial allowances and the free use of Government House (sometimes two such establishments), their lifestyle 'put them on a par with poorer peers at home'.[83] One exception to this monetary reticence is the fact that over a century the pension of every ICS officer stood unchanged at £1000 a year, for any length of service between 25 and 35 years and, uniquely, irrespective of the rank he had reached within the service – Mason's graphic range of 'the dullest clod-hopping Collector [or] the most brilliant twice-installed Governor'.[84] Against this apparent discrimination must be set the arguable advantage that on the death of an ICS officer, the pension was paid to his widow and then passed on to his unmarried children. In Britain today there remain, among the several thousand people still drawing an Indian pension, many children in their sixties and seventies whose fathers retired fifty years and more ago. Hence the long-standing jest among British 'empire' families and 'fishing fleet' friends and daughters in the first half of this century, counselling them not to overlook the eligibility of ICS young men, worth a thousand a year dead or alive.

Those who subscribe, like Curzon in one of his many piqued moods, to the belief that the Government of India bureaucracy was picturesquely both labyrinthine and elephantine, will not be surprised to discover that nearly one hundred pages, some 10 per cent, of the ark-of-the-covenant *India Office List*, published every year, was taken up by reproducing in minute typeface 'The Civil Service Fundamental Rules', covering the usual items of pay, leave, dismissal, and suspension, compulsory retirement and general 'conditions of work', together with an abstract (no more) of the 'Civil Service Regulations relating to Pensions, etc.'

There was a consensus among British undergraduates thinking of an overseas career in a Crown civil service, among universities' Appointments Boards, and frequently among serving ICS officers (even though this might be expressed more often in retrospective memoir than in current conversation) that the ICS salaries were reasonably generous and that, up to the Royal Commission of 1924, the ICS offered considerable security of tenure. Even when the concept of a 'career' was undermined by the unambiguous implications of the 1935 Government of India Act, the salaries were still substantial. They were published each year, though not always with the 'compensatory' allowance displayed. To indicate the mid-1930s level for some of the posts referred to in this chapter, the Governor of each of the three Presidencies received 120 000 rupees a year, the Governor of the Punjab and of Burma 100 000, and of Assam and NW Frontier 66 000. The 29 Secretaries to the Government of India were on 48 000 rupees, Joint Secretaries were on 36 000 rupees, and Puisne Judges on

48 000. In the provinces, Commissioners were earning a salary of 36 000.[85] But it cannot be denied that post-World War I disenchantment in the ICS was compounded by real economic hardship. Pay, not ungenerous, was not the whole criterion. Unlike Britain's other overseas civil services, ICS officers were expected to pay their own passages, a burden enhanced by the collapse of the rupee in the 1920s. The depression of the 1930s, of course, hit all of the imperial civil services and retrenchment followed. ICS recruitment was cut back from 35 in 1929 to 24 in 1931, and to only 14 in 1932. Furthermore, when Britain went off the gold standard in the 1931 crisis, a 10 per cent reduction in salary ensued.

THE DISTRICT OFFICER

Despite the caveat entered earlier, that in strictly technical terms the pan-imperial 'District Officer' is more properly replaced in the ICS context by the 'Collector', the former term is steadfastly used by the leading historian of the ICS to describe his role and office.[86] As one might anticipate from arguably the sole – and longest administered in any depth – British overseas possession to have excited a certain pride and stimulated a positive (lasting, as 'the Raj', well into the post-imperial era) interest in the British Empire, both its military and its civil manifestations, the literature on the DO in India and his centrality in the memory of the ICS is enormous; and it is, all but four hundred years after the East India Company earned its charter to act as a British imperial surrogate, still accumulating. With personal memoir, fiction and scholarly analysis; with studies by Britons and North Americans, by Indians, and now by at least one Japanese; and with the focus on the post-imperial legacy as well as research into the nineteenth- and twentieth- century life of the ICS, it is impossible to present a complete picture within a matter of pages. In some respects, straight reference to other sources may be the most rewarding advice. For example, few if any ICS chronicles have reached – and none surpassed – the magisterial Mason (its intense readability enhanced when set beside the staid, standard Service histories by O'Malley and his all-too-soon successor Blunt) or equalized the verbatim, I-was-there self-analysis of the essays edited by Hunt and Harrison or matched the sparkling collage of Charles Allen's *Plain Tales from the Raj*. Invaluable, too, are the memoirs like Beames' *Bengal Civilian* and Kisch's *A Young Man's Country* from the nineteenth century or Griffiths' *Servant of India: Impressions of an Indian Civil Servant* and Humphrey Trevelyan's *The India We Lost* for the twentieth. Nor have lesser but no less vivid and valuable reflections like, to mention but the latest (1990s) in a long line of personal accounts, R. V. Vernède's *Collector's Bag*, J. Stewart's *Envoy of the Raj* and D. H. Crofton's *Competition Wallah* failed to find a publisher – or readers. Other manuscript memoirs, some outstanding, others more pedestrian, lie in the archives of the India Office Library and the Centre for South Asian Studies in the University of Cambridge. In terms of biography, the life of the Viceroy of India remains an irresistible magnet, whether in person (Ziegler, Dilks, Gilmour, Moon and

Rizvi) or in prosopography (Mersey, Bence-Jones and Tinker). As for historical and analytical scholarship on the ICS as an institution, much of it rooted in post-imperial deconstruction, the earlier broad sweep of Misra has been informatively supplemented by the narrower focus of Potter and Dewey (see Bibliography). From such an array, it is possible to distil some – but by no means all – of the views about what the District Officer in India was and did.

The DO was unequivocally, in the title of Kipling's less than happy ICS story, 'The Head of the District', an entity described by the Government of India, somewhat delphically, as having 'a very definite meaning in official phraseology'.[87] The official pronouncement that 'upon his energy and personal character depends ultimately the efficiency of Indian government ... [upon the] stimulus of his personal example ... the work of his subordinates largely depends' was well and widely rendered into the shorthand sense of 'the DO is the Government and the Government is the DO'. Reduced, if that were possible, to further brevity, his duties were threefold: fiscal (revenue), magisterial (law and order), and executive – everything and anything that related to the directed administration of the District. Until the DO's functions were progressively handed over to a body of professionally qualified civil and sessions judges (many of whom, as we have seen above when noting the young Civilian's need after five years or so to determine the future direction of his career in the ICS, came originally from within the DO cadre), he was also responsible for the administration of civil as well as criminal justice in his District. He was very much the hyphenated Collector-Magistrate. And more often than not, everything was very much a matter of 'his' District. That the DO's duties were 'so numerous and so various as to bewilder the outsider' is not only a valid statement for those brought up in the post-colonial age: it was also an irrefutable definition of what the DO did (or was expected to do), whether in common shorthand (Jack-of-All-Trades) or official longhand:

> His title by no means exhausts his multifarious duties. He does in his smaller local sphere all that the Home Secretary superintends in England, and a great deal more; for he is the representative of a paternal, and not a constitutional government. Police, jails, education, municipalities, roads, sanitation, dispensaries, the local taxation and the imperial revenues of his district, are to him matters of daily concern. He is expected to make himself acquainted with every phase of the social life of the Indians, and with each natural aspect of the country. He should be a lawyer, an accountant, a surveyor, and a ready writer of state papers. He ought also to possess no mean knowledge of agriculture, political economy, and engineering.
>
> (India Office List, 1920)

Here, then, is the presentation of the work of the DO, responsible, powerful, colourful, purged of suburban routine and arguably preferable to the proverbial Surbiton society. It was an image along these lines that had probably inspired the young Civilian to apply for the ICS in the first place. Yet two aspects of that life tended to differentiate the idealized image from the blunt reality. One was

social, and likely a bit of a shock: the inclination of the British abroad to reproduce their home society, furnishings and conventions of protocol, sports and
clubs, attitudes and all, meant that there was far more Surbiton in Sialkot and
Seringapatam than the probationer had ever bargained for. That it was a
context which he soon adapted to rather than stand out against is another
matter. Secondly, though there was little to challenge the romanticized but
'real' cool days (and especially moonlit nights) out on tour or in camp, this
turned out to be only part of the DO's work and life. At some time or another,
ambitiously or protestingly, he could expect to spend some years in the
Secretariat in the headquarters city of his Presidency or Province, say Madras or
Lahore, or else in the initially awesome corridors of the central Secretariat of
the Government of India in Delhi. Often the best remained there, rising to
become one of the powerful nine Secretaries to the Government of India: few
high-flyers of the stature of Hailey did – or could – 'escape deliberately'[88] from
cold season Delhi and summer Simla to get back to the rural peasantry, the
fields and irrigation schemes and settlement duties which were to the average
DO 'the real India' and where many had left their hearts.

As with all of Britain's overseas civil services, the ICS took a firm stand
against sustaining a dual administrative service, with one cadre specializing in
district administration and the other confined to the Secretariat. Far better,
they argued against those who promoted the alleged commonsense of a bifur-
cated field and headquarters administration, to maintain a continual circulation
of mutually beneficial and supportive experience between field and headquarters, with each DO probably doing three years in the Secretariat before returning to district administration all the better educated for what he had learned
there. But just as good schoolteachers have – and generally expect – to become
headmasters and so do less of what they like doing best by having to administer
rather than teach, and good regimental officers quickly end up in staff posts just
because they have shown themselves to be good company commanders, so were
DOs transferred away from their beloved personalized Districts to assume more
anonymous and sedentary duties in the Secretariat. With them they often took
not only for themselves their district nostalgia, quickly forgetting the suffocation
of that first hot weather and the blessed breaking of the monsoon, but also
brought for their Provincial Secretariat or the Government of India that intimate, up-to-date, and irreplaceable knowledge of the periphery without which
the centre would be directionless and ineffective. Indeed, as Secretariat work
became more complex, with economics and elections, political parties and
constitutions, adding fresh layers to the problem of public administration in
countries with underdeveloped infrastructures and communications, a certain
mental image, often among their senior officers but sometimes in their own
mind, began to take shape in all the overseas civil services, of who was the 'good
bush DO' and who the 'bright Secretariat wallah'. In the end, when administration became predominantly political in the nationalist sense, for some once
dyed-in-the-wool District Officers the allure of the action-packed Secretariat
began to dim the image and subdue the mystique of the bush life.

But, DO or Secretary, Lyallpur or Lahore, the *esprit de corps* of the ICS was unambiguously a force of life. To endorse and to encourage it (again in a way rarely known to the rest of the colonial empire) there was in each Presidency and Province the institution of the Civil Service week. Held generally in the New Year, or at least in the so-called 'cold weather', every District Officer was summoned from the Districts to spend a few days in the provincial capital and take part in a week of festivities. There might be a durbar, there were always dances and discussions, with the climax of the annual ICS dinner at Government House and the junior officer being called on to propose the toast of 'The Indian Civil Service' before His Honour addressed the assembled guests.[89] Most big stations outside the provincial capital also held some Week or other – Christmas Week, Races Week, Polo Week – which provided 'valuable opportunity for talking shop with neighbouring colleagues rarely seen as well as for partying'.[90] For the chosen few, too, the ICS *esprit de corps* might be further bolstered by an invitation to His Excellency's Christmas Camp or even the prized *entrée* to the sumptuous Viceroy's Ball.[91]

THE DISTRICT OFFICER AT WORK

There are three classic vignettes of the DO in India. One is of him presiding over the magistrate's court, overwhelmed by heat and contradictory witnesses, yet determined that British justice shall prevail over all knavish tricks. Another is of him 'galloping over sunlit fields in the invigorating air of the cold weather in northern India, with a highly supportive retinue, and among a friendly if not subservient peasantry'.[92] The third is of the DO, unarmed and sporting a solar topee, fearlessly standing between a mob of shouting, sweating, swearing rioters in front and a thin line of nervous policemen armed only with *lathis* and the odd rifle well behind him, striving by his personality to keep the communal groups from tearing one another apart and loudly (if unheard) calling on the crowd, in the name of the King-Emperor, to disperse before the police are ordered into action.

Excerpts from personal testimony furnish convincing insights into the work of the DO. From within the considerable literature they could virtually be taken at random. First, two accounts of life in the ICS of the nineteenth century.

John Beames ranks as not only one of the first entrants into the ICS (he joined the Bengal Service in 1858) but also as one of the most eloquent of its memorialists. He spent his first months in Calcutta, principally to learn Hindi and Persian before being sent up-country to what was then the North-West Provinces. It is the socio-domestic rather than the work aspect which catches the imagination:

We usually got up between five and six in the morning and sat in our sleeping jackets and pyjamas on the veranda having tea. Then we dressed in riding breeches and went for a ride until seven. We usually rode on the *maidan*, the

broad plain round which Calcutta is built, but sometimes went for long scram-
bling rides in the country ... At seven we came in and got into pyjamas again.
Many of our old Haileybury friends would drop in and our cool, shady
veranda was full of men drinking tea, smoking, reading the papers or letters,
talking, laughing and enjoying themselves. At nine the *chota haziri* party
broke up and we went to have our baths, put on clean clothes and went down
to breakfast. This was rather an elaborate meal consisting of fish, mutton
chops, cutlets or other dishes of meat, curry and rice, bread and jam and lots
of fruit – oranges, lichis, pineapples, papitas, or pummelos – according to
season. Some drank tea but most of us had iced claret and water. After this
we returned to our rooms and worked at languages until twelve. The *munshis*
appeared and read with us one hour each, daily.

About twelve we usually went out either in a buggy or a *palki*, custom having
appointed this, the hottest time of the day, for making calls. Buggies are
seldom now seen in Calcutta, the present generation preferring dog-carts. But
a buggy has a hood which a dog-cart has not, and it is therefore more suited
for going out in the middle of the day. It is a light gig on two wheels with a
hood ... We each had, besides, a saddle horse. We went out at twelve and
made a round of calls on the principal ladies in the fashionable quarter of
Calcutta – Chowringhee. We were often asked to stop to tiffin (lunch) at some
one or other of these houses. If not we returned to 3 Middleton Street for that
meal. This was also an elaborate meal of soup, hot meat, curry and rice,
cheese and dessert, with claret or beer. After this we felt (naturally) lazy and
drowsy and lay about idly dozing – a sort of siesta in fact – under the punkah.

About five o'clock we got up and dressed, for during the heat of the afternoon a good deal of clothing had been dispensed with. Then we ordered our
horses and rode on to the course. This is a road along the banks of the river;
on one side of it were the Eden Gardens ... where the band played. All the
rank and fashion of the town collected here in carriages or on horseback.
Round the Eden Gardens there was at that time a turf road for riders ...
After meeting our numerous friends and acquaintances, and having a canter
round once or twice we dismounted at the bandstand and went and talked to
the ladies in their carriages which were drawn up in rows, or fetched them
ices from a refreshment pavilion in the gardens. We got home to dinner at
half past seven and were generally in bed by nine unless, which often happened, we were invited to dine out or to a ball.[93]

G. O. Trevelyan's account is hard to beat for depicting the work of the generic
DO in Indian field administration:

He rises at daybreak and goes straight from his bed to the saddle. Then he
gallops off across fields bright with dew to visit the scene of the late dacoit
robbery; or to see with his own eyes whether the crops of the *zamindar* who is
so unpunctual with his assessment have really failed; or to watch with fond
parental care the progress of his pet embankment ... Perhaps he has a run
with the bobbery pack of the station, consisting of a superannuated foxhound,

four beagles, a greyhound, the doctor's retriever, and a Skye terrier belonging to the assistant magistrate, who unites in his own person the offices of M. F. H. , huntsman and whipper-in. They probably start a jackal, who gives them a sharp run of ten minutes and takes refuge in a patch of sugar-cane; whence he steals away in safety while the pack are occupied in mobbing fresh fox and a brace of wolf-cubs ... The full field of five sportsmen ... adjourn to the subscription swimming-bath, where they find their servants ready with clothes, razors and brushes. After a few headers ... and tea and toast ... the Collector returns to his bungalow and settles down to the hard business of the day ...

He works through the contents of one dispatch-box after another, signing orders and passing them on; dashing through drafts, to be filled up by his subordinate; writing reports, minutes, digests, letters of explanation, of remonstrance, or warning, of condemnation. Noon finds him quite ready for a *déjeuner à la fourchette*, the favourite meal in the districts, when the tea-tray is lost amid a crowd of dishes – fried fish, curried fowl, roast kid and mint-sauce, and mango fool. Then he sets off in his buggy to the courts, where he spends the afternoon in hearing and deciding questions connected with land and revenue. If the cases are few and easy to be disposed of, he may get away in time for three or four games of rackets in the new court ... By ten o'clock he is in bed, with his little ones asleep in cribs enclosed within the same mosquito-nets as their parents.[94]

Next is Alban Way's diary (1891):

'I am going out by myself on a tour of inspection. I have to inspect everything, schools, roads, hospitals, dispensaries, ferries, police-stations and most important of all, the records of fields and cultivators kept by the village accountants, commonly called *patwaris* ... I am out all by myself and on my own resources. I inspected the liquor shop and the school. These appear to be the only inspectable institutions in the place ... During the day I examined some patwaris' registers.'

Mason goes on to gloss and elaborate Way's account:

He was quite right in thinking the patwaris' papers important. They were the mainstay of the whole system. An Indian field was usually not much larger than an English allotment, half an acre being a good field, and the problem was to keep a record of every crop and every payment for every field in an allotment area covering hundreds of miles in every direction. The tenure of each fragment of land was unbelievably complicated and shared in varying proportions by a bewildering number of relations.

The business of checking the record did not change much in a hundred years. The young man with a liberal education takes his stand in the middle of the allotment area with a map. It is drawn in Indian ink on cotton cloth and falls over his hand in limp folds like a cheap pocket-handkerchief. There is perhaps a road, a well or a temple to give him a starting-point and this triangular field on the map must surely be the one where he stands ...

When he feels satisfied that the field book and the map agree, at least for a score or so of fields, the youth will perhaps go into the village. A bed will be dragged out for him to sit on; there are no chairs in all the village. It is a wooden frame, with four legs, laced across with hairy string like binder-twine. A tall thick glass of greyish tea, generously sugared, generously stirred, is brought him, and there are oranges and perhaps hard-boiled eggs, peeled already and marked with grimy finger-prints. The villagers, in their coarse white cotton, sit closely on the floor and the young man proceeds to verify the shares of everyone…

That was the kind of thing Way – and every young man in the service – had to do.[95]

Writing home in 1936 Saumarez-Smith, on his first tour in one of the 'most important and heaviest subdivisions' in Bengal, outlines a daily routine familiar to every DO in his office down the ages and across the Empire:

My daily programme is: 7–11, confidential work & interviews in my bungalow; I have a most helpful confidential clerk. 11. 30–4. 30 or 5, office work, the most important being the 'General file'. This is the management of the pre-liminary stages of criminal cases before they get to the stage of actual taking of evidence – e. g. hearing complaints, and dismissing them as false, or sending them for local enquiry, summoning the accused, etc., etc. I shall have practically no time for criminal work myself; the bulk of this is done by my Deputy Magistrates. Actually, I've just taken up an extremely important case, at the request of both parties, an alleged abduction of a Hindu girl by a Moslem; all the people concerned are *bhadra-lok* (gentry) and my successful (or otherwise) handling of the case will probably decide the opinion of the local Bar about my judicial capacity.

After office, I usually have to pay a visit to the Jail, of which I am in charge. There are only about 80 prisoners, mostly people awaiting trial or under trial; those convicted go to Faridpur. Then I frequently have a school committee-meeting or some other meeting. I am president of all the high schools in the subdivision, and this will be an important side of my work. I probably do a little more correspondence before dinner at 8. 30. After dinner, I am going to keep free as far as possible, but early to rise means early to bed too.[96]

That was the pattern for half the month: the other half he was expected to spend out on tour in the 'district' (the opposite to headquarters, whether they were the Secretariat in the provincial capital, the District HQ city, or the sub-divisional town). Throughout the empire, touring, in all its variants, was not only the ultimate fulfilment of the romantic in the young imperial administrator, it was also the intimate realization of that personal touch so dear to British imperial administration anywhere and everywhere. It was, writes one ICS officer in his retirement fifty years on,

the best part of one's life in one's early days. Very few failed to enjoy it because you were completely independent. You camped outside a particular village for four or five days, dealing with all its problems and disputes, and then moved on to the next village perhaps ten or fifteen miles away.[97]

In India, the grandeur of the scale of touring added the final touch.[98]

Of the multiple and varied components in the work of the DO – the field administrator, that is to say, not his transformation into a Secretariat-wallah – three played a more conspicuous, even more consistent, role in the ICS than they did in the life of the DO in the other overseas civil services. These were 'settlement' work, a prominent feature of district administration in the Punjab; famine control; and communal disturbances. 'Settlement' (the word had none of the residential encampment connotation of a geographical settlement) was the term used for settling the cash value of the Government share of the produce. This was based upon a five-year period when prices in the nearest market were at their most stable; that fixing or 'settlement' might remain in force for 30 years. The resultant figure was thus among the Government's principal financial resources. The rent was not uniform but varied from village to village according to the crop records. Provision was made for postponement, and for remission should a major natural disaster strike the district. In the Punjab, where the emphasis was on Settlement work, the settlement was made with the *zamindar* or landowner rather than, as elsewhere, with individual farmers.[99]

Hermann Kisch had been in India only a year when in 1874 he was posted to Bihar on famine duty. The rains had – once again – failed. 'If I stopped the sale of Government grain', he told his parents, 'the air would be so foul with the dead that it would be impossible to move outside the house.'[100] Kisch had a further assignment on famine duty, in 1877; still under thirty, the impression the disaster made on his mind was all-pervasive: 'it is hardly possible to drive from one's thoughts for one single moment the terrible calamity that has fallen upon the country.'[101] In the middle years of the century the DO was called in to cope with more than a dozen major famines, notably in Orissa (1866), Bihar (1874), Madras (1877), in the north-west and central area in 1868 and again from 1876 to 1878. It has been estimated that, apart from the miracle decades of 1880–1905, it was rare during the first half-century of the ICS's existence to have five consecutive years free from famine.[102] Famine Commissions and Famine Codes issued from the Government of India in dizzy succession. The DO and famine relief measures were the first reaction, a stopgap. Railways were the first solution, for the movement of foodstuffs and medical supplies into the areas from those unaffected by the drought. The building of canals and barrages and irrigation works was the next. The scale of these in the Punjab and Sind did more than reduce the risk; they added to the reputation of the civil administration, as deserts blossomed and DOs were appointed to the new post of colonization officers. The creation of the prosperous district of Lyallpur was, it has been suggested, the monument the British could well choose by which their years in India might be most gratefully remembered.[103] If so, a *per contra* administrative entry must be the government's lamentable failure to handle the appalling Bengal famine of 1942–3, when women and children were dying in the streets of the modern, one-time capital, city of Calcutta.

Responsibility for law and order was a primary duty of the DO in every imperial territory and few DOs completed their career without having had some experience of a 'disturbance' to handle, all the way from the armed insurgencies in Malaya, Kenya and Cyprus in the 1950s and Aden in the 1960s to numerous one-off demonstrations, both rural and urban, where perhaps nothing more than a minimal police presence or just 'showing the flag' might be involved. In the life of the ICS DO, however, the riot – nearly always a communal riot – was more frequent, often more destructive and generally on a bigger scale. The violence in, say, Calcutta in 1946 and in the Punjab at the beginning of 1947 were affairs too massive to be included here.[104] Outside a limited number of easily identified 'events' in the Sudan Political and Colonial Administrative Service history (for instance, Khartoum 1924, Kano 1953, N. Rhodesia and Nyasaland in 1959), the military were rarely called on in support of the civil power and martial law declared. In India, on the other hand, few DOs escaped their baptism of fire. The standard chronicle of the ICS goes so far as to devote 40 per cent of the chapter 'District Officer, New Style', treating of the inter-war period, to the topic 'Riot'.[105] Its conclusion is that 'the DO in most of India and through all this time had to consider almost every day one abiding danger – feelings between Hindus and Muslims were getting worse; almost anything might serve to touch off angry feeling into riot, loot and murder.' There is, Mason notes, nothing unusual in the detailed description by R. V. Vernède of the 'typical' riot which took place in Benares in 1939: 'two hundred men at least could tell it'. Too long to quote here, the lessons he drew for younger DOs deserve to be noted:

> As a matter of technique, I think the three most difficult things are: timing the precautionary arrests, which you make beforehand as a preventative; being in the right place at the crucial time; and knowing which communal leader to trust and which to arrest.

Another riot, that at Cawnpore in 1913, triggered by the municipal Board's decision to demolish the projecting corner of a mosque in the interests of street alignment, is described by C. Skrine, whose senior officer, H. G. S. Taylor, acted 'in a way which has brought a lot of native opinion round to his side by ordering that no indiscriminate arresting was to be done and that the dead and wounded be immediately cared for'.[106] The mob was estimated at 30 000; the police contingent consisted of 14 mounted men and 50 on foot, their rifles loaded only with buckshot. The casualties were 16 killed and 50 badly wounded among the demonstrators, and two killed and 30 wounded among the police, including the DSP, R. S. Dodd. No troops were called in, but 'there is no doubt that it was a very near thing', concluded Skrine. From the Punjab, Colin Garbett's account of the Multan riot shortly before the Great War, although again too long to quote, is characteristically underwritten and may serve for them all.[107]

If the authority, influence and prestige of the DO have been emphasized, it needs to be noted that he was not only the head of the District but equally the leader of the District team. His relations with the local heads of the departmental services were critical to his success or failure as DO. While these professional officers were directly responsible to their own provincial chiefs, such as the Inspector-General of Prisons, the Chief Conservator of Forests, the Surgeon-General, etc., they were also expected to keep in close and regular touch with the DO. It was perhaps with the District Superintendent of Police that he was in nearest and most frequent contact, not only because the ICS and the IP were the two All-India Services to whom the provincialization introduced under the 1919 Government of India Act did not apply, but because the DO's primary responsibility for law and order was shared in its implementation by the DSP. 'It is not possible', one ICS officer summed it up, 'to think of the ICS District Officer without thinking of the IP District Superintendent of Police: in the District Team the ICS man was only *primus inter pares*.'[108] Any reading of what was involved in the common-or-garden Indian riot considered above makes this instantly clear.

At the very heart of the District team concept lay the realization that, for all the necessary groundwork of law and order, revenue and justice, administration had to be something less static than the conventional 'Steel Frame' metaphor of British rule in India. Much has been written in the post-imperial age about 'development', with even latter-day ICS officers asking whether the DO, with all his touring, inspecting, verifying and encouraging, his court cases over and his office work done, would have much time, energy or inclination left for the intense demands of development work.[109] It is thus of interest that a recent study of the ICS should not only have selected for its focus the contrasting contribution of two DOs zealously committed to – however contrastingly – rural uplift, M. Darling and F. L. Brayne, but also chosen for its personification of the dual ideology which inspired the ICS the title of 'The Mind of the Indian Civil Service'.[110]

Ultimately it was, as with the DO across the Empire from Karachi and Kuala Lumpur to Kampala and Kumasi, the life away from home and cantonment that really lived up to the romanticized expectations of the putative DO, namely touring and trek and life in camp and bush. This was the underlying influential element in the imagined composition of a career in the ICS or, as we shall see in Chapters 5 and 6, in the CAS and the SPS. It was, too, as that career ended and retirement recollections grew fewer but firmer, the imagery that flourished as other incidents faded or were forgotten. In a letter written home in 1877, H. M. Kisch described, in a matter-of-fact tone, the 'simple' joy of living an *al fresco* life while on duty. 'Camp life', he concluded,'is quite as comfortable as living in the house... I take all my horses and stable servants with me, besides a cook, *massalchi* (scullion), *kitmurgar* (butler) and water-carrier'.[111]

Sixty years on, and despite the excitement of social and infrastructural development and the agitation of nationalism and constitutional advance, 'in the greater part of India', writes Philip Mason, 'the life of the peasant and of the

District Officer went quietly on'.[112] There is romanticism besides continuity in the prose of reminiscence; colour and glamour, too; and more than a hint of magic in the memory of what generations of ICS officers would often talk of and think of as the essential India: 'a scene', Mason concludes in a stunning purple passage, 'unchanged since Akbar's day'.

INDIANIZATION AND THE TRANSFER OF POWER

In one influential way, the demission of power in India was less of an about-turn in civil service policy than it was in the rest of the Empire. This is in the context of the staffing of Britain's overseas Administrative Services, the focus of this book. In sharp contrast to conditions obtaining in the colonial territories, Indians had been admitted into the ICS for 80 years before independence; within a decade, too, of the Service's inauguration. By 1947, Indians were in the majority in the staffing of the ICS. Indians and Britons had long worked side by side as DOs and in hierarchical situations, regardless of race and dependent on objective seniority of rank alone. To their loss, nothing even remotely comparable existed in Britain's other civil services abroad. It was a contested breakthrough when the first two Africans were appointed Assistant District Officer in their own country (Gold Coast) in 1942, fifteen years before independence, and it was not until three years before independence that the first British DC handed over a Division to a Sudanese administrator. When, as we shall see in Chapter 8, localization of the administration did come about in the colonial empire, it was precipitate, patchy and plugging. The ICS was saved the CAS's trauma of having to 'kidnap', scrape around for and crash-train competent successors, and spared the tragedy of the Sudan where, uniquely in the history of imperial administration, the British DC was publicly relieved of his office *before* independence (Chapter 6).

Yet despite its deliberate recruitment policy which contained, from the 1920s onwards, positive evidence of what a later age might label equal opportunities (in this case of race, not gender), the ICS was subject to a number of preliminary tremors even if it did succeed in insulating itself against the final impact of independence. Its members endured successive crises of career which were arguably more damaging to morale than the single thunderbolt of post-haste localization that was the lot of its sister Services, up to then more comfortably removed from the hurly-burly of vociferous nationalism.

Over the second half, and above all during the final third, of its life, the ICS's image as Britain's leading overseas civil service received a series of shocks and setbacks at the level of career choice in answer to the final-year undergraduate question 'Do I want a civil service appointment abroad?' The constitutional concessions implemented by first the Morley-Minto and then the Montagu-Chelmsford reforms and the consequential Government of India Act of 1919, exacerbated by the post-war reduction in remuneration and the value of the rupee and the decline in the perquisites and terms of service, all made their mark on the future of the ICS. The successive assassinations of officials, including the actual or attempted murder of three DOs, a District Judge, a DSP and the Inspector-General of Prisons all in Bengal, and an attempt on the life of the Governor of Bengal and earlier on the Viceroy, along with the Moplah insurrection in Malabar and the repercussions to the Amritsar massacre reaching out to England, where a former governor of the Punjab, O'Dwyer, was gunned down in London, all took their toll of the traditional recruiting catchment areas of Britain. If the morale-denting Lee Commission's recommendation of 1924 on raising the number of Indian appointments to the ICS was a pessimistic precursor of the structure and limitation on the promotional opportunities which could now be expected, the Government of India Act of 1935 spelled out the message in capital letters: ICS, goodbye. What, the aspirant undergraduate asked himself and his tutors, had happened to that attractive career as a District Officer in India? Dyarchy and power-sharing called for different skills ... and likely different kinds of men for the ICS.

The sense of administrative failure which hung over the Bengal famine of 1942 and the intensity of the riots in Calcutta and Lahore in 1946–7 came at a time when the ICS was already overstretched and no longer confident of the validity of its authority or the viability of its future. As for the nightmare of partition in 1947, the Service's principal historian has dealt sensitively with the imputations cast, equally by the Congress and the Muslim League, on the ICS in the agony of its hectic final months in the Punjab cockpit. 'They saw a mighty empire divided much more swiftly and with far less attention to the interests of the parties,' Mason sums up. 'All their assumptions, all their experience, seemed to be ignored. In such circumstances,' he concludes, maybe mindful of Brigadier Dyer's defence over the horror that was Amritsar, 'a man might well hesitate before taking that robust action which might avert calamity but might also be pilloried as brutality.'[113]

Among this catalogue of checks and setbacks to ICS morale, it is the 1924 Royal (Lee) Commission report on the Indianization of the Civil Service which calls for individual attention here. It was, of course, an extension and a climax of policy, not an introduction. Racial feeling had, inevitably, been heightened by the Mutiny – mutually so, that murderous Sunday in Meerut and the treachery at Cawnpore countered by the brutality of blasting suspect sepoys strapped to a gun barrel in the presence of their comrades drawn up on the parade ground to witness ... and to wonder. Single incidents apart, echoes of the racial language of 1857 were heard again in 1883 in the furore over the Ilbert Bill, whereby Europeans could now be tried by Indians sitting as judges and magistrates in place of their previous right to transfer the case to a European-presided court.[114] The ICS, which had been declared open to all races well before the Mutiny when it was still the Company's civil service, accepted its first Indian officer in 1864. Three more, all Bengalis, joined in 1871, O'Malley's 'vintage year for Indians',[115] R. C. Dutt becoming a Commissioner and B. L. Gupta a Judge of the High Court. By the end of the decade, there were seven Indians in the ICS (1 per cent), a figure rising to 33 in 1899 and nearly 60 (now 5 per cent)

in 1909. The 1870s and 1880s had witnessed much debate and lobbying for
faster and more flexible procedures for Indianization, culminating in 1887 with
the report on the Public Service by the Aitchison Committee, which, it was
hoped, might ensure some stability in policy as well as do justice to Indian
claims for more positions. The appointment of Indians to the Governor-
General's Council and to that of the Secretary of State in 1909 breached the
ICS monopoly of top policy-making posts. Indianization came to the fore again
in 1912 with the appointment of the Islington Commission which, though it
rejected the idea of an ICS examination held simultaneously in India and
London, did propose that 25 per cent of the posts in the ICS should be held by
Indians. This proportion was raised by the Montagu-Chelmsford report to one
third in 1920, geared to reach just under a half by 1930. Just how disturbing
such a fading, or at least fractured, dream of the ICS as a career for young
Britons was to the new entry becomes clear in the recruitment figures of
1915–23, which registered a shortfall of 125 among British entrants.

But if the Montagu-Chelmsford figure was a timebomb, its timed fusing, set
for 48 per cent posts in Indian hands within 15 years, was at least graded enough
to allow many middle-rank and all senior officers in the ICS to see their way
into their pensionable age. The explosion came when the Royal Commission
on the Superior Civil Services in India (Lee) reported in 1924. Now Indian
recruitment into the ICS would be enhanced to 40 per cent and a target set of
50:50 in the composition of the ICS by 1939. 'In the days of the Islington
Commission [1912]', commented his successor, Lee, 'the question was "How
many Indians should be admitted into the Public Service?" Now it has become
"What is the minimum number of Englishmen which must be recruited?"'[116]
Records in the India Office Library show that in 1922 the ICS suffered the high
figure of 54 British officers taking premature retirement, followed by more than
20 in each of the next two years and 11 in 1926. Again, 1929–31 averaged 10, but
thereafter the number remained in single figures.[117] The appointment of the
Simon Commission in 1927 to review the working of the 1919 Government of
India Act left few members of the ICS in any doubt that Lee's minimum was
heading for zero.

Post-imperial analysts of the falling-off of the ICS after 1919, in numbers,
morale, and arguably by the 1940s effectiveness, are unambiguous in their
choice of language to describe the impact of Lee on the European members of
the Service: disenchantment, dismay, discontent, and decline, but not fall until
the ICS's undermining and its ultimate dethronement by the mid-1930s from its
recognized position as the pre-eminent choice among Britain's imperial civil
services.[118] In the job to be done, too – the nature of the work, that centrepiece
of life in the ICS – change was transparent, and not necessarily welcomed by the
DO in the field however much he might, liberally and broad-mindedly, go along
with constitutional advance in principle. It is an Indian member of the ICS (he
joined in 1922) who unerringly put his finger on the bruise. He located it in the
politician, who 'now stood forth as the mediator and had displaced the District
Officer ... The decline in the Collector's position was visible'.[119] And the men

who became or had thought about becoming DOs were everywhere congenitally sceptical, at the best suspicious and at the worst contemptuous of the political class, at home just as much as abroad. Yet the impression that by 1935 the ICS was irrevocably lost in a fog of gloom and that for the hitherto underpinning Oxbridge undergraduate, in the assessment of the Cambridge Appointments Board a decade before, 'wild horses would not drag them into the ICS',[120] is erroneous: one-third of the 60 British contributors to the India Office Library retrieval project[121] had joined the ICS between 1930 and 1940 because they had enjoyed a family link with India and because they still believed that the ICS had something to offer them.

So it was that a compôte of disenchantment with the imperial scene in post-1920 India, dismay over pay and promotion, despair at career prospects,[122] and here and there just a dash of racial prejudice, had taken the edge off what many felt, like their predecessors down the years, were the best years of their lives and the best career a young man could have: that of a DO in India.This was despite the noble and genuine belief by those British officers still in the ICS in 1947 (and no potentially revealing analysis of the number of premature voluntary retirements as opposed to those occasioned by normal wastage or termination of career has yet been published) in the motto of 'a job well done and now it's time to go'. To preside over the transfer of power and break-up of Empire might be a novel and a noble assignment, but it could hardly be presented as a career. Suicide is rarely encouraging. Indian Administration was a career no longer open to non-Indians. For them the pleasure was in the memory and the pride would be in the legacy of the DO ideal they left behind and its adoption or adaptation by their successors. The echoes remain, unforgettable and unforgotten, in a score of final paragraphs on the concluding page of ICS memoirs;[123] in Philip Mason's surprisingly subdued, domestic requiem, 'It was over. The long years of partnership and strife were ended and divorce pronounced';[124] and in the appropriately higher profile wording of the plaque in Westminster Abbey dedicated to the ICS and unveiled by the Queen in 1958, for all to see.

A final reflection. In a deeper attempt to grasp the essence, now not of India but of what life meant to the ICS official, a promising but so far untried approach might be to analyse the vocabulary – significantly, often in the vernacular – of his experience, whether in contemporaneous correspondence or in the recall of retirement, and consider the implication of its unambiguous indelibility. Even office work, with its basic similarities in Calcutta, Colombo and Croydon, carried for the DO, in service and much more in retirement, an emotive vocabulary rarely enjoyed by Home Civil servants: organization and method, files and flimsies, were colourless beside what complaints and *chaprassis*, *dafta* and *kucherry* could mean to the old ICS hand. Riot and famine, furlough and passages, godowns and *dak* bungalows, tanks and *thanas*, *zamindars* and *hartal* all brought a richer, racier dimension to the idiom of public administration and government institutions. Beyond work, sport and domestic staff added their own extra spice to the common vocabulary of off-duty leisure back home and in retirement: to the *pukka* ICS Collector Sahib, polo and *shikar* or *jheel* and *chukker* in sport, bearers and *khidmagars* in the house, the *mali* and *sais* and the *dhobi* and the *darzi* outside, all were far more than words: they were images, associations, recollections, individuals. Loudly heard in the 1930s and 1960s, less so in the 1990s, this idiom of empire could echo as a mini-vernacular of its own among the 'Koi Hais' in Cheltenham and Tunbridge Wells: a word in Urdu, an expression in Bengali, a Pushtu proverb dropped unconsciously into the conversation in the right, closed circle could at once crystallize the memories of yesterday in the ICS. In the longer-term study of the Indian imperial administrator, a lexicographical approach may open up some of what India – better, 'India' – meant to the ICS mind and memory and so complement the serial biographical one of the generic DO so tellingly exploited in Philip Mason's *The Men Who Ruled India*.

5 The Colonial Administrative Service, 1895–1966

The Colonial Service is not only the longest-lived of Britain's three pre-eminent overseas civil services under examination here, it is also by far the largest. On the other hand, while there is no room for argument over the exact dates of the life of the ICS, 1858–1947 (allowing for historians of bureaucracy to trace the pre-Crown continuities in administrative structure and system from the East India Company's Civil Service), and a largely academic question mark of no more than a matter of months hangs over the exact calendar of the Sudan Political Service, 1899–1955, both the beginning and the end of the Colonial Service are shrouded in indeterminacy.

ORIGINS

Although no precise date has yet been pinpointed for the founding of the Colonial Service, its history reaches back to at least the mid-1830s. There is in existence a set of 'Rules and Regulations for the Information and Guidance of the Principal Officers and Others in His Majesty's Colonial Possessions' dated 1837, indicating that the concept of a Service was, however indistinctly, recognized in the reign of William IV. In our chosen context of Crown employment, proconsuls were of course despatched overseas during Britain's first Empire well before the American Revolution, but this was far too early for any idea of a career or a Service. Each Governor was provided with a Commission, in the form of Letters Patent, passed under Royal Manual and Signet, as 'the source and general definition of his powers',[1] and with a supplementary set of Instructions relating to his duties and powers, principally in regard to trade. For instance, the governorship of the Bahamas dates from J. Wentworth's appointment in 1671, that of Jamaica from E. D'Oyley's arrival in 1655, and that of Bermuda to the commission granted to G. Somers in 1609. The American Colonies, too, each had a governor with his commission as the sovereign's representative. Often naval or military men, they were individuals and did not comprise anything like a Service.

Yet even to fix on a date of 'by 1837' does not lead to any swift clarification. To complicate the history further, though in no way to undermine the claim that the Colonial Service was the oldest of Britain's three overseas civil services, the single-titled Colonial Service, incontrovertibly in existence before the 1840s, primarily operated up to the 1930s as either a loose grouping of individual territorial Services (the Gold Coast Civil Service, the Nyasaland Civil Service, etc.) or else within the *sui generis* Eastern Cadetship scheme, a distinct unit recruiting separately for the Ceylon, Straits Settlements and Hong Kong Civil Services. It

was not until the unification scheme of 1930 that a single Colonial Service –
now in constitutional practice as well as in conventional theory – came into
being. Even then, as we shall see below, the now literally 'Colonial Service' was
to undergo a further sea-change to its title and structure in the 1950s.

When one turns to the other distinguishing element of the three administrative Services, that of numbers involved, the evidence in support of the Colonial
Administrative Service (CAS, established in 1932) as constituting the largest of
them all, is straightforward. On the eve of the Second World War, for instance,
in Africa alone there were some 1225 CAS officers, reaching nearly 1800 in the
whole of the Colonial Empire in 1947.[2] At the same period, the ICS cadre
totalled 1299, of whom 540 were Indian nationals. The SPS rarely if ever
exceeded 125 officers *en poste*.

Ironically, the end of the Colonial Service is no less imprecise. Though, in
literal terms, 'The Colonial Service' was abolished in 1954 and replaced, for
serving officers who transferred and for all new entrants, by Her Majesty's
Overseas Civil Service (HMOCS), there were in the 1970s ex-CS officers serving
in dependent territories in HMOCS, though their home administering office
was after 1966 the Foreign and Commonwealth Office and not the Colonial
Office. By the end of the 1980s, these HMOCS officers were overwhelmingly to
be found in Hong Kong. The handing back of Hong Kong to China in 1997
simultaneously marked the end of HMOCS and hence, after, a proven
minimum of 160 years of unbroken continuity, of the Colonial Service.

While none of these niceties and nuances in the argument over the lifespan
and history of the CAS contradicts its entitlement to seniority and size, its
spread, in contradistinction to the single-territory neatness of the ICS and the
SPS, does complicate its presentation here. At the height of empire, *c*.1939, the
CAS was responsible for the staffing of 37 colonial governments. They ranged in
character and condition from Antarctica to the Tropics and from Fiji to the
Falklands, with comparable extremes in size stretching from Nigeria and
Tanganyika, each over 350 000 square miles, to Pitcairn and Gibraltar, each
2 square miles. For convenience, these may be divided into broadly oceanic
zones, the exact number of CO territories being given for each.

Such globe-encirclement explains why, in strictly latitudinal terms, here was
an empire on which the sun never set: when it was dusk in one colony it was

Table 5.1   The geography of the colonial empire, 1939

Africa	11	Caribbean	7
South East Asia	5	Mediterranean	3
Central America	2	Pacific	2
Indian Ocean	2	Middle East	2
Far East	1	Antarctica	1
Atlantic	1		

dawn in another. Together, this multiple spread – in location, site, population, communication and territorial history – means that in its consequential administration the fundamental who and why and how of this inquiry is far harder to generalize and to synthesize than it is with the one-territory, one-Service nature of the ICS and SPS.

EVOLVING A COLONIAL ADMINISTRATIVE SERVICE

It is with the period roughly from the end of the Napoleonic Wars that the need for a corps of men with some experience of administering colonies began to be identified, in as yet a rudimentary fashion. The career of nineteenth-century governors like Sir George Grey, Sir Bartle Frere, Sir John Pope Hennessy and Sir Hercules Robinson, no longer 'one colony' men, demonstrates that from the mid-Victorian age, experience had become an integral element in the recognition of an evolving professionalism in the art of overseas government: as a norm, the caricatures of governors in *Vanity Fair* were on their way out. Nor was this growing sense of a career and a profession any longer confined to top administrators – Ceylon, the Straits Settlements and Hong Kong all developed their own civil services. In 1869 each began to recruit by open competition, combining in 1882 to offer a single Eastern Cadetship career in which officers could on appointment indicate a preference for one of the territorial Services. By 1896, a single competitive examination operated for the ICS and the Home Civil Service as well as for the Eastern Dependencies and now the Federated Malay States. It was not until 1932 that the Eastern Dependencies relinquished their cherished Cadetship scheme and accepted the Colonial Office plan for a single, empire-wide Colonial Administrative Service.

In the field, the structure of the growing CAS, in particular following the advance from evolution to expansion caused by acquisition of so many new responsibilities in Tropical Africa at the turn of the century, was similar to the provincial structure developed in the ICS and its predecessor Company Civil Service. It also echoed that practised in Ceylon and the Straits Settlements, both of which emerged from Company rule into Crown Colony, respectively in 1802 and 1867. Basically, a colonial possession – and for this purpose the legal difference between a colony, a protectorate and, after the First World War, a mandated territory is not relevant here other than in the substitution of the rank of Chief Secretary for Colonial Secretary in the two last-named forms of colonial government – was characterized by a ranked administrative hierarchy. At the top was the Governor (only occasionally and specifically Governor-General or High Commissioner), who up to the 1920s was frequently a military man or politician and sometimes a home civil servant. There was a central Secretariat under a Colonial/Chief Secretary, who from at least the turn of the century would be a career colonial civil servant. On the administrative side (as opposed to the professional or departmental), a field administration was set up, with each geographically defined unit headed by a Provincial Commissioner or

Resident supported by a number of District Commissioners or District Officers and Assistant DCs or DOs. As in the case of the ICS and the SPS (but not the Foreign Service), the Whitehall end was in the hands of a totally separate and differently recruited civil service.

Such was the Colonial Service scene by the end of the nineteenth century. If the West Indies and North American colonies had fashioned their own colonial government structures in the seventeenth and eighteenth centuries, and the Eastern Dependencies had established their own civil services in the nineteenth, it was in the new imperialism of the late nineteenth century that the opportunity for a career in a coherent and distinct, albeit still misnamed, Colonial Service became available and attractive. The bulk of the new empire to be staffed lay in Africa, West, East, Central and Southern. It was to be on that continent that, for the next seventy years or so (the last Colonial Office-staffed territory to be decolonized was Swaziland in 1968) the Colonial Administrative Service was at its largest and frequently, in the context of popular British culture, at its most prominent. Leaving the origins of the Colonial Service acceptedly but not quite satisfactorily identifiable in the indistinct mist of the 1830s, it is to Joseph Chamberlain's accession to mainstream office as Secretary of State for the Colonies in 1895 that the history of the modern Colonial Service can be firmly dated.[3]

THE MODERN COLONIAL SERVICE

One of the first tasks Chamberlain undertook was to set up a committee to establish whether there really was such an institution as a Colonial Service. True, Britain was responsible for 42 colonial governments. Many of them were self-sufficient, drawing their officials from local recruitment, especially in the former plantation colonies of the West Indies and in the small, outpost trading stations. Such territorial appointments lay in the gift of the local governor and called for no approval from London or membership of any centralized Colonial Service. Only the higher ranks in the administration, such as the Governor, Colonial Secretary and Chief Justice, were filled from outside and were appointed by the Secretary of State. Whether there truly was a Crown Service for young men to join and make a career of as they had been able to do in India for the past 40 years was something that the new Secretary of State, faced with the responsibility for administering huge tracts of additional dependencies in Tropical Africa, was unsure of.

The Selborne Commission found that, in so far as there was a recognizable Colonial Service, it consisted in 1900 of fewer than 1500 appointments.[4] These were made up of 434 higher administrative officers, of whom approximately 100 were on the books of the Eastern Cadet Service; 310 legal officers; and 447 medical officers. This left some 300 officials, designated as 'other' appointments in the Colonial Service. Among the options Selborne considered was that of continuing or 'allying' the Colonial Services either with the ICS or else with the Colonial Office, or else restructuring them, including the Eastern Cadets, into a single Colonial Service recruited through open competition. In the end Chamberlain felt these schemes entailed insuperable problems, particularly at a moment when West Africa, with its sinister reputation as the 'White Man's Grave', was calling for large numbers of new administrators who could only be volunteers.[5] The Colonial Service would continue.

RECRUITMENT

Patronage is generally held to have been progressively eliminated from recruitment to Britain's Crown civil services during the twenty years following the acceptance of the Trevelyan-Northcote reforms of 1854. In the Colonial Service, however, despite the introduction of a competitive examination for the Eastern Cadets, then making up at least one quarter of the Colonial Administrative Service, the principle of patronage steadfastly continued until 1930,[6] a fact not always realized in the context of the history of Britain and her civil services. Those officers who could be identified as Colonial Service appointments in Chamberlain's survey, and not as local appointments within the gift of the governor, such as those of governor and chief justice, were still held to be 'proper objects for the exercise of patronage by the Secretary of State', a remark quickly qualified by the Colonial Office historian Charles Jeffries with the rider that 'it need not be assumed that this patronage was normally exercised otherwise than in a public spirit'.[7] How formalized the system was in the Colonial Service – not the Colonial Office, which had been among the first Departments in Whitehall to adopt open competition in the 1850s – is evinced by the fact that right into the 1920s the Secretary of State for the Colonies carried on his staff the post of Assistant Private Secretary (Appointments). But with the increase in demand for colonial administrators in Britain's new and sizeable African acquisitions, patronage in its sense of family favouritism and personal protégés would be insufficient to find enough staff. A wider field was called for, and quickly. If not open competition, at least the universities could be sounded out and stimulated into enquiries from interested graduates. What is more, some sort of training should now be offered to this new kind of recruit into what was beginning to take shape as a real Crown civil service.

It was not until the seminal Committee on Appointments to the Colonial Service report of 1930[8] that patronage was replaced by a formal system of open recruitment, though for most of the 1920s the CO had been refining its basic system of unadulterated patronage by leaning towards more references and a less superficial interview. When the defining moment came in 1930, it was a sophistication and reform of the age-old patronage system rather than a total change. Interestingly, the key CO document in the life of an applicant remained the famous 'P/1', P now standing for 'Personnel' instead of 'Patronage'. The post of Private Secretary (Appointments) was abolished, in its stead a Personnel Division was created in the Colonial Office. A full-scale Colonial Service Appointments

Board was also set up, its members nominated by the Civil Service Commission. However, the mooted entry system of competitive examination was not adopted and the CO continued throughout its existence to put its faith in referees and interviews. Given his immense experience and acknowledged success within the CS, the official who had been Private Secretary (Appointments), R. D. Furse, was appointed to the new post of Personnel Officer in the CO, with subsequent recognition and regrading in 1931 as Director of Recruitment. He was thus responsible, in one capacity or another, for recruitment from 1910 to 1950 (apart from the years of the First World War), and is rightly acknowledged as the father of the modern Civil Service. The system which he evolved has been described by a leading member of his team as 'one of the secrets of the Empire'.[9]

Furse had not been slow to grasp the fact that with the decline in popularity that hit the ICS from 1919 onwards in both morale and prospects, the vacuum in Crown civil service careers overseas on offer to undergraduates could be filled by enhancing the image and opportunities of a career in the CAS. All the more so, he reckoned, if training could, as with the ICS, be integrated into a post-graduate year at a major university. It was to Oxford and Cambridge that Furse now turned. These universities were not only to train today's colonial administrators, they could also be instrumental in identifying and stimulating potential entrants for following years. Hence his enlistment of what he called his personal 'talent scouts', dons who could recognize the right type for colonial service and knew where to look – more often in the College sports teams than among the probable Firsts. Furse exploited, too, the formal agencies bringing the university, the undergraduates and the CO together, namely the respective Appointments Boards and their well-disposed staff. Many an open-minded second-year enquirer who went in to talk in general terms with his Appointments Board came out with his mind made up: 'If I can get in, it's the Colonial Service for me.'

The next stage was to write to the CO for an application form (P/1). No daunting document, and calling for no lists of work experience of the kind considered *de rigueur* in today's graduate c.v. or résumé, it nevertheless sought information on more matters of hinging dependence than most applicants realized at the time. Along with questions about captaincies, of school or house or in sport at school or college, and hobbies, went the critical requirement to give the names of three people to whom the applicant was well known. The fear of patronage advised against naming a relative or an MP: a frank opinion could well be expected from housemaster and headmaster, senior tutor or head of college, or (in those days) family doctor and bank manager. After 1945, the applicant's colonel or war service equivalent became an important referee. A wise candidate would apply at the end of his second or early in his third year so that initial interviews at the CO could be held in good time before the final selection was held in London during the summer. A successful candidate could then hear, maybe as early as in August, which territory he had been provisionally assigned to and which university he would be required to attend for his training course. Such timing meant that the candidate could update his record and inform the Board what class of degree he had just obtained. Right into the 1950s, the favoured method of communicating the result was by telegram from the CO, followed in due course by a letter from Mr Secretary of State confirming the offer. In the 1930s, possibly as part of Furse's strategy for keeping up with (if not getting ahead of) the ICS, he persuaded *The Times* to publish a list of the year's successful candidates, though not of course in any ICS-like order of merit.

The preliminary interview would be conducted on a one-to-one basis in a small office by one of Furse's skilled assistants, probably taking on the aspect of a relaxed, friendly, quasi-tutorial discussion but in reality allowing the interviewer to fill in any gaps in the data supplied, by applicant or by referees, and press the candidate further on areas of uncertainty. Somewhat surprisingly in today's presentation-driven interviews, candidates for the CS were not recommended to mug up on the minutiae of colonial policy and the details of imperial history. The CO Personnel Division compiled an in-house handbook for its staff on how to interview and what to look for in candidates for the CO.

It was, of course, the final Colonial Service Appointments Board (CSAB) that counted in the end, however make-or-break the preliminary interviews could be. This consisted of what to the candidate must have looked quite a formidable assembly, some six to ten distinguished-looking gentlemen (rarely any ladies then) seated in a row at (not round) a table. It would have been even more daunting had he been in a position to recognize the several colonial governors, retired or serving, and captains of industry among them. Certainly after 1945, the CO made a point of bringing in a younger serving officer, a DO who happened to be on leave or one who was currently on secondment to the CO, to elicit a more contemporary view on whether this was the kind of person he would welcome as a colleague or junior. Furse, with his celebrated gift of being able to turn his deafness on or off according to the situation, regularly sat in and often liked to throw in a parting question just when the candidate was thankfully making his way out.

The CO never announced how many CAS vacancies it wished to fill. Each colonial government would 'indent' for the number of cadets it required in the coming year, based on setting the number of retirements against the number of junior posts approved in the territory's annual Estimates or budget. In the Gold Coast it was said that Sir Gordon Guggisberg, an enthusiastic cricketer, once signed his indent for five cadets with the condition that one of them must be a slow left-hand bowler.[10] Successful candidates were probationers and were not admitted into the CAS until they had passed the examination at the end of the course. The date of their appointment, and subsequent date of seniority in the long grade, was the day they sailed from England for their colony.

One recruitment technique was more pronounced in the case of the CAS than of the ICS or SPS. This was the targeting of potential applicants through the medium of what can best be described as recruitment or promotional literature. By this is meant not so much the standard printed regulations dotting the i's and crossing the t's of conditions of service but a deliberate effort to try and tell prospective candidates just what the life and work of the District Officer was all about. In the inter-war years the CS, of course, had its authoritative, profoundly historical, and often uninspiringly dull texts, in the same way as the ICS eventually did: Anton Bertram's legalistic *The Colonial Service* (1930) and Charles Jeffries' worthy *The Colonial Empire and its Civil Service* (1938) set beside L. S. S. O'Malley's *The Indian Civil Service* (1931) and E. Blunt's *The ICS* (1937). One glance at the chapter headings told all – or nothing. In the case of the Sudan, MacMichael's comparably entitled *The Sudan Political Service* (1930) turned out to be nothing more than a school- or college-like register of biographical details of its members, invaluable 60 years on but meaningless to the would-be recruit still at university. One notices that all of these were written in the Service-competitive 1930s. Each Service did make some contribution to the 'My Life in XYZ' literature. Yet arguably the most arresting and influential of recruitment texts, namely memoirs from ordinary DOs rather than eminent proconsuls, were few and far between in the inter-war period. It took the demise of each Service and the stimulus of the last look-back, with a touch of unrepeatable nostalgia, to generate the flourish of imperial service memoirs which has characterized the final quarter of this century.

But it was the CS which carried this recruitment medium to the extreme, as an outgrowth of Furse's determination to put the new-look Colonial Service of the inter-war years at the top of the career choices for young Britons wanting to serve the Crown overseas. The publication of Kenneth Bradley's *Diary of a District Officer* in 1943, with a paperback edition quickly following, though *prima facie* a work of fiction, was in fact a genuine and effective piece of propaganda. In the immediate post-war boom of CS recruiting, there was no need to conceal the message of 'here is the life for you' under the cover of creative literature. Bradley followed this up with *The Colonial Service as a Career* (1950), aimed at 'young people who are thinking of making their careers in the Colonial Service' and bearing the CO's imprimatur. At the same time the CO's own post-war recruitment literature was substantial and impressive. It supplemented *Colonial Service* (1945) with its Colonial Service Recruitment I, *Appointments in HM Colonial Service* (1953) and the pamphlet *HM Overseas Civil Service: the Administrative Branch* (1955). Again, numerous articles in *Corona*, the journal of the Colonial Service (1949–62), on the life of the DO helped to offer the widest, clearest and most attractive career description there had ever been of what a DO's job was all about. Nor were colonial governments themselves slow off the mark, with Kenya, Tanganyika and Northern Rhodesia each producing revised editions of their *Life and Duties of an Administrative Officer* as late as the mid-1950s.

TRAINING

Formal CS training in Britain prior to arrival in a territory is best considered in the three main stages of the development of the modern Colonial Service. Pre-posting training did not feature in the CAS vocabulary before Chamberlain's review committee of 1900. Between 1908 and 1925 post-selection training, when it was required, was centred on the Imperial Institute in South Kensington, London;[11] many new officers went straight from service in the Boer War or brief, post-university work into the Colonial Service. The Imperial Institute course lasted for eight weeks and consisted of instruction in law, tropical hygiene, surveying, accounting and tropical products. Forty years later, the first three still featured in the curriculum of the CS course at Cambridge. Furse was of the opinion that the Imperial Institute course was 'not a very satisfactory piece of cramming and discipline was slack'.[12] Furthermore, he felt that by being 'tucked away in a corner' it lacked the high profile that the CAS needed, among recruits and their teachers alike. He had put forward a proposal in 1922, originally drafted in 1919, to transfer the training course to Oxford and Cambridge but the post-war slump brought about a reduction in recruitment, and it was not until 1926 that he was able to persuade the CO and the two universities to take on the Tropical African Service training course. Faithful to his aim to raise the CS career in the undergraduate mind in the same way that the SPS was so successfully doing by its informal contacts in the Colleges, Furse had more than just a better quality of teaching and training in mind: what he hoped for was 'a snowball effect'. Yet at that time, and for the next forty years, the underlying view of the Colonial Office, of influential proconsuls like Milner and Lugard, and overwhelmingly of the colonial governments impatient to reinforce their overworked staff and understaffed administrations with new blood, was that while a course in Britain could provide a useful educational background and furnish a valuable headstart in language learning, the real – and the best – training was training on the job. The sooner the cadet abandoned the classroom and cloisters and got out to bush, the better.

The 1926 Tropical African Service (TAS, from 1933 CAS or Colonial Administrative Service, reflecting its opening to the Eastern Cadets too) course at Oxford and Cambridge was fundamental to the revised thinking on the CS introduced by the Warren Fisher Committee report of 1930. At first, it lasted for two terms, which in Oxbridge language meant only four months – 20 per cent less than two terms spent at a Scottish or provincial English university. This structure was designed so that a probationer could embark on his training in either October or January. This proved cumbersome for the university, so the CO abandoned its biannual entry and the training period now coincided with the full academic year. In keeping with the CO and CS endorsement of the Aristotelian precept that the best way to learn to play a flute was to play a flute, recast in the ICS philosophy of being given a job and then left to get on with it, the training at the university was moved away from the practical subjects taught at the Imperial Institute and premised on providing a theoretical introduction to colonial government. An African language, anthropology, law, agriculture and forestry, and 'British Rule in Africa' now dominated the syllabus, under the enthusiastic aegis of the imperial historians Professor Sir Reginald Coupland at Oxford and Professor Eric Walker at Cambridge. The services of the Imperial Institute were retained for the teaching of tropical medicine and accounting during the otherwise long Oxbridge vacation (six weeks at Christmas and Easter). The last set of pre-war CAS probationers attended their training course in 1940/41. It is interesting to speculate on the might-have-beens of history by recalling the proposal made in 1926 by Philip Kerr (later Lord Lothian), Secretary to the Rhodes Trust, that the proposed Rhodes House might appropriately become a centre for the training of Britain's overseas civil services or at least assume responsibility for the ICS and TAS courses already provided by Oxford University.

The third and final reconstruction of training for the CAS was introduced in 1946, as part of the post-war reorganization of the Colonial Service.[13] Since 1934 the constituent colleges of the University of London were beginning to think that, with their second-to-none resources in exotic languages and an unequalled record in colonial education, along with the formidable fame of their departments of anthropology, whose professors like B. Malinowski, Lucy Mair, Margaret Mead and Daryl Forde had all been consulted on indirect rule and colonial policy, they were in a strong position to challenge the Oxbridge monopoly of colonial studies and CAS training. Inter-university wrangling and proposals to concentrate government and law at Oxford, history and agriculture at Cambridge, and then 'leave' languages to London, appealed to few and scared the CO into wondering whether it might not be best to sever the university link and establish some kind of Colonial Service Staff College along the lines of France's prestigious Ecole Coloniale. Accordingly the CO set up the Devonshire Committee, charged with making recommendations for the post-war training of the Colonial Service. Under the Chairmanship of the Duke of Devonshire, Parliamentary Under-Secretary of State at the Colonial Office, it included four members each from Oxford, Cambridge and London, and four CO representatives.[14]

Its influential report opened with the memorable initial sentence from Furse's own 1943 memorandum to the Committee: 'When the [anti-aircraft] balloons come down for good, the curtain will go up on a colonial stage for a new act.'[15] The Furse proposals were radical. He envisaged three stages of training for colonial administrators. The first would be a foundation course similar in content and focus to the pre-war Oxbridge CS courses. On graduating from this, the cadets would undergo an apprentice year, learning their job under supervision in their colony. The third and final year would be to return to the university and attend an advanced course in colonial administration, enlightened and fortified by their year or *stage* of practical experience in the field. But CS training was not something for probationers alone. Furse envisaged the provision of another kind of course, aimed at a selected number of officers of middle seniority, say in the 7–10 years bracket, who had been identified by their governments as high-flyers. They would be awarded what amounted to a sabbatical year, to be spent back at the university on research in colonial studies and in writing it up. By now other universities had brought their imperial expertise and opportunities to the notice of the Committee, such as Liverpool in tropical medicine and perhaps, it was felt in the CO, a redbrick university might become involved to relieve the Oxbridge association with elitism and class bias.[16]

The Devonshire Committee sat throughout 1944 and 1945 before it issued its major report on post-war training for the Colonial Service. The First Course, now to be called Devonshire 'A' Course and scheduled to start in October 1947 (the post-war pressurized universities could not manage the hoped-for start of October 1946),[17] would be held for two terms at Oxford and at Cambridge. All the probationers would then move to London in the third term for language training. With the ever further expansion of CAS recruitment from 1948, this two-part setting was abandoned in favour of a full year's course, including language training, at Oxford, Cambridge and London. There was now to be a Devonshire 'B' course, Furse's sabbatical year, also offered at all three universities. Before this was developed into its planned year for high-flyers, it proved a valuable conduit for those who, having had their university education interrupted (or perhaps cancelled) by war service, had joined the CAS in 1945 or 1946 and been sent straight out to the colonies without the opportunity to attend the Devonshire 'A' course. The casualty in all this was the proposal for a single, coherent, three-year course, above all the sandwich one-year apprenticeship *stage*: no colonial governor, least of all one facing a staff shortage of postponed recruitment, wartime invalidings and casualties, and additional administrative responsibilities, was willing to wait another whole year before the arrival of his desperately needed cadets.

But 'Devonshire' had taken off and the training of the post-war Colonial Service was being taken seriously by the CO and by the universities, to their mutual benefit. Over the whole Colonial Service, there were 1400 officers on training courses in 1950. This number rose to 2000 in 1952. So far beyond the Devonshire remit had the training moved, in numbers and directions, that by 1955 the 'Devonshire' courses had been restyled Courses 'A' and 'B'. They continued, in all three universities, until 1969, when Cambridge moved to a course in Development and Oxford to a training course in Diplomacy.[18] By then, their members had for some time been predominantly from independent overseas governments and British cadets were a thing of the past.

SOCIAL AND EDUCATIONAL BACKGROUND

The CAS has so far proved too large a Service and territorially too amorphous to elicit the level of research into the family and educational backgrounds of its members which has been so tellingly undertaken by scholars in respect of the ICS and the SPS. Pending the analysis of a recent data collection[19] – itself a far harder task than that involved for the ICS, whose personal records have been retained in a way totally unknown to the CAS – the following generalized profile carries a qualified validity, incomplete but yet to be statistically or seriously challenged.

In family terms, Heussler's finding of a predominantly landed gentry provenance is arguably distorted by an American's inability to apprehend and interpret the nuances of the British class system as it obtained up to 1939.[20] His data, on the other hand, are beyond reproach. Both those and the data into the CAS gathered by others support the finding that its members were very much the sons of the [upper] middle class, the meritocracy and the bourgeoisie. 'We were mostly', observed a typical member of the CAS and a future writer on the Service, who joined in 1926, 'the younger sons of the professional middle class, and had been given a Sound Old-Fashioned Liberal Education in the Humanities or preparatory and public schools, ending with an arts degree from one of the older universities.'[21]

Most of the colonial possessions, in particular the African territories which together employed perhaps 75 per cent of the CAS, came into existence some fifty years after the ICS had been formed. This meant that that marked element of family continuity in Crown Service, be it Military or Civilian, which characterized the British presence (the 'Raj') in India, was either absent or came a generation or two later in the CAS. By the 1950s there had been but a short time in the unified CAS (1932) for the son of a CS father to join. Furthermore, with the spread of the CS, sons might follow their father's career but might not do so in the same territory, in contrast to the 'single' ICS experience. Yet by 1939, and even more demonstrably in 1949 following the post-war expansion of the CAS and the concomitant search for employment with responsibilities of command by demobilized officers whose normal entry date onto the job market had been postponed by anything up to seven years, most colonies had among their administrators a scattering of men whose fathers had served with distinction in the Colonial Empire: men like R. L. Peel, H. G. Jelf and P. J. Cator in Nigeria, whose fathers had been in the Malayan Civil Service, or A. R. Creasy who followed his father to the Gold Coast, J. Waddington who followed his to Northern Rhodesia, and G. M. Baddeley, H. F. Patterson and P. I. Bourdillon who followed theirs to Nigeria. Others were sons or nephews of ICS officers. Family tradition, of imperial service overseas, was conspicuous in the make-up of the Colonial Service.

Whereas the 's/o father' records for the CAS are either destroyed or designated as 'no access', obliging the researcher to rely on little more substantial than oral history and personal knowledge, those on educational background – though not performance – have long been incorporated into the biographical details assembled in the official *Colonial Office List*'s 'Records of Service'. Broadly speaking, in Edwardian and ensuing Georgian Britain up to 1939, a *prima facie* correlation could be established between school attended and social class. Using this aspect of provenance, in the case of the CAS a pattern emerges of the alumni of the socially topmost Clarendon Schools less and less choosing a career in the CAS after 1914. In contrast, from the turn of the century and markedly after 1919, it is the rest of the Clarendon Schools and the younger public schools with nineteenth-century foundations that dominate the posts in the CAS: in Clarendon vocabulary, less Eton and Harrow, lots of Winchester, Rugby, Charterhouse and Shrewsbury, and much non-Clarendon Marlborough, Wellington, Cheltenham, Clifton and Haileybury. After the First World War, a third shift occurs, the attraction of a career in the Colonial Service to what might be termed the major-minor public schools, like Sedbergh and Radley, Eastbourne College and Monckton Coombe, Sutton Valence and Rossall. Now, too, the leading grammar schools were making their contribution to a career in the Empire, notably Manchester and Leeds Grammar Schools. The Scottish schools, like Edinburgh Academy, Fettes and Loretto had long sent their alumni out into the Empire. Table 5.2 offers a preliminary estimate of schools provenance of the CAS in its final thirty years of existence.

This is no more than a framework: too ready a connection between school and class is a progressively dangerous finding, the further the twentieth century advances beyond the end of the Edwardian era. Any assumptions of such a correlation are even less probable when the focus is on university education. A further caveat needs to be entered by the fact that the one-year training course at Oxford or Cambridge between 1926 and 1940, and again at Oxford, Cambridge or London from 1946 to 1969, could allow the CO List's biographical entry of 'Oxf. Univ.' or 'Trinity Hall, Camb.' to relate, in fact, not to a three-year degree course but to a one-year CS training course. What is more acceptable, and more important, is the positive upgrading in the intellectual quality of those accepted into the CAS following the establishment of the Oxbridge training courses from 1926. Soon it became possible for the CO, still reluctant to recruit through open competitive examination, to lay down that the expected standard for colonial administrators was at least a Second Class honours degree. In the accelerated recruitment by the CAS at the end of the Second World War, the same principle was upheld, in the argument that a candidate

Table 5.2   Leading school provenance of the CAS, *c.* 1926 – *c.* 1956

Marlborough	64	Uppingham	22
Winchester	43	Eton	21
Cheltenham	42	Malvern	21
Charterhouse	40	Sherborne	20
Rugby	40	Repton	19
Wellington	39	Westminster	18
Haileybury	36	Tonbridge	17
Shrewsbury	31	Sedbergh	15
Clifton	30	Radley	14
Fettes	25	Edinburgh Academy	13
Christ's Hospital	23	Campbell College	11
Harrow	23	Merchant Taylor's	11
St Paul's	23	George Watson's	10
Lancing	22		

Source: Calculations by Nile Gardiner, derived from data in A. H. M. Kirk-Greene, *A Biographical Dictionary of the British Colonial Service, 1939–1966*, 1991, based on the *Colonial Office Lists*. However, after 1948, officers with under ten years' service no longer appeared in the annual *List*.

Table 5.3   University affiliation of the Colonial Administrative Service *c.*1926–*c.*1966

Oxford	643	Durham	11
Cambridge	568	Wales	11
London	72	Bristol	8
Dublin(TCD)	69	Birmingham	6
Edinburgh	45		
Glasgow	29	RMC Sandhurst	55
St. Andrew's	22	RNC Dartmouth	14
Aberdeen	19	RMA Woolwich	13
Manchester	17	RNC Greenwich	4

Source: Calculations by Nile Gardiner derived from data in A. H. M. Kirk-Greene, *Biographical Dictionary of the British Colonial Service, 1939–1966*, 1991, based on the *Colonial Office Lists*. However, after 1948, officers with under ten years' service no longer appeared in the annual *List*.

would be eligible if he could show that had the war not interrupted his university education he could have expected to achieve a Second. The principle neither excluded a number of Thirds who revealed ample compensatory qualities at interview nor ruled out a number of Firsts. C. P. Snow's Senior Common Room witticism of the College Bursar's anxiety that if only his son could scrape a Third he stood a chance of getting into the Colonial Service because he was good at games,[22] may reveal a perception but does not justify its portrayal of the CAS as a Crown career of last resort. Table 5.3 sets out the university of the CAS over its last thirty years.

At the core of the post-First World War CAS, which attracted an increasing number of university graduates into its ranks, lay the question of what the CO was looking for in its potential cadet entry. Hand in hand with this key question of attributes went the complementary one of assessment: just how should the CO judge whether applicants had (or had not) the important yet imprecise desideratum of 'what it takes' – Furse's '"imponderables" of character or personality'.[23] In general terms, widely accepted as being near enough the reality without claiming susceptibility to precise statistical information – and there are enough proven exceptions to challenge any dogmatic schema – the career ranking among graduates thinking of a civil service appointment overseas lay within the primary boundaries of the ICS as the first choice of those with a superior academic record; the SPS for those with a superior athletic record, as well as the ability to achieve a good degree; and the CAS for the mix-and-match all-rounder, a bit of brain, a bit of brawn, and, first and foremost, the Fursian desiderata of 'character' and 'leadership'. Whatever those elusive attributes might mean to latter-day, psychology-driven, testability-led interviewing personnel (and the cherished public school, pre-1939 society recognition and endorsement of 'leadership' has today been arguably replaced by the concept of 'team management') and now the vibes-testing technology of 'corporate psychics' evaluation,[24] there was in the CO mind little doubt about the objective and the virtually unerring validity of what Furse called his 'hunches'.[25] Such inspired deduction was, of course, likely initially to be set within Furse's own clear class concept. 'The kind of man who usually proves most fitted', he told the conference of colonial governors in 1923, 'needs certain personal qualities and an educational background mainly to be found in the type of family which has been most severely hit by the war'.[26] It was widely believed in the CO/university circles where Furse exercised his recruiting genius that the CO would rather leave territorial posts vacant than fill them with young men who did not measure up to his quality control.

Different desiderata thus called for differing processes of selection. The formal and formidable Burlington Gardens open competition inevitably picked out those gifted with above-average intellectual capacity, and the SPS's personalized recruiting by contacts with undergraduates invariably resulted in the Service-endorsed outcome of like choosing like. The CAS placed all its eggs in the twin baskets of anything-but-perfunctory references and probing interviews, a weeding-out process culminating in the anything-but-rubber stamp Colonial Service Appointments Board. When Furse submitted his testimony to the Warren Fisher Committee and urged the superiority of his reference-cum-interview method of selection, it was the damning dismissal by the Under-Secretary of State in the CO of the inadequacies of the competitive examination that likely tipped the balance. They were fresh in his mind on his recent return from the Southeast Asian colonies. The impression he brought back was that all it achieved was to attract 'those who have specialized in classics or pure mathematics ... [leading to] the accumulation of an impossible array of miscellaneous uncoordinated information, none of it complete or profound, about a large number of subjects'.[27]

It is from those in-depth references, from housemaster and college tutor, from solicitor and doctor, from bank manager and clergyman in the 1930s and after 1945 from colonel and commander too, which – if the key P/1 form and its revealing attachments were still extant today – would furnish the building blocks with which to construct the *beau idéal* DO. Such a portrait would reflect not only the prototype of the CO mind but also what the Colonial Service meant in the imagination of Britain's schoolmasters and university teachers. Given the absence of such critical documentation, it is left to a cross between chance and deduction to come up with at least some testimonial evidence to assemble a passable identikit of the kind of young man the CO wanted, or at least the kind of candidate schools and universities thought the CO wanted and hence commended to them. Excerpts from the 'chance' discovery of isolated Submissions – the files submitted to the final Selection Board for recommended appointment – are unequivocally indicative of what referees and the recruitment staff thought the career of District Officer was all about: 'Heart definitely better than his head', 'Speaks in a clear, even voice and appears to be essentially a serious man who knows what he wants and will probably get it without turning aside on the way', 'Lacks personal charm ... would probably be an efficient but unpopular colonial official', 'Doubtful if he has the temperament for heart-breaking work in difficult climatic conditions', 'I cannot see putting himself across to a disinterested or truculent audience – a man must be ready to accept responsibility in our Service', and the all-embracing, self-revealing 'He looks the type'. Heussler, who was given privileged access to a file of submissions by a member of the CSAB in the 1950s, has commented on the frequency of allusions to appearances and mannerisms: 'A weak and selfish mouth', 'His appearance seemed to me to be a good gauge of his character', 'He has a strong face, inclined towards selfishness, and might incline to short temper with fools or uneducated primitive peoples'.[28]

What were those qualities? Apart from reading between the lines of the recruitment literature and perusing the 'Once a DO' accounts of what the work consisted of and hence what attributes and attitudes were required, the CO came out in 1930 with a frank but visionary description of what the colonial administrative cadet needed to have and to be. These were 'a liberal education, a just and flexible mind, common sense and a high character'. There was, they went on to concede, 'no calculus by which these endowments can be accurately assessed'.[29] Furse, gladly noting the Committee's endorsement of always acting in accordance with the traditions of an English gentleman, added his own ingredients to this cocktail of 'character': there could be nothing better on the applicant's c.v. than 'Head Prefect' – unless it also read 's/o F', i.e. son of a CS father. To have 'character' and the readiness to accept responsibility were precepts which he and his practised staff never forgot. Furse was the last to suggest that 'his' intuitive method was objective; yet if his capacity to spot the winners was hugely subjective, it was also for the most part successful. He and his assistants in the recruitment branch were perpetually conscious of the fact that they were selecting colonial administrators at the field level and not looking for tomorrow's stars alone: 'We are not only picking Governors', commented one of them.[30] Failures were few and far between, and disasters minimal. The in-house guidance contained in the CO's confidential *Appointments Handbook* issued to CO staff assigned to interviewing candidates for the CAS, drawn up by Furse's right-hand man and son-in-law Francis Newbolt, offers important insights into what kinds of candidate the CO had in mind for the CAS as well as making intriguing reading for those involved in scientific personnel selection fifty years later.

His physical appearance will, of course, have been noted at once; the cut of his face and the extent, if any, to which he has the indefinable quality of 'presence.' Colouring, build, movement, poise will have come under review, and even such superficialities as style of dress and hair, health of skin and fingers. But your scrutiny will be directed chiefly to eyes and mouth, for they, whether in repose or in action combined with speech and gesture, may tell you much. You will have in mind the truism that weakness of various kinds may lurk in a flabby lip or in averted eyes, just as singlemindedness and purpose are commonly reflected in a steady gaze and firm set of mouth and jaw. If need be you will search for any signs of nervous disorder, in the knowledge that an even temperament counts at least equally with a sound physique as a bulwark against the strains of a tropical or solitary existence.[31]

Reference has already been made to Furse's objective of heightening the popularity of the CAS as a career fit for the best of young Britons as that of the ICS declined after 1919[32] by offering a postgraduate year at Oxford or Cambridge. But the university link went beyond this, a bonus already in force for the ICS and SPS. His strategy was to give the universities a central role in the identification as well as the training of colonial administrators. This he did by establishing a personal network among selected dons, who would not only compile reliable references but would make a point of searching out and getting to know the 'right types' among the undergraduates.[33] He himself was a regular passenger on the GWR's Paddington–Oxford line and a frequent guest at High Table in some of the Colleges, including All Souls. Though all were prominent men, notably W. T. S. Stallybrass, Sir John Masterman, P. A. Landon and K. N. Bell at Oxford, Furse had his own mental order of the reliability of recommendations received from his recruiting sergeants. His triumph in his Oxbridge initiative was twofold: one to have secured their cooperation in setting up the TAS, later CAS, courses in 1926, and secondly to have involved the Oxford academic Margery Perham and the Registrar, Sir Douglas Veale, so closely in the plans of the Devonshire Committee for the training of the post-war Colonial Service.

Emphasis has been placed here on the selection of CAS officers in the inter-war period, when official patronage gave way to formal interviews and proba-tionary training became institutionalized. This was the central era of the modern Colonial Service. Taking it back to the inauguration of our chosen period of 'modern', that is to say the turn of the century, it is possible to outline some kind of generational characterization of the make-up of the CAS over the period 1900–55.[34] To begin with, many officers came in with the qualification of having served in the Boer War, developed a taste for the 'frontier' life of emer-gent colonial Africa, and having, as they proclaimed, 'an ability to handle natives'. In Nigeria and Kenya, their ranks were swollen by those accepted on transfer from the terminated Chartered Companies (see Chapter 3), men of considerable African experience. Within the decade this cohort was replaced, still through the patronage system, by university men, who from 1909 could undergo a short course of training at the Imperial Institute. Next was the post-war generation, of men who had seen action and been abroad, and who recog-nized that responsibility overseas could be the life for them. Unpublished records suggest that having been on military service during 1914–18 was *de rigueur* in a successful application to the Colonial Service job right through to 1924. This was the period when it was hard to read through the administrative Staff List of say, Tanganyika or Nigeria, and find an Assistant District Officer without military or naval rank.[35] In Northern Rhodesia, too, the CAS cadre was considerably enhanced in 1922–4 by officials transferring into the administra-tion from the departing British South Africa Company.

In 1926 another generation came on the scene, those who had just graduated and were willing to spend a further year at the university on a CAS training course. Some observers, particularly among those who joined in the 1920s, distinguished a further cohort among those who were recruited around the end of the slump in the mid-1930s, when Crown appointments were still few and the CO was offered and able to select the very best. The last regular intake was in 1938/9. However, there is a record of how a group of some 20–30 cadets, selected in 1939 but then sent for military training instead of being despatched to their colonies, were retrieved by a desperately staff-short CO in 1940 and, exceptionally, were entertained to tea by the Secretary of State prior to being sent on their way into the CAS.[36]

The next two recognizable generations were those selected immediately at the end of hostilities, in 1945 and 1946, often going straight from the army, in response to a positive CO recruitment programme under agencies set up in Cairo and New Delhi, into the CAS without any training; and those who, having on age grounds joined up in the early 1940s rather than in 1939, were demobilized later and either resumed their interrupted university education or else took a degree course before applying to the CAS in *c.*1947–50. A good proportion of these had served enjoyably either with colonial troops or with British regiments in parts of the Empire and, apart from those whose reactions had been along the lines of 'If that's the B—— Empire, they can keep it', had felt that a career in imperial administration was just the life for them. Finally, there was a last CAS cohort, of those who in the 1950s did national service after graduating and, often having done it in Africa or South East Asia (India was, of course, no longer an option), liked the tropical life enough to make it the wished-for context of their career. Surprisingly, CAS appointments on permanent and pensionable terms were still being offered by the CO as late as 1957 for Tanganyika and the early 1960s for the Western Pacific.[37] But for all practical purposes the idea of a 'career' as a colonial administrator had, despite the plugging measures of a corps of specialists advocated in 1956–9 (see below), faded by the time the Gold Coast attained independence in 1957. Those members of the HMOCS who 'saw out the Empire' in the Western Pacific and Hong Kong were frequently serving officers on transfer from territories now independent, supplemented by officials appointed on contract terms.

CONDITIONS OF SERVICE

Until the unification of the CAS in 1932, the terms of service – salary, passages, promotion, pension etc. – were regulated territorially and lacked ready comparability. After 1932, while local conditions continued to obtain in a number of cases (housing, allowances, length of tour and leave) and uniformity in no way predominated, there was enough common ground to enable the CO recruitment literature to speak with meaning of the CAS as a worldwide career.

There are three different types of documentation to draw on. The *Colonial Regulations*, which originated in the 1830s and were periodically revised (last reprinted 1966), laid down general principles in specific matters. Apart from regulations pertaining to Finance, Correspondence, Ceremonies, etc., a separate chapter related to 'Officers'. This was divided into sections, e.g. Appointments, Discipline, Salaries, Leave of Absence, Passages, with (cf. 1925 edition) a special section devoted to 'Leave and Passage Rules in West Africa', where an 18-month tour of duty instead of one year had been introduced. After the Second World War, Colonial Regulations were no longer reproduced in the annual *Colonial Office List*, instead they were issued individually to all serving officers.

At the same time, detailed data on the nature of appointments, including guidance on how to apply, recruitment and training, qualifications and salary scales, were set out in the new Colonial Service (Recruitment) series of *Appointments in the Colonial Service*. This second compendium of information also carried an extensive section on 'General Conditions of Service'. One difference that could – and did – affect the young man, about to leave England for perhaps the first time, in his choice of territory was the substantial variation in the length of tour and leave. In the 1950s, for example, a DO in West Africa would be on a 12–18 month tour, with seven days' leave on full salary for every completed month in the territory, whereas his colleague in Kenya would normally do a tour of 40–48 months before returning to the UK for leave earned at a ratio of four and a half days per month served. In the Western Pacific, the tour was of three to four years with a spell of paid leave in Australia or New Zealand, or of two to two and a half years without any mid-tour leave. In Hong Kong in the 1950s a normal tour was three years, with two days' leave for every 11 days of resident service, soon to be revised to a four-year tour and a 1:7 day leave ratio. Conditions relating to what was known as local leave, i.e. within the colony, were a matter of local regulation under the third administrative 'Bible', *General Orders*. This was a major source of territorial regulations in which cadets were required to pass an examination, along with law, financial regulations and a language, before they could be confirmed in their appointment.

A potentially equally determining factor in recruitment when read in conjunction with regulations governing leave was the question of salary. In the early 1950s starting salaries in the CAS ranged from £550 p.a. in East Africa rising to £1320 after 15 years on what was known as the long scale, through £750 in Nigeria rising by annual increments to £1560 after 18 years, to £870 in Malaya reaching £2044 at the end of 19 years and £1043 in North Borneo and Sarawak. A common saying within the African services was that an officer wise in financial planning would aim to spend his final years in one of the South East Asian colonies. Above the long scale, which it was not necessary to complete before promotion, were superscale posts, for Senior DOs upwards, with a few top posts below Chief Secretary placed on the staff scale. Still in 1955, the superscale posts could reach £1850 p.a. in East Africa, £3400 in West Africa, and £2912 in Malaya. In West Africa, Malaya and Hong Kong but not in East Africa, an additional expatriation (earlier called inducement) allowance was payable to overseas civil servants.

In pensions, too, though not many potential recruits paid much heed to these provisions, territorial variation predominated. In general, the 1950s' officers were entitled to retire – or be retired – on pension at the age of 45, with compulsory retirement at 55. The amount of pension, which in the case of married officers contained a Widows and Orphans Pension Scheme (WOPS) element deducted monthly from their salary, depended on the emoluments drawn over one's last three years of service. In the late 1950s pension schemes were further complemented by the introduction of 'Special List' schemes and lump-sum compensation payments for premature loss of career (see Chapter 9).

THE WORK OF THE COLONIAL ADMINISTRATOR

Shrewdly in the context of recruitment, and even more appositely in attempting to write a history of the District Officer, the CO prepared its literature with a caveat:

> Colonial administration in terms of actual work in the daily round is usually the most elusive in official literature, though hardly of less importance in considering a career than salaries and other factual terms of service ... The work of the Administrative Officer in the colonies has never lent itself easily to general description. Attempts at generalisation are confronted sooner or later with the infinite diversification which is one of the job's chief attractions ... It would be an ambitious undertaking to attempt to cover ... the whole gamut of administrative work in every colonial territory. But it is hoped that you may be able to judge whether anything appeals to you in the work and life.[38]

The following paragraphs are written with that necessary warning of the dangers of summarizing in mind.

Classically, the CAS was divided into two classes of work, on an interchangeable rather than separate staff basis. At the heart of the matter lay field administration, sometimes called provincial administration and frequently linked with subordinate native administration or chiefly rule as a form of local government. Here the nomenclature of the CAS was the common hierarchy of Provincial Commissioner (PC) or Resident, District Commissioner (DC) or [Senior] District Officer (DO), and Assistant District Commissioner or Officer (ADC, ADO). Central government work was carried out at headquarters, usually known as the Secretariat. For nearly all purposes the non-departmental branches of the Secretariat were staffed by officers seconded from the provincial administration for a limited period before returning to the field. While in the Secretariat, the field titles of rank changed to Secretary, Senior Assistant Secretary and Assistant Secretary respectively. In the last decade or so of colonial rule, when Ministries under elected Asian, African, Caribbean, etc. Ministers were established, the rank of Permanent Secretary along the lines of the Home Civil Service was created. At the same time, many a DO found himself as Private Secretary to a Minister. A modification of Secretariat work occurred when DOs from the field were posted to headquarters to serve in emerging specialist departments, for example Information and Public Relations, Cooperatives, Broadcasting. The nearer the transfer of power, the more varied the posting of the generalist administrator: Elections Officer, Community Development or Adult Literacy Officer, Census Officer, Antiquities Officer, Local Government or Native Courts Training Officer, Vice-Consul, ADC to UN Trust Territory Visiting Missions, etc., all were usually filled by DOs. In the Secretariat, too, were based all the departmental heads, like agriculture, education, forestry, medical, public works, etc., supported by and responsible for their professional officers in the territory.

Not surprisingly, proposals were intermittently put forward to split the CAS into two, a field or provincial branch and a headquarters or secretariat branch. This was resisted by colonial governors, who preferred the obvious strength of the knowledge of the locality which the DO brought with him on his posting to the Secretariat, to the evident drawback of a lack of continuity, of departmental know-how, and of professional skills notably in finance and economics. How far was the CAS right not to separate out its functions into administrators in their traditional imperial meaning and civil servants in their standard domestic sense? The latter, of course, was often the very career in Whitehall which the CAS cadet, his imagination fired more by the role of Sanders of the River than of Assistant Principal in the Ministry of Agriculture and Fisheries, had spurned for West Africa or the Western Pacific. Ironically, by the time of the 1950s and 1960s, the last years of most DOs' service were spent in the essentially Whitehall functions of elected ministerial government. Yet, it could be argued that once the Secretariats really got under way in the mid-1930s,[39] and infinitely more so once 'pure' colonial administration became 'tainted' with nationalism and partisan politics in the early 1950s, the work of the DO in the Secretariat became novel and stimulating.

As for the 'actual work in the daily round' of the DO mentioned in the official pamphlet quoted above, any acceptable attempt at such a description is at once ruled out by the spread of territories involved. In one sense, the work of colonial administrator in Hong Kong or Cyprus was as different from that in Sierra Leone or Uganda as it was from that in Aden or Malaya ... and so on, for 30 countries. In another sense, as officers transferred from say Nigeria to Malaya or Kenya to Aden quickly recognized, there was a comfortable sense of uniformity within diversity. For all the differences, the principle of a DO is a DO was instantly recognizable. Given this continuity, and accepting the premise that *mutatis mutandis* any DO in the CAS would immediately feel at home in the descriptions of the daily life of the DO presented by his brother officers in the ICS literature (Chapter 4) and that from the SPS (Chapter 6), this section will highlight three areas where the basic work of the

DO in the CAS differed substantially from that ascribed to the generic DO everywhere.

The first relates to the common underdevelopment of the governmental infrastructure in the Colonial Empire, particularly when set beside the context in which the ICS administered. This led to the common-or-garden description of the DO as a Jack of all Trades (nationalist schoolchildren could gigglingly enjoy completing the saw). What were known in the Service as 'one man stations' were commonplace in most large colonial territories into the 1930s; as late as the 1950s the DO could still find himself one of just two or maybe three government officials in the station. In the Devonshire courses after the Second World War, CAS probationers were still being taught the rudiments of field surveying and how to mix cement, just as in the 1930s attendance at a hospital operation had been a gruesome part of the curriculum.[40] No DO posted to Africa, where three-quarters of the CAS were to be found, up to at least 1950 could fail to recognize – possibly to have shared in – the definition of one of his predecessors posted to Nigeria, the largest of the CO possessions in Africa, in 1914. 'I am the [military] Censor', wrote J. Cary, ADO, 'as well as Builder, Surveyor, Road Constructor, Police Inspector, Assessor and Collector of Taxes, Magistrate, Meteorologist and Doctor.'[41] Initiative and versatility, or at least adaptability and the gift for improvization, were necessarily among the variables in the ongoing Fursian search for 'character' in the aspirant DO. In the end, as in much of his service when the DO might find himself assigned to the duty of hangman (1910s) or census superintendent (1920s) or locust control officer (1930s) or Clerk to the Legislature (1940s) or first-ever national elections supervisor (1950s) or Principal of an Institute of Public Administration (1960s), the DO was successfully to invoke his talent of adaptability to find himself a second career at home when his first abroad came to a sudden end with the transfer of power (Chapter 9).

The other two major differences in the life of the generic DO in the ICS and in the CAS, with the SPS coming in between in the first case (indirect rule) and equally out of it in the second (work opportunities in the Pacific Islands), relate not to his general responsibilities outlined above but to the specifics of the nature of his work as a DO. In the same way that we isolated 'riot duty' as a prominent though in no way exclusive feature in the life of most DOs in the ICS, so in the CAS a prominent, though not ubiquitous (e.g. never in Kenya nor of course in the Caribbean or the Mediterranean) feature of the DO's work was the emphasis laid on the policy of indirect rule and the application to his continuing and central involvement with the Native Authorities and their Native Administrations – basically, the emir or paramount chief and his local government machinery. It was here, a policy observed in more than three-quarters of the colonial empire, that the thrust of Heussler's meticulous study of *Yesterday's Rulers* comes to an abrupt halt: under the principles of Native Administration, the DO was *not* the ruler. The ruler was the chief; the DO was the adviser. The DO administered, the chief ruled. Granted the obvious nuances in when advice is not advice, there was nevertheless a clear appreciation, by DO and Native

Authority alike, of the principles and protocol of indirect rule. Lugard adopted the usage of Resident and District Officer over the standard Colonial Service ranks of Provincial Commissioner and District Commissioner in order to emphasize the advisory and less executive role of the administrative officer in the system of indirect rule.[42] Well into the 1920s, the governor of Northern Nigeria did not conceal his disapproval of the 'direct rule' type of administrator in his Service: 'As regards qualifications for promotion and passing efficiency bars,' minuted one Resident, with his superior's approval, 'I put first the question whether an officer is imbued with the spirit of indirect rule'.[43] And as late as the mid-1930s a leading official in the CO was still able officially to declare that 'It is to the furtherance of this policy [indirect rule] that a man entering the Colonial Administrative Service may be expected to be asked to dedicate himself.'[44] By then, too, under the governor-generalship of Sir John Maffey in the Sudan who had, uniquely, been brought in from the Indian Political Service, and his determined Civil Secretary, H. A. MacMichael, indirect rule and Native Administration had been adopted, albeit not without question, by the hitherto 'direct rule'-driven Sudan Political Service.[45]

A final disadvantage in leaving the ICS experience to represent the work of the DO is that it would exclude one other feature – and a highly popular recruitment attraction to a certain group of young Britons bent on a life in imperial administration – which only the CAS could offer. This was service in the Western Pacific, in Fiji or the Gilbert and Ellice Islands, where the shared ICS and SPS pleasure of the DO going out on tour or trek, on foot or bicycle, on horse or camel, or at one time by hammock, was here undertaken by ship or 'sitting in a beautiful thirty-two-foot surf-boat... "This is the life", I thought'.[46] For those many Britons who liked 'messing about in boats', in the Western Pacific a career in the CAS offered, both in post-colonial tourist terms and in daily colonial life before, a unique opportunity to realize the imagery of the conventional Pacific Paradise.

SIX MILESTONES IN THE DEVELOPMENT OF THE COLONIAL SERVICE

Apart obviously from their termination, the ICS and the SPS manifest overseas civil services with a straighter history than that experienced by the CAS. The ICS could point to, say, the Lee Commission of 1924 or the Government of India Act of 1935 as milestones, just as the SPS might wish to refer in the same way to the introduction of indirect rule from 1927 or the Southern policy of 1930. But these were milestones, moments of shift in policy, and not total turning points to the extent that the change in the whole name and identity of the Colonial Service was in 1930 and again in 1954 or the closure of the Colonial Office in 1966 was while the Service was still, and for another thirty years to come, in existence. Six defining moments in the history of the CAS are dealt with in outline below.

Dominion Selection Scheme, 1923

The first was the introduction in 1923 of the Dominion Selection Scheme.[47] What this brainchild of L. S. Amery as Secretary of State (supported in full measure by his Patronage Secretary, in due course Recruitment Director, R. D. Furse) did was to open the hitherto exclusively – and culturally very – British Colonial Service to qualified young men from the Dominions. It was applied first to Canada, then in 1928 to Australia and New Zealand, and with less public profile and formality to South Africa. There Smuts had extracted a promise of posts for South Africans in British East Africa and the Governor, Sir Edward Northey, had had it in mind to replace his legendary J. Ainsworth with a South African as Chief Native Commissioner rather than appoint his unfavourite O. Watkins (instead he got G. V. Maxwell, all the way from Fiji).[48] Progressively through the 1930s and noticeably in the 1950s, one could find a few Canadians, many Australians and New Zealanders, and a lot of South Africans as DOs in Africa, in Malaya and, above all for those from Australia, in the Western Pacific. What had started as a desperate measure to staff the expanded Colonial Empire at the end of the First World War, when Britain's own 'right age' man-power was grievously depleted, with young men from the Dominions soon became institutionalized as an integral and valued part of the CO recruiting system. Many made a full career of the CAS and achieved high office, others used the experience – and were not discouraged therefrom by the CO – to enhance a career in their own national civil or diplomatic services. Two New Zealanders recruited under the Scheme, and two Canadians appointed before its inception, became colonial governors.

Warren Fisher Report, 1930

Leo Amery was to play an influential role in the next two reorientations, too, of the Colonial Service. One was his setting up of the Warren Fisher Commission in 1929, charged with inquiring into 'the existing system of appointment in the Colonial Office and in the public service of the Dependencies not possessing responsible government'.[49] Its replacement of the century-old patronage system by a public process of application and interview under the auspices of a Civil Service Commission-approved formal Final Selection Board was only one of its recommendations to impact on appointments to the CAS. So influential and so wide-ranging was the effect of the Warren Fisher Committee that it has been called the Magna Carta of the Colonial Service.[50]

Unification of the Colonial Service, 1930

Though the next turning point, just as fundamental as the outcome of the Warren Fisher report, did not take place until 1932, it was the end product of a plan that Amery had first broached to the Colonial Conference in 1927.[51] Aware that there was, in the event, no such career entity as *the* Colonial Service, rather a series of territorial civil services loosely grouped for recruitment and executive purposes under the Colonial Office, and conscious that this separate box structure considerably militated against the idea of building up a Service which could compete with a career and promotion prospects in the ICS, the CO decided to effect what came to be called the Unification of the Colonial Service. New officers could be transferred to any colony within the Empire. They would, too, be considered for promotion across the colonial board and no longer only within their own territory. The first branch to be unified was the Colonial Administrative Service, in 1932. Symbolically, though regretted by the Eastern cadets rightly proud of their proven intellectual qualities, the competitive examination for those destined for Malaya and Hong Kong was dropped in 1932 and that for Ceylon in 1935. The Eastern Cadetships could undoubtedly justify separate treatment from the rest of the CAS (predominantly African) in a study of the CAS; but 'unified' it now was, and that particular Eastern identity was deliberately, if slowly, submerged into the wider CAS identity. This unification was followed by the eighteen other professional branches during the 1930s. Prior to 1932, only the Colonial Audit Service had operated on a unified system. That left one aspect of unification which only came about just before the end of the Colonial Service, and then but spottily. This was the opening of the CAS to women. Two women were appointed as Assistant Colonial Secretary in The Gambia towards the end of the First World War, and in the mid-fifties appointments as Assistant Secretary were opened to women in Tanganyika and Northern Nigeria. There is no record of any woman becoming a field DO.[52]

HMOCS, 1954

Compared with what was yet to come, the bumpy ride that the CAS had undergone in the inter-war period (that it was all to the Service's advantage is not at issue: change, for better or for worse, can always be convulsive) was a smooth run. In 1954, with the advance to independence now imminent in many of the colonial possessions, especially in Africa and South East Asia, and discernible in most of the rest, the Colonial Service was in one sense coming to the end of its shelf life. Yet in another, the need for professional manpower in the age of transition and into the era of independence was, if anything, greater than during the period of colonial government. The upshot was the abolition by the British Government of the Colonial Service and its simultaneous replacement by Her Majesty's Overseas Civil Service (HMOCS):[53] a bureaucratic objection in the Colonial Office meant that the name started life as 'oversea', the preferred CO adjective, rather than the CO adverb 'overseas'.[54] Those who argued that the change in name was nothing more than cosmetic (the concept of 'political correctness' was not then current) had to accept that it did involve two major changes. Serving CS officers had to apply for acceptance into HMOCS, since membership was not automatic; and HMOCS was no longer open, as the CS had been, to locally recruited officials, such as West Indians, Asians, Africans, and Kenya-born Europeans.

An Overseas Service

The ramifications of the linked legislation on Special Lists and compensation for retrenched colonial civil servants are considered in Chapter 8. However, in terms of the existence of a Colonial Service, attention must be paid here to the fifth – and final – trauma. This took place in public controversy, interdepartmental struggle in Whitehall, and debates in Westminster on how fairly members of the Colonial Service were being treated. In particular, disquiet was expressed at the regulations governing their admission into the Commonwealth Relations Office or the Diplomatic Service, and whether the British Government ought not, in the post-colonial era, to establish a British Overseas Service or a Commonwealth Service to ensure that the newly dependent territories had access to all the manpower aid they required and that the talent and experience accumulated in the outgoing Colonial Service should not be permitted to go to waste. It was, in fact, a scheme that had been put forward back in 1947 by a retired governor of Ceylon, Sir Andrew Caldecott. Writing in the context of staffing the colonies after independence, he argued that the so-called unification of 1932 had left the CAS as 'nothing more than a nominal nexus' of disparate Services. Instead, he suggested the creation of a central pool of qualified CS staff who could then be seconded to newly independent governments.[55] The idea of a Commonwealth Service came to nought.

Amalgamation with the CO?

The sixth, and last, upheaval in the structure and spread of the Colonial Service remained till the end a possibility rather than a happening. This was the *prima facie* logical amalgamation of the Colonial Service with the Colonial Office. The model seemed clear-cut enough to its advocates. From 1945 on, the Foreign Service staffed the Foreign Office at home as well as missions abroad, and members of the Diplomatic Service expected, under their terms of service, to have alternating tours at home as well as abroad – in a way similar, as we have seen, to DOs, who spent some of their time in the field with spells at the Secretariat in between. The same CAS argument for bringing local knowledge into the conduct of business at the centre rather than forming a split field/headquarters Service could be applied to the case for merging the peripheral CS with the central CO. A major stumbling block, apart from a feeling among the CAS that they had opted for an imperial career abroad (CS) and not for a colonial career in England (CO), was the question of method of entry. The CAS, doubtless endorsing many a DO's widely held argument that he chose the CS because at the end of his Finals at Oxford he was determined never to swat and sweat for another exam in his life,[56] eschewed the need to sit a competitive examination. On the other hand the CO, often drawing on the high-flyers in the CSC open examination, were not prepared to accept a reduced academic standard of entry achievement. Many had passed high, and frequently higher than those who had gone into the ICS. Others had subsequently applied to transfer from their Department into the CO. Amalgamation was a proposal examined periodically throughout the existence of the modern CS, by Selborne in 1900, by Warren Fisher in 1930, internally by Sir Thomas Lloyd within the Colonial Office in 1948, and again by the wider Whitehall of the CO, FO and CRO in the 1960s. Just as regularly it ended in nothing.

Julian Amery, son of L. S. Amery who had shown himself such a forceful remoulder of the CAS during his tenure of office as Secretary of State for the Colonies in 1924–9, observed after his own experience of both the CO and the FO at the end of the 1950s: 'Two years at the Colonial Office taught me to value the creative if sometimes unanimous dialogue between Whitehall and "the field". I was to miss it at the Foreign Office a decade later.'[57] To the end, the Colonial Service and the Colonial Office remained two distinct, separately recruited, separately staffed and separately managed, Crown Services. This was probably to the satisfaction of both. It has certainly contributed to the mystification of outside observers and the continuing incomprehensibility by foreign students of Britain's imperial bureaucracy.

THE BRITISH DISTRICT OFFICER AND THE FRENCH COMMANDANT DE CERCLE

In another context, research could usefully be undertaken into a comparative study of the British and other Colonial Services – French, Belgian, Italian, German, Portuguese, etc. Restrictions of space preclude such an inquiry here, but a brief look at the DO's often neighbouring *Commandant de Cercle* in West Africa can throw further light on the generic British DO who is at the centre of this study.

France, with Britain, constituted the largest colonial powers in the century under review. In Africa and North America, in India and the Middle East, in the Pacific and the Caribbean, the two nations had historically been in imperial competition and often in military conflict. There were more French colonial possessions in Africa than there were British ones; in West Africa the French Empire was several times the size of British West Africa; and in North Africa it was France which reigned as the sole colonial master of the Maghreb from Rabat to Tunis. If France could claim no possession on the East African mainland south of minuscule Djibouti, Britain could claim no African offshore island anything like the size of Madagascar. India may have been Britain's allegorical Jewel in the Crown but Indochina was France's Pearl of the Orient. Again, both these imperial giants suffered a monumental trauma in the Second World War. The capture of Hong Kong, and then of the would-be impregnable Singapore, by the Japanese was considered by Winston Churchill to be the greatest blow suffered by the British Empire since the loss of the American colonies in 1776. To the French, the German occupation of Paris – for the second time, at the same hands, within less than a century – compounded by the subsequent sight of a nation at war with itself, both in France and in its African empire, was a nightmare scenario on a scale impossible to have imagined in half a century of confident colonialism ... that is, until in the 1950s the equally unbelievable colonial tragedy that was Indochina and then Algeria shook the very foundation of France's imperial pride. In none of these colonial calamities was the dent to national prestige, that psychological commodity so critical to the maintenance of colonial rule everywhere, lost on the subject peoples, anglophone Malays, Chinese and Indians and francophone Africans, Arabs and Vietnamese alike.

The case for comparison, however, transcends geographical and historical grounds, situated as it is in the profound differences inspiring the basic principles of the two colonial policies. In theory, and in the tunnel-vision of a rigid London and Paris, the difference between the precept of indirect rule and the policy of cultural assimilation was as unmistakable as that between ale and wine, tea and coffee.[58] Inevitably, then, following from the argument that it is the national policy and milieu that make both the DO and his Service and not, for all the influence of the man on the spot, the other way round, the personnel and performance of France's colonial administrators were bound to be something different from – at times perceptibly antipathetic to – the British model, whether it was that followed in India or in the Sudan or in the colonial Empire. History, society, culture, philosophy and education all play their part in sharpening the contrasts. In the end, too, each empire, well on the way to *de facto* dissolution by the 1950s and to being undisguisably *de jure* ex-colonial powers by the 1990s, left behind the imperial legacy of a major, but separate, world language and the respective, but mutually exclusive, world clubs of the viable (so far) Commonwealth and the vibrant (as yet) *la Francophonie*.

The size and spread of France's overseas empire called for a commensurable colonial service: the British model of quite separate Services for the empire within an Empire that was India, for the Anglo-Egyptian Condominium, for the Colonial Empire, and for the Far Eastern dependencies up to 1932, may not have been one to appeal to the logical French mind. Yet logic does not always rule, and in the end the locus of France's imperial responsibilities was on occasion as scattered across the metropole as Britain's complementary India, Foreign, Dominions, Commonwealth and Colonial Offices. Since empires, like mushrooms, have a habit of growing willy-nilly, historical accretions played their part in the metropolitan arrangements for administering the French empire.

Up to 1914, the French too organized their overseas possessions through a multiplicity of Ministries. The protectorates of Laos and Cambodia were the prerogative of the Marine until a Ministry of Colonies was established in 1894. In North Africa, the protectorates of Tunisia (1881) and Morocco (1912) came under the Ministry of Foreign Affairs. *Sui generis* Algeria, although considered a colony when it was conquered in the 1830s, had a spell under the Ministry of War before being transferred to the Ministry of the Interior and finally, in 1848, being integrated into it like any *département* of metropolitan France. Further bifurcation characterized the administration of the overseas territories, shared between no less than five colonial services. In the Maghreb, the two protectorates were staffed by the Corps of Civil Controllers, while Algeria was administered first by a Corps of Administrators of Mixed Communes and then by *Préfets* employed by the Interior Ministry. In the Orient, the Civil Services of Indochina were established in 1887 when they took over from the navy: in William Cohen's terse phrase, 'men who made good ship's officers did not necessarily make satisfactory administrators'[59] – and in any case, they were constantly liable to be recalled to sea. In the same year, 1887, a uniform Corps of Colonial Administrators was formed. This Corps was the nearest equivalent to the British Colonial Service. Its officials were not only liable for posting across the oceans from the Pacific to the Indian (including the Goan enclave) but also to the Antilles and Guiana in the Caribbean. Predominantly, like their Colonial Service counterparts, their work lay in the new empire of Afrique Noire and in Madagascar, occupied in 1895. The first French territorial administration overseas appeared in Algeria, at the initiative of Governor Bugeaud who in the 1840s established *bureaux arabes* in every occupied region. An attempt by the Governor of the oldest West African settlement, Senegal, to establish his own corps of administrators came to nought when they turned out to be no better at administration than their military colleagues. It was the work of Governor Faidherbe, who had served under Bugeaud, in Senegal in the 1850s that was to influence the colonial administrators throughout the emerging Afrique Noire.[60] Starting with some 40 members in 1887, the Corps d'Administrateurs Coloniaux (CAC) reached 200 by 1900. It then rose steadily to 600 in 1910 and 860 on the eve of the First World War. In the 1920s the Corps passed the one thousand mark.

French West Africa (FWA, AOF) was created in 1904, formed out of eight separate territories, and the smaller (four territories) French Equatorial Africa (FEA, AEF) was set up in 1910. After the First World War, the greater part of German Togo and Kamerun were placed by the League of Nations under French mandate, as was what were to become Syria and Lebanon in the Middle East. Each Federation was in charge of a Governor-General and each of its constituent parts was headed by a Lieutenant-Governor (High Commissioner in the case of the mandated territories). In Tunisia and Morocco the administration was headed by a Resident-General, and in Madagascar by a Governor. In Indochina the post until the end of the Second World War was that of Governor-General. A common administrative structure was to divide the colony into a number of *cercles* under a *Commandant*, comparable to the generic District Officer in the British system. There were 118 *cercles* in FWA but only about 20 in FEA. Below the *cercle* came the *subdivision*, known up to 1934 as *circonscription, département* or *région* in FEA, in charge of a *chef de subdivision* or junior DO. The FWA carried some 200 *subdivisions*.[61] In the early 1920s half of the CAC, some 500 officials, were serving in FWA, with only 112 administrators in the less popular and less prestigious FEA, where as many as 250 posts remained unfilled. By the mid-1950s administrative reforms had reduced the number of *cercles* in FWA and FEA together to 182.[62] Allowing for changes in nomenclature over time and place, it may be said that the office of *Commandant* in his *cercle* corresponded to that of the DO in his Division in

West Africa but, as one of them felt, 'freer, and with more initiative and autonomy than the neighbouring British District Officer'.[63]

An integral part of the Colonial Service reforms initiated by E. Etienne
during his influential period of office as Under-Secretary of the Colonies from
1889–92 was his plan for a training programme for French colonial administrators. This was primarily aimed at those assigned to the Civil Services of
Indochina, France's most important and most prestigious overseas possession.
A proposal had been made that the short-lived *Collège des Stagiaires* in Saigon
(1874–8) should reopen in Paris as the *Ecole d'Administration annamite*.
Etienne's preference was for extending the small *Ecole Coloniale*, which had its
roots in an informal school, the *Ecole cambodgienne*. This had been founded in
1885 by A. Pavie for young Asians of noble birth brought from the Orient to
learn French, and was renamed the *Ecole Coloniale* in 1887. To its largely language curriculum Etienne added in 1889 instruction in colonial history and
administrative law. In 1892 the Indochina corpus was extended by the addition
of an African section. The *Ecole Coloniale* marked its centenary in 1985, dating
its foundation from the *Ecole Cambodgienne* and its renaming as the *Ecole
Nationale de la France Outre-Mer* (ENFOM) in 1934.[64] Recognized as one of
the seven great French bureaucratic *Ecoles*, ENFOM was the kind of College
that the British Colonial Service never had, though it had momentarily toyed
with the idea.[65]

Together, the *Ecole Coloniale* (1885–1926) and ENFOM (1923–59) graduated some 3000 administrators for service overseas. Colloquially they were
known in French student circles as *les colo*. Starting with a three-year course,
when the object was simply to acquire the *baccalauréat*, the course was reduced
in 1896 to two years, with an exacting preparatory year offered at the *Ecole* and
a diploma awarded at the end by examination in law and French colonial history
– and above all (a legacy from its origins) in the ability to write and speak in
faultless French. Students were ranked on entrance, with the best ones ear-
marked for Indochina and the bottom ones usually assigned to the African
section. It was not possible to opt for a change later in the course. The number
of places in the *Ecole* was limited, and the number of applicants high: in the
late-1930s, about one in ten applicants succeeded in gaining one of the 40
places available;[66] in 1934, after the slump, over 400 candidates applied for the
27 vacancies.[67] Following the tradition of the French civil service, and in contrast to the method used for selecting entrants into the British Colonial Service,
the *Ecole*'s oral examination was used exclusively to test knowledge and not to
assess the potentials of character and personality. Once admitted to the *Ecole
Coloniale*, which was tantamount to gaining entry to the Colonial Service since
few students failed to reach the standard required in the final exams, *les colo*
were required to supplement their professional training by taking a *licence de
droit* from the Faculty of Law in the University of Paris. Within the vigorous
public debate in France on what was the 'best' colonial policy, ENFOM soon
assumed the role of a strong advocate for *association*, with its indirect rule
echoes of the recognition of the different needs of colonial societies, in opposi-

tion to the assimilationists. This leadership in the colonial controversy was largely due to the influence of the staff of the *Ecole Coloniale* and later of ENFOM, with such distinguished names as G. Hardy and R. Delavignette among the Directors and H. Labouret and M. Delafosse among the professors. Their service in the colonies and their study of colonialism had persuaded them of the faults and fallacies inherent in a rigid policy of assimilation and gallicization.[68]

Socially, membership of the French colonial service was markedly lower middle-class and, according to a latter-day historian, himself from within the Service, peopled by Republicans (*'issus d'une petite bourgeoisie républicaine'*).[69] The aristocracy for the most part looked to the army and diplomacy,[70] while the cost of spending three years in Paris and putting oneself through the *Ecole Coloniale* was far beyond the means of most rural and working-class families. Thanks to the existence of the *Ecole Coloniale*, the French colonial service was able to disengage itself from the anti-imperialist image of a ragbag of patronage which had characterized it up to the turn of the century when 'a hairdresser, a chestnut vendor, a ditch digger, depending on his contacts (the concierge of a [colonial] administrator on leave, the bath attendant, the friend, etc.), can be appointed *commis des affaires indigènes* without anybody caring about his capacities ... or his aptitudes'.[71] To begin with, up to a sixth of the CAC were required to be drawn from the military: the army and the marine had played a notable role in creating France's African empire. The rank of *Commandant* for the generic DC of French Sub-Saharan Africa and the uniform adopted indicate the military origins of the French Colonial Service. But from 1905 the military were gradually eliminated from the CAC, and by 1907 they accounted for only 34 out of the 465 serving officials, seven of them being from the marine. While few civil servants employed in the metropolitan bureaucracies were attracted by a period of secondment overseas, a number of the new Corps came into it from working as *fonctionnaires* in the colonial secretariats-general, where two years' employment rendered them eligible for promotion into the CAC. But they did not prove up to it and the practice was soon dropped. By far the largest source up to 1914 had been from among the *agents*, often poorly educated, administrative assistants to the *Commandant*. Here, too, some were more successful than others. Up to 1914, it was still possible for men of scant education to seek a post in colonial administration, for the colonial vocation was unpopular and the health conditions were horrendous: 'if they did not die [in the colonies], the administrators' lives were nevertheless dramatically shortened' is Cohen's epitaph on the vital statistics showing that between 1887 and 1912 sixteen per cent of the 984 men appointed to the CAC died in the colonies and most required prolonged hospitalization when home on furlough.[72] Those who survived died on average 17 years earlier than their contemporaries in metropolitan civil service posts. But it was the *Ecole Coloniale* graduates who confirmed both the reputation of the Corps of Colonial Administrators and their own ranking as *la crème de la crème*. By 1912 the Ministry of Colonies was ready to rule that henceforth the CAC would be open only to those who passed out from the *Ecole Coloniale*, whether as direct entry or as *agents des affaires indigènes et civiles* selected for the Paris programme.

In France colonial service never attained the popularity and recognition it enjoyed among the products of Britain's public schools and universities. The writer André Maurois went so far as to ascribe France's lack of enthusiasm for colonial service to the absence of a national poet like Kipling to inspire the country's youth by deeds of derring-do empire. Even after 1945, when the ENFOM had carried the famous *Ecole Coloniale* to new heights of prestige, the social composition of the Service differed very little from the emphatically middle class origins which it displayed in the 1930s, when approximately a third of the CAC cadets were the sons of fathers in the higher civil service, 15 per cent from white-collar families, and under 5 per cent from the artisan and small farmer class. If the decennial cohorts showed a rise in the last-named class from 3 per cent in 1920–29 to 13 per cent in 1930–39, those coming from families in high administration dropped from 25 per cent to 24 per cent and those from the *rentier* and *propriétaire* classes remained at 12 per cent. The most noticeable decline was among the liberal professions, preponderantly doctors and engineers: in 1929 these families accounted for 30 per cent of the *Ecole Coloniale* intake, a proportion which fell to 17 per cent by 1936. Like the metropolitan bureaucracy but quite unlike the British Colonial Administrative Service, the French service was characterized by men with a degree in law, a compulsory qualification for entry to the Colonial Service.[73]

The comparison by Lyautey – the French equivalent of Britain's Lugard in the colonial service pantheon – of the commonness and coarseness of his subordinates in Indochina with the gentlemanly qualities of British colonial administrators is too early (1894) to validate any general standard, coming as it did when the *Ecole Coloniale* was not yet ten years old and did not yet enjoy the monopoly of staffing the CAC. Yet two generations on, another *grand personnage*, no less than the Director of the *Ecole Coloniale*, the eminent G. Hardy, could relate how a frequent reaction from those who learned that his students had opted for a career in the colonies was wonderingly to exclaim 'What crime must he have committed? From what corpse is he fleeing?'[74] Another Director, Robert Delavignette, (1937–46), one-time *Commandant de cercle*, ultimately High Commissioner of Cameroun, and an intellectual committed to a positive democratic discourse, argued the case for a more open recruitment, claiming that it was self-evident that 'we were not representatives of a high social class as some British colonial administrators or Dutch patricians might have been, we came from middle-income families where most members were minor civil servants'.[75]

The CAC reflected a distinctive regional provenance, outstripping even the proverbial role of the Scots in the making of the British Empire. Paris apart, a large proportion came from the areas round Bordeaux and Marseilles, from Brittany, Normandy and Gascony, and, out of all proportion, from Corsica, peoples who easily identified with the maritime tradition. By the end of the 1930s, however, it was overseas Réunion and Guadeloupe which provided the largest number of colonial administrators after Paris, Corsica and Brittany, with Martinique and Bordeaux about equal.[76] A well-travelled observer of the francophone West African scene in the 1930s was of the opinion that there was little to attract men of ability into the French colonial service,[77] while the reputation of the administration in French Equatorial Africa remained at the bottom of the list, in the eyes of both Paris and Libreville, for most of the inter-war period. There was an impression that all that the poorly paid *Commandant de cercle*, earning a salary of a mere £200 a year in 1927 (before the cuts of the slump hit the Service), was interested in was to save as much as possible and to retire to a little property in his own native town as quickly as he could.

Despite Governor-General van Vollenhoven's proposal[78] in 1917 to amalgamate the personnel of the Colonial Ministry in Paris (Rue Oudinot) with the field staff of the Corps of Colonial Administrators, no such merger took place until the wartime exigencies of 1942. In Britain it never took place at all. The Front Populaire (1936–8), which made its mark on the colonial service all the way from recruitment into the CAC to the replacement of incumbent governors-general by liberals like the new-look de Coppet, set itself the wider task of total colonial reform under the Rue Oudinot's Socialist Minister for Colonies, Marius Moutet. His commission, set up in 1937, to study the colonial problem, did not get very far before the Blum government fell. However, in the field of colonial service training the Front had time to establish the *Centre des hautes études d'administration musulmane* (CHEAM) in 1936, an institution providing additional academic orientation for administrators serving in North Africa and in the Middle East mandates.[79] After the war CHEAM's writ was extended to include administrators serving in Afrique Noire too. Between 1936 and 1959 twenty-six colonial administrators were awarded the Centre's *brevet* through examinations and the submission of a dissertation. When ENFOM succeeded the *Ecole Coloniale* in 1934, it secured its first colonial service Director when the outstanding Robert Delavignette ('*le grand Bob*') was appointed in 1937. Prestigious as it was, ENFOM never achieved the status of the *Ecole Nationale d'Administration* (ENA), founded in 1945, nor did it indicate any wish to merge with it in the decolonizing decade of the 1950s. Instead, in 1959 ENFOM was transformed into the *Institut des hautes études d'outre-mer* (IHEOM), a school to train civil servants from the former colonial territories. In 1966 this was renamed the *Institut internationale d'administration publique* (IIAP), now designed to train any foreigner anxious to pursue a career in public administration. At the end of the Second World War, when the French colonies were restyled France Outre-Mer and, more generally, in the French colonial vocabulary *indigènes* everywhere became *autochtones*, the CAC was transformed into the Corps of Overseas Administrators (CAOM) in the same way as in Britain the Colonial Service was redesigned as Her Majesty's Overseas Civil Service (HMOCS) in 1954. None of these changes prevented the ex-members of the CAC celebrating the centenary of the *Ecole Coloniale* at its former address in the Avenue de l'Observatoire in the very post-colonial year of 1985.[80]

But, as any student of French colonial history knows, the post-war changes impinging on the Colonial Service were far from being merely cosmetic. The epochal Brazzaville Conference of 1944 – in no way the prelude to decolonization that it is sometimes represented as being, yet in one respect years ahead of anything comparable in the British experience, namely the presence of a Guianese, Félix Eboué, in his capacity as a governor-general[81] – saw any hopes of accelerated localization of the colonial service blunted by the declaration that 'positions of command and direction cannot admit any but French citizens'.[82] In the extensive colonial service reforms of 1950 approved by Delavignette in 1938 but postponed because of the war, the apprenticeship scheme was now introduced into the training of the new CAOM cadres. This meant that the training programme for colonial administrators was split into *stages*. The initial four months in Paris were followed by an eight-month attachment to one of the colonial governments in FWA, FEA or in Madagascar. The *stagiaires* were sent in pairs to rural districts, where they worked in various departments and had their performance evaluated by their supervisors. They then returned to Paris for two more years, with a six-week stint in their final year either in the Colonial Ministry or in private industry. A further post-war impact came when the strength of the colonial service was limited in size by law, recruitment now being permitted only to fill vacancies caused through retirement and not for newly created posts. By 1957 the Corps had been reduced to some 1700 officials, considerably less than Britain's 2300 in the same year. ENFOM's recruitment declined from 367 in 1945 to 240 in 1947. The 1953 total of 120 administrative *stagiaires* turned out to be high when set against subsequent opportunities for a colonial career after the traumatic loss of Indochina in 1954.

The final influence in the shape and size of the French colonial service was that of Africanization. An intensive programme was started in 1957, when it was decreed that two-thirds of the Corps of Overseas Administrators were to be from the territories and only a third from the metropole. There had, of course, been a good number of black officials in the CAC, though these were overwhelmingly from the Antilles: in 1945 there were no more than six African administrators in the Service. In 1956 a protest was staged by ENFOM students, largely Socialist in affiliation, who demanded a reform of the still decidedly generalist curriculum.[83] This called for the teaching of economics and sociology, and recommended that issues relevant to the contemporary evolution of the French Union should be studied instead of the continuing style and spirit of the 1930s, with its 'colonial' emphasis on ethnology and administrative law. At the same time they urged the speeding up of the Africanization of the Corps of Overseas Administrators and the implementation of internal autonomy in the territories. Their hope was that ENFOM would be transformed into a part of the ENA.

Apart from the sociology, structure and formation of the French colonial service, there are a number of differences in its field organization which call for comment. Behind them lie the mainstream divergencies in the declared policy aims: British indirect administration and French assimilation, which continued at

the personal and cultural level even after its replacement at the national level
by *association* – a policy originally designed for Indochina – often seen as the
opposition of indirect and direct rule. Such a divergence persisted in the national
attitudes towards the end-game of empire, with the British assumptive but unde-
clared (till 1943) goal of eventual self-government within the Commonwealth –
always within the vague context of 'indefinite time ahead' – contrasted with the
unambiguous and eternal vision of *La France une et indivisible*. That view had
been reinforced by Charles de Gaulle's blunt warning at Brazzaville in 1944 that,
bringing gifts though he was, there was no point in asking for *autonomie* since the
word did not exist in France's colonial vocabulary.[84]

Two of the principal contrasts affecting the Colonial Services derived from
the opposition of direct and indirect rule, principally played out in the two
African empires. One is the relative size of the colonial administrations, with
the two policies frequently rubbing shoulders in contiguous Anglo-French possessions. Among the expediencies of indirect rule was the attraction of it being
far cheaper in terms of DO posts required than direct rule: less officials meant a
lesser cost in salaries and pensions and quarters, and on passages to and from
Europe. This is borne out by the comparative ratio of colonial administrators to
local population, running in the 1930s from 1:27 000 in 'direct' FWA and
1:19 000 in settler Kenya to 1:54 000 in 'indirect' Nigeria and 1:35 000 in 'mixed'
Congo. Raising these figures from the Administrative Services to all Colonial
Service officials, the proportions were as shown in Table 5.4.

The second difference affecting the colonial administrators was their
required attitudes towards natural rulers, and hence the critical relationship
between the DO/*Commandant* and the emir/chief.[85] In a nutshell, the French
administrators looked on chiefs as auxiliaries within the colonial administration,
whereas the British saw them as recognized (if regulated) rulers. It was a case of
Governor von Vollenhoven's insistence on chiefs being no more than an auxiliary instrument – 'they have no power of their own of any kind... The native
chief never speaks, never acts, in his own name but always in the name of the
Commandant de cercle'[86] set beside the Lugardian precept that chiefs were to be

Table 5.4   Ratio of Colonial Service officers to population: Africa, *c.* 1935

	Population	Colonial officials
FWA	15m	3660
FEA	3.2m	887
Congo	9.4m	2384
Nigeria	20m	1315
Kenya	3m	1214

Source: R. Delavignette, *Freedom and Authority in French West Africa*, 1950, 18.

'supported in every way and their authority upheld' and their 'prestige and
influence, position and authority' consistently maintained.[87] In the system of
indirect rule, 'the cardinal principle' of native administration was 'rule *through*
the chiefs',[88] not the French rule *over* the chiefs. In practice, while the
Commandant customarily and, by French conventions, 'correctly' treated his
chiefs as if they were NCOs, the DO was expected – and himself intuitively
expected – to treat his chiefs (at least in public) with the accepted courtesies
between officers, if not perhaps quite from the same regiment.[89] Delavignette
never forgot the 'brusque manner' in which the *Commandant* treated the Sultan
of Zinder, nor his own surprise at how the DO in Kano found nothing out of the
ordinary in inviting the emir back to his house for a cup of tea.[90] The sociological analysis sketched earlier of the two Colonial Administrative Services, sug-
gesting that most *Commandants* were Republicans and many DOs likely
Conservatives and largely monarchist in their politics and coming predominantly from etiquette-bound schools for young gentlemen, explains the
common colonial suspicion that in the art of ruling native races the French had
never really forgotten the meaning of 1789.

In addition to the distinct differences which heightened the sense of *autre
pays autre moeurs* in colonial rule, the French practice of having a colonial
inspectorate, either sent out from the Colonial Ministry or posted in the territorial headquarters to undertake regular inspections so as to make sure that governors and their staffs were complying with regulations, was utterly alien to
Britain's overseas administrations. Acceptable in the Foreign Service, it would
have been anathema to the Colonial Service. In Afrique Noire, the French colonial service was characterized by another administrative peculiarity. This was
the practice of *rouage* or rotation, introduced into FWA by Governor-General
Carde in 1924, whereby, in the name of reducing exposure to corruption and
partiality or the risk of becoming uppity towards superiors at headquarters,
administrators should serve no more than two tours running in the same colony
and were regularly liable to transfer. Thus whereas a British DO might well
expect to spend the whole of his career in, say, Uganda or the Gold Coast or
Nyasaland, to which he had been assigned as a cadet and would rise to
Provincial Commissioner unless he were high-flying enough to be transferred
on Secretariat promotion to, say, the West Indies or the Western Pacific, his
French colleague could serve in two, three or four colonies while still in the
rank of *Commandant*. A defining result of this mobility, which in itself ran
counter to the Lugardian insistence on continuity as the best insurance of sound
administration, was that while the British DO was required to learn the principal local language fluently enough to dispense with the need of an interpreter,
his French colleague relied on French as the language of colonial communication. Such an administrative necessity was at the same time a boost to the
metropolitan policy of positive cultural assimilation.

British administrators generally conceded that their French colleagues were
far more systematically trained than they were, though whether that led to
better performance remained a matter of amicable argument. Certainly Britain

had nothing in its one-year Colonial Service course at Oxford, Cambridge or London to compare with the *Ecole Coloniale*, in intensity or length of training. Similarly, any attempt to equate the Second Devonshire Course with CHEAM overlooks the far deeper and more demanding academic content, rightly culminating in the award of a well-earned *brevet* instead of a not-too-demanding certificate in Britain. At a personal level, the typical DO's enthusiasm for, and frequently accomplishment at, competitive team sports which he often carried over from Fenner's or the Parks to Nairobi and Accra and which marked him out as a member of what has been identified as the imperial 'athletocracy',[91] was rarely matched by any claim to or interest in a *rôle sportif* on the part of *Commandants* and their junior officers. For the French administrator, while sport was compulsory at the Ecole Coloniale, the emphasis was on individual sports like fencing and riding, and not the team games of British cadets like rugby, cricket and rowing. In yet more personal terms, the typical British DO's view of the stereotype *Commandant* taking a measurably different attitude to 'sleeping dictionaries' and *marriage à la mode du pays* received some endorsement through the contemporaneous but contrasting official guidance on such matters issued to colonial administrators. Dr Barot's 1902 manual of helpful hints on tropical hygiene, concubinage, miscegenation and *moussos* can be set beside Lord Crewe's warnings of what 'ill conduct between Government officers and native women' could lead to, including 'grave injury to good administration'.[92] Post-imperial research suggests, not surprisingly, that British and French habits may have come closer to one another in what the BBC has called matters of 'Ruling Passions'[93] than in the more formal aspects of comparative colonial administration viewed so differently by the Colonial Offices in London and Paris.

The last two areas of Anglo-French comparison in the context of colonial administrators are located in the era of the transfer of power. Once again, both bear on – possibly reflect – a difference in and for the administrators. The first relates to policies (or at least politics) and the second to the personnel. No student of the post-war relinquishment of empire by the European powers can fail to be struck by the bloodshed and the bitterness that erupted now and again, here and there, as the process evolved. India saw the massacres of partition, the Dutch were ejected from Indonesia, the Belgians fled from a Congo precipitated into a civil war, Spain left a dangerous power vacuum in the Sahara, and the Portuguese ended up with half of Guinea in rebel hands and a war of independence dragging on in Mozambique and Angola. The British were confronted by emergencies in Malaya and Kenya, and more or less fought their way out of Palestine, Cyprus and Aden. For all this conflict, and for all the subsequent record of civil war and collapsed states over the whole of that spectacularly colonial continent of Africa, the end of France's empire was second to none in the scale of its military turmoil: a battlefield defeat in Indochina, an all-out savage war in Algeria, massive casualties in Madagascar, a full-scale campaign in Cameroun.[94] What this legacy has meant to the emergent nations is regularly discussed. What, on a smaller but no less personal scale, this trauma meant to the British and French colonial administrators (Dutch, Belgian and Portuguese too) who believed in the worthwhileness and integrity of their mission and indulged in dreams of proud success, has yet to be analysed and evaluated.

Secondly, there remains the question, equally under-studied but far shorter in its duration, of what became of all those thousands of civil servants from the European colonial powers when, unexpectedly and often against what they had been led to believe by the eager recruiting staff of Colonial Offices in London and Paris, they found their career prematurely terminated. The situation of the three British overseas civil services is treated in Chapter 9. Little attention has as yet been paid to the case of the other European civil services nor is this the appropriate place to rehearse what events are known. But given the prominence of the French colonial experience and of its colonial service, a summary account will be in order pending further research.[95]

The French government proved far more flexible than the British. Of the three alternatives on offer when the Corps was abolished in 1959, the majority of its members opted for transfer to and integration into the metropolitan civil service. This was not an opportunity instantly available to British ex-colonial administrators. Over 350 former colonial administrators, approximately 20 per cent of the remnant overseas cadre, joined the Corps of Civil Administrators, from which the highest ranks of the metropolitan bureaucracy were filled. Among the Ministries, the largest numbers were taken into those of Finance and of Economic Affairs. Thirty were taken into the elitist Prefectoral Corps and four of these held the rank of *Préfet* in 1967. The French governmental arrangements allowed many others to continue serving the new, independent governments, in central (not provincial) administration *en service détaché*, secure in the knowledge that when their service was no longer required in Dakar, Abidjan, Yaoundé, etc. they would be reabsorbed into the home civil service from which they were now seconded. It was an arrangement and a security unknown to their British counterparts.

Those who did not choose to retire or join the metropolitan civil service could apply to enter either of two newly created Corps. The Corps of *conseillers des affaires d'outre-mer* was set up within the Ministry for Overseas Departments and Territories. However, most of the *conseillers* worked for the Ministry of Co-operation, which had special responsibility for channelling aid to Afrique Noire. More senior ex-colonial administrators were enrolled into the new Corps of *administrateurs des affaires d'outre-mer*, acting as advisers to African governments.[96] In 1967, well after France's decolonization of Africa, ENFOM still had more than two hundred of its alumni working on technical assistance in successor states, with a further 45 in charge of co-operation in the Ministry of Foreign Affairs. Some senior ex-*Commandants* actually became Ministers in the new states, for example in the Ivory Coast, Senegal and Chad. Others were appointed ambassadors, sometimes accredited to countries where they had served as *commandant de cercle*, e.g. in Togo and Dahomey in 1965. The former governors of Niger and of Gabon returned respectively as ambassador to Niamey and Libreville in 1962. ENFOM recorded that in 1967 nearly one hundred of its alumni were in the French diplomatic service, half of whom had been at the Quai d'Orsay and a quarter of whom were *en poste* in one or other of the former African colonies.[97] Here was African experience called on as a resource in a way generally eschewed by the British Foreign Office.[98] In the same year, a further 65 ENFOM graduates were working in international organizations, over twenty of whom were with the UN. Eleven won a seat in the 1968 election in France, mostly on the UDR ticket, and in the 1960s three held Cabinet posts: P. Messmer, J. Sainteny and Y. Bourges. It had been a common perception of the French colonial service by their British opposite numbers that as a Service they were, while not politicized, much more politically conscious.

In discussion of the European colonial services it would be fair to claim that one fact is incontrovertible. The differences, often substantial, in the recruitment, training, attributes, attitudes and performance of the colonial administrators, depend primarily on divergent colonial expectations and policies and not on simple stereotypes of national behaviour. National traits could play their part in the minutiae of imperial administration, especially when they bordered on the mythology of self-caricature as in Mason's ultra-British 'Gambit of the Second Reminder'[99] or the unlikelihood of ever finding a French colonial governor who was also a team athlete of world class. But below the surface the difference was deeper and deliberate. It called for a different philosophy of training, maybe a different social provenance and intellectual upbringing, to become a successful colonial *administrateur colonial* in the context of direct rule and cultural assimilation. It required a different kind of outlook and expectations after the continuity of twenty years as a DC and then PC in Uganda or the Gold Coast from a career and experience built on periodic transfers across Africa and to the Antilles.

In London and Paris, once one set aside the shared colonial purpose to which each country made its bow and paid constant lip service, encapsulated in the ancient pan-European prayer of *a bello, peste, fame, libra nos Domine*, each country's policy may have seemed, or been deemed to be, more apart than close. Yet once the metropolitan scenario was transported overseas, it was no less true that though the generic DOs were unlikely literally to speak the same language, they shared an overriding common concern and idiom: justice, tax, good rains and bad harvests, crops and corruption and communications, health and education, 'my' chief and 'my' people – in brief, the catechism of native administration at its most devoted. In the final analysis, there was more truth in the mini-mantra that 'a DO is a DO is a DO' than in the witticism that the ultimate difference between the British DO and the French *Commandant* was revealed in the priority question put to colleagues just back from home leave: 'Did you see the Test Match at Lord's?' against 'How are this year's *vendanges*?'

6 The Sudan Political Service, 1899–1955

Of Britain's three principal overseas civil services considered here, the Sudan Political Service – the key provincial administration – was at once the youngest and the smallest of them all. Established in 1899, forty years after the Indian Civil Service (ICS), and abolished in 1955 (indeed, no British officers were recruited after 1952), forty years before the one-time Colonial Service (later HMOCS) approached the end of its time in Hong Kong, and never numbering more than 150 on duty in any one year and with less than 500 members in the whole of its existence,[1] the Sudan Political Service (SPS) was characterized by a certain *sui generis* character in the history of Britain's overseas civil services.

On three further counts, too, the SPS was something of a Service apart. First – admittedly expressed in no more than generalities – in respect of its attractiveness to those in search of a civil service career overseas, its recruitment process appeared to emphasize athletic achievement as much as academic ability. Its own guru, Sir Harold MacMichael, did not hesitate in declaring that its *beau idéal* was 'the undergraduate of good health and reasonable ability'.[2] The SPS thus eschewed the conventional perceptions of the ICS aiming for the cerebral Double First and a Colonial Service content with, *inter alia*, a sound Second. A friendly pecking order among Britain's three overseas civil services would put the average-sized ICS at the top, the large Colonial Administrative Service (CAS) lying third, and the small SPS contentedly located in between. But the ICS also had its Blues; the SPS also recruited its Firsts;[3] and the CAS numbered both categories in its ranks. Yet not for nothing did the quipping sobriquet of the Sudan as a 'Land of Blacks ruled by Blues' or 'a Two [Second Class Honours] and a Blue' Political Service gain currency among British undergraduates after the First World War. One opinion, as expressed by a District Commissioner (DC) from the Sudan, was positive enough: between the wars the SPS became 'the true successor in merit to the ICS'.[4] A more liberal, less ranking view is derived from the number of applicants who, being offered an appointment in both the ICS or the SPS, opted for the latter, or from the even larger number who applied for all three Services and sometimes took the one which completed the process quickest and put them on the payroll first – often the SPS. Often, too, it was a favourite choice.

Secondly, the SPS offered exceptionally generous leave terms, with home leave once a year against anything up to seven years for members of its competitor services, along with the opportunity for retirement on full pension at the early age of fifty. Against this was the fact, plain for all to see, that the chances of promotion within a self-contained territorial Service were severely limited when set beside the possibilities inherent in a unified (from 1930) and more or less worldwide Colonial Service. That this potential brake on high-flyers rarely seemed to bother them once they were in the Service is itself a testimony to the SPS's own perceptions of its worth as a career. Thirdly, the SPS was under the aegis of neither the India nor the Colonial Office; nor did it have any office of its own among the Whitehall ministries. Uniquely, the SPS came under the jurisdiction of the Foreign Office through the High Commissioner in Cairo. This arrangement had two effects to which Khartoum was continually sensitive. One was that, to the FO, what mattered above all in the Sudan was Britain's relationship with Egypt.[5] Second, because the Sudan administration was on its own, it could find itself out of touch with comparable developments in Britain's other African territories, suffering, as one senior official summed it up, from the FO's 'lack of interest in internal administration' and lacking the 'authoritative advice' which the Colonial Office made available to its other territories.[6]

On a number of counts, then, the SPS could justify its own perception and its projected image that here was a British-recruited overseas civil service which was demonstrably 'different' – and, in its own eyes, almost certainly preferable. In Britain's post-colonial age of retrospect and reminiscence, just as ex-ICS officers have questioned the introduction of the term 'colonial' and the very concept of 'the Raj', so has there been a readiness for former members of the SPS to be quick to point out to latter-day critics and unsympathetic analysts of Britain's age of empire that they were never part of any 'imperial' or 'colonial' Service or scene. The Sudan was not part of the British Empire; it was not a Dominion or a Mandate, neither a Colony nor a Protectorate. On no school atlas was it coloured completely red. For all the prominence of its British personnel, and despite the unbroken succession of Britons as its Governor-General vested with supreme military and civil command, the Sudan was, from first to last, constitutionally a joint Anglo-Egyptian Condominium. If there was but one other such hybrid in the complicated legal vocabulary of Britain's overseas relationships, namely the Anglo-French Condominium of the New Hebrides, then this status neatly confirmed the SPS argument and easy assumption that the Sudan was indeed 'different'.

STRUCTURE AND TERMINOLOGY

For all its undeniable points of difference, however, the administrative terminology and territorial structure of the SPS would have been instantly recognizable by, and often comfortingly familiar to, any member of the ICS or CAS who, *rara avis* though he would have been before the dissolution of the ICS in 1947, transferred from (as it were) Karachi to Khartoum or, after the demise of the SPS in 1955, moved from Khartoum to Kano or Kampala.

Allowing for alterations to provincial boundaries and responsibilities inseparable from the growth of a rudimentary administration in 1900 to a sophisticated government guiding the country through constitutional change to self-government fifty years later, the fundamental pattern of administration could be looked on as standard among Britain's overseas bureaucracies. Basically it consisted of a Governor-General and his central Secretariat under a Civil Secretary in Khartoum (unlike India and several of the African territories, the civil service was involved in no traumatic move from, say, Calcutta to New Delhi or Zungeru to Kaduna – nor in the annual hot weather exodus from the Indus plains to the hills of Simla), with authority substantially delegated to a group of Provincial Governors. They in their turn devolved much of their responsibility to a cadre of subordinate District Commissioners, supported by Assistant DCs. Thus, by 1930, approximately the half-way mark in Britain's administration of the Sudan, the country was divided into 12 administrative Provinces, twice the number extant at the turn of the century. By 1950 these had been reduced to nine: three in the north, three in the south, two to the west and one to the east of Khartoum. For this area of almost a million square miles carrying a population of some nine million there was a civil service of 9625 established posts.[7] In 1950 this included 993 British officials. Of the remainder, 87 per cent were Sudanese and 2 per cent Egyptian, with eighteen from other nationalities. The junior executive rank in the Administration, operating at the level of the sub-district, was that of *mamur* or sub-*mamur*, initially held by Egyptians and then, from 1915, progressively filled by Sudanese nationals. Right up to 1952, all the Governors and most of the DCs and ADCs (in other words, the Sudan Political Service) were British. In that year, an accelerated Sudanization programme was introduced (see below).

The elite of the British elite in the Sudan (and many of the British departmental staff were of noteworthy calibre: for instance the Railways, Surveys, Medical and Education, where names like Sir James Farquharson, Sir Eric Pridie, Sir James Currie and Sir Christopher Cox achieved international recognition) were the Sudan Political Service, as the administrative service was restyled after the first World War.[8] At about the same time the initial titles of *mudir* for Governor and *mufattish* for Inspector gave way in 1922 to the generic rank of District Commissioner and in 1924 *Sirdar* was replaced by Governor-General. In the text that follows, the terminology of SPS, Governor and DC are for convenience used throughout, regardless of the 1922 watershed in administrative vocabulary. Similarly, while many of the so-called 'Bog Barons' (as the inter-war DCs of the riverine southern provinces were affectionately known) were not officially members of the SPS, and accordingly are excluded from Tables 6.1–6.4, they have, along with the contract DCs as well as those on permanent appointment, unhesitatingly been included here under the rubric of the SPS, on the grounds of duties and deserts if not of bureaucratic Establishment regulations.

ORIGINS

The Egyptian factor was an integral part of the history of the modern Sudan, from the signing of the Condominium Agreement in 1899 stipulating that the

Governor-General should be appointed by Khedival decree with the consent of Her Britannic Majesty's Government (a subtle balance of approval devised by Lord Cromer) through the traumatic international events of 1924 and 1953 to the lowering of both codomini's flags on the Palace roof on 1 January 1956. If the Egyptian connection had its low points, such as the Allenby declaration of 28 February 1922 in which Britain had publicly affirmed its restoration of matters relating to the Sudan 'to the discretion of HMG until such time as it may be possible by free discussion and friendly accommodation on both sides to conclude agreements'[9] and the ultimatum presented in November 1924, following the assassination of the Governor-General of the Sudan, Sir Lee Stack, in Cairo, which abruptly required the Egyptian Government to withdraw all its units and all its officials from the Sudan, it was nevertheless from the Cairo connection that the impetus for the formation of the SPS came. For this much of the credit lies with Cromer, who was Adviser to the Khedive and was the influential British Agent and Consul-General in Cairo from 1883 to 1907. His role was crucial following the defeat of the Khalifa at Omdurman and the British reoccupation of Khartoum in 1898.

Initially, the Sudan was administered by military personnel transferred from the largely British-officered Egyptian Army. Kordofan Province was occupied by 1900, and in provinces other than Bahr-el-Ghazal in the extreme south governors were *en poste* and the process of consolidation was well under way. Not unexpectedly, these *mudirs* were primarily military commandants and only secondarily administrative officers of the emerging provincial governments. Likewise, heads of the new technical departments were mostly drawn from the Egyptian Army. Indeed, between 1899 and 1905, a commission in the Egyptian Army was qualification enough for the military to secure as many as 12 out of 28 appointments on secondment to the incipient SPS. Furthermore, both the first Governor-General, Sir Herbert Kitchener (himself the *Sirdar* or Commander-in-Chief of the Egyptian Army), and his long-serving successor, Sir Reginald Wingate, were men with substantial Egyptian experience. Although the Governor-General was supported by several civilian advisers in Khartoum, such as Edgar Bonham Carter and Wasey Sterry on the legal side, E. E. Bernard for finance, James Currie in education, and the colourful Austrian, Rudolf Slatin, appointed by Wingate as Inspector-General of the provincial administration, when Cromer visited Khartoum as early as January 1899 he quickly came to the conclusion that, in the long run and the sooner the better, a corps of civilian officials was essential to carry out the regeneration of the Sudan adopted by the Governor-General in his first directive to his provincial Governors and Inspectors. Cromer's own rationalization, genesis and vision of a new civil service for the Sudan speaks for itself: his search was not to be for 'the mediocre by-products of the race but the flower of those who are turned out from our schools and colleges'.[10]

Disturbed by the fact that hardly had the cadre of Egyptian military officers been seconded to the tentative Sudan administration than they were recalled by the War Office for service in South Africa (a transfer from which even the

Governor-General himself, Kitchener, was not exempt) and worried by the fear
that, 'through ignorance of the language, [such youthful soldiers would] fall into
the hands of scheming native subordinates',[11] Cromer argued that in the interests of continuity – that fundamental principle of sound administration and, in
Lugard's classic conception, nowhere more so than in the context of 'native
races' – the Sudan must have its own civil service. He warned London that in
this 'hazardous experiment in the Sudan', the popularity and success of British
rule would be dependent on one or two qualified British officers in every district; to leave it to Egyptian officers alone was to stimulate corruption and complaints. If his general model was probably the ICS, of which he had had
experience during his years as Private Secretary to Lord Northbrook as the
Viceroy in 1872–6, rather than the Egyptian Civil Service which he knew well,
Cromer brought to its creation his own recruitment priorities. What he envisaged, in words much quoted in discussion of the origins and calibre of the SPS,
was a cadre of officials who would 'carry out successfully an imperial policy ...
active young men, endowed with good health, high character and fair abilities'.[12]
Dissatisfied with the low degree of sensitivity to local conditions shown by military officers aware that their tour of duty in the Sudan would be but brief,
Cromer concluded that 'the only remedy [was] gradually to train up a number of
young English civilians ... prepared to stay in the country and acquire a thorough knowledge of the language'.[13] At the same time he argued for two other
conditions over and above the basic requirement of high character: good pay
and generous leave. A period of nine consecutive months, it was argued, 'was
quite long enough for any European to remain in such a climate as the Sudan'.[14]
Finally, in the search for officers to work in Britain's newest overseas civil
service, Cromer declared it to be 'a matter of complete indifference whether
they had received their early training at Sandhurst or Oxford or Cambridge'.[15]
The mould was set: 50 years later, the SPS entrants had totalled respectively 19,
180 and 103 from these three sources, with 29 from 12 other universities.

   The first civilians were recruited for the new Sudan administration in 1901,
bringing the total of British officials to 67, 46 of them being military personnel.
Three of the new intake were from Cambridge (C. H. Armbruster, G. H. Iles
and G. C. Kerr), aged between 25 and 29, and two had graduated from Oxford,
C. E. Lyall (24) and K. C. P. Struvé (25). The sixth, Lt-Colonel C. H. Townsend,
was a graduate of RMC Sandhurst, while E. W. D. Drummond (24) had no
degree. They joined three officers who had been seconded from the Egyptian
Army in 1900 and a further two who had come into the SPS the same way in
1899. The very first civilian was J. H. Butler, transferred from the Egyptian
Government in 1889. Three more civilians were recruited in 1902, including –
significantly, in view of the Service's eventual reputation for athletic prowess –
its first Blues, R. E. More, who had played cricket for Oxford, and
S. A. Tippetts, who had represented Oxford at athletics. Cambridge's turn came in
1903, when one of the two graduate entrants was J. W. Sagar: for good measure,
he had not only captained the university at rugby football but was the first member
of the SPS – and in no way the last – to have earned an international cap,

playing for England in 1901. As early as 1904 the SPS recruited its first officer to have graduated with a first-class honours degree, E. M. Corbyn. Clearly the Service was well on its way to making its mark among British undergraduates in search of a challenging career overseas.

As was the case with the advent of the Competition Wallahs on the Indian scene, so the academic-civilian dilution of the markedly military composition of the first cadres of Sudanese administrators did not escape sharp criticism. Sir Sidney Low's contemporary portrait of Service scepticism is unrivalled:

> Jones, of Balliol, and Smith, of Trinity, who attained the supreme distinction of a university Blue, and possibly also the minor honour of a First Class, may be disposed to give themselves airs at the outset. It does not last. They speedily discover that these unpolished products of the orderly room and the barrack square have learnt a good many things which are not, as yet, imparted beside the Isis and the Cam. The soldier's training, for instance, teaches those humble but necessary virtues of order, punctuality and discipline, which are, perhaps, as useful for practical purposes as the best public school or university 'tone'. Such attainments as he does possess may also inspire rather less respect than they did at home, and they do not always impress his older military mentors. One of them, a veteran of thirty-seven, who held high office under the Sudan Government, had no esteem for the New Civilian, and imparted to me unfavourable opinions of this young gentleman.
>
> 'I am not a university man', said this unbeliever, 'so perhaps you can tell me what they do learn at Oxford and Cambridge that can be of the smallest use to anybody? When we get them out here we have to begin teaching them the simplest things, which we stupid British officers learnt before we left Sandhurst... We have to teach them book-keeping, office accounts, map measuring, how to docket papers, and draw up reports, the element of land-surveying; surely these are things that their schoolmasters might have taught them before they sent them out to us? Of course, they know all there is to know about Latin and Greek... They can play cricket, I believe, but that isn't much use in a country where there's no turf. They had much better teach them to ride decently and to shoot, and give them some military drill, which, you know, we have to put them through when they have come out. It seems to me that their real education only begins when we take them in hand.[16]

But by now the process of total civilianization of the SPS was well under way and not to be halted or reversed.

RECRUITMENT

Just how Cromer's 'active young men' were so carefully selected over the years has, in the case of the SPS, become the study of close scrutiny in the post-imperial era by academics – and by Sudanese as well as by their own chroniclers

– all exercised by how influential the character and make-up of the 'rulers' was on the style and quality of the administration of the ruled. A leading American historian of the Sudan, R. O. Collins, has argued that critical to an understanding of the official mind of imperialism is an intimate acquaintance with just who the imperialists were, whether as statesmen at Westminster, policy-makers in the departments of Whitehall, or as proconsuls and agents in the field.[17] M. W. Daly has gone further, basing his history of the Anglo-Egyptian Sudan on the premise that it was personality rather than policy which determined the history of the Condominium. '*Sharati* and *Shaykhs*, governors and ungoverned,' he concludes at the end of all of half a page of names associated with every walk of life in the history of the modern Sudan, 'their collective stories and relations mock the notion of policy, defy generalization, cry out to the biographer, and illustrate what was meant by empire'.[18]

In terms of total entry into the SPS – and, as has been noted, the corpus is officially held to have been under 400 all told between 1899 and 1952 – the recruitment divides into a five-part calendar (Table 6.1).

Such a chronology reflects a periodization characterized, in the Sudan as in the dependent Colonial Empire, by the big-dipper progression of short spasms of steady development, with the consolidation of administration interrupted by two world wars, the slump and depression of the 1930s, and the transfer of power. Yet each Service has one qualification to such a common periodization. In the Indian case there was an extra determinant in the choice of a potential career in the ICS for young graduates. There concern generated by the violence and demands for advance in the immediate post-First World War years led to genuine doubts over how much longer Indian administration could go on offering a full and worthwhile career to the young civilian. One recalls the testimony of the last Civil Secretary of the Sudan, J. W. Robertson, who in 1920 decided against following his father into the ICS on the grounds that 'India seemed very unsettled, with the papers full of the Amritsar affair and other disturbances'.[19] In the case of the Colonial Service, the time-span of decolonization is considerably lengthened, with surges in South East Asia in the 1950s, Africa in the 1960s and the Pacific in the 1970s. In the Sudan case, the period of 1919 to 1933 is frequently referred to as the Golden Age of administration, even – to borrow the imagery of its notable Civil Secretary, Sir Douglas Newbold – the Arcadian

Table 6.1   SPS recruitment, 1899–1952

1899–1918	94
1919–1933	179
1934–1939	43
1941–1944	8
1945–1952	72
Total	396

Years. Newbold, who had cautioned his officers over the Service's 'temptation to linger in the countryside' and close its eyes to the bustling political undercurrents of nationalistic feeling in the cities and mounting elite discontent, had warned against wistfully harking back to a 'gilt-edged period … lest the paradise of the Sudan of the Golden Age becomes a Fool's Paradise'.[20]

Examining this periodization in more detail, one discerns the gradual build-up from three recruits to the SPS in 1899 and the same number in the following year to a regular five or six a year in 1901–4 and thereafter to eight. SPS recruitment reached double figures twice before the First World War, in 1905 and again in 1910. Depending on a combination of vacancies and funds, up to 1930 the SPS expected to take in between four and twelve new Political Officers each year. Unsurprisingly 1920 saw the intake rise to 23, with wartime casualties, postponed retirements, and four years' ban on recruitment, all to make amends for. Because of its formidable record of all-round competence, and ultimately the highly successful career of many of its members, the cohort of 1920 was locally labelled 'The Twelve Apostles'.[21] The severity of the depression can be measured by the fact that in 1932 recruitment was down to four; it then halved again in 1934. War years apart, such a minimal entry had not been seen since 1911. Yet worse was to come. In 1933, for the first time ever until 1940, not one person was offered a post in the SPS, while in 1941 and 1944, as in 1915, a single vacancy was filled – and this at a time when staffing suffered yet another blow when three men recruited in London lost their lives at sea on their way out to the Sudan. If, with the war over, 1946 proved to be the bumper year the SPS had been waiting for, with 13 probationers recruited, recruitment to the Service experienced a hiccup in 1947. Khartoum had its doubts about the quality of the candidates, pointing out how it had declined presumably because the SPS could no longer offer a career. The counter-proposal of the Foreign Secretary, Ernest Bevin, was that applicants might be offered a career in the Diplomatic Service when that in the Sudan came to an end. Understandably, this found no favour with the Foreign Office. In the event, the quality of applicants in 1948 impressed Khartoum and the Civil Secretary, who himself chaired the Board, was so 'greatly taken' with them that he offered, on his authority, contracts of 20 years to some who might otherwise have been lost to the Service.[22] The Board was equally enthusiastic over the field in 1949, 'as good as ever'; those selected in 1950 were recruited without any advertising; and the 1951 group were also ranked as 'a good lot'. Yet by now the end was unmistakably in sight. In the face of rumours of approaching self-determination and the release of the report of the Anglo-Sudanese establishments committee, which in 1946 laid down that the proportion of Sudanized posts in the First Division Administration (i.e., the SPS) should be increased from its current 14.3 per cent to 21.4 per cent within the next four years and attain a target of 54.5 per cent in 1962, recruitment plummeted from 16 in 1950 to four in 1951 and only three in the following year. In the aftermath of the British-Egyptian Agreement of February 1953, which unambiguously presaged the dissolution of the Condominium, 1952 turned out to be the last intake of British officials into the SPS.

In any anatomy of the SPS, there exists one special kind of DC (and some-times a subsequent Provincial Governor) which is integral to an understanding of the Sudan's provincial administrators, yet which may easily elude commen-tary because of a certain fixation with (and, it must be admitted, amplitude of data on) the permanent and pensionable cadres of the SPS. In vulgar but affect-ionate parlance, these DCs were known as the 'Bog Barons'.[23]

Although there was no doubt by about 1905 that the SPS had established itself as an overseas civil service competing with its sister ICS and CAS in recruitment directly from British university graduates, the social impact of World War I had its effect on the composition of the Service. As we have seen, a number of military officers serving with the Egyptian Army transferred to the SPS in its formative years, with one or two still being seconded right up to the 1920s. However, from 1919 'War Service' progressively began to oust 'Egyptian Army' as a *prima facie* qualification for the Sudan and a positive military element was reintroduced into the DC ranks. These were generally older men, in the 27–35 age bracket. Many of them had held a commission in the King's African Rifles, the colonial regiment of East Africa, and quite a few had a mili-tary decoration to their name. All were appointed to the SPS on contract terms only, usually for two years at a time with the possibility of extension, or, particu-larly at the beginning of the scheme, on a single contract of ten years (with a few instances of semi-permanency). Here seemed to be the ideal type of administra-tor for the *sudd*-clogged marshes of the riverine southern provinces of the Equatoria, Upper Nile and Bahr-el-Ghazal ('the Bog'), where trouble was still most likely to occur, where amenities and administration were sparse, and where 'the government' was usually – and effectively – symbolized in the fear-less and commanding figure of the proverbial 'lone DC'.

These, then, were the Bog Barons, unique to the Sudan as a class of DC though replicated on an individual level in many other parts of Africa as the 'Rustybuckle' syndrome.[24] Their patriarchal rule was enshrined in semi-feudal fame and in-service balladry. They epitomized, too, that 'Southern Policy', of protectionism to the point of separatism, which Khartoum developed in what it believed to be the best and protective interest of the non-Arab population but which in the end was condemned by Northern nationalists as a classic example of the perfidious British ploy of *divide et impera*. Because the Bog Barons are as inseparable from an understanding of the pre-1939 administration of the Sudan as the south was from the *sudd*, it is important to direct attention to the exist-ence of such a genre of DC before passing on to the standard recruitment crite-ria and procedures of the SPS. The Bog Barons will, of course, reappear, now and then larger than life, in later sections where the work of the DC in the Sudan is considered.

The essential bio-qualifications of the 400 or so members of the SPS recruited between 1899 and 1952 have been distilled into four tables.[25] Besides identifying their educational background (and hence, in pre-1950 Britain, partly a corre-sponding social one) in Tables 6.2 and 6.3, Tables 6.4 and 6.5 emphasize two further features, the academic and the athletic, commonly attaching to the home reputation of the SPS and spelled out at the very outset in Cromer's triple criteria of health, character and ability. If Table 6.2 comfortably substantiates Cromer's belief that 'the system of education adopted at our Public Schools ... is of a nature to turn out a number of young men who are admirable agents in the execution of imperial policy'[26] and Table 6.3 confirms the predominance of Oxbridge as their 'finishing school', Table 6.4 gives the lie to any mischievous accusation that, consequent on the so-called 'Blue's imperative' revealed in Table 6.5, the SPS was made up of nothing more than 'a bunch of first-class hearties with third class minds' – the British equivalent of the American campus cartoon of guys who make the football team but have a problem in chewing gum and thinking at the same time. On the contrary, the SPS would seem to have exemplified the inter-war ideal of the 'best of British youth', within whatever social restrictions and middle-class boundaries were then in fashion at its breeding ground of Oxford and Cambridge.

A look at some of the SPS stars, already shining at their moment of application and often (but not always) burning yet more brightly by the end of their career, may suffice for the lower galaxies in the SPS firmament and will illustrate some of the underlying qualities looked for among its intake. By common

Table 6.2   School provenance of the SPS, 1899–1952

Winchester*	30	Sedbergh	7
Eton*	21	Rossall	6
Rugby*	20	Glenalmond**	5
Marlborough	19	Merchant Taylors*	5
Edinburgh Academy**	14	Repton	5
Charterhouse*	13	Sutton Valence	5
Haileybury	11	Bedford	4
Clifton	9	Fettes**	4
Shrewsbury*	9	Monkton Combe	4
Wellington	9	Radley	4
Cheltenham	7	St Paul's*	4
Christ's Hospital	7	Sherborne	4
Harrow*	7	Tonbridge	4

Three each from Berkhamsted, Blundell's, Downside, Durham, Glasgow Academy**, Lancing, Malvern, St. Bee's, St. Edwards, Uppingham, Westminster*
Two each from 14 other schools
One each from 57 other schools

Overseas schools:
Two each from Geelong(Australia) and St. Andrew's (South Africa)
One each from Sydney Grammar School (Australia), Wellington (New Zealand), Houghton (South Africa), and the English School, Cairo

Notes:
*Clarendon Schools **Scottish Schools

Table 6.3   University affiliation of the Sudan Political Service, 1899–1952

Oxford	180	**Cambridge**	103
Other Universities:			
Trinity College, Dublin	7	Wales	2
Edinburgh	4	Aberdeen	1
St Andrew's	4	Sydney	1
London	3	Victoria	1
Glasgow	2	Poitiers	1
R. M. C. Sandhurst	19	Lincoln's Inn	1

consent, H. A. MacMichael was a giant even among a group of tall men. To his First in Classics at Cambridge he added a fencing Blue. After eight years in the key post of Civil Secretary in Khartoum (and an earlier six as the influential Principal Assistant to the Civil Secretary), he went on to become Governor and Commander-in-Chief of Tanganyika and finally High Commissioner of Palestine. Among his successors to the top SPS post were A. Gillan, who had rowed for Great Britain – and won – in the 1908 and again in the 1912 Olympic Games (though by then he had served for three years as ADC in the exacting Kordofan Province), and J. W. Robertson who, with an Oxford rugby blue to his credit, became Governor-General of the Federation of Nigeria. There one of his subordinates, G. W. Bell, who had captained Oxford's Rifle Club, followed him as Governor of the Northern Region after being HM Political Agent, Kuwait. Yet another one-time Civil Secretary, the scholarly and popular D. Newbold, would surely have gone on to higher office had not an early death overtaken him in Khartoum. L. O. F. Stack rose within the SPS to become Governor-General of the Sudan; W. Luce became Governor of Aden; and among the fifteen officers who, obliged to retire prematurely in the early 1950s, gained admission to the Diplomatic Service, half of them went on to reach ambassadorial posts.[27]

   Among examples of the promise of an above-average career within the Sudan as reflected by a record of outstanding athletic achievement at the moment of entry, the legendary P. Munro (1908) had captained Scotland at rugby football, while his coeval R. K. Winter had played for his university (St Andrew's) at golf, football and hockey. From the penultimate intake (1951), R. M. Cooper and R. L. Crole were both hockey internationals, and eve-of-First-World War probationer N. S. Mitchell-Innes had played cricket for England on the MCC tour to New Zealand as well as captaining Oxford at both cricket and golf. Quite exceptionally, the oarsmen J. H. T. Wilson and W. G. R. M. Laurie had not only represented Great Britain in the 1948 Olympics – both, be it noted, like Gillan before them, *after* several years as DC in the Sudan – but won gold medals in the Coxwainless Pairs twelve years (and a war) after they had together rowed for Cambridge. They thereby earned the headline in the British press of 'Desert Pair Set Thames on Fire'.[28]

Table 6.4 Class and subject of degree-holders in the Sudan Political Service, 1899–1952

	First-class Honours													Second-class Honours													Third-class Honours													Others
	Classics	History	Law	Pol/Econ.	Eng. Lit.	Geog.	Mod. Lang.	Anthrop.	Maths	Nat. Sci.	Mech. Sci.	Chemistry	Agric.	Classics	History	Law	Pol/Econ.	Eng. Lit.	Geog.	Mod. Lang.	Anthrop.	Maths	Nat. Sci.	Mech. Sci.	Chemistry	Agric.	Classics	History	Law	Pol/Econ.	Eng. Lit.	Geog.	Mod. Lang.	Anthrop.	Maths	Nat. Sci.	Mech. Sci.	Chemistry	Agric.	
Oxford	3	2	3		1	1	1		2				1	28	22	6	5	3	3	2		3	3		2	1	22	22	3	9		1	3		1			1		Classics IV: 2; Law IV 1; PPE IV: 1; Moral Sci. II: 1; Econ. II 1; Medicine II: 1
Cambridge	5	1	1				1		2	1				6	18	5	1	4	6	4		3	3			1	1	8	3	1		3	2	1	4	5		1	1	Theology III: 1; Orient. Lang. III; History IV: 1; Medicine 1 (no class)
Trinity College Dublin		1							1								1																							
St Andrew's	1								1								1																							
Glasgow						2																																		
Edinburgh															1					1																				Vet. 1 (no class)

Table 6.4 Class and subject of degree-holders in the Sudan Political Service, 1899–1952

	First-class Honours													Second-class Honours													Third-class Honours													Others
	Classics	History	Law	Pol/Econ.	Eng. Lit.	Geog.	Mod. Lang.	Anthrop.	Maths	Nat. Sci.	Mech. Sic.	Chemistry	Agric.	Classics	History	Law	Pol/Econ.	Eng. Lit.	Geog.	Mod. Lang.	Anthrop.	Maths	Nat. Sci.	Mech. Sic.	Chemistry	Agric.	Classics	History	Law	Pol/Econ.	Eng. Lit.	Geog.	Mod. Lang.	Anthrop.	Maths	Nat. Sci.	Mech. Sic.	Chemistry	Agric.	
Aberdeen																																								
London															1		1			1			1																	
Wales			1												1					1																				
Totals:	10	4	5	0	1	1	3	1	5	1	0	0	1	34	41	11	9	4	7	9	4	17	6	2	1		23	30	6	9	1	4	5	1	5	5	1	1	0	
	32 Firsts													140 Seconds													93 Thirds													5 Fourths

Note: Under subject, a commonly understood terminology has been used rather than any specialized vocabulary. For example, at Oxford, Law is called Jurisprudence, Classics are known as Lit. Hum. or Greats, and Politics is subsumed under PPE (Politics, Philosophy and Economics), also known as Modern Greats. Anthropology was not offered as a first degree at Oxford. Engineering has been grouped under Mechanical Science.

Table 6.5 Number of 'Blues' in the Sudan Political Service, 1901–52[a]

Period of recruitment	Number appointed[b]	Blues gained in:								Total[c]
		Rugby	Cricket	Athletics	Rowing	Hockey	Soccer	Shooting	Other	
1901–18	63	6	5	4	5	3	3	0	2	28
1919–44	193	14	7	7	6	3	3	6	12	58
1945–52	54	1	1	1	0	2	0	0	2	7
Totals:	310	21	13	12	11	8	6	6	16	93

Notes:

[a] Predominantly gained at Oxford or Cambridge, these also include the comparable distinctions earned by members of the Service at Trinity College Dublin, Edinburgh St Andrew's, Sydney and Rhodes Universities. The term here includes 'half-Blues' awarded for minor sports.

[b] This total excludes appointments offered to those who did not attend a university but went to the Military College, Sandhurst, or Royal Military Academy, Woolwich, or, occasionally, to no post-secondary institutions. They numbered about eighty over the period.

[c] These include 12 men who gained a double blue and one who had a triple blue.

By such colourful standards, double Blues like A. K. Maitland and J. D. Burridge may have seemed a little pale, while mere Blues may have felt they were after all but two a penny. Yet two-thirds of those appointed in 1902, 1909 and 1913 were Blues; almost half of those entering the Service in 1906, 1914, and 1923, and again in every year from 1934 to 1939, were Blues; and, in 1932, the proportion reached three-quarters. In only twelve years did a Blue not feature among the personal achievements of those recruited into the SPS. One other Sudan DC, though never a member of the SPS, who earns a mention in any such catalogue of achievement is Hugh Boustead. He represented Britain in the Olympic Games and his series of remarkable travels culminated in his selection for the 1933 Everest expedition. Wilfred Thesiger, too, achieved a traveller's fame far beyond his DC days in the Sudan.[29]

While those with a Pass degree were rarely accepted (less than 2 per cent in 50 years) and those with a First Class Honours degree were courted by such competing career services as the Diplomatic, Home Civil and ICS (though the SPS's record of over 10 per cent Firsts among its 270 university graduates is high), it was men with a Second or Third Class degree who made up the bulk of those summoned to and successful at the final Board assembled by the Sudan Agency in London, essentially an 'in-house' affair. And among them it was acknowledged that the final choice generally settled on those who had achieved some form of athletic distinction. The SPS never wavered from a firm faith in those endowed with athletic ability: not necessarily Blues but, perhaps even more attractive to the Board and suggestive of a sound performance ahead, it sought that evidence of 'getting on with' and leadership that come from having played in – better still, having captained – a college team. 'The reason', as the doyen of the Service sought to explain the importance it attached to distinctions in sports, 'is that we were proud of them and did not regard them as altogether irrelevant... Hence the relevance of athletic details'.[30]

The account by one of the entrants into the SPS in 1907, looking around his probationer companions on the Desert Express as it trundled the hundreds of miles from Wadi Halfa to Khartoum, must rank as more representative than rare. Counting them (one international, one Army Champion, three university captains and one Fourth Wrangler), he reflected that 'I think we have been chosen mainly because we were athletes'.[31] Against this, equity calls for a view that the sporting imperative was not all, nor did athleticism constitute an indispensable ingredient in the make-up of every SPS officer recruited. Many an SPS officer has confirmed this view, and one post-war applicant has recorded how, despite the fact that his Oxford talent scout did not think much of his candidature because he did not play games or come from a public school, he succeeded in convincing the Board that he was what they wanted.[32] There is a case to be made for the neat – though unintended – balancing act in the formal qualifications of the four civilians recruited in 1910 and 1911: on the intellectual side, one First, one Senior Optime, a Second and a Third Class, and on the athletic side two Blues (one a captain) and two 'ordinary' undergraduates content to be neither muddied oafs nor flannelled fools.

If all this was the end product of recruitment for the SPS, what was the actual process? For students of public administration, the formation of bureaucratic cadres, regulatory Public Service Commissions committed to the Trevelyan reforms of the 1850s and the replacement of patronage by ability demonstrated through competition, the immediate surprise must be the total lack of any competitive examination in the selection of the SPS. The contrast with the ICS selection process is polar. Instead of being compelled to sit for one of the most searching and weeding-out intellectual examinations facing British graduates in the inter-war years, an applicant for the SPS had to satisfy – often no less searchingly – a small *ad hoc* interviewing committee meeting once a year in London. This Selection Board nearly always included one or two serving officers home on leave from the Sudan. The whole exercise, in the concise comfort of the recollection of one of their number, was 'from first to last informed and sensible'.[33] It might not be too extreme a reading to suggest that the only hint of anything as constraining as rules in the selection process was the reverent observance of the original Cromer criteria. True, much spadework would have been done by the positive yet quite personal talent-spotting within the university among men in their second or final year, carried out by tutors such as the Arabist Professor Margoliouth at Oxford and the Orientalist E. G. Browne at Cambridge, who had been quietly invited by those in Khartoum to keep their eyes open for likely types (especially among the Blues). This was valuably supplemented by visits from DCs – better still by ADCs, nearer in age and undergraduate generation to the prospective candidates – to their old College while on leave to make what informal reconnoitring or contacts they could. Sometimes the 'old boys' might co-ordinate their trip to Oxford or Cambridge and constitute themselves into a preliminary yet unofficial Board on the last day of their visit. One candidate dolefully wondered what impression he had made on the two representatives who had called him to their preliminary selection visit at Oxford:

> On opening the door I fell down two steps into the room, cursing volubly, and on looking up found myself facing the two laughing officials. However, it can't have done me much harm for I was asked to attend a final selection board in London... I do not remember much of what I was asked, but the members of the board were friendly and I know we had some discussion about bridge.[34]

Those who survived this local taking of soundings and the formal if perfunctory interview with the University Appointments Board, considered by some SPS applicants as being designed for nothing more than to weed out the irredeemably unsuitable, were summoned to the final Board in the early summer. This might consist of several Provincial Governors (the SPS leave conditions were such as to allow senior officers to spend the summer, the Sudan's restricting wet season, in Britain). One applicant, a graduate of Dublin, took the precaution of putting on a morning coat when summoned to something as formal as a Whitehall Selection Board during the Edwardian era. To his amazement,

he found the other candidates, from Oxford and Cambridge, resplendent in
their Leander colours and Hawks ties, making him feel like a crow among
peacocks.[35] Even in the 1920s, by which time the selection process was well
established, the hallmark remained that of informality. Another recalls how,
when called in by two selectors (J. D. Craig and P. Munro, both DCs on leave),
he seemed to be interrupting a discussion about the Kirk. They at once brought
him, as a fellow Scot, into the argument, quizzing him on the difference
between the United Frees and the Wee Frees as he had read of it in the works
of J. M. Barrie. A brief but amicable conversation ensued, after which he was
courteously dismissed, 'having presumably demonstrated my comparative lack
of interest in the intricacies of Presbyterianism, my reluctance to pretend to a
greater knowledge than I possessed, and, I suppose, something of my taste in
books'.[36] Unapocryphal, too, is the account of the joy which other candidates
waiting in the anteroom to be called before the interviewing board felt when
they subsequently learned that the one of their number who had ostentatiously
left his copy of *The Times* open so as to reveal the crossword completed had not
been accepted.[37]

Among the advantages of such a 'family' Board was that they were able to
correlate their findings with the university Class Lists published in July and then
inform candidates of the result of their interview within a week. Such an almost
in-house procedure was possible for a Service which not only recruited no more
than a handful of probationers in a year but which also, on the ground, rarely
exceeded a hundred and fifty officers. Unlike the ICS, and impossible in the
CAS within some of its larger territories, in the SPS the odds were that you not
only recognized the name of every brother-officer, but if you did not meet this
year you would surely come across him next year. Thus a close-knit family relationship was effective in the ranks of the SPS and easier to establish right from
the moment of interviewing.

It is not hard to conclude that, in a phrase, in its selection the SPS favoured
its own kind. The selectors, themselves all members of the SPS, understandably
tended to favour those in whom they could recognize the same qualities which
they believed had gained them entry a few years before and which had proved
just what was needed in the Sudan. And were these not, as they now knew from
experience, the very attributes which made not only for a good and successful
officer but also for a happy and efficient Service? It is not surprising then that
the SPS provides a telling example of a self-perpetuating elite, endowed with
'the values, habits and inclinations of the earlier civil recruits admired by
Cromer', all drawn from the leading, and often the top, English and Scottish
public schools 'an elite within an elite', the image of 'a solid performance'.[38] In
this schools connection, the terminology is, as Honey and Mangan have argued,
somewhat wider than the standard nineteenth-century classification of the
'Great' or 'Clarendon' Public Schools.[39] Instead, they set up chronological categories, of Early Leading Schools, Early Lesser, Peripheral, Recent and More
Recent Schools, a total of some 600. Following Mangan's findings, the 393 SPS
officers recruited between 1899 and 1952 were drawn 302 from Early

Established Public Schools and 29 each from Later Public and Non-Public/Colonial Schools. Mangan summarizes his findings thus:

> In short, fashion, upbringing, and education did play a part in determining the composition and character of the Service, but so did similarities of temperament, character, physique and achievement. Virtually all achieved distinction at school and university in games and in terms of leadership rather than in terms of academic honours, were physically and mentally robust with an inclination towards outdoor adventure rather than indoor study.[40]

The golden opinion of a Sudanese observer, too, is not without interest:

> To the Recruitment Board, good birth and good manners counted more than abnormal intelligence; strict morality and distinguished sportsmanship carried as much weight as academic honours. Still, good educational qualifications were taken for granted, and none could be selected who was not among the leaders of his class on graduation. Under such a rigid system of selection, only the cream of British universities and British families went to the Sudan, and never has such a splendid selection of men been assembled to do a single job in any part of the world.[41]

Perhaps all these strands of the underlying Cromerian ethos, of marked athleticism, a fair mind, and good social class, come together in the off-the-cuff quip of a senior SPS official who confided that Ted Dexter but never Ian Botham would have made the Service.[42]

MOTIVATION

Given this account of who the SPS officers were on entry, it is legitimate to integrate catchment area and recruitment machinery in the creation of a given Service with a third, less practical yet equally influential factor. This is the psychology of the Service's appeal to those seeking to join it. What did its potential recruits think the job offered them by way of opportunity (the job satisfaction of later generations) and just how, in their mind's eye or at second hand by way of reading books about the Sudan and snatches of in-Service folklore among relatives or neighbours, did they perceive the kind of work they would be called on to undertake?

In, as it were, apologizing for having written one of the first personal accounts of 'the sort of experience which coloured and enriched the lives of members of the Sudan Political Service', Reginald Davies, who went out to Khartoum in 1911, accurately estimated that by the end of the century there would be few if any of his colleagues left to record or recall that experience.[43] He based his narrative on what constituted a challenging yet intangible reward to those who chose a career in any of Britain's overseas civil services, 'that human interest which was ample compensation for the hard physical conditions of life in the outlying parts of the Sudan'. Of all the activities, he went on, the one aspect from which he gained the profoundest knowledge of what really lay under the surface was his work as a magistrate, 'touching life at many points and sometimes at strange angles'. To the excitement – for an undergraduate just turned twenty-one – of responsibility for law and order, of getting under the skin of 'native life', and of a certain degree of physical challenge, Davies added an element calculated to appeal to the kind of young man the SPS wanted to attract, the exoticism of travel often in unusual ways and back-of-beyond places. Calculating that in the first half of his service he had ridden over 20 000 miles on his camel, he argued that, for all his personal dislike of the camel's back, here was a unique 'means to experience' (it also furnished him with the title of his autobiography). Here was arguably the symbolized quintessence of a life in a career government service overseas generically known as being 'on tour', with individual Service language variants of trek, camp, circuit, safari, *ulendo*, etc. Here was the very essence of reminiscence recounted, with that air of nostalgia breathed by all but a handful of overseas administrators as they recall their life; 'such were the days of my youth'. With men like Davies and Jackson recalling inspirationally 'the rough and the smooth, the sunshine and the storm'[44] of service in the Sudan as they chatted in the quads and courts to third-year men, or recounted such routine experiences to nephews or the sons of neighbours, what possible recruit whose social and intellectual identikit has been sketched in the preceding pages could miss the tinge of romantic adventure as such storytellers reached the end of their tale?

> The farewell parties were over. The final speeches had been made; the last presents exchanged... A henna-bearded sheikh had thrown his arms about my neck, kissed me on both cheeks and burst into tears when the ceremony was over! As I left my house (to a salute of nine guns) for the steamer that was to take me on the first stage of my homeward journey, I thought of the day when first I looked upon the Nile, and on which I was now to look for the last time. Except for a brief period of service in the Red Sea Province the Nile had always been with me, threading its way through the desert and the swamp, but woven into the fabric of my life ... the River of Destiny that determined the fate of millions of people in Egypt and the Sudan.
>
> Dusk had fallen as I reached the landing-stage and the foreshore thronged with the usual crowd of people waiting to bid their Governor farewell, each one of them anxious to shake him by the hand. For hours before my arrival the luluing and the chanting had continued; but as the departure of the steamer was unexpectedly delayed, I suggested to the people that they should all go home to their evening meal. After more shaking of hands and last-minute expressions of goodwill, the crowd gradually dispersed and I went to dinner myself.[45]

Others stressed other attractions and appealed to other motivations. The pay was good, though not extravagant; leave was generous; the great outdoors was extensive; and the life was an active, healthy one for young men who were likewise both. The Permanent Secretary at the Foreign Office was not afraid to draw attention to the sacrifices inseparable from a career in the SPS, with its call to take up the challenge and face the possibilities of privation and even death.[46] Yet compensations there were, among them – and here his recruitment message was as loud and clear to young Britons of the inter-war years as it is to Africa's safari holidayers today – 'a superabundance of animal life ... a profusion of birds and butterflies ... a paradise for the naturalist'. Overall, the judgement of a latter-day (1942) entrant remains valid throughout the Service's existence:

> The British administrator in the Sudan is no martyr. He stays there because he is happy; because in some strange manner and almost in spite of himself he finds, in the service of the Sudanese, fulfilment of life.[47]

It is an epitaph which, *mutatis mutandis*, applies to the majority of Britain's imperial administrators.

Finally, frills apart, what young man 'of the right type' and of the time could, when it came down to the nuts and bolts of the job itself, hesitate longer over his choice of career after exposure to this kind of almost idyllic description of what was, after all, apparently no less and no more than just another 'Day in the Life of a District Commissioner'? And what a day every day might seem to be to the young DC in the making: 'It would start at dawn [after a night spent under the stars, sleeping on the open roof] with a gentle awakening shake from the houseboy bringing him a cup of tea followed [after breakfast and probably a canter down to the office] by a very long morning dispensing justice.'[48] If that was routine, with camel and stern-wheeler thrown in for good measure, what price the 7.52 to London Bridge every morning? Many could not wait to exchange the imagined view of Whitehall for those 'feelings of lively expectations [as they] stood upon the north bank of the Nile and gazed across the waters to the palm-fringed city of Khartoum'. That was indeed the life for them!

TRAINING

If there is far less to be said about SPS training than the commentary generated by the case of the ICS or the CAS, this is partly because there was a lot less of it for the probationer accepted into the SPS and partly because what there was came somewhat later than that long provided for the entrants to the ICS. To an extent, the SPS above all preferred the commonly endorsed Aristotelian precept about how to learn to play a flute. Certainly in the early days, the sooner the new entry got out to the Sudan and down to the work, the better both for a stretched Service and his own experience.

The one area where some kind of pre-posting instruction was recognized as valuable was in learning Arabic. Before the First World War, preparatory training for SPS probationers could not be said to have been streamlined. True, those selected were expected to spend an extra year and a half at Oxford or Cambridge, learning the language – but at their own expense.[49] In 1908

Dr E. G. Browne of Pembroke College, Cambridge, found to his chagrin that more basic teaching of the language was necessary before he could move to what he had planned as his opening tutorial, handing to his two SPS probationers a copy of *The Arabian Nights* in Arabic and inviting them to read it aloud.[50] Perhaps Oxbridge Arabic as then professed by learned dons was not what was really wanted. To borrow a judgement from a probationer who experienced such teaching, the first thing one learned on reaching Khartoum was that colloquial Sudanese was as different from the classical Arabic one had laboriously acquired as Italian from Latin.[51]

After The First World War, the course was reduced to three months at the new School of Oriental and African Studies in London, principally in Arabic, and the probationers were given a small grant. Instruction was also given in anthropology, tropical medicine, first aid and mapping. There is some evidence that book-keeping was also tentatively included in the later Cambridge syllabus, but few seem to have attended the lectures, finding them 'unprofitable' (*sic*). Nor were they exactly enthused at Cambridge by the anthropologist Professor Haddon, who reputedly greeted his special probationers with the news that he had mislaid the notes on the Sudan which he thought he had but would be much obliged if they would attend his lectures on the totem men of New Guinea.[52]Another probationer, this time at Oxford, where the SPS probationers were encouraged to prepare themselves for the sight of blood and amputated limbs by attending operations at the Radcliffe Infirmary, had to be laid out on the floor of the operating theatre to recover from a fainting fit.[53] Probationers were also encouraged to brush up on their horsemanship 'if necessary' (a socially revealing proviso). From 1930, those who had not yet reached their twenty-second birthday were sent back to the university to join the Colonial Office cadets on the new (1926) Tropical African Services Course.

CONDITIONS OF SERVICE

New appointments were on probation for two years. Seniority and salary dated from the date of arrival at Port Sudan, earlier in Port Said. If the probationer did not pass the mandatory Government examinations in Arabic and law within this period, he would not be awarded any increment to his salary. Generally, however, the SPS requirements for confirmation, as for training, were simpler than those demanded by the ICS and CAS, as C. W. North found from the unusual experience of having been in all three services.[54] For many years young officers were expected not to get married, but later on these regulations were modified to allow an officer to marry either after two years' service or when he reached the age of 27. During the years of the slump the ban was extended to a wait of five years. Other conditions of service included compulsory retirement at the age of 50, or at 48 if an officer wished, always provided that he had completed the minimum number of years to be entitled to draw a pension. Climatic and health reasons apart, the aim of this concession was to sustain the morale of young officers in a Service of very limited promotion prospects as well as to enable those retiring to find, if they wished, further employment in the UK. There had always been a core of SPS officers recruited on short-term or contract terms, at first those seconded from the Egyptian Army and then after 1919 the ex-military Bog Barons. From 1945 on, with political question marks beginning to gather over the future of the Condominium, more and more officers, however satisfactory their qualifications, were offered contract and no longer pensionable terms. Once self-government had been promised as a realizable objective, it was no longer desirable either to recruit a continuing cadre of pensionable expatriate officials who might be entitled to compensation when they made way for Sudanese DCs, or to encourage recruits to believe that they had a full career ahead of them in the SPS. Thus of the 70 appointments made by the SPS after 1947, only a third were offered pensionable terms. The rest were given contracts.

Members of the Sudan Civil Service, administrative and departmental officers alike, wore a collar and tie when out on trek in the districts. The custom of wearing uniform was not widespread in the CAS, other than for a while in Kenya. This uniform consisted of a blue puggaree (to distinguish them readily from military officers whose puggaree was red) wound round a Wolseley helmet, with an SCS badge in the front and a provincial one at the side. In the office, civilians were required to wear a jacket, trousers (not shorts), and for many years a *tarboosh* too. In later years a bush shirt and shorts were acceptable attire for trek and office alike, and the dress uniform of a *tarboosh* and '*stambouly*' frock coat became a thing of the past. However, attendance at the Governor-General's levée in Khartoum still necessitated a frock coat, surmounted by a *tarboosh* in recognition of the Egyptian element in the Condominium.

While most SPS officers expected to spend the largest part of their career as a DC (after all, that was the kind of life they had joined for) and probably with promotion to the cognate post of at least Deputy if not always Provincial Governor, a spell of duty in the Secretariat was looked upon – in the headquarters at Khartoum, though not always so enthusiastically in the districts of, say, Dongola or El Fasher – as a necessary and important part of an officer's career formation. Although the SPS was in theory a unitary service in the sense of provincial postings, there was at times a tendency for an officer to spend most of his field career in one of the Southern (3) or in one of the Northern (6) Provinces. This was, of course, very much the case of the soldier-administrator Bog Barons. For them, the South rather than the Sudan was their Service, and wide was the lore about such DCs who insisted on going on leave via Uganda and on to Mombasa rather than risk contamination by having to pass through Khartoum en route for Port Sudan. As for a 'training' posting to the Secretariat, it was a matter of conjecture who would have been the more alarmed at such a suggestion, the Bog Baron or the Secretariat.

It is arguable that, with a single Service of no more than 150 or so posts on the establishment, with the Governor-General always coming from outside the

Service (Stack was the only exception to this practice), the prospects for promotion were considerably less than in the much larger ICS or than in the unified CAS with its inter-territorial transfers and several dozen territories complete with superscale staff posts. In the event, apart from the gubernatorial appointments of MacMichael to Tanganyika in 1934 and the no-return secondment of S. Redfern to Ottawa in 1935 (J. H. Driberg's transfer from Uganda and early departure from the Sudan were rather special), few SPS officers before 1945 transferred out of the Sudan into a comparable career elsewhere. However, the abolition of the ICS in 1947 attracted one or two of its officers into the SPS. *En revanche*, when the time came for its own liquidation in 1953–5, a number of SPS officers found familiar posts in the CAS, including appointments at the gubernatorial level in Nigeria (J. W. Robertson and G. W. Bell) and Aden (W. Luce) as well as in the DC and Secretariat cadres (see Chapter 9).

THE DC

As with all Britain's overseas civil services, the life of the DC or his equivalent furnished the heart of the matter. One joined the Service – beyond-the-pale careerists apart – to become a DC, not a Financial Secretary or a Governor. It was the DC image which was highlighted in the appeal to potential applicant, projecting the kind of life that he was looking for and for which he might just be the 'right type'. It was emphasized in the policy decisions emanating from the Secretariat: provincial administrators were the backbone of good government, at once the generator and reflector of a contented populace. And, as we have seen, it coloured the DC's own recollections, whether from retirement or from his temporary desk in the Secretariat: those incomparable (and the remoter the rosier) days out on trek. From beginning to end – and one might well add beyond – what dominated both the perception and projection of the Service, be it ICS, CAS or SPS, was the work and responsibilities of the generic DC. As a consequence, the image of the DC, however partial and however romanticized, assumed in Britain the manifestation of the be-all of imperial administration, the quintessential symbol of the responsible, resolute, reliable and ever-ready 'man on the spot'. The DC was the government and the government was the DC.

And so, as the new SPS entry stopped off in Khartoum anticipatedly to learn their destination – was it to the deserts of the north, distant Darfur, or one of the remote 'Bog' provinces? – and filled in the days with a round of what more modern management would call orientation briefings and familiarization visits to various Departmental headquarters in the capital, impatiently they waited and wondered when, with a year's training behind them, more background files to read up and still more homilies to receive from the Great and the Good all the way down from the Palace itself, the moment would come for them to put learning behind and at last start on the real job, that of becoming a DC. One typical probationer calculated that in 1922 it took him and his fellow probationers three weeks kicking their heels in Khartoum before they were dispatched to the districts:

> We were accommodated in the Grand Hotel, and as was customary for young probationers, spent about three weeks in Khartoum before going out to the provinces. During that time we were introduced to senior officials, shown something of the way in which the country was administered, and bought kit and stores for our new life. We visited the main Government offices and spent a day in Omdurman with the District Commissioner seeing how he dealt with the various problems which came to him. We also visited the Agricultural Department research station at Shambat, and had lectures from departmental officials and from the Deputy Governor of Khartoum – Robin Baily who told us that we should model our behaviour on that of a 'genial baron'. We were instructed in our responsibilities for tax assessment and collection, district accounts and budgets, and our duty to see that government money was kept securely in the town treasuries and checked by us at frequent intervals.[55]

A decade later, the induction was reduced by half, with care taken to learn, besides the general working of government, 'the necessary shibboleths of social life in an overseas territory', paying evening calls on senior officials (and hoping they were out), wearing tropical suits in the office, white dinner jackets in the evening and stiff shirts if it were a formal dinner.[56]

In the Sudan, with but a handful of newcomers to deal with and a limited number of older hands in the field, it was possible for the Civil Secretary to take a personal interest in whether A should go to work with Y at Kassala or which of B or C might be the better man for Equatoria Province under Z. The SPS could afford the luxury – and the bonus – of greater intimacy and a personal matching up of probationer with post, taking account of the known traits of the receiving DC with the conjectured strengths and vulnerabilities of the probationer. Few ADCs ever forgot their reception by and impressions of their first DC, and few failed in retrospect to admire qualities if not, sometimes wisely, always to reproduce all their characteristics or repeat their performances.

There is an inherent obstacle in attempting to describe a typical day in the life of a DC in the SPS. This is that not many days were typical and there were few typical stations – and, for that matter, few typical DCs. It was often the very absence of routine, the challenge of the unexpected and the allure of novelty and variety, that lifted the DC's life out of the common humdrum of administration and made it what it was. The principal impression that emerges from the synthesis described by one experienced SPS administrator under the heading 'The Run of the Mill' is precisely how untypical and unroutine such a life was.[57] District life was nothing if not varied. Perhaps the best way of grasping what that work was is to divide it, as every DC did, into its two very different lifestyles: his work when in station and his work when on trek.

In station – and this could sometimes be a town with a minimal number of government colleagues and he maybe the sole member of the SPS – the DC would spend much of each day in his office. Yet this was no hub of VDUs, no hum of machines; sometimes there was not even a telephone, and maybe but a single typewriter, with pins and thorns standing in for paperclips and staples. Three areas of responsibility were likely to dominate a DC's station work.

One was his formal judicial responsibilities, sitting as a magistrate, sometimes in summary cases and sometimes in conducting a full trial, including a meticulous record of the evidence, and as often as not acting as judge, jury and counsel for the defence. Crime, especially theft of livestock as much as of domestic property, robbery and affray (including murder) accounted for most of the DC's time spent on court work. Even junior ADCs dealt with up to a score of judicial cases in one day. While the introduction of Native Courts presided over by their own *alim* or legal expert subsequently relieved the DC of having to spend so much of his time in court, though in no way reducing the critical value of local knowledge when it came to sitting in on cases heard in the native courts or inspecting their court records, the DC never lost that pivotal responsibility – indeed, arguably his ultimate insignia of status as 'the Government' – for law and order. In civil cases, knowledge of the law was more likely to outweigh knowledge of the locality, and so in many civil actions a prudent DC would adjourn such cases for hearing by the professional judge when he next came on circuit. Islamic personal law, *Shari'a*, was of course something quite apart. In the Sudan, this was administered by a *kadi* or trained Islamic judge, and the DC was involved only if a breach of the peace had taken place. On the other hand, the DC was frequently called on, as a case of first and often of final instance, to adjudicate in matters of litigation over land, a common cause of dispute and not infrequently of disturbance. 'I used to go out to the scene and hear the evidence on the spot,' records one DC, 'making the plaintiff walk along the boundary he claimed, carrying the Koran on his head', with a shouting crowd of both supporters and adversaries following him while his friends restrained him from perjuring himself.[58]

The post-colonial concern over the undesirability of combining judicial power with executive authority in a single office rarely constituted a matter of anxiety for DCs. Most of them were satisfied that, despite their limited legal training (though many qualified as members of the Bar), in the final analysis the accused was exposed to a far greater danger from the absence of local knowledge by a professional judge on circuit. However, in the case of the SPS, as in the ICS but less markedly in the CAS, a fair number of appointments to the judiciary came from within the ranks of the administration, thereby combining the best of both professions. For instance, posts of Judge of the High Court, Provincial Judge and Police Magistrate were frequently filled from within the SPS.

Besides 'law' and the exercise of justice, the DC was responsible for the other half of the equation, 'order' – classically, for keeping the peace. One way of trying to ensure this was in 'hearing petitions'. The DC, at prescribed hours when in station and virtually at any or every time when out on trek, would make himself available to listen to petitioners. The colourful variety of such requests was matched by the scale of their importance, together providing – and calling on – an unparalleled reservoir of local knowledge. In the eyes of many a Provincial Governor, time spent by a DC on petitions was never time wasted. Such activity may be said to have represented the core of the DC's art of human relations and the ultimate manifestation of his primary responsibility for keeping his finger on the district's pulse. While hours spent listening to grievances, whose petitioners often had more time on their hands than had the DC and for whom, it was surmised, a day out on a visit to the *merkaz* or district office offered an agreeable form of entertainment, could be tedious, for many a DC this was the best, though frequently the hardest, initiation into his work, in terms of both social learning and language practice. At a higher, and fortunately rarer, level, keeping the peace could involve police operations and, in the early days, acting as the Political Officer accompanying a punitive expedition. This extra responsibility was paralleled in later years by a new one, that of keeping the peace when protest marches or political party processions were planned and a licence to hold them had to be issued.

The third aspect of station life, besides judicial work and listening to petitions, was inspection. Institutions, buildings, markets, public works, prisons, etc., all might expect a visit from the DC when he was in town. In the Sudan, this visitation took a special form known as 'The Town Ride', notably performed in the township of Omdurman. This weekly inspection ritual, 'trotting around [the town quarters] accompanied by a retinue of *mamurs* and sheikhs', was one of the features which differentiated the work of the DC in the Sudan from that of his fellow DCs in other countries.[59] If at its heart lay the psychological principle of 'showing the flag', in practical terms the Town Ride served as an effective method of exercising authority over building control, a paramount requirement of sound urban administration everywhere. While in the 1920s spit and polish may have been to the fore in Omdurman, with the DC, in uniform, riding forth from his front gate to be greeted by the Sheikhs of whichever quarter was due for inspection that day and then escorted on his ride by a posse of mounted police dressed in spotless white, in later years the tempo and atmosphere were modified and tempestuous scenes (including the DC rebuking his ADC for having a button undone) gave way to more professional considerations, while never abandoning the readiness to hear petitions all the way.[60] The generally low level of rural discontent throughout the Condominium has been largely attributed to the ability of anyone to go and present his case to the DC in person.

Finally, of course, in station, whether it was a district or the capital, there was office work, the desk duties inseparable from the art of administration. In Khartoum – but not across the river in Omdurman, where the *merkaz* still functioned – Secretariat work was, indeed could be, nothing much more than office work. Yet office work was still safely removed from the stereotype drudgery of a 9 to 5 life in Whitehall or some Town or County Hall, however groaningly most DCs protested over their transfer from provincial work to a spell in the Secretariat. In the Sudan there was always, even in the highest-powered Secretariat offices, a strong element of across-the-desk personal contact, often without the impersonality of the telephone and frequently, as constitutional advance accelerated, with people one had known and worked alongside in provincial Native Administration or Local Government contexts. Office work, then, whether in the Secretariat or the district, was better described as regular rather than routine, despite the fact that, as DCs often felt, the only really regular feature about it was the irregularity of office hours, generally ignoring the official closing hour of government and frequently taking in weekends.

While accepting, as the writer himself did, the atypicality of a typical day in the life of a DC in the Sudan, the following description gives as good a representative picture as any of the classic Arcadian years up to the eve of World War II:

> Before breakfast the District Commissioner would go out on a tour of inspection of his station, police lines and local prison, and of any building, road-making or other type of work which was in progress in the neighbourhood. After having breakfast at about 8.30 a.m. he would then leave for his office where he would spend a very long morning dispensing justice as a magistrate and dealing with a miscellaneous host of administrative matters. He would have to interview anyone who wished to see him, bringing a wide variety of requests and complaints for settlement. He would be lucky if he got back to his house for lunch by 2 p.m.
>
> After a brief rest the afternoon brought recreation and exercise in the form of riding or a game of polo, tennis or squash, if his station provided such facilities. Occasionally there might be the opportunity to shoot duck or sandgrouse. The DC's day did not always end at sunset, which in those latitudes was around 6 p.m. throughout the year, and he might have to return to his office to complete the morning's correspondence, or to write up criminal or civil cases. If not so employed he might invite some friends to join him in a game of bridge or in making music, or he might have a small dinner party.
>
> Every DC would expect to leave his station periodically and to tour his District, camping for days on end in different parts of it, in order to meet his headmen and their people in their own surroundings and, where necessary, to settle difficulties and disputes on the spot and supervise the work of the traditional native courts...
>
> It was a tradition that a DC should be on duty at all times.[61]

If office work everywhere took up progressively more of the DC's time as the Condominium moved forward and sophisticated development and constitutionalism overtook rural administration as the primary focus of government, there remained one aspect of every DC's work which lasted a full fifty years. This was going out on trek, the Town Ride writ large on the countryside and its few hours transformed into days, even weeks. It could be by camel, horse or mule; by steamer on the Nile or by 'saloon' on the railway. In the southern provinces, it might be by bicycle[62] but more usually was on foot. Whether a trek lasted weeks or a month was of little significance; in those days administrative duties were not undermined by a failure to move about quickly.

That trekking by camel was more than a memory of the past is evidenced by the touring diary of another DC, Brian Kendall, who in 1946 spent ten days checking the tax collection among the nomads in Singa, Blue Nile, and outstripping them all on his own camel as well as 'confounding them by mounting without the camel being held'.[63] While trekking may have become less leisurely both as office work increased and the motor-car replaced slower methods of transport, its priority in the DC's life and its primacy in his post-career recollections remained second to none. For most if not all, that was what much of being a DC was ultimately about.[64] 'I think', mused one for many, 'the proper context … is that we shared a love of the open air and wide open spaces. That prospect had been a main factor in applying to join the Service, whatever one's background.'[65] Significantly, even a DC of a much later period could reflect, in tallying up his balance sheet of a life as a DC in the Sudan:

I have always wondered why a reasonable Government is willing to pay high salaries to able-bodied men who live an open-air life, just for gratifying that propensity. There could, in my imagination, be nothing nicer than riding a camel through the gum gardens of Darfur on a nice warm sunny day in winter, stopping to take a pot-shot at a gazelle and spending the middle of the day in the shade eating breakfast and lunch. Then at sunset halting in a beautifully sheltered valley, well wooded with acacia and everything as comfortable as camp life can be, with a large wood fire for warmth and hot water brought for washing and shaving after tea. Then guinea fowl for dinner and early bed out in the open under the stars. It's ideal; people take their holidays doing it – if they can. And yet here am I, not only being paid my normal £E1.6.8d a day, but actually an extra 7/- a day for living this life of hardship and toil. There is, of course, a fallacy somewhere and it lies in the fact that one isn't always young, one's liver is not always working like my Rolex Oyster and one is not always in the best of tempers in consequence.[66]

SPECIAL DUTIES

While a spell in the Secretariat at Khartoum came the way of nearly every DC – other than the special cadre of Bog Barons – as part of his professional education and could become a more permanent posting once one reached the staff officer rank, there were in the SPS a small number of postings which were, so to speak, *hors série*. These are typically described as Special Duties.

Some of the posts were inaugural. That is to say, as new policy directions were charted and directives implemented, it was in nine cases out of ten someone from the DC cadre who would be summoned to Khartoum and given responsibility for getting a fresh Department off the ground. R. Davies, for instance, became Secretary for Economic Development in the dire days of the early 1930s and W. P. D. Clarke officiated as Director of Posts and Telegraph before returning to Berber as Governor in 1931, while A. J. Matthew, who had been Deputy Governor of Berber Province in 1925, transferred to the Railways and Steamers Department in 1927 and ended up as its Assistant General Manager. A. J. Arkell became Commissioner for Archaeology and Anthropology after twenty-eight years as DC and Deputy Governor. After 1945 such special assignments proliferated, generated by the call for Labour Officers, Local Government Officers, Electoral Officers, and a Public Service Commission machinery. When after 1952 the Civil Secretary's and Financial Secretary's Offices and Departments were transformed into embryo Ministries, the SPS was further 'raided' to establish and man them. For instance, in the turning-point year of 1953, when self-determination was translated into a specified timetable, the new Ministry of Interior took in three junior (1949 entry) ADCs, G. F. Cox, M. Ward and R. G. C. Young as Assistant Secretaries, as well as the senior A. C. Beaton, G. W. Bell and B. D. Dee to become respectively its Permanent and Deputy Secretaries. The embryo Ministry of Local Government had had the young P. H. C. Pawson and M. P. Whitlock assigned to it in 1954. J. S. Owen became Commercial Director in the Ministry of Agriculture in 1952 and D. Vidler Commissioner of Lands in 1953. Many of the post-war probationers were transferred to Khartoum with much less field service than their predecessors.

Three Departments of the Sudan Civil Service had a particular link with the SPS. These were the Legal, Education and Intelligence Departments. While the transfer of the DC to the magistracy was never such a clear-cut career choice as with the ICS, it was natural that a number of officers might wish to build on the considerable judicial work they had undertaken as a DC and develop it professionally. Typically, T. Creed was, after three years in the provincial administration, first seconded to the Legal Department as a District Judge and then transferred to it after another three years. Less typically yet more significantly, he became Chief Justice of the Sudan in 1935 and, as Legal Secretary from 1941 to 1946, was one of Khartoum's bureaucratic Trinity. Yet another DC who became Chief Justice of the Sudan (1950) was W. Lindsay, who transferred out of the SPS in 1938. W. C. McDowall joined the Legal Department, after seven years as a DC, becoming Deputy Legal Secretary in the Advocate-General's Office in 1947 and a Judge of the High Court in 1951. D. F. Hawley, who had joined the SPS as the sole probationer in 1941 (and was immediately commissioned into the Sudan Defence Force as Bimbashi), joined the Legal Service after two tours in the provinces and in 1952 became Chief Registrar of the Judiciary. C. J. Treadwell and D. H. A. Wilson were among those who became Police Magistrates, while J. M. Hunter and H. C. N. M. Oulton became Resident Magistrates.

Leaving aside the fairly regular secondment of post-war probationers to the Middle East Centre of Arabic Studies (out of the enhanced 1944 intake of 10 ADCs, a third were so assigned), it was not uncommon for ADCs to be seconded, and sometimes transferred, to the Education Department. In particular, several moved to Gordon College (later the University of Khartoum).

K. D. D. Henderson was seconded for two years as Principal of the School of Administration and Police at Omdurman, where J. P. S. Daniell went as Dean in 1950 before moving on to the University College of Khartoum. Among others who transferred from the SPS to Education were G. C. Scott, after 10 years as DC, who in 1944 became the first Vice-Principal of the University College of Khartoum; D. H. Hibbert and A. B. Theobald, the former becoming Director of Education in 1950; and, from a pioneer generation, E. N. Corbyn, who became Director of Education in 1927 after twenty-three years as DC and Provincial Governor. More rarely, J. W. Meadows did it the other way round, transferring to the SPS in 1951 after spending four years as an Inspector of Education in the Southern Sudan.

Right from the beginning, with Kitchener and Wingate, then L. O. F. Stack in 1908, F. C. C. Balfour in 1921 and R. Davies in 1924, a tradition developed for the Intelligence Department to have DCs seconded to its Directorate. Two other posts that were nearly always filled from within the SPS were those of Private Secretary to the Governor-General and those relating to the country's outside representation, specifically the Sudan Agency in Cairo and in London. During the 1940s, DCs like J. A. A. Blaikie, P. P. Howell, W. G. R. M. Laurie, M. S. Lush and D. H. Weir, were seconded to the OETA (Occupied Enemy Territory Administration) in Eritrea and Cyrenaica. Assignment to the Palace as Private Secretary, while not every DC's cup of tea, could be rewarding for the right officer, and was always looked on as – and often found to be – recognition of a high flyer. It was usually no more than a two or three year appointment. Stack had been Private Secretary before returning to the Palace as Governor-General himself. Other notable DCs to have served as Private Secretary included M. W. Parr (twice, in fact, between 1928 and 1933, with a spell out as Deputy Governor of White Nile Province in between), M. S. Lush, E. O. Springfield and, the last of the line, J. S. R. Duncan. E. A. Pearson followed W. S. M. Johnston as Aide-de-Camp to the Governor-General in their early tours, the post being filled by an officer junior in rank to the Private Secretary. During the war years, P. P. Howell, R. G. McComas and J. W. Kenrick each combined the post of ADC with that of Assistant Private Secretary. The position of Sudan Agent in Cairo was generally held by a serving Provincial Governor while the corresponding London post was often given to a retired officer, possibly one, like R. C. Mayall, who held it for ten years, having been invalided out of the Service. This was an important link in the recruitment process at the London end each summer. Transfers out of the SPS into a sister Service were rare; the one-off SPS injection into the Colonial Service in the early 1950s is discussed in Chapter 8.

THE TRANSFER OF POWER

Britain's demission of authority in the Sudan in 1955 was characterized by at least three features which distinguished it from comparable events in her mid-twentieth century retreat from empire. First, it was the sole experience of a formalized transfer of power by the Foreign Office, in contrast to the India Office and in particular the Colonial Office, whose primary role this was in post-war South Asia and Africa from 1948 to 1966, with lessons to be learned for the Caribbean and Pacific in the 1970s and beyond. Secondly, here was the first dependent British territory – whatever the caveats needed to hedge such a definition of that rare constitutional hybrid, a Condominium – in Africa to become independent since the Union of South Africa was established in 1910. Thirdly, UN Trust Territories with their Visiting Missions and supervising plebiscites apart, here was the only occasion in Africa – until Southern Rhodesia (1980) and Namibia (1990) – where international concern was translated into an international presence. This took the form of three outside Commissions charged with guiding and overseeing the co-dominis' withdrawal from the Anglo-Egyptian Sudan and its dissolution ... a mission, in the mocking words of the British member of one of the Commissions, 'to frustrate British knavery'.[67]

It is this unusual international dimension which led to a situation unique in the dismantling of Britain's imperial administrations. One of the three Commissions was required to effect the localization ('Sudanization') of the Sudan Political Service, the Sudan Defence Force and the Police. What this meant, in short, was all Government posts likely to influence Sudanese decision-making, or, as the Agreement had it, posts which might affect the freedom of the Sudanese at the time of self-determination. In Khartoum, the embryo Ministry of the Interior, under whose jurisdiction the SPS now came, was set to working out a withdrawal plan (the military overtones of an evacuation were not inappropriate) whereby the process of Sudanization would begin at the lowest level of the Administration, the ADCs, and then work up through DC and Deputy Governor to the Provincial Governors and the top SPS posts in the Ministry itself. The need for young Sudanese administrators to gain some measure of experience in their accelerated advance to promotion posts was critical in the non-Arab South, long the fiefdom of the archetypal 'lone DC' and heir to the domain of the now-legendary Bog Barons.

Translated into practicality, what this meant was that alone in Britain's history of dismantling her empire in the twentieth century, her overseas civil servants (in this case, her widely respected SPS) were no longer seen to be trusted to be objective and supportive in their commitment to the transfer of power. The fact that this mistrust revealed a positive Egyptian rather than a popular Sudanese chemistry brought little comfort to the demoralized SPS officers *en poste*. The result was that, for the first and last time in the history of Britain's overseas civil services the Administrative Service was dismantled, localized and evacuated *before* independence.

In general, the SPS were less affronted by the brusqueness of the decision than engulfed in despair at the impracticality of the speed it envisaged. A policy of positive Sudanization had been in force since the seminal Administrative Conference of 1946, when a committee had been set up to make recommendations for the phased replacement of expatriates in the senior posts of the Sudan Civil Service. By 1952, out of the 136 established DC posts, 41 were held by Sudanese. All 39 governors and deputy governors were British.[68] The timetable aimed to reduce the number of Britons in the Civil Service from 694 in 1948 to 232 over the next 16 years. Now any hope of such a calculated and careful handover of the administration was gone. The SPS's successors would within a matter of months move into posts which would normally have come along in seven to ten years. Yet the Sudanization Committee, hell-bent on its determination to secure 'a free and neutral atmosphere', felt that even three years was an unnecessarily long time; their first assessment was that eighteen months should suffice. For the Egyptian press a mere fortnight would have been quite enough.[69] The British representative on the Commission, Colonel Burnett, found himself in a perpetual minority of one. Though many an expatriate would have cheerfully done what hundreds of his Colonial Service colleagues were to do elsewhere and stayed on to help the new nation through its independence, even accepting a transfer into the national civil service, this was not to be an option in the case of the Sudan.[70] In the absence of any such invitation, rumours spread that the SPS were closing ranks and, even among Sudanese officials, were coming out in favour of a rapidly promoted *mamur* (after all, could they not remind one another how Tiger Wyld, DC Yambio, had seen fit to leave his police sergeant-major to run his district when he went off on leave?) or a young graduate straight out from the School of Administration rather than take on a more senior and experienced official from one of the Departments as a DC or Provincial Governor.[71] In the end, the Ministry of the Interior succeeded in completing the accelerated Sudanization programme within nine months. Only seven British ADCs had been recruited in 1951–2, and none at all after the signing of the Anglo-Egyptian Agreement; over a hundred members of the SPS retired or were retired; not a single DC was left in the field; and by the end of 1955 the last half-dozen SPS officers were grouped into the Governor-General's personal staff in the Palace.[72]

The impact on the SPS was as deeply psychological as it was immediately practical. Members of the Service have variously described the implementation and the implications of the notice to quit implicit in the terms of reference of the 1953 Sudanization Committee as 'a major problem', 'a rude shock', 'a sudden end', 'an abrupt expulsion' and 'a bitter blow'.[73] The Sudanization Committee had, in the opinion of another member of the Service, simply 'run wild'.[74] Yet, in a major Service assessment gathered in retrospect many years after the event, the debate was marked by little bitterness and the complete absence of any vitriolic rhetoric about personal betrayal.[75] It was left, in 1953–5, to the more philosophical, likely to have been the younger DCs, and the occasional cynic among the Old Guard, to shrug their shoulders and, as they said goodbye to their chosen *sans pareil* career and began to look for a good second-best, to relapse into doggerel – that mental safety-valve to which so many of their predecessors had had recourse in moments of stress and despair that versification became part of the SPS tradition – and, as they penned their ballads on 'Sudanization Blues' and 'Roll on, Self-Determination', stoically reflect that

>We end our term imperial
>A trifle sooner than we thought before.[76]

A REPUTATION IN RETROSPECT

In attempting any such evaluation, sight must not be lost of the point made at the beginning of this chapter, namely that the SPS was at once the youngest, the shortest-lived, and the smallest of Britain's principal overseas civil services: no more than 500 Political Officers at work over 50 years all told.

Assessing a reputation is like buying a house: one must look at the inside as well as the outside. Though never on the tourist track, in contrast to neighbouring Egypt where the Pyramids and archaeological wonders provided a continuous attraction for visitors all the way from Thomas Cook to Agatha Christie and where European society could enjoy a long, leisurely and luxurious winter season in Cairo just as self-indulgently as in Cannes, the Sudan nevertheless had its share of travellers. Curious, observant and given to writing, they furnish some outside opinion on the role and reputation of the SPS.

Among such travel-writers, one of the most unusual was a Dutch journalist born in Constantinople called Odette Keun. Foreign, female, fearless and fanatically anti-British (she opens her monograph with the ringing declaration of 'I am not British ... most emphatically do I wish to state how I hold no brief for the British system ... when I went to the British Sudan I had *a priori* no disposition to enthusiasm'),[77] she nonetheless concluded her 1930 fact-finding tour of the Sudan and interviews with members of the SPS on a very different note. Contrary to her earlier affirmation that 'every single colony, protectorate and mandate-run country I have visited has invariably moved me to anger or despair and to expostulatory writings', here was a unique experiment in colonization. Internal as well as external evidence implies that at the root of her conversion lay the SPS. While she never ceased to wonder how that 'little body of alien men' did it, her conclusion, at the end of several pages of hero-worshipping, culminates in a paradox of praise: 'That [British] youth we know in Europe as a Nuisance and a Stupid has become one of an order of Samurai... The record is sterling throughout.' Such adulation was neither appreciated nor reciprocated by the Service. In Egypt the book was promptly banned.

Visiting in the 1930s too, the French writer Pierr Crabites was content to record his inspirational doubt 'whether any civil service in the history of the world has ever attained that degree of real merit, efficiency and usefulness which characterized the bureaucracy of the Sudan ... a model government'.[78] Another *a priori* anti-British writer was the American John Gunther. In his 1000-page encyclopaedic travelogue on the African continent in what was to turn out to be the dying days of the Condominium, he too succumbed to the allure of the SPS. Under the heading 'In Memoriam', his judgement is short and simple: 'This was probably the most elite body of its kind in the world … carefully chosen, impeccably trained … even more powerful and exclusive [than the ICS].'[79] The chief grievance that Gunther found in nationalist Khartoum was that the SPS was too expensive to maintain:

> The Sudanese resented the salaries and pensions the British got, their beautiful houses along the Nile, and also the fact that its members were part of a rigidly closed circle, all powerful and immune to criticism.

Yet he could discover among the Sudanese little of that 'active animus' against the British that pervaded neighbouring Cairo.

Another American, this time a historian, has been so fascinated by the Sudan DCs, including the Bog Barons, that from a lifetime's work on the country he has established himself as an authority and a sought-after consultant on the contemporary Sudan. Robert O. Collins' fourth volume in his quintet covering the past 100 years of the history of the Southern Sudan is a mine of information about Southern DCs. Of their individualistic and informative role Collins leaves his audience in no doubt. 'In the saga of the British in the Sudan, [British officials] were as important as paper to understanding what happened and why. Evening whiskey and dinner conversations were a vital part of the machinery of government.'[80]

A comparable approach is found in the mind of another, younger, American scholar who has devoted his writing to a study of British rule in the Sudan, Martin Daly. In his two-volume history of the imperial Sudan he develops the argument made elsewhere in the context of proconsular prosopography, that one cannot explain imperialism without an understanding of who the imperial agents were, and reaches what may be its ultimate rationalization in his conclusion that 'Personality not policy determined the course of the Condominium'.[81] Yet Daly has his reservations about the SPS, whose over-cited, close-knit and unique character and 'obsessive loyalty' to the Sudan may, he believes, have covered up 'the deficiencies of a one-career service'.[82] Emotion, he charges, not human logic or imperial imperative, ruled Khartoum's constitutional and political strategies in its final decade. Would, Daly pointedly asks, 'a transferred bureaucrat have answered the Graduates' Congress as Newbold did in 1942?' Daly concludes that when the SPS came to liquidate itself, 'it was not in favour of a new system but in order to take the Sudan, their Sudan, away with them'.

Two rather special kinds of outsider were C. S. Jarvis and Margery Perham. The former, a consular official in the Middle East and so arguably half-way to an understanding, tartly (and perhaps with some animus) accused the SPS of having 'accumulated practically all the male paragons of virtue in the Empire … 100 per cent cock-angels and nothing else'.[83] Their noble reputation he archly explained by the clever way in which Sudan DCs blew their own trumpet without ever playing their own instrument:

> If you should meet Brown of the Service he will not say a word about himself (though he may think a lot) but will tell you instead what marvels of efficiency

and foresight Smith and Robinson are; Smith will tell you the same thing about Robinson and Brown; while Robinson will play a French horn solo on the topic of Brown and Smith.

Margery Perham, scholar and acknowledged authority on colonial administration, somewhat lyrically concluded that Britons 'created one of the supreme types of their nation, that of the Colonial District Commissioner', nowhere more conspicuously so than in the Sudan.[84] Like Keun and Jarvis, though for different purposes, Perham had a personal interest in the Service, and in all probability she accorded the Sudan preference over Nigeria and Kenya in her ranking of imperial love affairs.

So much for some of the influential assessments of the SPS from the outside. In turning to the insiders, there are two distinct groups of observers to take into account: the SPS and the Sudanese. Further subdivisions, such as the opinion of the SPS held by Departmental officials, missionaries and commercial agents, or any variation in the views of Southern as opposed to Northern Sudanese, are not, for all their justifiable research validity, part of the equation here.

The SPS was proportionately a notably literate Service when it came to writing its memoirs. Significantly, perhaps, this turns out to have been a more frequent exercise after it was disbanded than during the normal tenure of a career job. A preliminary analysis of this insider literature has recently drawn attention to its potential for generating an additional view on nationalism in the Sudan, noting how the *post hoc* memoir is likely to contain more criticism of the SPS than anything written while the Service existed. In particular it devotes attention to the social gap between the urban, educated elite and the DC, whose heart and happiness may have been too long cocooned in the rural districts.[85] To that rich and generally consistent image of the Service revealed in their autobiographical writing, one may add the encomia from the top at either end of the SPS's existence, setting the Earl of Cromer's initial determination to create a cadre of '... active young men ... the flower of those turned out from our schools and colleges',[86] beside the tribute paid by the Permanent Secretary of the Foreign Office, in whose jurisdiction the SPS lay, to the Service on its termination as 'the finest body in the world ... all picked men, scholars and athletes'.[87] There is room, too, to recall the retrospective judgement of the most distinguished member of the Service at its dissolution, Sir James Robertson. Commenting on the legacy of the SPS, with its officers imbued with the highest standards of duty and honesty, his tribute lay in Virgil's epitaph to a colonial ideal nobly achieved: *pacisque imponere morem, parcere subjectis et debellare superbos*.[88] Overall, if, as the record positively implies, the average DC lived up to the homely homilies of that gentle giant of the Service, Douglas Newbold, then maybe their memorialist need look no further for the measure of their success:

> I only ask you to work hard, appreciate other viewpoints, keep calm and unruffled in the face of difficulties and setbacks ... respect continuity, and identify yourself with the Province... Don't be precipitate or inconclusive but

go ahead with reasonable reform... I want you to say 'I am a member of an important and honoured Service with moral and official responsibilities to the government and people of the Sudan...' Be compassionate, considerate, discriminate, impartial and philosophic.[89]

Yet, as one has the right to expect from members of an anything-but-yes-man Service, the SPS had its own critics too, dissenters rather than dissidents. If, in contrast to the articulate stormy petrels in their sister Services like Eric Blair (Burma), Leonard Woolf (Ceylon), Walter Crocker (Nigeria), or Norman Leys (Kenya), they preferred to keep quiet while their Service was still in being, once the Condominium was past history some were ready to speak up. One such analyst, an informed commentator rather than a critic *pur sang*, comes, significantly, from the post-war entry. After premature retirement, G. Balfour-Paul went on to three ambassadorial posts in the Middle East, and in his study of Britain's withdrawal from the region he allocates a complete chapter to what is effectively an epitaph on the SPS.[90] He reckons that the Service was able, intellectually, to combine a dedicated concern for the welfare of subject peoples with a light-hearted awareness of the irrationality of the whole business – 'the SPS laughed at itself from a position of supreme self-confidence'. To support his querying of the high reputation which the SPS had certainly acquired ('and relished: some of its members may have relished it more openly than was seemly'), Balfour-Paul invokes the criticism of an American student of the Service,[91] together with confidential comments by the first British Trade Commissioner despatched to Khartoum on the eve of independence. The latter accused the SPS of being merely in contact with rather than under the control of HMG, and concluded by asserting to HMG that its members had already 'outlived their usefulness as the autocratic rulers of the country'.

And what of the final, and most telling, element in this reputational synthesis, the view of 'the other' insiders, of the Sudanese themselves? In the crucial and continuing discourse of how 'they' viewed 'us', where insufficient attention has as yet been paid to the two-way imagology between the rulers (here the ICS, CAS, SPS) and the ruled, the case of the Sudan has achieved a pioneer status by narrowing the research from the generalized view to the specific of the relations and image of the governing elite. This represents a welcome, more considered, advance on the instant, 'expatriate' Sudanese view expressed, under the title of 'In Fairness to Them', where in fulsome terms which no member of the SPS would have dared to write as his memorial, 'the chivalrous, dignified withdrawal of the Englishman from the Sudan passes down to history as a monument of modesty' and leaves behind, as relic, 'the Englishman of the Sudan as a specimen of human perfection'.[92] In a preliminary evaluation appropriately written by a Sudanese and aptly titled 'In the Eyes of the Ruled', Francis M. Deng developed his premise that 'first encounters are frequently the most memorable', and through a series of verbatim recollections and reflections he reaches the moment when he can aver that the Sudanese have not forgotten the style as well as the substance of the departure of the imperial presence.[93]

Throughout the interviews there runs an accepted boundary between social barriers and well-remembered personal friendship. Deng stresses generational differences in the way individual DCs conducted their dealings with the Sudanese. He discerns a general feeling that, while in the 1930s and 1940s the DCs were 'more comfortable' with the Shaykhs in Sudanese society, for a brief period they began to switch their interest to the educated class who were also civil servants, yet rarely ever did anything but look down on the political elite when it operated outside the civil service. In a subsequent attempt to evaluate what they call 'the human factor in the British administration of the Sudan', Deng and Daly widen their enquiry – without, however, extending the very narrow base of their informants, a mere 17, all elites and all virtually successors to the British – and match it with the views of the rulers (twice as many), all former members of the SPS.[94] The dual conclusion is unchanged. One, the 'distaste' many SPS officers felt for the emerging, new, urban, intellectual elite of the 1930s. Two, while personal relationships of trust and even admiration developed, in most cases they simultaneously remained formal and impersonal. That last word suggests that perhaps there was, in reality as well as in the mind of the ruled, here and there too loud a resonance of the advice given as late as 1949 to a young SPS officer by one of his seniors on his transfer to Omdurman: 'My boy, always do your Town Rides and never have a Sudanese in the house.'[95]

This key relationship between the DC and the educated elite has also been explored within the context of the DCs' awareness of nationalism as revealed in their memoirs.[96] Here the dominant feature is the extent to which the average SPS officer (and the very concept of average implies exceptions) concentrated his enthusiasm and affection on the rural and chiefly classes at the cost of empathizing with, or at least striving to understand, the aspirations of the new, young, urban elite whom he and his administration had brought into being. The complementary opinions of a (Young Guard) SPS probationer and of a man-in-the-middle official of the Sudanese Government can be tellingly juxtaposed: J. S. R. Duncan's verdict on how his colleagues viewed the educated elite, 'It was their human failing to be aggressive and precocious; it was our human failing to underestimate their importance and, more reprehensible, to be impatient of their precociousness', set beside Edward Atiyah's shrewd judgement, from his position with a foot in both camps, that 'the average Englishman, like an old-fashioned parent, ... had little insight into the psychology of the new generation which he himself had educated'.[97] If such an image is generally correct, then that particular interpretation of how the ruled saw the rulers is far wider than a Sudan phenomenon. It is likely to have coloured – still with documented exceptions – the whole of Britain's overseas civil services' institutional (as opposed to individual) relationships.

What is still lacking in any such evaluation is the voice of the majority of the Sudanese, those who were not numbered among the elites: not only the semi-ruled, semi-ruling classes, the tribal chiefs and *mamurs* and civil service subordinates well down in the hierarchy (clerks, messengers, constables, drivers), but also the urban workers and the rural peasantry. There a different voice, another view, is likely to be manifest. Meanwhile, this chapter closes with Chief Babu Nimr's moving verdict on the pathos of the parting, 'We felt sad, not for love of colonial rule but for love of them as friends',[98] balanced by the caution of a latter-day DC that maybe after all the SPS were 'deceived', through Arab courtesy and their traditional technique for 'answering questions with more regard for giving pleasure than for brute fact', into believing that they enjoyed the respect and even the affection of the ordinary Sudanese.[99]

Overall, the impression continues to hold good that the SPS was not only a first class Service but also, as is frequently asserted, 'unique'; that it did have Sudanese interests at heart,[100] even if this virtue was Daly's 'proprietary instinct'[101]; and that individual friendships derived from mutual admiration and affection between ruler and ruled were frequent and firm. If proof were needed, it may lie in the apparent determination and willing memory, on the part of the survivors from both parties, to have promoted a mental legacy from fifty years ago.

7 Proconsuls at the Top

Empire is frequently analysed under such contradictory concepts as trusteeship and exploitation or under such single rubrics as ideology, the diffusion of ideas and the transfer of technology, or, in more recent retrospect, race relations, gender and cultural imperialism. Other, secondary but popular, interpretations rest on the evidence of fiction, themes of adventure and 'deeds of Empire', brought to a peak in the writings of G. A. Henty and Rudyard Kipling, or else focusing on the underbelly of imperial life, as depicted by those less enthusiastic for empire but keener for good copy, like George Orwell and Somerset Maugham. Yet outside the pages of the colonial novel and, in a narrower circle, outside the coffee rooms of Pall Mall clubs or afternoon tea at homes in Taunton and Tunbridge Wells, interest in – even concern with – who the overseas civil servants were and what the work of those pillars of empire was diminished after the Great War and rapidly evaporated after the Second World War.

The partial exception to this continuing disregard for the activities and achievements of those whom the American Robert Heussler has labelled 'Yesterday's Rulers' and the British Michael Crowder 'The White Chiefs'[1] was to be found, still not much more than now and again, in a nodding acquaintance with the names at the topmost, individual level of administration overseas: some of the Viceroys, several governors-general, and perhaps a few colonial governors and high commissioners. These have often been looked on as the ultimate proconsuls of fact and fiction. From time to time just a handful reached the status of temporary household recognition.

Yet the irony of indifference and ignorance remains. Only a fraction of those who achieved the highest office in India and the Sudan, and only a proportion of those appointed to governorships in the colonial empire before 1930 were drawn from within the ranks of those career overseas civil servants who have been at the centre of Chapters 4–6. For instance, a mere four of the thirty-three Governors-General and Viceroys of India between 1774 and 1947 had had some previous experience of service in India; only one of them came from within the ICS. In the Sudan, only one of its nine Governors-General had previously been a member of the Sudan Political Service. Excluding the three 'fortress' colonies of Gibraltar, Malta and Bermuda, where the governorship traditionally lay in the gift of the armed services, two-thirds of the colonial governorships in 1851 were held by political or military nominees.[2] This proportion was still over half at the turn of the century. Even though the Colonial Office strongly endorsed the recommendation by the influential Warren Fisher committee on colonial appointments in 1930 that only in exceptional cases should it look outside the Colonial Service when it came to the selection of governors, of the 103 men who held gubernatorial office between 1919 and 1939, forty-nine had not started their career in the Colonial Service.[3] For a quarter of these, their first appointment to that Service was in the rank of Governor. In two principal dependencies, Kenya had never had a career Colonial Service governor before 1940, while only two High Commissioners of Palestine were career overseas civil servants. Even during the 'end of empire' period, between 1940 and 1960, career Colonial Service men held no more than 78 of the appointments made to a colonial governorship.[4] In a number of cases, the nomination of the terminal governor-general went to a politician.

Because these are the men (there were no proconsular women involved before Canada, in somewhat different circumstances, innovatively chose Madame Jeanne Sauvé as its Governor-General in 1984, shortly followed by New Zealand's choice of Dame Catherine Tizard for its governor-generalship in 1990,[5] in an age when female heads of state and prime ministers had become more usual) who did succeed for some of the time in eliciting some interest by some sections of the metropole about their role, responsibilities and record; who seemed to symbolize what was understood by ritual references back home to 'our Indian Empire' or 'our colonial dependencies'; yet who were in no way regularly drawn from the career civil services anatomized in the preceding chapters, they call for separate treatment in this study.

TITLES

The spread and status of proconsular titles were as varied as were many of the holders of the posts. While India was content to have its top post renamed from Governor-General in 1774, first of Bengal (where Clive had become the first Governor in 1758) and then of India, to that of Viceroy in 1858 (the rank was also introduced by Gladstone for the Lord Lieutenant of Ireland in the 1870s), and the Sudan retained the title of Governor-General throughout the fifty-six years of the Condominium, both territories also made use of the common colonial ranks of Governor or Chief Commissioner. In India, for example, each Presidency or Province was for most of the time headed by a Governor (Bengal, Bombay, Punjab, United Provinces among the larger ones, Assam, Orissa, Bihar among the smaller) answerable to the Viceroy in New Delhi (earlier at Calcutta). However, a common administrative evolution was to inaugurate a Chief Commissioner's Province before it was recognized as a full-scale Governor's Province. For example, the Punjab was administered by a Chief Commissioner in 1856, a Lieutenant-Governor from 1859, and a Governor after 1921. Similarly in Burma, the post went from Chief Commissioner in 1885 to Lieutenant-Governor in 1897 and Governor in 1923, finally separating from India in 1937 as a Crown Colony. On the other hand, the North-West Frontier Province and Sind had their status raised from a Chief Commissioner's to a full Governor's province in 1932 and 1936 respectively, whereas both Baluchistan and Delhi were headed by a Chief Commissioner right up to independence. In the Indian case, the changes in proconsular rank were sometimes consequential on changes in the administrative boundaries. In the colonies, particularly in the final years, such changes in upper-level nomenclature generally reflected a shift in constitutional arrangements.

The Sudan was the other instance of the constituent parts being administered by a series of Governors rather than the whole itself, as was characteristic of the colonial territories; Nigeria, which reverted to a governorship for each of its regions in 1954 after a lapse of over forty years, remained *sui generis*. In the Sudan each of the Provinces, nine for much of the time, was administered by a Governor (Kordofan, Darfur, White Nile, Equatoria, etc.) responsible to the Governor-General. In the colonial empire, on the other hand, Governor was the conventional rank of the sole and supreme administrative authority and the recognized representative of His or Her Majesty in the country. Thus, in pro-consular terminology, the title of Governor could involve a different status in different countries.

Nor was the rank of Governor-General, traditional in the four Dominions (in Canada and Australia subordinate Provincial or State Governors also existed) and in the Anglo-Egyptian Sudan, and coexistent in the letters patent with the more usually used title of Viceroy, exclusive to those countries. In Nigeria, the rank of Governor-General was conferred on Sir Frederick Lugard as part of the scheme for amalgamating the previous separate Protectorates of Northern and Southern Nigeria into the new Colony and Protectorate of Nigeria in 1914. It lapsed on his retirement in 1919 and was then revived with the constitutional reform of 1954. In the colonial context, the title was also used in the short-lived Federations of Malaya (1946–8), of the West Indies (1958–62) and of Central Africa (1953–63). In a number of colonial possessions, the rank of Governor-General was conferred, for the first and generally last time, on the final British appointee. This might be the incumbent, ultimate Colonial Service governor, who was simultaneously invited to stay on for 6–12 months and become the first Governor-General of the new, independent state. Examples include Sir Charles Arden-Clarke in Ghana, Sir Richard Turnbull in Tanganyika, and Sir Kenneth Blackburne in Jamaica. Occasionally, this appointment was succeeded by another Governor-General, this time a political figure following on the terminal Colonial Service one, for instance the Earl of Listowel in Ghana (1957–60). Exceptionally Sir Maurice Dorman became post-independence Governor-General of both Sierra Leone (1961–2) and Malta (1964–71). Uniquely, Malcolm Macdonald's rank of Governor-General of Malaya was redesignated High Commissioner in 1948 and then raised to Commissioner-General of South East Asia (1948–55).

Governor and High Commissioner were the most widespread top ranks within the British dependent empire. For most purposes they were of comparable status. However, just as Ambassador and High Commissioner can rank *inter pares*, and are in theory interchangeable as regards posting in the post-colonial hierarchy of Commonwealth Diplomatic Services while recognizing that there are grades within grades, so there were distinctions within the rank of Governor and High Commissioner in the colonial empire. The High Commissionership of, say, the Western Pacific was not on a par with that of Palestine. The key variables in this hierarchy at the top, essentially – but not solely – size of territory and population and hence the level of salary, are discussed later.

Before that, consideration must be given to the many titles used to designate quasi-gubernatorial office, locally recognized as sole administrator yet not invested with sole command, i.e., still retaining accountability to a higher authority somewhere in the territory, and hence not entitled to correspond directly with the Colonial Office. Examples of this quasi-gubernatorial office include Lieutenant-Governorship, for instance the Colonial Service or Office appointment as second-in-command to the traditionally military Governor of Gibraltar or Malta, the number two in Hong Kong from time to time, or the senior regional administrators in Nigeria responsible to the Governor in Lagos; between 1933 and 1951 these alternated from Lieutenant-Governor and Chief Commissioner and then back to Lieutenant-Governor of the Northern and Southern (later Western and Eastern) Provinces. Chief Commissioner was a regular high rank in the Gold Coast, too, whereas in India it was usually found in provinces which had yet to be (if ever) upgraded to a governorship, e.g. Assam or the Andaman and Nicobar Islands. In territories like Uganda, Nyasaland and Kenya (then still British East Africa) which had started out under the jurisdiction of the Foreign Office and then been transferred to the Colonial Office, the change-over was marked by the retitling of the post from H. M. Commissioner to colonial Governor. The Resident Commissioner of the Gilbert and Ellice Islands or of the British Solomon Islands Protectorate both came under the High Commissioner of the Western Pacific. A similarly quasi-gubernatorial rank obtained in the High Commission Territories in South Africa: Resident Commissioner in Botswana, Basutoland and Swaziland, subsequently restyled Her Majesty's Commissioner. The title of Resident, as in Brunei, implied a more advisory than administrative responsibility; it was also used for those Indian Political Service officers appointed to the Indian States. The British Resident of Zanzibar was awarded gubernatorial recognition, after its serial nomenclature from Consul in 1840 through Consul-General in 1873 under the Foreign Office to Resident under the Colonial Office in 1914. In the Arab states, the most common proconsular title was Resident or Political Agent. Largely drawn from the Indian Political Service, they were to be found in, for example, Kuwait, Bahrain and Aden. When the last-named territory was transferred from the aegis of the India to the Colonial Office in 1937, the senior post was restyled Governor. Sir Bernard Reilly's proconsular career was thus exceptional, having been appointed Political Agent of Aden in 1931, promoted its Chief Commissioner in 1932, and upgraded to Governor of Aden in 1937.

The lowest of these quasi-subordinate, quasi-gubernatorial superscale proconsular ranks was that of Administrator. Examples of its usage include those officials in charge of the smaller islands in the Caribbean, for instance the latter-day British Virgin, Cayman, or Turks and Caicos Islands. The Seychelles were also under an Administrator between 1889 and 1903, when the post was redesignated Governor. In the case of the Andaman and Nicobar Islands under the Indian administration, the chief official was a Superintendent until he was upgraded to Chief Commissioner in 1872.

The lesser, in no way quasi-gubernatorial and emphatically subordinate ranks of Provincial Commissioner, Provincial Governor (Sudan) and Resident (with, in the Federated Malay States as in the Indian princely states, a slightly more 'diplomatic' role attaching to it than in the lineally linked Nigeria or even the *ad hoc* case in Uganda), were, in contrast to the top echelons of proconsular appointments under examination in this chapter, filled almost without exception by promotion from within their respective career Services and not by appointment from London. They are accordingly left in their respective Service Chapters 5 and 6.

Among the gubernatorial class, then, while there is sufficient, though by no means exact, comparability to allow the Sudan data to be handled alongside that of the Colonial Service, the case of the Viceroys of India is distinct enough to require separate treatment.

INDIA: THE VICEROYS

With a proconsular history covering almost 200 years, twice the span of the colonial empire created by the 'new imperialism' and four times that of the life of imperial Sudan, and with an influential image projected since Disraeli's day of India as the centrepiece of the British (especially Queen Victoria's and her son King Edward VII's) crown, it is not surprising that the post of Viceroy of India was recognized as the premier British appointment overseas.

Between 1758 and 1947, thirty-three Governors-General and Viceroys were appointed, fourteen by the East India Company and twenty by the Crown – Canning was, uniquely, appointed by the Company in 1856 and two years later confirmed by the Crown in his reappointment. Unusually, too, Cornwallis was reappointed in 1805, having already held office from 1786 to 1793. The mean age on appointment was 49; Dalhousie was only 35 and Curzon 39. However, both Willingdon and Reading were over 60 when they assumed office, and Cornwallis was 66 when he went out for the second time. The average tenure of the Viceroyship was five and a half years. At the two ends of the spectrum, Warren Hastings held it for thirteen years (1772–85) if one includes his period in the antecedent Governorship of Bengal, and the elder of the Elgins and Mountbatten for less than two – indeed, the latter held office for only six months. As many as a tenth of the Viceroys died in office.

Six of them had had a military career before their appointment, and one had been an admiral. Another five had been diplomats. Only four had previously had professional career experience of Indian administration. It is widely believed that Sir Malcolm Hailey, Governor of the Punjab (1924–8) and then of the United Provinces (1928–34) could have become the second appointment from within the ICS had it not been for his wife's problems.[6] Only one Governor of an Indian Presidency (Bentinck) was ever made Viceroy, and only

Table 7.1 Governors-General and Viceroys of India, 1758–1947

Governors of Bengal

1758–1760 & 1765–67	Lord Clive
1772–1774	Warren Hastings

Governors-General

1774–1785	Warren Hastings
1786–1793	Marquess Cornwallis
1793–1798	Sir John Shore, Lord Teignmouth
1798–1805	Earl of Mornington, Marquess Wellesley
1805	Marquess Cornwallis
1807–1813	Earl of Minto
1814–1823	Earl of Moira, Marquess of Hastings
1823–1828	Earl Amherst
1828–1835	Lord William Bentinck
1835–1842	Earl of Auckland
1842–1844	Earl of Ellenborough
1844–1848	Viscount Hardinge
1848–1856	Marquess of Dalhousie
1856–1858	Earl Canning

Governors-General and Viceroys

1858–1862	Earl Canning
1862–1863	Earl of Elgin
1863–1869	Lord Lawrence
1869–1872	Earl of Mayo
1872–1876	Earl of Northbrook
1876–1880	Earl of Lytton
1880–1884	Marquess of Ripon
1884–1888	Marquess of Dufferin
1888–1894	Marquess of Lansdowne
1894–1899	Earl of Elgin
1899–1905	Marquess Curzon
1905–1910	Earl of Minto
1910–1916	Lord Hardinge of Penshurst
1916–1921	Viscount Chelmsford
1921–1926	Marquess of Reading
1926–1931	Lord Irwin, Earl of Halifax
1931–1936	Marquess of Willingdon
1936–1943	Marquess of Linlithgow
1943–1947	Earl Wavell
1947	Earl Mountbatten

Source: Viscount Mersey, *The Viceroys and Governors-General of India*, 1949, 163.

one member of the ICS (Lawrence), though, as Curzon commented, 'many have hoped for and even been promised the elevation'.[7] Between 1859 and 1899 no less than five Viceroys had been Under-Secretaries for India. All but four of the Viceroys were political and not Service appointments. The link with politics was underlined by the fact that nearly half had sat in the House of Commons and a similar number in the House of Lords before their appointment to India, and more than half had held Cabinet Office or subordinate office in the Administration. Curzon was Under-Secretary for Foreign Affairs, and after leaving India became Foreign Secretary. On his retirement, Bentinck declined a peerage and went into the House of Commons. In the Canadian case, on the other hand, no less than half of the British Governors-General appointed between 1867 and 1947 had previously been Members of Parliament or had held ministerial office. Three Viceroys were sons of a Prime Minister and a fourth was a brother. Canning's father, Prime Minister George Canning, had declined the Viceroyalty. Two were related by marriage to Prime Minister Castlereagh and another two had been friends and close associates (one a godson). No Viceroy ever went on to become Prime Minister of Britain, though Curzon, in presenting his anatomy of his predecessors, took care to hedge such a statement with 'has ever yet'.[8] Similarly, no Secretary of State for India ever became Viceroy, though two holders of the predecessor office of President of the Board of Control did. One Viceroy was a member of the royal family, against two in Canada's case and one each in the case of South Africa and Australia, though it now appears that the Prince of Wales was offered the Governor-Generalship of Australia in 1988.[9] According to Mersey, 'during the Regency, friendship with the Prince of Wales was occasionally an element in their choice'.[10] It is also said that the fact that Willingdon had been a regular lawn-tennis partner of King George V was not forgotten when names were under consideration to succeed Byng in Canada and Irwin in India.[11] Curzon, arguably *plus royal que le roi*, did not favour the idea of a Royal Viceroy.

The viceregal India–Canada link is substantial. In less than fifty years, four Viceroys, the supreme imperial appointment, had held previous office as Governor-General of Canada, the senior Dominion. Lansdowne, Minto and Willingdon all went straight from Ottawa to Calcutta (later Delhi), while Dufferin held ambassadorial appointments at St Petersburg and Constantinople between leaving Canada in 1878 and becoming Viceroy in 1884. Furthermore, both Lorne, married to a daughter of Queen Victoria, and Tweedsmuir had hoped to crown their proconsular career in Canada with the prize of India. While it is unlikely that we shall ever learn the names of all those who were discreetly sounded out or shortlisted for the post of Viceroy, or who actually turned down a post looked on in the public esteem as second only to that of Prime Minister, researchers of the viceroyalty have hinted at Sir Henry Norman and Lord Milner among the latter category. Curzon devotes a half chapter of his close study of the Viceroys to 'the story of contested or abortive appointments to the Governor-Generalship'.[12]

Two-thirds of the Viceroys were English, with six each Scots and Irish. The link between the Irish Peerage and the Viceroyalty is marked. Even more unusual than the fact that 14 were educated at Oxford University (and, less surprisingly perhaps, over 40 per cent at Eton) and seven of them successively from 1884 to 1910 against only four at Cambridge, is the statistic that ten of these were at Christ Church. In familial terms, the prosopographical data are equally remarkable. In the case of the Elgins both father (1862) and son (1894) were Viceroy; with the Hardinges, grandfather (1844) and grandson (1910) were both Viceroy; and with the Mintos, great-grandfather (1807) and great-grandson (1905) each held the office of Governor-General. As Governor of Bombay, Lytton's son once acted for the Viceroy when he was on leave in England. Another close blood relationship was nephew and uncle, as with Auckland and the first Minto.

SUDAN: THE GOVERNOR-GENERAL

The top proconsular corpus of the Anglo-Egyptian Sudan constitutes approximately half of the Indian data in time and a quarter of it in the number of office-holders involved. In the Sudan's 56-year history as the locus of one of Britain's overseas civil services, there were only nine Governors-General. Of these, two held office for one year apiece; one, Wingate, occupied the Palace in Khartoum for seventeen years.

Only one Governor-General had risen through the ranks of the Sudan Political Service. This was Stack. The proportion is thus similar to the case of the Viceroys, where only four of the thirty-three came in from the Indian Civil or its anterior Company Service. As became a possession brought under British control after a colonial war which stirred the imagination of the British public, the Sudan, immortally connected in the British mind with the name of General Gordon, looked to the military for its first Governor-General. Military men spanned the first 25 years (and, by the end, just about half) of its existence. Kitchener, Wingate, Stack were all generals; Symes, too, came from the army; and the military tradition was revived towards the end of the Condominium with the appointment of another general, Huddleston, to the strategically sensitive Sudan during the Second World War.

Of the rest, Archer came in briefly from the Colonial Service. The last two Governors-General, Howe and Helm, were career diplomats, selected because of the latter-day difficulties with a post-monarchical revolutionary Egypt over the future of the Anglo-Egyptian Sudan. They were, too, the only appointments to reflect the link, hitherto however gossamer, with the Sudan's 'parent' Ministry back in London, both of them having previously held senior diplomatic posts.

Maffey, who was Governor-General from 1926 to 1933, represents one of the more unusual appointments in the context of proconsular promotions among Britain's overseas civil servants. Not only was he the single member of the Indian Civil Service to have been appointed to the Governor-Generalship of the Sudan (he went from the Chief Commissionership of the North-West Frontier Province), an example of Lord Swinton's radical thinking in Whitehall that one-Service top proconsular appointments would have much to gain from a touch of imperial cross-fertilization;[13] he was also one of only four Governors in

Table 7.2   Governors-General of the Sudan, 1899–1955

Herbert Horatio (Lord) Kitchener	19	Jan	1899	–	22	Dec	1899
Sir Reginald Wingate	23	Dec	1899	–	31	Dec	1916
Sir Lee Stack	1	Jan	1917	–	20	Nov	1924
Sir Geoffrey Archer	4	Dec	1924	–	17	Oct	1926
Sir John Maffey	24	Oct	1926	–	13	Nov	1933
Sir Stewart Symes	10	Jan	1934	–	14	Oct	1940
Sir Hubert Huddleston	15	Oct	1940	–	7	Apr	1947
Sir Robert Howe	8	Apr	1947	–	10	Mar	1955
Sir Alexander Knox Helm	11	Mar	1955	–	31	Dec	1955

Source: M. W. Daley, 'Principal Office-Holders in the Sudan Government, 1895–1955', *International Journal of African Historical Studies*, 17, 2, 1984.

the British Empire to have held the traditionally Home Civil Service post of Permanent Under-Secretary at the Colonial Office. The others were Sir John Anderson, earlier Governor of the Straits Settlements, General Sir Samuel Wilson, one-time Governor of Jamaica, and Sir John Macpherson, previously Governor-General of Nigeria and the sole career Colonial Service man to have occupied the post.

GOVERNORS OF THE COLONIAL OFFICE TERRITORIES

The Colonial Office data, even when covering the same fifty years or so of the Sudan corpus and extended over just about the same century as the Indian viceroyalty, generates statistics of many times the combined totals of those pro-consular office-holders. With over thirty colonies to be governed at the turn of the century, and further responsibilities added after the First World War (Palestine and a number of ex-German colonies in Africa and the Pacific) bringing it up to nearly forty territories by 1947, the total of people holding a colonial governorship between *c.*1866 and 1966, the year in which the Colonial Office closed its doors, exceeds 400. Of these, perhaps half held African governorships at one time or another. Thus in presenting and interpreting the multiple gubernatorial data, greater selectivity is imposed than for the less populated 'single' contexts of the Viceroy of India and the Governor-General of the Sudan. It is also more meaningful to periodize rather than total the appointments to colonial governorships.

With such a huge number of colonial appointments to dispose of, it is not to be wondered at that the range of occupation from which their holders was drawn is far more varied than that obtaining in the case of the India or Sudan appointments. While the Colonial Service can point to a regulatory rulebook dating back to 1837, no such unified Service existed in practice before 1930.

There were numerous territorial Services but no single Colonial Service. Consequently, professional Colonial Service appointments to a governorship, identifiable from the mid-nineteenth century, do not dominate the field until what, in the event, turned out to be the last quarter-century of the Colonial Office's existence.[14] Out of the 110 colonial governors appointed between 1940 and 1960, seventy-eight came to this office at the end of a full-time Colonial Service career. Forty-nine of these had served principally in tropical Africa and twenty in the Eastern Cadetship colonies of Ceylon, Malaya and Hong Kong. Nevertheless, in the same period another 17 governorships went to persons who had come into the Colonial Service laterally – but still below the rank of gover- nor – from another career. Among these gubernatorial appointments, five came from the legal profession, four from the army, and three from the Home Civil Service. A further 15 were appointed from outside the Colonial Service direct to a colonial governorship. This included three each from politics, the army and the Home Civil Service (again, not necessarily the Colonial Office). Only one, C. N. E. Eliot, ever came from the Diplomatic Service, and that was to British East Africa in 1900.

When we turn to the generation covering the years 1920–40, while the total number of appointments to a colonial governorship was virtually the same (103 against 110), the distribution was significantly higher in those appointed from outside. Nearly twice as many came from other careers, predominantly the army (22), and three times as many appointments were made from MPs – pre- empting Patten to Hong Kong fifty years later – including one cabinet minister, H. L. Samuel; one journalist (admittedly *The Times*), E. Grigg; and one trade unionist, J. O'Grady. Only 54, less than half, were able to count a governorship as the peak of their full Colonial Service career, compared with nearly three- quarters in the period 1940–60.

Taking the analysis back to before the First World War, expectedly appoint- ments to colonial governorships are dominated by military and political men. The proportion of Colonial Service promotions is correspondingly lower still, though there was emerging a small number of what one can justifiably identify as 'professional' governors, men with long experience of administering overseas populations on behalf of the Colonial Office and, in some cases, as employees of one or another Chartered Company where names like Lugard and R. T. Coryndon furnish leading examples. Cromer and Milner, too, were every inch professional proconsuls round the turn of the century. Many of the new breed of colonial professionals had learned their apprenticeship in the Eastern dependencies, where Crown rule was established far earlier than in Tropical Africa – for example, W. E. Maxwell. This was also the period when the pre- Dominions colonies were very much part of the colonial governorship pattern of transfer: W. F. Hely-Hutchinson governed the Windward Islands, Natal and Cape Colony; Matthew Nathan was successively governor of the Gold Coast, Hong Kong and Queensland; the highly experienced Hercules Robinson in turn governed Hong Kong, Ceylon, New South Wales, New Zealand, and Cape Colony; and Arthur Havelock went one better than them all by including the

Governorship of an Indian Presidency (Madras) in his tally of six governorships between 1881 and 1904. Stretching the inquiry back to the middle of the nineteenth century, one notices the high number of military appointments from the 1860s to the end of the century, averaging 25 per cent and peaking at 40 per cent in the 1860s, and the steady proportion, about 15 per cent, of political appointees, reaching 30 per cent in the 1870s. The number of the new breed of professionals appointed grew from three in the 1850s and a third between 1860 and 1880 to about half of the 30 posts available in the 1890s.

While, in modern Colonial Service circles, the appointment of a military man was sometimes acceptable (after all, in the aftermath of the Great War and again after the Second World War there was ample military experience throughout the ranks of the Service to understand and sometimes endorse the hierarchical and disciplinary attitudes often displayed), and that of a politician, especially in the tricky terminal phase of empire, could now and again be positively welcomed, most of the Service suspicion and hostility seems to have fallen on those Colonial Office officials who were appointed to a governorship. G. H. Creasy, for instance, able home civil servant and an official respected by Colonial Service governors while he was at the Office, and, more arguably, A. B. Cohen, one of the outstanding CO officials of the day, were held by many to have come to grief in their respective governorships. Some officials in the Gold Coast still hold Creasy responsible, however unfairly, for the eruption of the Accra riots in 1948, while in Uganda, for all the positive developmental advancements of Cohen, some older officers gleefully indulged in the game of asking what would have happened to *their* careers had they mishandled the senior chief in the same way as Cohen had summarily deported the Kabaka in 1953.[15] The use of the word 'gleefully' here is not accidental: the possibility of jealousy and *Schadenfreude* should not be dismissed from any consideration of the Colonial Service view of Colonial Office governors.

If the Colonial Service threw up no proconsular titans or neo-household names like Clive, Warren Hastings, Lawrence, Curzon and Wavell in India, or Kitchener and Wingate, 'The Master', in the Sudan, this was arguably attributable to a very different context. Yet big names there were among governors. Lugard was a legend in his lifetime, with twenty years as colonial governor and then the influential British Delegate to the Permanent Mandates Commission of the League of Nations. Nor was the publicity achieved through his writings and through the shrewd lobbying of Westminster and Whitehall by his wife Flora Shaw, formerly *The Times* Africa correspondent, a handicap. In the immediate wake of the First World War, H. C. Clifford, who had held four colonial governorships, was publicly acknowledged by the Secretary of State for the Colonies as the doyen of his Service generation. Different criteria of assessment would obtain for a post-Second World War list, but in the difficult 1950s and delicate 1960s the Colonial Office saw to it that its Colonial Service had many a first-rate governor for its new objective of the transfer of power.

So much for the personalities; next the practicalities. The normal term of appointment was five years. Because the retiring age was 55, in the normal process this meant that a colonial civil servant might expect no more than one – if any – governorship. A term of office could be extended, usually by two years. This was not always a success. The most widely instanced case is that of P. E. Mitchell, who, one-time rising star of the Colonial Service and appointed to the first of his three governorships well before he was fifty, served out his last renewed tour of duty in Kenya at a time when fresh – and healthy – blood might have produced sounder policies. Clifford, too, who held major governorships for 17 years, was sorely troubled by health problems in his last years of office in Nigeria and Malaya. To spend more than five years in the same governorship was unusual, and when it did occur it was more common before rather than after 1914. H. L. Galway spent nine years in the unexercising post of St Helena, G. C. Denton eleven in the mini-governorship of the mini-Gambia, and H. C. Sloley fifteen years as Resident-Commissioner of the fairly isolated and slow-moving Basutoland. Longevity in one Government House was not necessarily a matter of declining competence – nor, for that matter, the hallmark of irreplaceable distinction. Nonetheless, on the assumed link between marked ability and length of gubernatorial tenure (serial rather than the single post of the Sudan), it is remarkable how many men held colonial governorships for between two and three times the standard term of five years. R. T. Coryndon, A. E. Havelock and W. F. Hely-Hutchinson were all colonial governors for more than twenty years, two-thirds of the normal length of a Colonial Service career.

Having given consideration to those career aspects of the ultimate proconsuls which are best presented on an individual territorial (India) or Service (Sudan and Colonial) basis because of their several particularities, it is now possible to move to other prominent aspects of 'life at the top'. These can be usefully subsumed under general rubrics, despite the clear differences within the basic similarity of the wider context.

APPOINTMENT

How were appointments made to these supreme proconsular posts, held in the Indian instance as ranking only after the Prime Ministership, and commonly acknowledged in the case of major colonial governments like Ceylon and Malaya, Palestine and Hong Kong, Nigeria and Kenya as 'the plums of the Service'?

Although Mersey, in his summary of India's Governors-General, is adamant that the Viceroyalty was only rarely a political reward,[16] few would deny that political considerations were prominent in the selection. Even if a comparison between the ideology of the political party which appointed him and his own previous partisan preference on the one hand, and on the other a change in the complexion of the incoming administration and the timing of a change in the Viceroyalty (where the average term of office was less than six years) does not respond to an immediate correlation, there is little doubt that in making up their mind whose name to recommend to the sovereign, the party, policy and political needs of Westminster were not to be overlooked and were nearly always instrumental, sooner rather than later. The Viceroyalty may not have been a political prize for services already rendered, but it was surely an anticipation of political loyalty to come.

While it is unlikely that we shall ever have access to the most conclusive evidence of all on the criteria for nomination, namely the names and credit/debit qualities on the government of the day's short list of candidates for consideration – not excluding those who were no longer on it because of their negative reaction to a preliminary, probably quite personal, sounding out – it is not hard to build up a persuasive 'political' argument to explain the eventual appointment of each Viceroy. To take just one example, if one adds to the general requisites the particular position of India in 1943, with its very safety under grave threat of invasion on the eastern front by the Japanese so successful in overrunning Burma and Malaya and capturing the *soi-disant* impregnable British base of Singapore, it was inevitable that military (in no way the simple antithesis of political) considerations would prevail for a successor to the already-overdue-for-retirement Linlithgow. The solution was, continuing an earlier tradition of the Viceroyalty in Cornwallis (1786), Moira (1814) and Hardinge (1844), another serving general, Wavell. That his successor should have been a serving admiral was, by 1947, on the other hand a purely political one. Mountbatten was, not so much also but above all, royalty; and this was a moment in Britain's imperial history when a unique experiment in the transfer of power called for a unique appointment as the last Viceroy of India.

Finally, whether over and above all this or just as one more desideratum, the Sovereign's indispensable assent to the appointment carried an endorsement that here was a fit and proper person to be, quite literally, His (Her) Majesty's personal representative, the *vice-roi*.

In the case of the Sudan, although this was a Foreign Office responsibility, it was inconceivable, both in its origins and during the two world wars during which the country enjoyed an acknowledged strategic importance, particularly in 1939–45, that the military factor would not be brought into play in tandem with personal and administrative qualities. This was the incontrovertible reason for the appointment of the Sudan's first governor-general, Kitchener, in 1899. Experienced in military intelligence in Cairo, *Sirdar* or Commander-in-Chief of the Egyptian Army, and the general who led the spectacular Sudan campaign of 1898 to wrest the country from the Mahdi, who better – who else – could there be for the new governor-generalship of the Anglo-Egyptian Condominium of the Sudan than 'Kitchener of Khartoum'? When Kitchener was despatched by the War Office to South Africa, now a Field-Marshal and subsequently (if calamitously in personal relations with the Viceroy)[17] Commander-in-Chief of India, it was still too early for London to contemplate the appointment of anybody but another military man to Khartoum. In choosing Wingate, his record fitted exactly. He it was who had led the Nile expedition of 1885, who had been Director of Military Intelligence in Cairo, and who had succeeded

Kitchener as *Sirdar* of the Egyptian Army. But whereas Kitchener occupied the Palace at Khartoum for less than seventeen months, Wingate remained in it for seventeen years. When he left to become High Commissioner for Egypt, it was in the middle of a world war which witnessed major campaigns on African soil, all the way across from the west (Togo and Cameroon) to east (Tanganyika) and southern (Nyasaland). Once more, London looked to the Directorate of Military Intelligence in Cairo for filling the governor-generalship, finding their man in General Lee Stack. Yet again, in 1940, with first a large enemy presence in neighbouring East Africa (this time, Italian rather than German-led *askari*) to be dealt with, and then the contiguous Egypt emerging as the critical theatre for the turning-point North African campaign, the Foreign Office and the War Office had little difficulty in agreeing that the right thing to do would be to appoint another military man to Khartoum. General Hubert Huddleston had not only been officer commanding India's Western Command since 1945, he had also commanded the Sudan Brigade in 1924.

Among the non-military governors-general of the Sudan (and if the civilian appointments outnumbered the military ones by five to four, they accounted for but 24 years of office to the military's 32), two appointments were directly attributable to the personal lead of Cunliffe Lister (later Lord Swinton) as Secretary of State for the Colonies. In bringing in J. L. Maffey, a career Indian Political Service officer, and G. S. Symes, who had held a number of Colonial Service appointments though not as part of a career structure, Cunliffe Lister gave shape to his feeling that the Sudan Political Service, for all its sterling qualities, inevitably suffered from a degree of isolation and career-capping. Several times smaller than the ICS and lacking the world-wide opportunities for transfer opened up by the unification of the Colonial Administrative Service since 1932, the SPS could, in Cunliffe Lister's opinion, neither benefit from interaction, let alone interchange, with members of its sister services, nor offer its high-flyers anything like the same scope for promotion when all they could aspire to was less than a dozen provincial governorships and one Civil Secretaryship. So the marked break with tradition initiated by the importation of Maffey in 1926 was widened by the transfer in 1934 of Symes after only two years in the governorship of Tanganyika. To consolidate this radical policy of Service musical chairs, in 1934 H. A. MacMichael was promoted out of Khartoum, first to the governorship of Tanganyika, and then to the major colonial post of High Commissioner Palestine. It is likely that B. H. Bourdillon, who had moved from the ICS to Ceylon and then as governor to Uganda in 1932, would have completed the shake-up by becoming Governor-General of the Sudan had his putative successor in Lagos, Sir John Shuckburgh, not been diverted to special wartime duties in London.

The Foreign Office came, as it were, into its own in the two final appointments to the Governor-Generalship of the Sudan. Both R. G. Howe and A. K. Helm were career diplomats, with Howe enhancing his African experience – in itself a rare attribute in the ranks of the Foreign Service before the 1960s – of Minister at Addis Ababa with a spell as an Assistant Under-Secretary

Governance

at the FO so as to help him with his upcoming delicate negotiations with Cairo. Helm, on the other hand, represented the more usual end-of-empire colonial posting, that of very much a last-act governor-general, for whom many of the decisions behind the moment of the final curtain had already been made. Symbolically, his departure from Khartoum was as abrupt as his residence was brief.[18]

It is when we turn to the colonial governorships, in particular in the wake of the decision of the Warren Fisher Committee of 1930 to purge the whole procedure of Colonial Office appointments by ridding it of any hint of hangover from nineteenth-century patronage, that one finds a concise and relatively clear procedure for the appointment of top proconsuls. For the final thirty-five years of Colonial Office responsibility – that is to say, two Colonial Service generations and half a dozen colonial governor 'generations' – a formalized pattern evolved for selection to gubernatorial office.

In the new Colonial Service Division of the CO, charged with such vital personnel matters as promotions and transfers and specifically the appointment of governors, two critical confidential lists were cumulatively compiled and meticulously maintained. List 'A' comprised the names of Colonial Service officers who, being under the age of 55, had enjoyed a career record which enabled them to be considered for promotion to a governorship as soon as such a vacancy occurred. Negative factors (other than passing the age when an appointment to a governorship might carry them too far into the fifties) could prevent the inclusion of a name on this list, almost certainly stemming from some earlier adverse report from the governor or another senior officer in the territory commenting on his subordinate's sins of commission or omission: for instance, failure to have acted promptly in an emergency such as a potential outbreak of violence or a temperamental inability to get on with local traditional rulers or maybe with the incipient political elite. Undesirable personal traits, such as alcoholism, short-fuse temper or marital infidelity, would likely have ruled a man out earlier in his career from eventually getting on to List 'A'. Those on it had usually already attained the threshold ranks of Chief/Colonial Secretary or Senior Provincial Commissioner/ Resident. Holders of lesser governorships would also appear on it, to be considered for preferment to a major governorship depending on their record in their current post of independent command.

Posting as Colonial Secretary (in effect, second-in-command and chief executive) to a smaller African or an island territory was a frequent testing ground and, if successful, a stepping-stone to a gubernatorial appointment. It was these men, often high-flyers, who comprised the essence of List 'B'. This register, again confidential, was maintained in the CO for use as a panel from which to draw potential Chief/Colonial Secretaries, from whom in turn the next series of colonial governors would likely be found. The Colonial Office unofficial talent spotters might well make a note of some fast-stream District Commissioner, from a perusal of a report in the files and, after 1945, often from an official tour to a territory and a not-really-so-casual personal encounter. The development of air communications now made possible such critical contact visits.

Career planning thus became institutionalized as part of the Colonial Office machinery for its highest appointments. In some instances, it already had a higher post in mind when initially appointing an individual to a smaller governorship. This was the case with E. F. Twining, when he was offered St Lucia in 1944, en route, as it were, to Tanganyika. It was a long way from the turn-of-the century procedure whereby it was legitimate, as R. Williams did to secure Newfoundland, to offer oneself for the next colonial governorship that fell vacant.[19]

Physically, these two Lists took the form of a credit and debit card index maintained in the Colonial Office. This was basically derived from the annual confidential reports which every governor was required to submit on each member of his administration. Inevitably, and valuably, great reliance had to be placed on the reports of officers submitted upwards to the Governor by the Provincial Commissioner, for he was in a position to know most about the qualities of the officials serving directly under him. When the annual reports were received in the CO, they were scrutinized by both the geographic (e.g. Pacific, West Africa, etc.) and the subject (e.g. economic) departments. An officer of sufficient seniority and outstanding merit would have his name passed to the personnel department, with the suggestion that it be 'noted', that is to say added to List 'A' or 'B' as appropriate. Once noted, officers might be invited to call at the CO when they 'happened' to be on leave, quite informally and often innocent of why or how or even that they had been privately sized up. Colonial Office officials were not allowed to feature on either List.

Six months before a governorship fell vacant a small *ad hoc* committee of senior officials in the CO would scrutinize List 'A' and draw up a short-list. The personnel department added comments against the competing names and, if necessary, included a gloss to explain why certain names had not made the short-list. As the file passed upwards, further minutes might be added to the specific recommendations of the head of the relevant Department of the Colonial Service Division, for many years Sir Charles Jeffries and then A. D. Garson. The final recommendation for promotion to the governorship was made by the Permanent Under-Secretary. However, since the actual appointment lay with the Secretary of State, the Minister was sometimes – and could insist on regularly being – consulted. The Prime Minister himself had the right to be consulted about the name finally recommended. Some of the recommendations in which Attlee and Macmillan took a personal interest reputedly did not count among the most successful governors. Post-war Secretaries of State, from Creech Jones onwards, also had positive views on many of the governors they inherited, appointed or removed during their time in Sanctuary Building. Macmillan, too, unimpressed by what he encountered in Nyasaland in 1959, was influential in the retiral of the governor. In the last resort it was the Sovereign who endorsed the supreme appointment. Queen Victoria took a close interest in many of them, far fewer as they were before 1900, while it was from the King himself that Curzon learned of the acceptance of his offered resignation in 1905, 'with deep regret I have no other alternative'.[20] Yet there is no known case in recent history of Buckingham Palace actually having turned down an appointment. Up to its closure in 1966, on the other hand, the Colonial Office was careful not to submit the name of a person who would not have been admitted to the royal enclosure at Ascot, principally divorcees. Queen Mary had been forthright in her injunctions on the social standards she expected in Government House when she approved Grigg's appointment to Kenya in 1925.[21]

THE RESIDENCE

There is enough evidence, from the extensive and superior vocabulary attaching to the official proconsular residence in the capital, to justify at least the first part of the cynical remark uttered by a colonial judge during the heyday of British imperialism, 'To a colonial governor, two things are of supreme importance. One is Government House, the other the Government yacht'.[22]

In the nineteenth century the Viceroy lived in Calcutta.[23] The viceregal residence was first Fort William and then the palatial Government House built, complete with superb marble hall, for Wellesley in 1799. The fact that it was based on – indeed, likely copied from – Kedleston Hall in Derbyshire is enhanced by the coincidence that its occupier in 1899 was Curzon, whose ancestral Scarsdale home Kedleston was. The anecdote goes how Curzon, when this was pointed out to him, commented, with his flat Derbyshire 'a's, that whereas the pillars of his old home were made of alabaster, those in his new house were merely made of lath and plaster. In 1912 the central administration took the decision to move to a building designed, not by the Public Works Department or a military engineer but by the celebrated Edward Lutyens, in the generously laid-out site of New Delhi. It was called Viceroy's House.[24] Palatial throughout, it measured nearly an eighth of a mile along its two main fronts and covered $4\frac{1}{2}$ acres. It enclosed a dozen courtyards and its dome rose nearly 200 feet above the ground. The approach was along the magnificent two-mile ceremonial King's Way, framed by the huge All-India War Memorial arch, lined with parks and canals. Against the £60 000 spent on Government House in Calcutta in 1803, the Viceroy's House cost over £1 million. It took more than a decade to build and was not ready for occupation (by the Irwins) until 1929. Entering the circular Durbar Hall one faced the viceregal thrones surmounted by a canopy of crimson velvet – Bence-Jones's 'climax' of the two-mile approach along King's Way. Behind the vast State Dining Room (itself divided by the largest of the three State Drawing Rooms) rose the stunning grand staircase open to the sky. A week-end residence was also available, in the pre-Delhi era, at Barrackpore, fifteen miles up the Hooghli river. Nevertheless, for almost half the year when the hot season seemed to make European life intolerable on the plains, the Government of India – which in this physical instance meant the Viceroy, hundreds of senior officials along with their families, and tens of thousands of official files – had since 1864 moved up to the cooler hill-station of Simla. There the Viceroy lived, first at Peterhof and then, from 1888, at Viceregal Lodge, a cool and curious country house, part stately Scottish Hydro and part enchanted castle.[25]

In Khartoum, the Governor-General's residence was known as the Palace. This was no proconsular invention, for the splendid building fronting the Nile had earlier been the residence of the Mahdi. There, too, General Gordon had lived, and died there when the city was stormed by the Mahdi's troops in 1885.

Throughout the rest of Britain's colonial empire, the generic term for the governor's residence and place of work was Government House (GH). However, in some territories this building, generally splendid and often noble to look at, yet (at least in the mind of the incumbent) not always comfortable or convenient to live in – Sir Richard Burton wrote off Government House, Lagos, as 'a corrugated iron coffin or planklined morgue, containing a dead consul once a year'[26]) – was known locally by another name. In Ceylon, the Governor resided at Queen's House. Malaya and Jamaica had their King's Pavilion and King's House respectively. In St Helena it was Plantation House and in Gibraltar it was The Convent. On the Gold Coast, the Governor lived in Christiansborg Castle. India's hot-season Simla model was sometimes copied for a hill-station retreat, generally known simply as Government Lodge. Examples include Tudun Wada in Jos on the Nigerian plateau, hilly Lushoto well away from humid Dar es Salaam, or Le Réduit in Mauritius, described as a cross between a masculine shooting lodge and a private house built in the charming Dutch colonial style. Unlike the Viceroy's exodus to Simla, however, colonial administrations were spared the annual trauma of upheaving their Whitehall a thousand miles away to the hills ... and back again six months later. The term Government Lodge could also be used for the official residence of Lieutenant-Governors in territories where, like Nigeria, there was also a Governor.

Administration aside, Government House also performed a socially symbolic role. Levées and investitures were held there, and foreign dignitaries received. An invitation to dinner, or best of all to a ball, was a perceived mark of social distinction. For those visiting the country, an invitation to stay at Government House was something special. More than one Governor's wife frustratedly looked on Government House as a cross between a four-star hotel and a bed-and-breakfast boarding house, where on occasion a genuine crisis would blow up in the problem of getting the sheets washed and ironed between the departure of one VIP and the arrival of the next. It has been observed that 'a perennial problem at GH was not so much those who were invited to stay as those who thought they ought to have been'.[27]

STAFF

In writing about the staff attached to a top proconsul, it is necessary to divide the category into two: the personal and the public staff at Government House.

Taking the personal group first, the senior appointment was that of Private Secretary. Always pivotal on the Governor's personal staff, in India the post of Private Secretary to the Viceroy (PSV) reflected huge responsibility and importance. If one were to look for signs of a promising career, the man selected as PSV was as likely as not to be a proconsul in the making. In the Sudan and in colonial territories, the Private Secretary was usually a young District Officer, who had in one way or another caught the Governor's eye both as a potential high-flyer and as a person gifted with above average social sense and skills. Just now and again, an additional – but not an alternative – factor may have been at work, e.g. being the son of a former governor. Nor was this unreasonable, in a position which virtually converted its holder into a temporary but integral member of the family; at its unlikely lowest level, here was a safe choice. In Nigeria, Hugh Patterson and Imbert Bourdillon, one the son of a previous Chief Commissioner and the other of a Governor, became Private Secretary, and Sir Arthur Richards chose R. L. Peel as his PS, having served together with his father in Malaya. In promotional terms, once again the records show that many a Governor had himself, some twenty years earlier, done his apprenticeship at Government House, where the contacts made as well as the skills acquired and experience offered opened a network which would stand him in good stead for a future in the Service. In the Sudan, G. S. Symes, who became Governor-General in 1934, had been PS to Wingate in 1913. In India, PSVs like Evelyn Baring to Northbrook, held by Curzon to have been 'perhaps the most famous of all Private Secretaries',[28] Walter Lawrence ('Soapy Sam') and James Dunlop Smith at the beginning of the century and George Abell and W. H. Christie at its ICS ending, were names to be conjured with, exemplifying the reputation of the office as a power in the land. Among a score of careers in Africa, W. E. Jackson had started his life in the Colonial Service as Private Secretary to the Governor of Trinidad and then of the Bahamas. In turn G. F. Archer had been PS to Jackson, W. F. Hely-Hutchinson had been PS to Sir Hercules Robinson, A. E. Havelock PS to the Governor of Mauritius, H. L. Galway PS to the Governor of Bermuda, and E. B. Denham PS to two Governors of Ceylon. R. T. Coryndon had been Private Secretary to Cecil Rhodes. Other governors who had themselves been Private Secretary include R. S. D. Rankine, PS to no less than three successive governors of Fiji, and A. C. Burns, successively (and enrichingly) PS to Lugard, Clifford and Cameron in Lagos. A. C. Hollis, by contrast, felt so uncomfortable with Sir Donald Stewart after being PS to Sir Charles Eliot that he quickly asked to be moved out of Government House Nairobi. The tradition of PS as a stepping-stone continued beyond the colonial period proper: for instance, J. H. Smith, the last Governor of the Gilbert and Ellice Islands (1973–8), had twenty years earlier been PS to the Governor of Northern Nigeria. Sir Frederick Lugard and Sir Harry Johnston each appointed his own brother as PS. If tales of the tribulations and tumult of being Private Secretary to His Excellency around the empire are legion and not always legendary, they seem to be more often told by the PS than by HE.

If the Private Secretary's principal responsibility to the Governor was a cross between an executive adjutant and a protective watchdog, in larger colonies the responsibility for the complementary smooth running of Government House primarily rested with the Governor's Aide-de-Camp (ADC). Sometimes he, too, was a young administrator plucked from within the territorial cadre. Often he was a subaltern drawn from a British regiment stationed in the colony. Unusually, Sir Gordon Guggisberg disembarked at Georgetown to assume the governorship of British Guiana with a retired Rear-Admiral as his ADC. A common practice, especially in the final decade of localization of the security forces, was for a junior local officer to be seconded from the army or the police. The ADC accompanied the Governor on parades and military inspections, while the PS went with HE on official tours. The ADC was responsible for the protocol side of the Governor's official entertaining, such as placement at table, introducing guests and making sure none monopolized HE in the brief moments of personal conversation before dinner. He might also supervise the choice of menu and wines in consultation with the Household Comptroller and, of course, with the Governor's wife if she so wished.

For both Private Secretary and ADC, the secondment was a posting and not a rank. At the end of the assigned tour of duty – or sooner, if there had been some monstrous and memorable gaffe within GH – he was returned to his department. It was conventional in some territories to allow a successful PS (very much the majority) to have a say in his next posting, frequently a small, attractive, up-country station where the pace of life was measurably slower than it had been in GH and where there was a greater likelihood of enjoying a full night's sleep.

As for the staff who, as it were, went with Government House and were thus not initially of the Governor's appointing, their number affords one of the most telling insights into the pomp and circumstance which everywhere attached to GH and was generally inseparable from HE's lifestyle. It took an ex-diplomat Governor like Sir Charles Johnston in Aden or an unusual insider like Sir Richard Turnbull in Dar es Salaam to reverse some of the hallowed order of things.

At its apogee, the Viceroy's household numbered the best part of 2000, if one included – as awed visitors, ardent newspaper reporters and anxious comptrollers usually did – the contingent of the Viceroy's Bodyguard and the Viceroy's Band. For lesser proconsular figures like the governor of some small island in the Atlantic or the Pacific, the staff might still comprise a dozen or so household domestics. Elsewhere, a standard size of GH staff would easily run to 30 or 40, including a major-domo or butler, a head chef, a head steward and a head gardener – each with a subordinate staff – a chauffeur, an orderly, and half a dozen washermen. There would also be a group of government employees assigned to the Governor's office: personal secretary, confidential clerk, cypher officer, typists and messengers.

Many of the senior household staff were permanent, thereby providing a continuity and acquaintance with practice and precedent which could be a relief to changing HEs and their even more transient ADCs. In return, to dismiss a major-domo or head chef was an all the more difficult decision to make. Alexander Grantham made history in Lagos when he sacked two GH servants whose memory reputedly dated back to Lugard's occupancy a quarter of a century earlier – and he but acting for the substantive governor! But he likely lacked the art of handling such snobs as GH staff could easily become. When he was at King's House, Jamaica, the GH butler and one of the footmen gave notice minutes before the guests were due at a large official luncheon. In Hong Kong, too, where Chinese domestics have long been looked on, by colonial civil servants and contemporary tourists alike, as exemplars, Grantham felt it necessary to keep them up to the mark. 'The table boys, if not watched', he noted, 'might appear in grubby uniform, or during lunch and dinner stand around daydreaming.'[29] His conclusion, that Lady Grantham regularly held a post-mortem on No.1 Boy to review what had been done wrong (or right) at a meal, suggests that even with the châtelaine of GH the common coffee-party topic of conversation among colonial wives, 'servants', was likely to crop up. Governors who, like both Mitchell and Twining, returned as Governor of a territory in the region in which they had served their Colonial Service apprenticeship in the provincial administration, found a job in GH for their retainers who had served them thirty years before. Such an exercise in patronage was not always welcomed by the GH domestic staff. A visiting Secretary of State had a somewhat different view of how far his host trusted his domestic staff. Touring Malaya during the height of the Emergency, Lyttelton was horrified not so much by the careless talk around the Governor's luncheon table but by the assumption that the household staff, many of them Chinese, did not understand a word of English. The King's House butler turned out to be a communist. 'I had been lucky', Lyttelton noted, 'that he had belonged to the Intelligence and not to the Operational branch of Red China, for he could have shot me easily as he gave me the sugar [when handing round the coffee]'.[30]

POMP AND CIRCUMSTANCE

It follows from this brief consideration of the staff attaching to Viceroy and governor that the office was projected and perceived in an undisguisedly high profile. Such emphasis was neither unintentional nor unexpected. After all, was not the Viceroy the *alter ego* of the Sovereign (*vice-roi*) and was not a colonial governor the personal representative of His or Her Majesty? That was a fact of life not lost on visiting politicians. Macmillan, punctilious where protocol was concerned, had no trouble in giving his host the Governor the courtesy of the bow reserved for royalty whenever he first met Sir James Robertson each morning.[31] Just to make the point clear lest it should be overlooked by some colonial subject or non-colonial visitor, the Viceroy and governor had their entitlement of royal salutes (21 for the Viceroy, 17 for a governor, 15 for a Commissioner 'acting in subordination to a Governor'), their own quarter guard to turn out and present arms each time they drove through the GH gates, a fleet of Rolls-Royces or Daimlers (save in the Falkland Islands, where for many years the GH car was a much-loved London taxi), an ensign to fly over Government House and a pennant to fly on the bonnet of the car. There was, too, a gorgeous uniform to wear for official occasions, or else a frock-coat and top hat. No wonder that a popular colonial anecdote, variously attributed to this or that royal personage in respect of this or that governor, is how His Royal Highness remarked, after being received by His Excellency the Governor, 'Now I know what it is like to be royalty.'

Protocol and procedure defined much of the proconsul's life. For India, the Order of Precedence printed in the annual *India Office List* exceeded fifty pages. For colonial governors, the whole of Part II of the official *Colonial Regulations*, dating back to the first half of the nineteenth century and regularly reprinted into the 1960s, was devoted to a close account of the public privileges of office.[32] The package of some three hundred regulations was set within the framework of 'Directions to Governors for General Guidance'. Of special application to His Excellency was Chapter II, starkly titled 'Governors' and relating to the terms of their appointment ('his tenure of office is as a rule confined to a period of five years from his assumption of the administration'), salary, leave, allowances and 'Passages in HM's Ships'. Part II refers to 'Public Business', focused on the Governor's code of conduct. Chapter V extends the guidelines to the office generally, assuring the incumbent that while 'As the Sovereign's representative he is entitled to give the "word" (parole) in all places within his government', he must remember that 'although bearing the title of Captain-General or Commander-in-Chief ... he is not invested with the command of HM's Regular Forces in the Colony.' This was so even if the Governor happened, as was sometimes the case, to be of a higher military rank than that held by OC Troops. Considerable attention was paid in these Regulations to matters of ceremony, correspondence and financial control. The last-named carried a separate section on the upkeep and expenditure of GH, set within the requirement that 'The Government House, together with its stables, garages, outbuildings, fences, and other appurtenances, shall be kept in substantial repair throughout at the cost of the Colony.' Britain was preoccupied with nothing if not the transparency of the financial honesty of its proconsuls.

At each territorial level, the *Staff List* (another public – and purchasable – document in the drive for open accountability) set out the name of each member of the civil service in strict seniority. It also showed their salaries, including that of the Governor. Precedence at Government House functions was rigorously based on this *List*, with wives willy-nilly taking the seniority of their husbands. Equally rigid were the unwritten conventions about who in the civil service was 'allowed' to invite the Governor to dinner – usually restricted to not many more than the Colonial Secretary, Chief Justice and GOC. It is not surprising that much of the recent interest in the invention of tradition and imperial ritualism has found abundant material in the colonial experience, notably in the lifestyle of Government House.[33] Yet while a later generation may smile at the 'performance' and the occasional nationalist might cavil at the expense of public funds involved, the rulers' message was clear: here is authority. It also expressed the precept inherent in the expectations of many a pre-colonial society: to be recognized as a chief a man must first be seen to be a chief.

THE FIRST LADY

Inevitably, though far from always being acknowledged, much of the care and credit in the smooth running of Government House fell on the shoulders of the one person who, unlike her husband and his staff, had not been specially chosen for the job. The wives of the Viceroy, Governors-General and Governors were a spectacular example of what latter-day feminist sociology has neatly termed 'the incorporated wife'[34] – the exemplar of an early generation's loyal lament about having married not the man but also his institution (regiment, college, Service or, as with the novelist Joanna Trollope's Anna Bouverie, 'the church').[35] What in a post-imperial, perfect world would be looked on as a full-time, fully paid, management-cum-diplomatic appointment, the châtelaine of Government House was, in the age of colonial governors, at the worst looked on as evidence of nothing more than presumed loyalty, at the best taken for granted. Often it could be as much make-or-break for 'her' as it was for 'him'. Contemporary feminism aside, what is touched on here is not the wider sociological and gender aspect that informs modern analysis of career husbands and [non-] career wives, but simply the complementary social feature of who the proconsular wives were, balancing the social insights opened up earlier in the chapter on who the husbands were.

Only the wife of the Viceroy or a Governor-General was entitled to the courtesy title of 'Her Excellency'. It was one of the Dominion Governors-General who used to quip that he had assumed the wife of a governor-general would be known as the Governess-General.[36] In India, the Viceroy's consort was officially styled the Vicereine. Yet for all the exalted position of and deference due to the First Lady, she was never allowed to forget in public who her husband was. In contrast to normal social convention, imperial protocol demanded that it was the Governor, not his wife, who should enter a public room first or, again in defiance of common practice, who should be served first at meals. There was to be no room left in the mind of the public about who it was the National Anthem was played for. The protocol that cocooned the First Lady and her husband could sometimes go to the proconsular head (of either). One such wife insisted on the ADC drawing up a table-plan when there were only six sitting down to dinner at Government House. Another confessed she was made to feel like a Victorian wax posy under a glass dome.[37] A defence by some consorts intimidated by doubts about their capacity to carry off the responsibilities of an often starched existence was to become daunting and semi-regal themselves, at least in the eyes of some of those they encountered or officially entertained. A few others simply collapsed into a bundle of nerves or else developed a tic or a trait to the point of eccentricity. Most of them coped superbly; many enjoyed every minute in GH.

The commonplace colonial quip that gubernatorial wives were aristocrats, actresses or Americans has, no less flippantly and no less factually, been brought a fraction nearer the truth by its reformulation as Caledonian, couthy, or slightly crazy. On occasion, it has been observed, one met in GH with 'a confusing tutti-frutti concoction of all the ingredients'.[38] Yet, spouse for spouse, such an artist's impression is no less valid for the male than for the female of the proconsular species. It was L. S. Amery who, as long-serving Secretary of State for the Dominions and Colonies, admitted that in the light of the many appointments he had made to Government House, the one thing he wished for was to be granted papal powers so as to divorce Governor X from his lady and remarry her to Governor Y, thereby creating the best colonial team for the best colonial occasions.[39]

No Governor-General of India ever married into royalty. This is in distinction to the Dominions, where one Governor-General of Canada (Lorne) was married to a daughter of Queen Victoria, and another (Athlone), Governor-General of South Africa as well as of Canada and himself brother to Queen Mary, married Princess Alice, one of Queen Victoria's grand-daughters. Mountbatten, royalty himself as a great-grandson of Queen Victoria, was married to the grand-daughter of King Edward VII's friend, the financier Sir Ernest Cassel. Nonetheless, and expectedly, the Vicereines were often, like their husbands, from the aristocracy or had been prominent society women before their marriage. If aristocrats abounded from the time the Crown took over in 1858 (Charlotte Canning had been Lady-in-Waiting to the Queen; Hardinge's wife, too, was attached to the Royal Household and the niece of a previous Viceroy; the mother of the Hon. Emily Eden, Auckland's sister, was sister to the first Minto, Governor-General in 1806; Edith Lytton was the daughter of Lord Clarendon, the distinguished Foreign Secretary), others too became Vicereine. For instance, Lord Cornwallis's wife was the daughter of a Colonel in the Guards; Lord Teignmouth, himself the son of a supercargo, married a doctor's daughter; Lord Lawrence married a clergyman's daughter; the Marquess of Reading, the second son of a fruit merchant of Finsbury Square, married the daughter of a merchant from Hamburg; and Lord Willingdon married the granddaughter of a wealthy contractor. The Colonial Service could point to few aristocrats in the female line. Nevertheless, just as Minto's wife was the grand-daughter of Lord Grey, the Prime Minister, so among the final governorships, the wife of Lord Soames, momentary Governor of Southern Rhodesia in 1980, was the daughter of Winston Churchill.

Prominent among the American contingent of proconsular wives was Lady Curzon, heiress to the Levi Leiter millions of Chicago's Marshall Field dry goods empire.[40] Lady Grantham, Lady Bede Clifford, and Lady Bradley all came from the USA (the latter two from Ohio).

Other gubernatorial wives enjoyed other claims to fame. Sir Hugh Clifford's second wife, Elizabeth de la Pasture, was a household name among Britain's readers of novels at the turn of the century; he himself was an amateur novelist. Before her marriage, Lady Guggisberg had been the popular actress Decima Moore. Lady Twining was a qualified medical doctor and Lady Lugard was very much in advance of her time, being *The Times'* Africa correspondent in the 1890s and contributing, as Flora Shaw, to the *Encyclopaedia Britannica*. Lady Willingdon was remembered, in Government House Bombay, Rideau Hall and the Viceroy's House, as a highly colourful character – quite literally, too, in her positive passion for purple furnishings.

The nature and needs of imperial service in the context of finding suitable appointments for Government House came to an end before feminism, affirmative action and the imperatives of equal opportunity had established themselves in British professional society. It was not until after the colonial era that the proconsular male tradition was breached, first in the Government Houses of Canada and New Zealand. By then, women ambassadors were well established as part of Britain's post-imperial overseas scene. Among the no more than speculative couple of pre-war possible names for top proconsular office (and the likelihood of such office was admittedly no stronger than speculation) a senior Colonial Service official once exclaimed, forty years on, 'Ah, Dame Margery Perham! Now there's a woman who should have been a colonial governor'.[41] Otherwise, there was nothing more than the occasional worry expressed by a furious or frustrated Colonial Secretary wondering, as his new chief took office, why a short-sighted Colonial Office had picked *him* as Governor without thinking about *her* impact or, to adapt a latter-day Washington joke, indulging in the belief that the only hope for the colony lay in the sudden death of Lady H so that Sir William could at last emerge as the real Governor.

THE GOVERNOR'S WORK

It is time to turn to what was after all the *raison d'être* of these top proconsuls, the work of the Viceroy and the Governor. The day-to-day structure and nature of the office were, it has been said, conditioned by a network of responsibilities and relationships which, though in part formalized, were in the final analysis qualified by His Excellency's personal and attitudinal characteristics, 'his traits and qualities and moods, his interests, his strengths and limitations'.[42] Within the necessary defining scenario of *quot sententiae, tot proconsuli* – a qualification enhanced by the fact that at any one time there were some thirty occupants of Government House, each conditioned by his own context and circumstances – it is nevertheless possible to separate the nature of the office into a number of principal and common areas. These were often too overlapping and intertwined to permit of any meaningful ordering of priorities.

If performance while in office rightly stands as the principal criterion of securing the reputation of a 'good' governor or not, such an evaluation at once involves two areas of assessment. How was His Excellency perceived in the territory and how in Whitehall or, particularly for Viceroys but sometimes for governors of colonies at unusually sensitive moments (Palestine, Cyprus and Aden, or Kenya and Nyasaland, all in the run-up to decolonization), in Westminster and at Number 10? Again, when one looks at the reputation 'in the territory', in whose mind is the reputation constructed? Is it the view of the Governor's civil servants, particularly those close to him in the Secretariat, or of his field agents, senior and junior alike? Is it the judgement of non-officials, business and banking, civil society, the professions (sometimes even the military)? Or does it reflect the opinions of the elected legislature, or of the maharajahs and emirs, or of 'the local population' at large? A good – or bad – Governor could too easily mean anything to everyone.

Ultimately these proconsuls were responsible for law and order in their territory. Nowhere was this capacity more closely watched than by London. At the same time, this was no *status quo* requirement; good government had to be combined with a sense of advance, be it constitutional (always a paramount responsibility of, and often a strain on, the Viceroys), economic (central in the colonial territories, particularly from the Colonial Development and Welfare Act of 1945 on), or the basic if blurred objective of 'leaving the place better off than when I assumed office'.

If the Governor was, then, head of the government, he still had many hats to wear in that office. In nearly every case, he was additionally Commander-in-Chief (in Jamaica, the title was Captain-General). The main exception to this pattern was India, with its separate Commander-in-Chief. There, the relationship erupted in bitter feuding when Curzon and Kitchener took issue on the appropriate appointment of responsibility between the Commander-in-Chief and the independent military member on the Viceroy's Council.[43] While the rank was largely titular in most colonies, in the three 'fortress' colonies of Malta, Gibraltar and Bermuda the Colonial Office made sure that there should be no misunderstanding by consistently appointing a senior serving officer from the armed forces as Governor. Constitutionally, the Governor might preside over a legislative council, with – at varying periods in various dependencies – a growing proportion of unofficials among the members, progressively moving towards an elected majority until His Excellency eventually shed his responsibilities to a President of the upper Chamber or Speaker of the lower House, and finally to an elected Prime Minister. In Executive Council, comparable to the Cabinet in London, he was likely to preside until the final stages of the constitutional transfer of power, even then retaining reserve powers for security and foreign relations in his own hands until the last minute. The extent of the localized and elected element of these Councils varied enormously in the colonial empire, with the Caribbean legislatures being chronologically well ahead of most of the African territories. There the first Africans were not appointed to Executive Council until 1942, in the case of the 'progressive' Gold Coast, while in Kenya no African was appointed even to the Legislative Council until 1943, twenty years behind the West

African case. In India, Indian Members had taken their seat on the Viceroy's Executive Council before the First World War.

One area where the Governor had a special and unhappy responsibility was in deciding on appeals against the death sentence. This prerogative of mercy had been described by one colonial legal luminary as the Governor's 'highest endowment'.[44] Even though the appeal could be referred to London, it could too, as Sir Alan Burns' trauma over what came to be known in the British press as 'The Juju Murder' proved, be a scarring experience.[45]

In the Secretariat, where the departmental work of administering the territory through the field administration was centred and co-ordinated, nearly all the correspondence and instructions went out over the Chief Secretary's signature, often invoking the Governor's name in the time-honoured bureaucratic phrase of 'I am directed by His Excellency the Governor to....' From time to time, a Governor took the unusual step of addressing a Minute to his subordinates himself – now and again directing that, for good measure, a copy should be sent to every officer on leave, too.[46]

Where correspondence with the Secretary of State was involved, it would be signed by the Governor. The Governor's personal office was not normally located in the Secretariat but in the residence. Correspondence to and from London was by despatch, telegram (in cypher or in clear), savingram and letter, the last-named also carrying a d/o or demi-official category. This was a useful device to allow each other's personal views to be revealed informally, with the governor addressing his letter to the Permanent Under-Secretary by name or the Secretary of State writing in personal terms to the Governor. There was also a 'Secret and Personal' series used between Government House and the relevant Office in London, particularly towards the end of empire. Viceroys and Governors-General, excluding those holding the rank *ad hominem* or who held it as part of the final constitutional change, were also required to write a monthly report to the Sovereign. It was Queen Victoria who started the practice of regular correspondence with the Viceroy. Curzon relates that she wrote to him once or twice a month (King Edward's letters were far fewer), and in her own hand.[47] Conventionally, the Viceroy would write to his Sovereign in the third person, but the Earl of Lytton, diplomatically censured by Curzon for such 'engaging disregard for the established etiquette', used the first person – and got away with it. 'Her Majesty was enchanted', Curzon concluded, 'with the unconventional and interesting character' of the literary Lytton's letters.[48] For every holder of gubernatorial office, two kinds of message from London caused the heart to beat momentarily faster: the intimation that a member of the Royal Family would be paying a visit to the territory, and the 'PQ' telegram, calling for information urgently required by the Secretary of State to enable him to handle a Parliamentary Question. In the opinion of many proconsuls, success was to be signalled by the lack of times one's fiefdom featured in Hansard or was named in official reports.

Every Viceroy and Governor, whatever the size of the territory, set great store by the need to keep in touch with his provincial staff. This was most effectively done by getting out of the capital on tour. Over the years, and especially as the speed of constitutional change accelerated, tours primarily of inspection gave way to visits for two-way communications and consultation. Often, of course, this was a welcome break for His Excellency, away from the punishing routine (social as well as official) and sometimes oppressive climate of life in the capital. If, as was increasingly the case, His Excellency had himself 'come up through the ranks' and been a DC, then here was a wonderful opportunity to recapture – at least in spiritual terms – one's youth. Touring involved visiting institutions, opening new buildings, installing a paramount chief, discussions with people from all walks of life; and, *de rigueur* rather than maybe, a spot of recreation (duck shooting, fishing, tennis, hill-climbing – that youth again), official receptions and formal dinner-parties. In this last connection, it was traditional that His Excellency on tour provided all the food and drink for such parties. While such thoughtfulness meant he and his entourage were thus no financial burden on his host, typically the Resident or Provincial Commissioner, when HE was really up-country with no Government Lodge or Residency to stay in, it was equally a convention that the DC move out of his quarters and let the gubernatorial party have the use of the house.

Such tours were undertaken by all means of transport. At one time His Excellency would ride out of the capital on horseback to undertake a tour of inspection in the hinterland. Elephants and camels were kept for ceremonial, shorter occasions – one Viceroy, Lord Hardinge, and his wife were the subject of an assassination attempt as they sat splendidly in the howdah on a state entry into Delhi in 1912. The railway generally preceded the motorcar as the next standard form of transportation for official visits. The Viceroy had a sumptuous viceregal train at his disposal, and in the larger colonies the Governor's special coach could be attached to scheduled (express was not always the correct term) services. In the Pacific, a Government House steamer, often known as the Governor's yacht, was essential, just as it had been earlier in African rivers and estuaries. Just how strenuous a gubernatorial tour could be is evident from Sir James Robertson's journal of his first visit round the country after his appointment to Nigeria, 15 days of being, as he expressed it, 'on the job' without intermission.[49] In the course of time, and a boon to the governor though not automatically so to his subordinates, a visit could be made by air. In Northern Nigeria in the 1950s the innovative Sir Bryan Sharwood Smith, who in the First World War had served with the Royal Flying Corps in India, established the Northern Region Communications Flight for VIP visits to the remoter parts of his region.[50] Air transport was, of course, not an unmixed blessing for governors. From the Second World War onwards, they found themselves more and more on the receiving end of the BOAC flight from London. When constitutional problems began to dominate a governor's life, and in particular where the Cabinet was taking an interest in the situation, a senior official from Whitehall or even the Secretary of State himself could fly in within a matter of hours, or else have the Governor recalled for immediate consultation with him or, as Wavell found to his cost in 1946, 'disastrously' with the Prime Minister himself.[51]

As Governor, His Excellency was technically responsible for his civil service. The Secretary of State may have appointed the members of that Service, but it was the territorial government (hence, the Governor) who employed them, posted, paid and pensioned them. While each Secretariat gradually developed its Establishment or Personnel Division, it was to the Governor that civil servants were required, following the territory's General Orders, to forward their requests, submit their petitions (on, for example, promotion – or the lack of it), and address their memorials on conditions of service. And it was to him that the annual confidential reports on staff were forwarded. Only in the final decade or so were bodies like Public or Civil Service Commissions set up to take personnel affairs off the Governor's shoulders. Individual cases of misdemeanour or temperamental unsuitability or compassionate grounds among his civil servants were constantly brought to the Governor's attention for a decision, either locally by way of reprimand or reporting, or after referral to Whitehall, likely ending in transfer or just occasionally dismissal. A spectacular case of the Viceroy's power to punish was Curzon's volcanic banishment to Aden of the West Kent Regiment after a raping incident in Rangoon in 1899 and his humiliation of the famous 9th Lancers in 1902.[52]

Yet for all their importance in the administration of the government, the civil servants were in no way the only recipients of the governor's personal relations. In India above all, the business community's relations with and access to HE, together with their reports conveyed to Directors at home, combined to take up a lot of the Viceroy's time. In the colonial territories the need was also pressing to find time for the non-official community. Sometimes, as with Sir Arthur Grimble's encounter with the Ocean Islanders (Banabans) over the sale of phosphates or Sir Hugh Clifford's rebuff of Lord Leverhulme in Nigeria, it was a multinational company at work; in other instances, it might be a powerful missionary body who criticized the government, as with the Church of Scotland Mission in inter-war Kenya or the ambitions of the Church Missionary Society in the largely Muslim Nigerian emirates. These relations between expatriate business and territorial government call for closer attention than has so far been accorded them by post-colonial scholars, notably as an aspect of the governor's function and responsibilities in the run-up to the transfer of power.[53]

If little emphasis has been placed here on the work of the governor vis-à-vis 'his' subjects, this is because that was principally the realm of his field agents, the provincial administration and the professional and technical departments. To them, the Lat Sahib in far-off Delhi or the Governor away in Lagos or Dar es Salaam was as remote a figure, now and then invoked but mostly invisible, as was the Queen of England whom His Excellency was said to represent and who, he assured them, constantly had their interests at heart. Nevertheless, there remains one aspect of the proconsular relationship which could touch on every one of the territory's inhabitants, from expatriate civil servant to fellow box-wallah and from prince and rajah down to peasant and ryot. This is what His Excellency could, and frequently did, do in projecting himself and his office in the realm of sport. It was a field in which the fundamental colonial art of the practice of race relations, critical at the periphery, could be most effectively practised – at the very centre. As a recent detailed analysis of the proconsular association with sport in the British Empire, whether at the field agent or Government House level, concludes:

> Myth or half-truth, when we finally learn what 'they' thought of us, the sporting enthusiasms of His Excellency and of so many of his officials seem destined to play a positive part in the shaping of 'our' image and reputation in 'their' collective memory of the *dramatis personae* of imperialism.[54]

THE REWARDS OF OFFICE

Table 7.3 is designed to give an idea of the comparative value of gubernatorial emoluments at what could be considered the peak moment of imperial over-rule, 1947, before India, Ceylon and Palestine left the empire. As it happens, apart from the salary paid to the Governors of Tanganyika and Uganda, most colonial governors saw only a minimal increase in their pay and allowances between 1925 and 1945. While there was no inflexible or precise mathematical correlation between size of territory and salary of the post, it was incontrovertible that no other territory carried the stature and status vested in the Indian Empire. Similarly, the governorship of the smaller islands of the Colonial Empire, like St Helena, the Falkland Islands or the Gilbert and Ellice Islands, could not expect to match the expectations and prestige attaching to those of Ceylon, Nigeria or Malaya, rightly recognized as the plums of the Service. The governorship of a senior Indian presidency or province was, in financial terms, on a par with these top colonial governorships. Both these classes ranked some 20–25 per cent below the salary paid to the Governors-General of Canada, South Africa and Australia.

The salary given in Table 7.3 excludes that popular item of bureaucratic and business life both at home and abroad, allowances. For the most part these were designated as 'duty' or 'entertainment' allowances. These could be substantial, for example an extra £4500 in the case of the Governor-Generalship of Malaya and an additional 50 per cent of salary for the Governor of Kenya and the Resident of Zanzibar. A median figure in 1947 stood at a quarter to a third of salary. Unusually, that supplementing the salary of the Governor of the Bahamas was underwritten as an allowance towards the upkeep of Government House, possibly a carry-over from the 1940s when the Duke of Windsor was, somewhat curiously, given the post and so became the only member of royalty to become a modern British colonial governor. Salary and allowances were tax-free, as were Government House (civil servants were customarily expected to pay a nominal rent for their quarters) and a host of domestic perquisites. Following diplomatic practice, liquor consumed for official entertainment was imported free of duty. Some Government Houses, even in the tropics, could boast a fine cellar. This was an asset usually sold to the incoming governor. For the Viceroy, it was said, the purchase of another – if wasting – asset, the horses and carriages from his predecessor, might cost the new incumbent a fair proportion of his first year's salary. While the entertainment allowance could amount to a substantial sum, such was the burden of official entertaining that few twentieth-century governors managed to save much money. The eighteenth century cases of Clive and Hastings are well known, but somehow Lansdowne managed, a century later, to save £20 000 in five years.[55] All that Guggisberg could leave in his will, at the end of eleven years in Government House, was £1934.[56] An entry from a colonial governor's memoirs written at the turn of the century concludes, of his fellow proconsuls, that 'it will be garnered from my narrative that if they do their duty, the luxurious life they are supposed to lead is at least not an easy or idle one'.[57]

In course of time, consonant with a procedure followed in the Foreign Office as the post-Great War world called for more but not equally ranked ambassadorships, the Colonial Office too classified its governorships. Four classes were recognized. In 1947, a quarter of the colonial governorships were placed in the first class: Singapore had just been added and Kenya had advanced to Class I, a ranking later shared by each of the three regional Nigerian posts from 1954. Dependencies like Nyasaland and British Somaliland started off as Class IV governorships, though the former was subsequently to move to Class III in 1932 and Class II in 1955, following the creation of the Central African Federation.

Governors' pensions were a matter of separate legislation, dating back to the Governors Pensions Act of 1865, and susceptible to complex regulations, rendered all the more mathematically labyrinthine by their often split territorial service. No less maze-like were the rules governing their passage out to (paid by the British government) and home from (paid for by the colonial government) the colony. The rates were punctiliously prescribed by the Colonial Office, an improvement on a slightly earlier age when, it was said, a nineteenth-century official had the temerity, on being offered a governorship in West Africa, to enquire which government would pay his passage home on the expiry of his term of office. He was informed that the question had never actually arisen in the 'White Man's Grave'. On the other hand, no pension was paid to any Viceroy once the Crown took over from Company rule in 1858. Curzon elaborately researched the financial minutiae of Viceroy's allowances and outlay in the nineteenth century.[58]

Three more points can be subsumed under the rubric of proconsular conditions of service. Colonial governors, like their staff, were entitled to home leave. For the Viceroy, this was not usually the norm. In the colonies leave tended to be frequent, especially where, as in the Sudan and on the West African coast, the climate was particularly trying. When a governor went on leave, and generally during the interregnum between a retiring governor and a new appointment, the Chief (or Colonial) secretary was nominated to stand in for him. He was not, however, designated as Acting Governor but rather the Officer Administering the Government (OAG). Just occasionally, in earlier times, it

Table 7.3 Selected gubernatorial status indices in the dependent British Empire, *c.*1947

Office	Country	Population	Size sq.m	Salary (£)	Grade
Viceroy	India	430 000 000	1 808 679	19 000	–
Governor	Indian Pres/Prov	–	–	10 000	–
Governor-Gen.	Sudan	9 000 000	990 000	6 000	–
Governor	Nigeria	20 000 000	372 674	6 500	I
Governor	Ceylon	5 300 000	25 332	6 000	I
High Comm.	Palestine	1 800 000	10 157	5 500	I
Governor-Gen.	Malaya	4 900 000	50 350	5 000	I
Governor	Kenya	4 000 000	224 960	5 000	I
Governor	Jamaica*	1 400 000	4 411	5 000	I
Governor	Gibraltar	20 000	285	5 000	I
Governor	Hong Kong	1 600 000	391	4 800	I
Governor	Gold Coast	4 000 000	92 203	4 500	I
Governor	Tanganyika	5 500 000	362 684	4 500	I
Governor	Trinidad/Tobago	600 000	2 000	4 000	I
Governor	Uganda	4 000 000	93 981	3 500	II
Governor	N. Rhodesia	1 700 000	288 130	3 000	II
Governor	Aden	600 000	112 080	2 500	III
Governor	Gambia	200 000	4 003	2 500	III
Governor	Leeward Is.	110 000	413	2 200	IV
Resident	Zanzibar	272 000	1 020	2 000	IV
Governor	Falkland Is.	2 594	4 788	1 500	IV
Governor	St Helena	4 748	47	1 200	IV

Note: *While the full title of the colonial governorships was 'Governor and Commander-in-Chief', in Jamaica the traditional title of 'Captain-General and Governor-General' was retained.

was the Chief Justice. Lugard disliked the thought of having anyone acting on his behalf when he was on leave from Nigeria and tried to cajole the Colonial Office into letting him run the government in Lagos from a desk in the Colonial Office. He did not succeed in his innovation. In India, a senior member of the Viceroy's Council or else the governor of one of the three Presidencies (Bengal, Madras, Bombay) would perform this function. Whereas in the colonies it was a convention that an outgoing governor should have left the territory before his successor arrived – reportedly to satisfy Treasury officials reluctant to have two governors holding the same post on their books, but more likely to ensure that the new governor came with a *tabula rasa* in making up his mind on the state of play – this was not always the case with the Viceroy. Kipling's conversational poem in which Dufferin, reflecting on the achievements and anxieties of his Viceroyalty, addresses his successor, Lansdowne, may represent as much an imagined monologue as an actual encounter in Calcutta:

> 'I envy you the twenty years you've gained
> But not the five to follow...
> Four years and I forget. If *I* forget,
> How will *they* bear me in their minds?'[59]

Secondly, gubernatorial mobility. While no Viceroy could be transferred to an equivalent official post overseas – though at least two Dominion Governors-General moved on to the Viceroyalty – and no Governor-General of the Sudan was ever to find a senior overseas civil service post (one did become Permanent Under-Secretary at the Colonial Office), within the colonial territories it was commonplace for the ablest and younger of the governors to be transferred. This was made easier, too, not only by the substantial number of posts available but also by their grading into four classes, thereby enabling promotion within the same office. Indeed, migration was very much part – though never a norm – of the Colonial Service after its unification in 1930. Nowhere was this more marked than at the very topmost echelons, the practice among colonial governors stretching back to before the turn of the century. For instance, between the wars, H. C. Clifford, somewhat exceptionally, went on to Ceylon and Malaya after the Gold Coast and Nigeria; T. Shenton Thomas's gubernatorial route took him from Nyasaland through the Gold Coast to Malaya; and H. Monck-Mason Moore went steadily upwards (and eastwards) from Sierra Leone through Kenya and on to Ceylon, whereas A. R. Slater went in the other direction, from Sierra Leone and the Gold Coast to Jamaica. P. E. Mitchell, too, brought wide (and extra-African) colonial experience to his final governorship of Kenya, having previously been governor of Fiji. A. F. Richards moved from North Borneo to The Gambia, then back to Fiji and across to Jamaica before being posted to Nigeria. Intra-African cross-fertilizing, too, from West to East or Central and vice-versa, was quite usual in the name of widening experience. Sir Donald Cameron was Governor of Tanganyika before Nigeria, B. H. Bourdillon moved from Uganda to Nigeria, and J. D. Rankine came to Western Nigeria from Zanzibar. Sir Percy Girouard moved from Northern Nigeria to Kenya, two of whose other governors, J. A. Byrne and H. M.-M.-Moore, had likewise been West African governors. An analysis of the 134 men appointed to an African governorship between 1900 and 1965 – and Africa comprised the largest area, the biggest concentration of overseas civil servants, and one-third of the total governorships on offer within the whole colonial empire – shows that 22 came from holding a governorship outside Africa and another 20 came from another African governorship.[60] In the same context of the imperative of experience, 35 had been appointed to an African governorship from the key post of Chief or Colonial Secretary of an African territory, but only nine from such a post elsewhere in the empire.

Lastly, it would be impossible to leave this composite sketch of the top proconsuls of empire without giving consideration to one of the most public and cherished indications of a successful incumbency of the peak post, namely the award of honours by the British sovereign. No attention is paid here to honours bestowed from time to time to governors by other sovereigns, for instance within the Order of the Brilliant Star of Zanzibar or the Order of the Nile, or those awarded personally to an earlier generation of African proconsuls by King Leopold II. Nor does this commentary concern itself with military decorations, few of which are likely to have been awarded for service in a proconsular post.

India had its own orders of decoration, notably those of the Star of India and of the Indian Empire, established respectively in 1861 and 1886. Every Viceroy thereafter automatically became a Grand Master of each order, GCSI and GCIE. However, no more than half the Viceroys received the higher recognition of an honour in the orders of the Garter, Thistle or St Patrick (KG, KT, KP). All became Privy Councillor (PC).

Probably because the Sudan came within the annual quota of honours available to the Foreign Office, members of its Political Service seem in retrospect to have received fewer awards than their Colonial Service peers. At the top, however, the Governors-General of the Sudan were rewarded no less honourably than their gubernatorial colleagues elsewhere. Kitchener remains unique: his roll-call of honours were earned by his military prowess. Exceptionally, too, in the other-than-Viceroy corpus, he was made KG as well as KP and, along with Malcolm Macdonald, within the total proconsular class exceptionally elevated to the Order of Merit. Among his successors, Wingate held the highest honour within no less than three orders of chivalry (GCB, GBE and GCVO). Nearly all were made GBE. Maffey left the Sudan with the KCB and KCMG (his promotion to the GCMG came later, in acknowledgement of his work in London). Significantly, Archer's tenure of the Governor-Generalship of the Sudan was unmarked by any award.

Established in 1818 and then reorganized in 1864, the Order of St Michael and St George became pre-eminently the order of chivalry for rewarding British citizens who had given outstanding service in the colonies. Its further reorganization in 1879 extended the order to those who had performed meritorious service in foreign affairs, thereby bringing it within the purview of the Foreign Office. However, its Registry remained within the Colonial Office. The Chapel of the Order is in St Paul's Cathedral. The order consisted of three grades: GCMG, KCMG and, outside the knighthoods, Companion (CMG). The number in each class was limited by statute. In the public mind, a second order understandably attached to the overseas civil services, the Order of the British Empire. It has been looked on as pre-eminently the Colonial Order. Yet its sheer size, including two additional grades, Member and Officer (MBE, OBE), has meant that, despite the Order's title, just as great a number of awards since its creation in 1917 have gone to those with no empire service or interest, including actors, footballers and pop-stars.

With the last two orders largely available for colonial civil servants, it is perhaps not surprising that very few top proconsuls retired without being awarded a knighthood, the most frequent being KCMG. Senior governorships sometimes – but by no means invariably – earned advancement to GCMG. A slightly lesser form of knighthood conferred on a colonial governor was KBE or

Knight Bachelor (Kt.). While it would be unfair to describe a knighthood as 'going with the post', in the same way as the DSO was unjustifiably described as 'coming up with the rations' on the Western Front in 1914–18, the observation of one of the most experienced governors, Sir Alan Burns, who also had high-ranking experience in the Colonial Office, is relevant and revealing:

> I have always thought it would be wiser if the Secretary of State were to re-commend to His Majesty that [a knighthood] should be awarded to the Governor of even a small colony *before* he assumes office... Surprise is always expressed when each successive occasion on which such an Honour could be received ... passes without the Governor being awarded what is generally regarded as a routine Honour.[61]

The third order of chivalry, ranking above the Order of the British Empire, fre-quently found among the honours of colonial governors was that of the Royal Victorian Order (KCVO, CVO, LVO formerly MVO). Established in 1896 and lying in the personal gift of the Sovereign, its award here dates principally from the 1920s, when an Empire Tour became part of the royal programme, and reached its peak at the end of the 1950s and in the 1960s when the Queen visited a large number of her colonial possessions, often in connection with a ceremony to mark independence. Frequently she conferred the KCVO on her Government House host.

While the post-retirement occupations of overseas civil servants is treated in Chapter 9, one feature remains which is best considered as part of the honours system in so far as Viceroys and governors are concerned. This is elevation to the peerage. Since no career overseas civil servant outside the proconsular ranks ever became a member of the House of Lords (unless, of course, in rare cases, by inheritance), this is better treated here among the rewards of guberna-torial life rather than as an aspect of post-retirement activity and 'second careers'.

Out of the 33 Viceroys, 20 were either made peers or else, already in the House of Lords, were promoted within the peerage. Overall, by the end of their term of office (subordinate grades of advancement within the nobility are ignored), the viceregal corpus could point to 15 earls, nine marquesses, six barons and two viscounts in almost 200 years (1758–1947). Hastings declined a peerage in 1806 pending the revocation of his impeachment. Such a microcosm of Britain's aristocracy is unsurpassed in the holding of any public office in Britain over a similar period, including that of Prime Minister. Although in no way in the same league, nor reflecting the incorporation of the aristocracy to anything like the same extent, the gubernatorial record of the Sudan stands out. No less than one-third of its governors-general were rewarded with a peerage (Kitchener, Wingate, Maffey), though only in the case of Wingate, pre-eminently the longest serving of them all, was this directly consequent on his term of office in Khartoum.

In contrast, elevation to the peerage was very much the exception among colonial governors, and even more rarely while still in office. Early Alfred

Milner, midway Edward Grigg, and latter-day Christopher Soames all earned a baronetcy; none had been a career colonial servant. Proconsuls like Lugard and latter-day H. M. Foot gained theirs for services after their colonial governorships. On the other hand, Lords Twining, Howick, Grey and Maclehose had been career overseas civil servants (Baring coming to an African governorship after starting in the ICS), all elevated on their retirement. Exceptionally, Richards became Lord Milverton while still a serving governor. In contrast to viceregal pedigrees, E. Baring, both Hugh and Bede Clifford, W. F. Hely-Hutchinson, P. S. Methuen and W. W. Palmer were among the few members of the British aristocracy to end up as colonial governors. The Duke of Windsor's colonial appointment as Governor of Bermuda remained unique.

If this chapter has outlined a number of the salient features in the make-up of the holders of the top posts in Britain's overseas empire, after the gradual formalization of its structure and the progressive professionalization of its civil services since the abolition of patronage in the middle of the nineteenth century, the justification for its separate treatment and not as an integral part or concluding section of the specific chapters on each of the three overseas civil services remains compelling. First, the number of these career civil servants who internally reached the top was – could but be – very few in proportion to the size of each Service; four in India in two hundred years (Clive, Hastings, Shore and Lawrence), one (Stack) in the Sudan in fifty years. The Colonial Service figures are higher, with over five hundred governorships filled in the past 150 years, yet it is only since 1920 that a governorship began to be looked on by members of the Service as a normal – if still remote – promotional expectancy and only since the 1930s that career appointments seriously began to exceed those from the outside. All three of the Services continued to have outsiders – military officers, politicians, home civil servants – appointed to their top territorial post right up to (and often very much so at) the end. With only one SPS officer ever having been appointed to the Governor-Generalship of the Sudan (and he originally a military man, not a civilian) in the whole of its history as a Condominium and with no ICS official appointed to the Viceroyship since 1863 (and, in Curzon's tart estimate, 'his experience was not such as to encourage a repetition of the experiment'),[62] neither Service could seriously look on the top post as part of its career structure. If the numbers of holders of the supreme post of governor were higher in the Colonial Service, with perhaps 350 governorships *en disponabilité* over the same comparable period of 1900–60, so too was the strength of the competing Colonial Administrative Service – the resource from which an increasing number of governors were drawn after the First World War – its numbers rising from 400 in 1900 to 1800 in 1947 and 2300 in 1957.[63]

Thus, however ardently and ambitiously every ICS and SPS probationer and CAS cadet may on first appointment have felt – slightly to alter the Napoleonic analogy – a governor's plumes to be potentially in his saddlebag, he soon realized that statistically his enthusiasm, dedication and competence in his chosen overseas civil service career could in no way be matched by the chance of inter-nal promotion to the very top.[64] It was rare indeed for Malcolm Macdonald's prayer, when seeking a replacement for the assassinated Governor of Sarawak in 1949, to be answered in kind by the Colonial Office: 'Send me a first-class District Officer.'[65]

Part III
Relinquishment

8 The Transfer of Power and Localization

The first decade following the transfer of power to successive new nations from within the colonial empire was characterized by a glow of mutual congratulations on one feature above all in the imperial governmental legacy. This was the inheritance of a sound civil service derived from many years of the finest British traditions of efficiency, dedication, loyalty to whatever elected government was in power, and total incorruptibility. That at least was the image, promoted and generally perceived. The fact that different circumstances and needs had meant that Britain's successor civil services were not necessarily the same thing as the metropolitan Home Civil Service, in responsibilities as well as recruitment, was beside the point. The message, a two-way donor-receiver one, was clear and for the most part genuine: in the legacy of the British connection, 'we' gave 'you' the democratic model of a civil service second to none. In return the other 'we' are grateful to the other 'you' for such a priceless bequest. Parliamentarianism might need a little longer to take root. In the wake of a government which was by definition 'imperial', democracy might need a little longer yet. But the rule of law and its instrument of an upright, impartial and trained civil service were already in operation, ready loyally to serve the new government. Localization of the bureaucracy was as transparent a symbol of the transfer of power as was the new national flag.

If that was the accepted wisdom at independence, within a few years the view began to alter dramatically. In some cases the new public service, once the ambition of every local schoolboy in the colony, crumpled in the public mind as it came to be looked on as corrupt, nepotistic and incompetent, even obstructive and ethnically discriminatory. It progressively found itself replaced by the professions, by commerce and business, and here and there by the military, as the preferred career among graduates and school leavers. In the one-time metropole, post-colonial scholars too young to have known the Empire at first hand joined ex-colonial civil servants in 'witness' seminars[1] to identify among the Achilles heels of Britain's imperial experience the failure (outside India) to build up over the years a viable local civil service to which the departing colonialists could have handed over not only their authority but also their experience and their ethos. Despite the emergence of many outstanding civil servants from among the founding generations of the successors to Britain's overseas civil services, some of whom went on to make their mark again in the international civil service of the UN and its agencies, what Britain all too often left behind (with the ICS, with its long record of integrated recruitment, once again the exception) was numbers of able individual civil servants but always not an ongoing civil service.

241

If in retrospect the British themselves began to query whether they had after all done such a good job in preparing their civil service successors, the question that arises is just what had they done. India apart, the answer has to be that it was by and large considerably less than should – and could – have been done. Since the focus of this book is on the Administrative Services, epitomized by the generic District Officer in the field, it is on the localization of the administrators and not of the professional and technical cadres – where the record is often a far better one – that we shall concentrate in this chapter.

Before considering the Indian and Sudan experiences, each carrying one unique feature in the context of localization, and that of the Colonial Empire, certain general imperial factors need to be taken cognizance of in explaining the slow pace, almost seeming reluctance, in the localization of the senior ranks of the administrations.

One factor is the inevitability of paternalism in the classic colonial situation: 'we know better than you, but we will teach you so that one day you will be able to do it yourself'. Typically, fathers do not share authority with their sons, they show them instead how to acquire and exercise it in due course. Another factor is the clear principle of the pre-1939 doctrine of indefinite time ahead: 'maybe one day they will be able to govern themselves, but probably not for at least another fifty years and certainly not in my life time.'[2] A third influence, and this time one to which the Indian subcontinent was not immune, was frankly racist: white menfolk, particularly when it came to being tried in a court of law – as the reactions to the Jurisdiction Bill in India in the 1880s showed[3] – and white womenfolk, particularly in the area of medical care – as the sorry closure of the West African Medical Service unequivocally demonstrated[4] – too often equated the pyramid of authority (giving and taking orders) with the pigment of the skin. Not for nothing was the dichotomy of a colonial civil service sometimes officially demonstrated in terms of 'European' or 'Senior' and 'Native' or 'Subordinate' cadres. The mists of the White Man's Burden were as persistent and as slow to clear as the opaqueness of the monsoon.

In addition to these general considerations, two more attitudes proved peculiarly influential. The first is that the widespread British principle of indirect rule, which accorded primacy to consultation with and support of the 'natural' or traditional rulers, enabled the Maharajahs and Princes, Sultans and Tunkus, Emirs and Paramount Chiefs to exercise a subtle yet effective brake on any proposed localization of the civil service. In India, it was simple: Indian Princes did not have District Officers from the Indian Civil Service posted to their territory. There the role of adviser was the prerogative of the quasi-diplomatic Indian Political Service. Elsewhere, notably in Malaya and Nigeria, the executive rank of Provincial Commissioner was styled Resident, with its emphasis on advice and its echoes of the protocol of princely courts.[5] Following the onset of incipient party politics, some traditional rulers, with generations of monarchical authority behind them, may have been shrewd enough to prefer the devil they knew (the foreign overlord) and knew how to handle, often to hoodwink, to the one they did not, one of their own people either as political officer or as interventionist politician. Others in multi-ethnic societies read between the lines of the manner in which their British District Officer might frame the frank but confidential question: 'Would the [Northern] Emir really welcome a Southern DO here?' From there it was not hard for the Secretariat to draft a reply to the Colonial Office along the lines that the Chiefs seemed to evince little enthusiasm for Africans to be admitted into the Administrative Service.

The irony of this deprecating divide-and-rule suggestion is that it reinforced another attitude, possibly less entertained by the imperialists but undeniably prevalent among an impatient nationalist elite, namely that the British were reluctant to contemplate accelerated localization of the upper echelons of the civil service because it would deprive them of their jobs and terminate their career. That suspicion, already generated in the early years of the century by the abrupt ending of appointments of West African doctors to government service and of the handful of African District Officers in the 1880s, received further encouragement in the 1930s from the Colonial Office scheme to unify the territorial services into a single empire-wide Colonial Administrative Service. Thus a Gold Coast national who had achieved a post in the Secretariat in say Accra or Kumasi (in the twentieth century no Africans were appointed to the post of DC until the 1940s) could in theory now be transferred to Nigeria or even Nyasaland – and be dismissed should he decline. In Nigeria, resentment bubbled up again with the Yaba Higher College fiasco of 1934, when the African graduates found themselves appointed to nothing higher than *assistant* medical, agricultural, forestry officers, etc.[6]

Suspicion and scorn deepened in the 1950s, when localization of the civil services at last began to gain momentum. Now British administrators, from colonial governors downwards, publicly promised that easier access to the civil service would on no account be accompanied by any 'lowering of standards'. When this dictum was translated into terms of qualifications, a measure of hypocrisy became apparent. The noose round the nationalist neck was tightening. As both the emergent political class and the aspiring educated elite were quick to point out, how could an older school of senior DO or PC maintain that 'Of course, to be considered for appointment to the Colonial Administrative Service the regulations require that you have to have a good degree' when, after 1945 as after 1918, hundreds of ADOs whose education had been interrupted by the war were being recruited into the Colonial Service and sent straight out, degreeless, to the colonies? And when, as nationalist politicians were not slow to observe, not every colonial governor in the 1940s and 1950s held a university degree, having come in in the wake of WWI the Great War? So patronage and nepotism were not dead after all, and 'jobs for the boys' no longer need be confined to the British DO's standard view of chicanery in the Native Administration?

That direction of argument leads to the last of the official attitudes on localization to be noted here. This is the much-criticized 'scaffolding theory', in the event more assailed for its misunderstanding than for its message. Promoted if not actually designed by Margery Perham, respected authority on colonial

administration at Oxford University from the 1930s to the 1960s, devoted friend
of Lord Lugard, and confidante to countless colonial governors and successive
Secretaries of State, the principle maintained that no African should be admitted into the Administrative Service since the position of District Officer was
anomalous to that of 'a temporary scaffolding round the growing structure of
native self-government'.[7] Once the building reached completion, the scaffolding
would be removed and all the British staff withdrawn. After all, the argument
continued along the corridors of colonial power, just as local government in
Britain required no PC Sussex or DC Leamington Spa, so an independent
Nigeria or Kenya would no longer need a DO Kano or PC Rift Valley. In the
end, far from abolishing the provincial administration and its DOs, criticized by
the nationalists during the colonial period, the newly independent governments
found that they could not do without their field agents, and increased their
numbers, sometimes strengthening their powers.

It is arguable that in the whole transformation of a colonial civil service to the
modern bureaucracy of an independent state, the emergent nations could have
been appreciably helped by three measures. The first is to have purposely set
out to recruit, down the years, local graduates (as the ICS had done for eighty
years before independence) alongside the expatriate ones into the existing ranks
of the higher civil service. Guggisberg on the Gold Coast was twenty years
ahead of his time in his proposals for accelerated Africanization of the administrative service.[8] Those who point to the virtual non-existence of institutions of
higher education in the colonial empire before 1948 might like to calculate the
financial cost involved and results achievable from an alternative scheme,
selecting a handful of the best secondary-school graduates each year and educating them in British sixth forms and on to British universities, say from *c*.1935
onwards. This was never tried, yet its estimated cost could be interesting, set
against the human as well as national cost and results achieved in the crash
training programmes for local DOs-in-the-making undertaken by many colonial
governments on the eve of independence. Secondly, the position could have
been considerably eased and improved had the colonial governments established a junior field service, staffed only by local personnel, who by working
alongside their European DOs could have acquired more administrative experience and immediate know-how than any university degree in public administration could offer to its young entry. The *mamur* or administrative auxiliary
arrangement in the Sudan was one such approach.

It is this that leads into the third opportunity missed. Had that 'junior service'
not remained a junior service but served as a qualifying entrée for admission
into the senior service, then come independence the emergence of a national
civil service would have been strengthened by a corps, already in place, of experienced, able and older field administrators. By the time the colonial governments came round to thinking in terms of the Home Civil Service dichotomy of
Administrative and Executive grades yet with the clear ability to move from the
lower to the higher on merit and performance, it was too late to introduce such
a division without risk of the new Public Service Commissions being accused of

discrimination by the label of 'second class' perilously replacing the colonial bogey of discrimination by race.

If self-government within the Empire, later Commonwealth, really was at the heart of imperial rule, it was an aim which was not transformed from a tacit assumption to an explicit objective until 1917 for India and 1943 for the colonies.[9] Integral to such a new status would be the provision of an independent civil service to replace the former imperial one. Localization would need to be the order of the day, and the earlier it was introduced the better the chances of a stable transfer of power. It was in India that most was done, and was done soonest, to ensure that when 'that day' should come the departing imperial power would leave behind a functioning civil service as the administrative basis and the executive framework for the new nation state. In contrast, it was in the Belgian Congo that the result of little preparation and no planned training for localization was disastrously at its most negative.

An integral part of the study of the localization of any of Britain's successor civil services lies in an intimate reconstruction of the existing facilities for higher education. Yet one wonders whether the meaning of what 'education' was all about was the same for the aspiring new entry as it was for the departing colonial civil servants. It is easier shrewdly to surmise than statistically to prove that among colonial civil servants, whether in the ICS, CAS or SPS, there lingered a fundamental belief that preparation, above all for a career overseas, entailed another ingredient in addition to 'learning'. This was 'character', discussed at length in Chapter 5. The fact that the raw, local DO would not be operating in the old colonial context meant less to many of the departing colonial civil servants than the twin principles that a DO was a DO was a DO and that a DO needed 'character' as well as book knowledge and skills. Here was an educational philosophy long beloved of the British imperial elite, finding its expression in the words of the incoming Governor of Ceylon, Sir James Longden, who in 1880 took care to qualify the notable academic output of the schools system in the colony by conveying to the Secretary of State his fears about Ceylonese sitting the competitive examination in Colombo as well as in London for the Ceylon Administrative Service. This was not so much because it was 'impossible for any young man without leaving the Island to shake himself so free of local ties and local feelings of caste prejudices and insular narrowness as to acquire any independence of thought' as his belief that in the schools in Ceylon, despite their curriculum in the classics, 'the moral, physical and social training of an English Public School or University are wholly wanting ... an almost essential factor for the civil service'.[10]

THE INDIAN CIVIL SERVICE

Indianization, as the process came to be called, was in fact enabled in 1833, twenty-five years before the ICS came into being. A clause in the Charter Act laid down that no native of British India 'should by reason only of his religion, place of birth, descent, colour, or any of those, be disabled from holding any place, office or employment under the Company'.[11]

Although Clive had left much of the civil government to the Nawabs of Bengal and their Indian assistants (*diwans*) and Persian agents, all 'strangers to the customs and indifferent to the welfare of the people of the country',[12] and Warren Hastings was in favour of employing Indians in the administration, Cornwallis adopted a policy of excluding Indians from positions of authority and trust in the government of British India. In the States, too, opportunities were circumscribed as soon as Residents were appointed under the Crown and the host of Indian functionaries was replaced by a far smaller cadre of zealous British officials. In 1831, however, Bentinck had made the first change in policy when he created a higher grade of Indian judges and proceeded to open the executive branches of the administration to Indians by offering them the position of Collector.

But the most significant change came with the renewal of the Company's charter in 1833, after a Parliamentary Committee, noting that 'natives are only employed in subordinate positions in the revenue, judicial and military departments ... they are said to be alive to the grievance of being excluded from a larger share in the executive government',[13] persuasively argued that

> their admission, under European control, into the higher offices would strengthen their attachment to British dominion, would conduce to a better administration of justice, and would be productive of a great saving in the expenses of the Indian Government.

Yet it is doubtful whether the Directors ever went so far as seriously to consider admitting Indians into the Covenanted Civil Service. Defective education, as Macaulay diagnosed it in his celebrated Minute, ruled out the possibility of such a move. A sound, English-style education, with its character training component as vital as its intellectual contribution, would have to precede any move towards opening the prestigious Covenanted Civil Service to Indians. Meanwhile they were increasingly deployed in the other public services. In 1833 the post of uncovenanted Deputy Collector was opened, and from 1853, with the abolition of patronage and the introduction of a competitive examination, Indians now had equality of opportunity with Englishmen to compete for the ICS. The fact that the examination was held in London, of course, continued to exclude both orthodox Hindus, who could not travel across 'the Black Water' without losing caste, and the sons of anyone unable to afford to send their children to Britain.

The first Indian to be accepted for the ICS was in 1864, when S. N. Tagore, a Bengali, was appointed. His 915 serving colleagues were all European. He was posted to Bombay. In 1871, three more Indians joined the Service. Two of them went on to high office (one was R. C. Dutt, a future President of the Indian National Congress). One, the luckless S. Banerjea, was quickly dismissed the Service. This did him no harm, however, for he became a nationalist politician, was appointed a Minister in 1921, and received a knighthood.[14]

Agitation continued, not only for more Indians in the ICS but also that the examination should be held simultaneously in England and India. Proposals and piecemeal reforms continued throughout the 1870s, among them Lytton's scheme for a new closed civil service for Indians, to be filled by nomination of those considered to be *bene natiet modice docti*, of good family and fair education.[15] In the event, this Service soon fell into disrepute as nothing more than a second-class one and it was abolished. In all, 69 'Statutory Civilians', as they were called, were appointed to it. In the same period it was enacted that the monopoly of the Uncovenanted Service posts should go to 'natives of India', i.e. including Eurasians, subsequently restyled Anglo-Indians. This provision reserved for them over 2500 posts in the executive and judicial services at a time when there were less than 950 posts in the ICS. The reduction of the maximum age for ICS candidates from 21 to 19 was seen to be a deliberate obstacle in the way of Indians, whose knowledge of English at that age could not normally be expected to permit them to compete on an equal footing with British candidates.[16] After toying with a proposal to reserve for Indians 18 per cent of the posts annually filled, the Secretary of State appointed in 1886 the Aitchison Commission, with a remit to investigate once and for all Indians' claims to senior appointments in the public service. While their recommendation to divide up the general administrative personnel into the elite ICS, the Provincial Civil, and the Subordinate Civil Services passed substantially into practice over the next fifty years, their other proposals failed to assuage Indian feeling, in particular the refusal to countenance a simultaneous examination in London and Calcutta. At the same time, the British had their reservations about the wisdom of any forced pace. In Curzon's sonorous warning at the turn of the century there are tones and undertones of the imperial mission, of upholding standards and of Britons' natural talents, which echo on down the years and, in the case of the colonial empire, penetrate through to post-Second World War years:

> The first [principle] is that the highest ranks of civil employment in India, those in the Imperial Civil Service, though open to such Indians as can proceed to England and pass the requisite tests, must, nevertheless, as a general rule, be held by Englishmen, for the reason that they possess, partly by heredity, partly by upbringing, and partly by education, the knowledge of the principles of government, the habits of mind, and the vigour of character, which are essential for the task, and that, the rule of India being a British rule, and any other rule being in the circumstances of the case impossible, the tone and standard should be set by those who have created and are responsible for it. The second principle is that outside this *corps d'elite* we shall, as far as possible and as improving standards of education and morals permit, employ the inhabitants of the country, both because our general policy is to restrict rather than to extend European agency, and because it is desirable to enlist the best native intelligence and character in the service of the State.[17]

The Indianization issue was officially revived in 1912, this time with the appointment of the Islington Commission on the Public Services of India. Reviewing the statistics, it interpreted the slow progress made as a sign of failure. At its conclusion, by 1915, only 63 Indians had received appointments in the ICS in nearly sixty years, and they still did not constitute more than 5 per cent of the posts. The Commission recommended that rather than pursue the old hare of simultaneous examinations, which it rightly viewed as no more than a means to an end, at least 25 per cent of the posts should be filled by Indians. The war overtook their somewhat complicated system of allocated posts, and by 1918 the mood in India was such that Islington was already stillborn. The Montagu-Chelmsford reforms recognized that, to realize their declared goal of associating more Indians with every branch of the administration, the system of recruiting in England had to be supplemented by a defined percentage of new entrants to be found from India. They envisaged that one-third of all the ICS posts should be filled by Indians in 1920 (it was then barely 10 per cent[18]), followed by an annual increase of 1.5 per cent for the next ten years so as to reach 48 per cent of the Service in 1930. Provision was also made for Indians now to be promoted from the Provincial Civil Service. To ensure a measure of representation by religion and province, up to a third of all the appointments reserved for Indians could be filled by nomination. From 1922, a system of competitive examination was established in India, supervised by the Civil Service Commission, whereby those successful would be sent to a British university for two years' probationary training.

By now the pace was relentless. When the Royal Commission on the Superior Civil Services in India (Lee), appointed in 1923, again looked at the staffing of the ICS, a significant deterioration had occurred in its British ranks. A combination of wartime casualties among young Britons, a faltering enthusiasm among ex-servicemen who had survived the Western Front, ICS and family reactions to such grim events as the Amritsar massacre compounded by the outbreak of violence in Bengal, and personal unwillingness to commit oneself to a career where the pay was no longer attractive and the career prospects were clouded by constitutional and administrative reforms, all took their toll. Not all DOs took kindly to the dyarchy arrangements of 1919, which required them to work under Indian Ministers. Between 1915 and 1922 there was a shortfall of 125 British entrants for the ICS. In 1924, Indian appointments exceeded their quota by 15. In the same year, the Lee Commission recommended that out of every hundred ICS posts no more than 40 should go to Europeans, the balance going to Indians, with 40 by direct recruitment and 20 listed posts by promotion from the Provincial Posts. The Lee target was that by 1939 the ICS would be 50 per cent Indianized. This would compare with the previous decennial proportions of 884:12 in 1899, 988:33 in 1899, 1082:60 in 1909, and 1177:78 in 1919.[19] Accordingly, in the first five years of the 1930s, only 90 British were appointed to the ICS against 130 Indians. When 1935 came, with the defining Government of India Act finally passed and another bout of severe communal violence undermining Service morale, already lowered by the personal attacks on British officers in Bengal and the Punjab in 1928–31 – including two Governors assassinated and two Inspectors-General shot dead and culminating in the notorious 'Murder on the Punjab Mail'[20] – a mere 71 British candidates, along-side 221 Indian applicants, sat the examination. The parity at entry on which the Lee blueprint was premised was no longer viable.[21]

Nor was its target of 50:50 posts by 1939 quite realized. On the eve of the war, out of an ICS establishment of 1299 posts 540 were held by Indians, supplemented by 85 Listed Posts, and 759 by Europeans. The Indian figures had risen sharply, from 78 in 1919 and 241 in 1929 ... and from one seventy years earlier. In 1939, too, recruitment for the ICS virtually came to a close. By 1949 both the successor Indian Administrative Service and the Pakistan Civil Service were in operation.

THE SUDAN POLITICAL SERVICE

The Government of India may have been no pacemaker in the Olympiad of the localization of Britain's imperial civil services, with its record of one Indian to 882 Europeans in 1869 inching up to 33:988 thirty years on and not really taking off till it reached a fifth in 1929 yet still not a half by 1939. But in comparison with the speed of the rest of the empire's commitment to localization, in particular in all the African territories, India stands forth as a hare when set beside the African tortoise.

The Sudan, firmly a Foreign Office responsibility and, as its Political Service felt, always subordinated to the primacy of Egypt in London's view of the priorities of the Nile Valley, is an extreme case. Its administration, nominally carried out by the co-domini until the brusque repatriation of Egyptian officials after the assassination of the Sudan's governor-general in Cairo in 1924 and the consequent mutiny and riots in Khartoum, was reflected in a Political Service which recruited 100 per cent British (this term admits a couple of 'colonials', from Australia and New Zealand) all the way from 1899 up to 1952, just three years before independence. If that were not solid record enough when set beside the relatively progressive ICS and the accelerating latter-day CAS, the SPS was characterized by another once-only event. This was when an international commission ordered and supervised the enforced rundown of the Political Service, relieving the British staff of their functions and responsibilities as DOs and conventional 'fathers of their people'. Uniquely and humiliatingly, the reason publicly announced was that, in the run-up to independence, British DCs could not be relied on not to influence the Sudanese in coming to a decision on their future. The result, again without parallel in the history of the localization of Britain's overseas civil services, was the sky-rocketed promotion of subordinate *mamurs* and young graduates from the School of Administration in Khartoum to the rank of DC or deputy governor virtually overnight, compared to the years and years of service conventionally required to qualify for such posts.[22]

The commonplace imperial concern at any suggestion that 'standards' could (or should) be lowered, combined with the long-looming Sudanese problem of how best to 'protect' a backward South against an aggressively sophisticated North (in many respects the mirror image of the classic and calamitous Nigerian divide), were too influential to encourage much serious thinking about Sudanization of the provincial administration until after the Second World War. In SPS idiom, it was a case of 'How could you possibly expect the South to accept a Northerner as DC – and in any case how many Southerners are there capable of doing the job?' Within the Service there had been a view that it would be a mistake to promote any Sudanese above the rank of *mamur* or administrative auxiliary.[23] This was despite the fact that, with the luxury (or at least bonus) of annual leave for British DCs, *mamurs* had a regular opportunity to run a District for a couple of months or so as acting DC. The future lay, as A. H. Marshall saw in his landmark 1949 report on the Sudan (in which he also, acquainted with advocates of the scaffolding theory, wrongly foretold the end of the office of DC in the Sudan), in local government, not in provincial adminis-tration.[24] Sudanese officials might, he believed, take on the post of executive officer to rural or urban councils, but it would be unfair to expect them to exer-cise over their own people, especially with strong traditional rulers in the rural Sudan, the same kind of effective and acquiesced-in authority that British DCs did. Sudanese nationalists, however, were vociferous in their determination that the DC posts should be accessible to the Sudanese as *mutatis mutandis* they were to Indians: not for them the sop of the scaffolding theory and the replace-ment of provincial administration with local government as the answer to the DO problem. The demands of the 1942 Graduates' Congress were plain for all to hear who did not refuse to listen:

> [to give] the Sudanese an opportunity to share effectively in ruling the country; this is to be attained by the appointment of Sudanese in posts of political responsibility in all the main branches of the Government.[25]

A few years later the 'high Wagnerian drama'[26] of London's negotiations with Egypt over the Sudan Protocol and Egypt's decision to lay what was known as 'the Sudan Question' before the United Nations,[27] accompanied by Foreign Secretary Ernest Bevin's conviction that Egypt must be re-associated with the administration of the Condominium, introduced fresh fears into the SPS of knavish Egyptian intentions in the Nile Valley. The seminal Administrative Conference of 1946[28] committed itself to a plan for the reduc-tion of expatriates in senior civil service posts from 694 in 1948 to a target of 232 by 1962, not without some misgivings, of course, over 'standards' and 'quality'.

The Egyptian revolution of 26 July 1952 changed all that, and much more besides. With King Farouk overthrown, Cairo increased its pressure on Khartoum, and with the signing of the Anglo-Egyptian Agreement on 12 February 1953 the writing was on the wall for the SPS. Among the interna-tional Commissions now set up was one specifically charged with the Sudanization of the Administration, the Police and the Sudan Defence Force *before* self-determination. This ukase gave the Secretariat only three years in which to replace over a hundred British officials, in the key Ministries as well as in critical command posts in the provinces. Recruitment of British DCs was abruptly halted, the last three coming in in 1952. By 1954 three Sudanese had taken over posts of deputy governor and a number of Sudanese DCs were in place, carrying responsibilities that they would not normally be assuming until they had 7–10 years' experience.[29] Giddy pace that this seemed to outgoing British and incoming Sudanese DCs alike, the Commission found it unacceptably slow. Total Sudanization of the SPS was now ordered for accomplishment in nine months: not localization but liquidation was the order of the day. Soon not a single British DC was left in the provinces. In the words of one of the many Sudan DC bards quoted earlier,

> We end our term imperial
> A trifle sooner than we thought before.[30]

The SPS, which had never had a Sudanese substantive DC in its whole existence from 1899 to 1953, was totally Sudanized by the end of 1955. The rationalization of this abrupt localization – programme is too leisurely a concept – was as unambiguous as it was unique in the history of the British DO overseas. The decision was taken, by an internationally appointed Commission at the urging of the Egyptian Government, that if the British DCs were allowed to remain in their posts till independence, as they had done everywhere else in the British Empire (often following requests from the newly elected governments), they could not be trusted to be neutral in face of the question whether the Sudan should join Egypt or become independent. Accordingly, the DCs had to be removed from all 'sensitive' positions of authority, in the Police and SDF as well as in the SPS. It was, as the modern colloquialism has it, as simple as that. Despite the risk of a breakdown of law and order at a time of high excitement and tension, their place would be taken by rapidly over-promoted *mamurs* or inexperienced graduates. That the anticipated, and quite possible, collapse of administration did not take place (until, that is, after independence) reflects credit on a feature of the SPS which was not enjoyed in the rest of the colonial empire. This was the stalwart presence of the *mamur* cadre of Sudanese subordinates, used to authority and with a wealth of administrative experience. There was no such field service to support the CAS, though the partly comparable device of a separate Malayan Administrative Service (see below) provided that country with a lifeline at a time when a sudden withdrawal of British officers might have caused a breakdown.

Related to this was the existence, since 1949, of a special training programme for *mamurs* at the School of Administration and Police in Omdurman, under the direction of a senior SPS official. At least that precedent could be passed on to the emerging local civil services elsewhere in Africa, who from the late 1950s invested heavily in establishing Institutes of Public Administration as an integral and influential item of the localization of their administrative services.[31]

THE COLONIAL ADMINISTRATIVE SERVICE

The CAS was very much a latecomer in the policy of localization. True, in Sierra Leone Thomas George Lawson and on the Gold Coast George Ekem Ferguson held senior administrative posts and H. Vroom became Secretary for Native Affairs, all well before 1900.[32] There were too, in 1883, among the District Commissioners half a dozen Africans. In Lugard's Nigeria H. Carr rose high in the Secretariat. But a handful of *ad personam* nominations do not make a policy: it was, for instance, another sixty years before the Africans again became District Officers in the go-ahead Gold Coast. The fact that up to the 1950s practically every DO in the Gold Coast and Nigeria could name his African colleagues in the CAS underlines how few they were. All along the West Coast, from Bathurst and Freetown to Lagos and Buea, a number of Africans were accepted into the Administrative Services and their names appeared in the annual *CO List*; but they worked in the Secretariats, not in the prestigious provincial administration.

Uniquely, in the older territory of Malaya, a partial palliative was explored with the creation in 1910 of the Malayan Administrative Service (MAS) as an adjunct – for Malays only – to the Malayan Civil Service (MCS) for the staffing of subordinate posts in the administration.[33] During the colonial period the MAS had provided a valuable second tier to the European officers of the MCS and off-duty were looked on as social equals. Many of the latter were quick to acknowledge, like W. Goode, how on his first tour he had learned the ropes by really being put in the charge of the Malayan ADO.[34] This Service provided a reservoir of local talent on which the post-colonial MCS could initially draw. By 1962, 44 per cent of the new MCS were MAS graduates and were described as having been 'disproportionately influential' in shaping the character of the successor MCS.[35]

In the colonial empire, Ceylon was the first to have a career civil service under the Crown, in 1802.[36] Just before the First World War the Ceylon Reform League had agitated for all posts below that of Governor to be opened to Ceylonese. Realization took off in 1919 with the appointment of a Committee on Further Employment of Ceylonese in the Public Service. Finding that only 18 out of the 108 administrative posts in the Ceylon Civil Service were held by local officers, it recommended that one-third of the posts should be immediately reserved for Ceylonese and that in due course the proportion be raised to 50 per cent. From the 1930s Ceylonese began to be appointed Government Agents (as DOs were called on the island) and European recruitment to the Ceylon Civil Service was suspended following the introduction of the Donoughmore Constitution in 1931. It was momentarily resumed in 1935–7.[37] In 1940 Ceylonese already held most of the posts in the Civil Service, the Administration being 80:45. The Soulbury Commission of 1945 was worried not by the slow pace of localization, the normal complaint, but rather by the implications of the ethnic imbalance in the Civil Service as independence approached (1948), with 30 Tamils and 15 Burghers (in the local vocabulary, these were people of Dutch or Portuguese origin; 'Moors' were Malayans) against only 70 Sinhalese, who constituted 69 per cent of the population. A similar ethnic problem was to beset the localization programme in the Fiji civil service 25 years later.

Elsewhere in the British Empire it was the Gold Coast, sometimes held up as the 'model' British colony and envisaged in the post-war Colonial Office as the most likely candidate to be the first to become independent in colonial Africa, which witnessed the only positive planning for localization before 1940. An imaginative scheme was drawn by the Governor Sir Gordon Guggisberg, as early – in CO terms – as 1925.[38] Twenty-seven Africans were then holding appointments in the higher civil service, a solid advance on the one official, W. Bannerman, to do so in 1919: the enviable track record of the Gold Coast before 1900 noted above had quickly petered out as the number of European DCs was increased in the pre-war years. Working on an ambitious 20-year plan, Guggisberg envisaged that by 1931 seventy-six of the 543 European posts in the Gold Coast Civil Service would be held by Africans, a figure doubling over the following five years and reaching an estimated 229 out of 558 posts by 1946. Suitably qualified Africans would now be eligible for admission to any branch of the Administration ... except the judiciary and the Political Service, i.e. the DC cadre. In the event, the reformist Guggisberg plan fell victim not so much to prejudice or vested interest opposition from within the Service as to the economic slump. More than 250 officers were retrenched and another 327 posts were left unfilled. By 1933 there were still no more than 31 Africans holding senior appointments, less than a fifth of the total planned by Guggisberg. In 1948, less than a decade as it turned out before independence, Africans held only 98 of the 1300 senior appointments in the Gold Coast civil service. Small beer as it was, it was the Gold Coast which once more registered its lead in localization: following Ferguson's appointment in 1878 and Guggisberg's initiative in 1925, in 1942 the Gold Coast made CAS history when Sir Alan Burns appointed two local graduates, K. A. Busia and A. L. Adu, to the provincial administration as Assistant DCs. It was a step that India had taken 78 years earlier.

Undertones of racism and *non possumus* 'standards must be maintained' apart, it was the absence of any subordinate Service in the colonial territories (other than Malaya) which in retrospect strikes the historian of empire, and certainly the historian of decolonization, as a major weakness of governmental thinking. Those officers who came into the CAS from the ICS at the end of the 1940s and again from the SPS in the early 1950s found such a desert of administrative support hard to understand. Nor had Africans been behind Asians in presenting the Secretary of State with memorials calling for a greater share of appointments in the civil services to be given to 'competent and worthy natives'.[39] From the Aborigines' Rights Protection Society in the 1910s through that of the National Congress of British West Africa in the 1920s to that of the nascent political party, the Nigerian Youth Movement, in the 1930s, the standard petition was for more civil service positions for Africans.

It was left to Lord Hailey, bringing his authority and his vast Indian experience to bear on Africa in his hush-hush CO visit to every African territory in 1940, to face up to the localization problem. He opened his confidential report on what he called 'the association of Africans in the Government services' with the observation that

> It is in our readiness to admit Africans to such posts [Administrative Service] that they will see the test of the sincerity of our declared policy of opening to them the road of self-government.[40]

He went on to imply that an earlier concession of a substantial share in what he neatly described as 'posts of control' might well have delayed the demand in India for popular constitutions. Rightly unconvinced of the sincerity or likely success of the belief announced by the Governor of Nigeria in 1938, that the proper field for responsible Africans in administrative work was to take up service with their Native Authorities and that it consequently 'would not be reasonable to employ Africans in the Administrative Service since the Service is destined to disappear as Africans become able to manage their own affairs',[41] Hailey called for 'more substantial' grounds if the Nigerian exclusion of Africans from appointments to the CAS was to seek endorsement as policy. He commended the Tanganyikan initiative in appointing Africans to the judicial department as subordinate magistrates. But above all Hailey argued for the establishment in each colonial government of a locally recruited Intermediate Administrative Service. These officers would be given on-the-job training to top up their higher education and, critically, time spent in that Service would be regarded as one of the qualifications for promotion to the CAS. It is sadly the case that sometimes it was the local legislature which prevented such an Intermediate Administrative Service from getting off the ground, arguing that it would be a snub to Africans who were educationally just as qualified to become DOs as Europeans, some of whom were not even graduates. When, belatedly in the mid-1950s, some African governments turned to the solution of an Executive Grade to serve as an apprenticeship and accelerate advancement into the Administrative Class, the experiment met with little success because it turned out to be a dead-end berth for failed administrators rather than a springboard for the promotion of the brightest and the best.[42]

Africanization in West Africa and its parallel of localization in East Africa, where the policy of multiracialism initially ruled out the use of the term Africanization *pur sang* as long as civil service posts were officially open to Asians and locally born Europeans too, and its application to the rest of the colonial territories (Malayanization, Fijianization, localization in Hong Kong, etc.) was in the end distinguished by two things, one negative and one positive. On the debit side was the crash nature of the process when set beside its continuity in India (e.g., it was all over in a couple of years in the Sudan compared to the eighty-year process in India, while in Tanganyika and Fiji the CO was still recruiting European DCs on pensionable terms up to a few years before independence). On the credit side stood the establishment of effective Public

Service Commissions and the development of a number of critically influential Institutes of Public Administration throughout anglophone Africa, subsequently incorporated into the national universities but, starting with the pioneer case of Zaria in Northern Nigeria, initially created with the express purpose of training the new governments' own administrators. Their input was able to save their governments from what, given the spread and volume of the exodus of expatriate administrators as part of the decolonization process, encompassed the potential of a total administrative breakdown.

THE STATISTICAL PACE OF LOCALIZATION

What, then, characterized the transformation of the imperial civil services into national bureaucracies during the transfer of power across the colonial empire was not only the slow pace of the recognition of local claims to a share in appointments to the public service and the gradual, grudging admission of a handful of local elites into the Administrative Service. It was also conditioned in its final stage by the stream, on occasion threatening to be a flood, of expatriate retirements, exacerbated by the widening gap between posts available and posts filled. In contrast to the SPS's experience of what was little more than summary dismissal from their posts, an enormous amount of time and thought was spent by the colonial governments and by the Colonial Office in seeking to persuade expatriate administrators to ignore, or at least postpone, the blandishment of enhanced retirement benefits as compensation for premature loss of career, and instead to continue serving, for a few years, the new independent governments. What these schemes were all about and how they impacted on the last generation of imperial administrators is the focus of Chapter 9. The present chapter concludes by looking at some of the statistics on localization as an indication of the scale of the problem of staffing the Administration in the colonial territories in the run-up to independence.[43] While the timespan of this book is up to 1966, the date of the closing down of the Colonial Office, further colonial territories did become independent in the 1970s and 1980s and on to 1990, the year marking the independence of 'Africa's last colony' (Namibia). But the manpower problem of new nations like Zimbabwe, Namibia and South Africa never reached the dimension of that faced in the Colonial Empire 'proper', for they were blessed with large numbers of graduates-in-waiting (themselves 'expatriates') in North America, Western and Eastern Europe, available to staff the new civil services as soon as an independent government took over. It was a reservoir of educated and trained manpower unknown to the colonial territories as they hastened towards self-government in the 1950s and 1960s.

In India, the proportion of Europeans to Indians at independence was 3:2, in a total of 1300 posts in the ICS. In the Sudan, where the total of SPS officers rarely exceeded 150, there were no Sudanese DCs in the SPS before 1952, and all British DCs were withdrawn from the provinces by 1954. At the end of 1955 there were only half a dozen members of the SPS left in Khartoum, all on the

Governor-General's staff. Within the wider Sudan Civil Service, in 1954 the Sudanization Committee either Sudanized or abolished 650 of the 1030 posts held by Britons and 85 of the 150 held by Egyptians. In Egypt, peripheral and not central to this study yet clearly relevant in this context of the statistics of localization, when the British handed over the mandate/protectorate in 1922, 60 per cent of the top posts were still held by Europeans. In Malaya, the percentage of posts in the Malayan Civil Service held by Europeans dropped from 67 per cent shortly before independence to 9 per cent five years later. In Kenya, which had more European officers in the administration than either of the other two East African territories – including a large number of Europeans in the clerical grade drawing salaries that were not commensurate with their minor responsibilities – and which had its own civil service inflated first by the 'second colonial occupation'[44] and then by the Mau Mau emergency, Europeans accounted for 28 per cent of officers in the administrative and professional grade, compared with 16 per cent in Uganda and 18 per cent in Tanganyika. In 1960 there were only five Africans holding senior posts, but at independence three years later Kenya was able to replace every British permanent secretary with an African graduate, half of them with experience in the Ministry which they now ran. In Uganda, where Governor Andrew Cohen's wind of change blew the cobwebs away and where the standard of African education was higher than anywhere else in the region, Africans holding senior posts shot up from five in 1952 to 130 in 1961. In Tanganyika, the government announced six months before independence in 1961 that a number of posts would remain open to (but not reserved for) expatriate officers who wished to stay on and whose offer was accepted. These included 24 posts in the rank of DC and up to a further 50 posts at the DO level. Others, up to 48 in all, would be incorporated into the new Inspectorial Teams. Prime Minister Julius Nyerere addressed a personal letter to each expatriate DC, asking him to stay on for a while after independence. 'If you can stay indefinitely', he went on, 'that is what I would like best – subject only to our Africanization policies.'[45]

Two territories stand out, at opposite ends of the scale of success. In Singapore, localization recorded one of its most rapid (along with the enforced break-up of the SPS) results. Within a year of its inauguration the Singapore Malayanization Committee could report that every permanent secretaryship was in the hands of a local officer.[46] Furthermore, the number of Europeans in the civil service eligible for compensation plummeted from 415 *en poste* in January 1957 to 250 a year later and to 150 by the middle of 1959. This was a pace of localization in the colonial empire outdistanced only in the West Indies, where local officers had been in senior posts for some years before independence. Malawi, on the other hand, had one of the slowest ratios of Africanization. The first four Africans were not appointed to the Administrative Service until 1959. This figure reached 40 in 1964, the year of independence. But the Administrative Service was still 85 per cent European and did not drop to a third till a year beyond independence. In the superscale posts, remarkably no Malawian was appointed until 1970, and eleven years after independence two expatriates were still holding superscale posts in the District Administration.[47]

In turning to the Gold Coast and Nigeria, it should be remembered that not only were these non-settler territories, and hence not exposed to the multiracial problems which conditioned localization attitudes and policies in East and Central Africa and put a brake on the expansion of higher education for Africans, but at the time they became independent, in 1957–60, the Cabinet was still thinking in terms of independence for the East African territories in the period 1970–75 and expecting the Central African Federation (created in 1953) to continue.[48] As it happened, the Gold Coast was at last to achieve the localization sea-change that had eluded it despite Guggisberg's vision thirty years earlier, while Nigeria was only just salvaged from a staffing disaster direly envisaged by both the Governor-General and the CO. In the Gold Coast, permanent and pensionable (p. and p.) overseas officers rapidly and regularly reduced from 1300 in 1952 through 800 in 1955 to 400 in 1958, the year following independence. Of the last number, 130 had already given notice of the wish to take early retirement. African numbers rose – for everywhere the replacement of a colonial Secretariat by a Ministerial system called for an expansion of administrative posts – from 550 to 1950 over the same six-year period. In smaller Sierra Leone, where an Africanization Commission had been set up in 1949, Africans held 160 senior posts in 1958 against 380 on the eve of independence (1961).

To claim that it was in Nigeria that the biggest problem erupted, in size and severity, is true of only some of the governments in Nigeria. After 1954, the Nigerian civil service was regionalized (from 1914 onwards the Northern–Southern Service divide was *de facto* rather than *de jure* and experienced occasional exceptions in the posting of administrative officers, junior and senior) into four separate Services: the Federal, Northern, Western and Eastern. At the drop of a hat, the careful 1951 projections for 'Nigerianization' disappeared and 'Northernization', 'Westernization', etc. became the watchwords of staff development.[49] The regional variations were considerable.[50] In 1959, on the eve of independence, out of 230 superscale posts in the Western Region Civil Service, 70 were held by Nigerians and 120 by Europeans. Significantly and alarmingly, 20 per cent of the posts remained vacant. In the Eastern Region, where higher education had also enjoyed a long history, out of 175 superscale posts, 45 were held by Nigerians and 90 by Britons, with a quarter of the approved establishment unfilled. In the Federal Civil Service, which came late into its own recruitment (1954) and had had to rely heavily on transfer or secondment from the Regional Services, there were only 70 Nigerians in the 480 superscale posts. The Northern Region had on its establishment 220 administrative officers in the provinces and in Kaduna. Of these 160 were European and 60 Nigerian in 1959. In the Northern public service there were, on the eve of independence, 1396 European officers compared with only 148 Northerners and 267 non-Northern Nigerians. Such statistics will be revisited in Chapter 9, when their meaning not as indices of localization, as in the present chapter, but in influencing the decision of serving expatriate administrators whether to take early retirement or continue serving the new independent governments, will be considered.

There remains one extra dimension to the evolution of successor 'colonial' civil services not studied here. This is the Diplomatic Service. During the colonial period none of the territories (the partial Indian exception has been discussed in Chapter 3) had a diplomatic service: foreign affairs were the prerogative of the metropole, not of the colonies. Thus there is no justification here for such an analysis: no anterior Service means there could be no successor Service. However, one point germane to the thrust of this chapter calls for mention. In any discussion of the evolution of the Foreign Service of newly independent countries, attention needs to be paid to the way the early Ministry and missions often raided the now localized DO cadre to staff them, or else attracted into the new Foreign Service candidates who would otherwise likely have opted for a career in the Administrative Service.[51]

Throughout this examination of the localization of the former civil services and the replacement, at a gentle trot down the years or at a galloping pace in the last straight, of Europeans by nationals, one superficial misunderstanding of the process needs to be corrected. Whatever the Establishments or Personnel dichotomies – Covenanted and non-Covenanted, European and Native, Superior and Subordinate, Senior and Junior, Division I and II, Expatriate and Local Officers – the focus was similar: it was the DO cadre – Hailey's 'posts of control' – that lay at the heart of the matter and often attracted the brunt of the criticism about the slow pace or discriminating undertone of localization policies. In unmeasurable yet practicable terms, one European DO 'meant' far more to the nationalists than a dozen European Directors and Senior Inspectors or a score of expatriate technical officers. Common-or-garden riots apart, in East and Central Africa, where the settler context and a policy of multiracialism made decolonization harder to achieve, the DO was in the front line of political protest and nationalist assault more frequently and more frighteningly than was the average lot of his colleagues in West Africa. Yet for all the expression of fury and all those moments of injury and danger, and for all the ease with which the DO was pilloried as the obvious target of every 'Ruritania for the Ruritanians' protest – for the DO *was* the Government, in popular perception and in personal symbolism – and now and again became the passing scapegoat of nationalist rhetoric, what is incontestable by nearly all insiders and incomprehensible to many outsiders is how little bitterness was shown to the DO as an individual. To his office, maybe; to him as a person, rarely. No historian would want to deny the century's roll-call of DOs who were killed in the line of duty, putting down an affray or trying to separate armed mobs. A few were murdered, many were invalided. Yet come the adrenalin of nationalist excitement and the sophistication of modern weaponry compared with the spear-and-arrow culture of turn-of-the century 'punitive patrols', the wonder – the relief – must be that politically motivated crowds, inspired by the rousing slogan of 'Self-Government Now', so rarely turned their violence on the person of the DO – *their* DO, and hence maybe his protection.

But the surprise goes further than the DO's 'escape' from mob violence. Little animosity was displayed towards this prime symbol of imperial rule by the new, elected political class. They might have criticized him for his obstructiveness or cursed him for his nosy intervention, but they often went on to welcome him as their aide or ask for him as their Private Secretary, and they accepted and trusted him as their constitutional adviser. There were few victims of what was at the time called in the CAS the 'Singapore sack race', an allusion to the unusually fast tempo of localization there. In Tanganyika, the cordial personalized encouragement in May 1961 of the Prime Minister, Julius Nyerere, to members of the CAS 'to stay with us if you possibly can',[52] was brusquely reversed a year later when the incoming Rashidi Kiwawa undertook an accelerated Africanization of the civil service (among the immediate retirements was his Permanent Secretary, C. Meek), and again in July 1968 when the remaining 17 British administrative officers were removed from their posts, all but one being immediately retired.[53] Only in the Sudan were there hints of some sort of witch-hunt ('proscription lists'); even then the action was not so much motivated by personal animus as by 'a felt need to strike while the iron was hot'.[54] Those DOs who were no longer wanted – and if every colony had them, the negative opinion was sometimes shared by their colleagues as well as felt by the new political class – were often the ones who lacked the temperament for working with and under local officers and politicians. In the majority of the decolonizing situations, there was more pressure on the DO cadre to stay and serve the new government rather than get out while he was still young enough to find another job. Post-imperial memory suggests that, for all the happy exaggeration of the tales told under the moon in the village square, the DO, though the symbol of imperial rule, is not centrally remembered as its evil djinn.

9 Decolonization, Early Retirement and Second Careers

If the reverse face of the coin of decolonization has been the emergence of the Third World, equally the reverse of the primacy of localization in the public services was the withdrawal of Britain's Crown civil servants overseas from the independent nations-to-be. Chapter 8 considered the principle, process and pace of localization; Chapter 9 looks at the winding up of the respective Services, studied in their heyday in Part II, in the context of what became of the imperial administrators whose careers in government service overseas were dislocated or were prematurely terminated by independence. For, as one of the CO officials ultimately involved with the reduction and redeployment of the CAS put it, 'Of all practical issues that have to be dealt with in the transition from colonial to independent status, one of the most important is the problem of the public service.'[1] Nationalist politicians may well have felt that more time was devoted by the departing imperial power to legislation related to guarantees, safeguards and pensions for expatriate civil servants than that allotted to ensuring the political stability and economic well-being of the emergent nation and its population.

The argument for equity and justice in the treatment of serving members of the overseas civil services was a strong one. An appointment had been offered and accepted, in a personal letter signed by the Secretary of State, for service in one of His/Her Majesty's overseas administrative services (ICS, CAS, SPS) under specific and stipulated conditions of service which included a retiring age and pension. In brief, here was a classic 'career' contract. *Ergo*, if that Government career be prematurely terminated through no fault of the employee (naturally there was consistently provision for resignation, invaliding, disciplinary dismissal or, in some cases, of an officer 'who is proved unfit for further advancement'),[2] some form of compensation for such a loss should be looked on, especially by the model kind of employer that the Crown believed it should be, as right and proper, on moral as well as legal grounds. Thus the Civil Service Regulations for the ICS – a Covenanted, and hence a contractual, Service – specified that officers were *entitled*, after twenty-one years in the service, to a pension.[3] Under Colonial Regulations, it was stated that appointments to public offices were held during pleasure of the Crown.[4] While Regulations did not constitute a contract with the Crown, they were held to be an 'officer's charter of security'.[5] When, in the exceptional circumstances of the Depression, compulsory retirement was introduced into the Crown Services overseas, it was, as with the innovation of premature retirement in the 1920s for the ICS on the heels of the post-war reforms, accompanied by a measure of compensation.[6] The precedent had been set. Now a totally new set of circumstances arose, with target dates for independence and, as an integral and inescapable element in the transfer of power, for the accelerated localization of the administration and the complementary withdrawal of expatriate civil servants.

EARLY RETIREMENT AND COMPENSATION SCHEMES

The first occasion was India, in 1947. Expectedly, the ICS procedures for 'loss of career' established a precedent – a pattern rather than a model – for the SPS from 1953 to 1955 and for the CAS, variously from Ceylon and Palestine in 1948 through the Gold Coast and Malaya in 1957 and on, fifty years beyond South Asia, to Hong Kong in 1997. The hurly-burly of wartime India, the human pell-mell of partition, and the forcing of the pace by calendar-driven[7] Mountbatten's decision to bring independence forward by a year, 'giving the British a mere 73 days to vacate a subcontinent for which they had had supreme responsibility for 250 years',[8] together meant that it was not until 1947, the very year of the transfer of power, that the two governments were in a position publicly to set forth the options for members of the now terminal ICS.[9] Wavell, the penultimate Viceroy, records in his diary how it was only in January of that year, barely six months before independence, that the final details were worked out with the India Office on how to negotiate a settlement of compensation for the ICS.[10] He was only too conscious the British ICS were disheartened and 'the delay in settling terms for compensation, date for winding up, and future prospects has had an adverse effect'.[11] There were about 700 British officers on the ICS books at the time.

In the case of an ICS officer, the career choice was uncomplicated, apart from the ultimate dilemma of personal preference. He could either elect to join the new, successor Indian Administrative Service (IAS) or the Civil Service of Pakistan (CSP), not only with the guarantee that existing terms of service (of which, significantly at this juncture, promotion had never been one) would be honoured but also with the no less significant proviso that the officer would be acceptable to the new government, a matter ominously beyond the competence of the Secretary of State to ensure. Or else he could elect to leave the Service, at or immediately after independence or after a period of employment if accepted into the Service of one of the two new Dominions. In that case he would receive a proportionately calculated pension for service completed (and many officers had not yet acquired the minimum ten years' service) and receive what in the context of Crown service overseas was the innovation of lump sum compensation for loss of career, payable on a fixed scale. If this choice was exercised, the ex-ICS officer would face the uncertainty of taking pot luck in the hunt for a job. In the ICS case, too, the situation was made worse by the coincidence of India's independence with the wave of demobilized war veterans flooding the UK employment market.

In the event, and after some arm-twisting, a subsequent offer was made, allowing ex-ICS officers to remain on the continent and among the people they knew, by joining the staffs of the new UK High Commission in Delhi or Karachi. In that case, the applicant would be required to satisfy the rigours of the full selection process by the Civil Service Commissioners in London when he returned to London on furlough at the end of his first tour of duty in the High Commission. He would, of course, need to pass the preliminary selection held in India, which one of the Civil Service Commissioners would be flown out to conduct.[12] The one option that was never on the table, either to the ICS or in subsequent cases, was a lateral transfer into the British Foreign, Commonwealth or Home Civil Service. In the case of the ICS, but not the CAS or SPS, the irony was that the ICS officer had sat and passed the same competitive examination as his Whitehall colleagues. The SPS was arguably small enough, with less than 150 members to place and some of those ready to take early retirement on the not ungenerous terms worked out, to see through a largely successful exercise of relocation. Some statistics and individual case-studies, including transfers into the CAS, will be noted later on.[13] One thing they did achieve, coming after and learning from the ICS experience, was the importance of setting up in London a special bureau to help former members of the Service find another job.

The CAS, too, had a useful model of its own to turn to for precedent, dating back to the same period as the ICS. In Ceylon, which gained independence in 1948, a Public Officers' Agreement had been signed which closely followed the basic provisions of the ICS arrangement. The CO felt that should the Ceylon government renege on its undertaking to pay compensation and pensions it was the British Government and not the officers who would constitute the aggrieved party.[14] This was not a commitment the Treasury was willing to accept.[15] But one welcome improvement on the ICS scheme was that, although the CO did not adopt the ICS clause offering immediate attachment to the new British High Commission in Colombo, it initiated the system of offering serving members of the Ceylon Civil Service transfer within the CAS to other colonial territories. Some, like J. W. O'Regan, who had joined the Ceylon Civil Service in 1934, went on to enjoy promotion and postings in a series of colonial territories.[16] Another 'pilot' scheme was that worked out for the Gold Coast. By now a separate Public Officers' Agreement was the norm. Terms like 'Entitled Officers', 'Lump Sum Compensation' (LSC), 'Freezing' and 'Table of Factors' (age and length of service) became institutionalized as part of the defining vocabulary. In the case of the Gold Coast, the maximum sum payable in 1957, calculated on a formula of length of service and age, was £8000. In contemporary Malaya, where salaries were higher, the maximum compensation worked out at £11 000, payable on the age-related scale optimum of 39 years old and at least 8 years' service. It was Malaya that became something of a benchmark in negotiating compensation to overseas civil servants for premature loss of career.[17] By the time the staffing crisis in the governments of Malaya erupted, the CO had plenty of precedent to fall back on. It was to need it all – and more.

A CONTINUING CAREER?: HMOCS

Although recruitment for the CAS had risen to an all-time peak during the years immediately following the end of the war, and was still showing little or no sign of running out of steam as a full career even with the signals of the decolonization of India in 1947 and of the Sudan actively in train by the early 1950s, the Colonial Office was at the same time giving thought to how to run down the CAS without injuring the prospects of its members, virtually all of whom outside West Africa were still being offered permanent and pensionable terms well into the 1950s. Extensive discussions took place between the Colonial Office, the Commonwealth Relations Office, the Foreign Office and the Treasury, and in 1954 the Cabinet approved a statement on the reorganization of the Colonial Service.[18] It acknowledged that officers were entitled to ask what their position would be should the British government find itself, as the result of constitutional changes, unable to exercise control over their tenure and conditions of service. This personal uncertainty was balanced by HMG's own certainty that, despite the advance towards self-government in the colonial territories, the work of the Colonial Service was by no means over, and by the repeated reassurance that leaders of the emerging Commonwealth countries also recognized the fact that their service would be required for some time to come. The solution was therefore one of partnership between the British government and each government about to attain independence. In respect of responsibility for its public officers in the Colonial Service, what HMG now looked for from the about-to-be new administrations was set out in a series of expected guarantees which may be summarized as under:

- Conditions of service of expatriate officers not to be less favourable than those enjoyed prior to independence;
- Pensions to be safeguarded;
- HM Government to continue to regard expatriate officers as HM servants even when they were employed by the new state;
- Any reasonable request for transfer should be accepted without disturbing the officer's pension rights;
- Expatriates to be considered on equal terms with local officers for promotion;
- Expatriates to be given adequate notice of the termination of employment;
- HM Government to try and find them alternative employment;
- In the event of premature retirement at the hands of the new government, expatriate officers to receive adequate compensation for interruption of career.[19]

This constitutional *quid pro quo* was incorporated into a proposal in 1954 to reorganize the Colonial Service into a new Crown service, to be called Her Majesty's Overseas Civil Service (HMOCS). Membership would be open to serving members of the old Colonial Service as well as to new officers, although it would not be automatic and they would have to apply. HMOCS would not be open to local civil servants already in the CAS, who would be expected to transfer into their own new administrative services. Although the assurance, as we have seen, on the obligation of the Secretary of State to try and find alternative employment for Colonial Service officers made redundant through constitutional change was vague, the formalization of the principle of compensation was definitely encouraging. Indeed, in many instances it was to prove too encouraging. Offered a down payment of a lump sum, many officers – not only those who were likely to be compulsorily retired but also those who voluntarily decided to retire early – preferred the assurance of an immediate lump sum to the uncertainty of the 'guarantee' of acceptable future employment. As it turned out, too, it was often the mid-career officers, whose services were critical and whom the new government wanted to retain, who were among the first to go in search of a new job now rather than a few years later, instead of being, as was hoped, among the first to stay on a bit longer.

The creation of HMOCS in 1956 proved only a partial victory for the CO in its vigorous campaign within Whitehall for the realization of its dream of a Commonwealth or British Overseas Service, with a Commonwealth-wide remit for continuing service by members of the former Colonial Service. The FO and CRO were determined to draw an unmistakable line between the colonial then and the autonomous now; such a demarcation clearly excluded the re-appearance of Colonial Service officers under another Service name. Any question of a direct transfer from the CAS into the CRO or FO was a non-starter. If a DO wanted to seek a position in either of these departments of state, let him apply in the usual way, take the competitive examination and be interviewed by the Civil Service Commission – the very process many of them had deliberately rejected five to twenty years earlier. Some, as we shall see below, took advantage of the opportunity opened up for HMOCS personnel to sit the concessional competition,[20] i.e. they were allowed to deduct the time spent in the Colonial Service from their age up to the maximum entry age. In the Foreign Service this was 28. Many of these (see below) went on to a rewarding second career, once more in the preferred context of work overseas. Yet today evidence can still bubble up of the existence of bad blood between ex-CO officers (less noticeable among ex-CAS officers) and the other senior Ministries in Whitehall over the campaign waged by the CO to protect the careers of their people in the Colonial Service by offering them the element of continuity in Crown service.[21] This, as they and the CO saw it, would bring to Britain's mushrooming High Commissions and new Embassies in the Third World knowledge and experience of, interest in, and affection for that world.

Meanwhile, following what some saw as the damp squib of the HMOCS, a staffing crisis had blown up in Nigeria, the scene of the largest number of CAS personnel in the whole colonial empire. None argued more vigorously than the new Governor, Sir James Robertson, that the provisions of the 1954 reorganization of the Colonial Service into the HMOCS were utterly inadequate to stem what he prophesied would be an exodus of 'compensated' – frequently the best – officers. What added to the dire and doleful assessment was that not a single

British DO had been recruited since the new Nigerian constitution of 1954. Alarmed by the prospect of an administrative breakdown of mammoth proportions, Robertson in person added his weight (which was considerable in all ways) from Lagos. The CO, led by its new Secretary of State and an admirer of the Colonial Service, Alan Lennox-Boyd, showed itself willing to stand up to the Treasury (whose Chancellor, Harold Macmillan, was not without experience of the CO, having been its Parliamentary Secretary during the post-Atlantic Charter scuffle and scurry). In May 1956 the Cabinet approved the issuing of a further statement of policy regarding the 1954 Colonial Service reorganization.[22] In it, the government acknowledged the point made by Robertson, that compensation schemes were having an arguably reverse effect, and accepted that fresh arrangements would have to be made so as to help create conditions which would encourage officers to remain. The new Special List scheme primarily had the acute staff situation of Nigeria in mind, but its presentation was flexible enough to permit it being adapted to other instances. Essentially it established a Special List of HMOCS officers who would be in the direct service of HMG and be seconded to the employing government. HMG would pay their pension and any qualifying compensation, recovering the cost from the employing government. Those transferred to the Special List would accept an obligation to serve the British government, up to the age of 55, in any post to which they might be assigned from time to time. Finally, while HMG declared its hope of finding continuous employment for these officers until they were 55, any officer unemployed through no fault of his own would be kept on full pay for five years or up to the age of 50. Lump sum compensation in the Nigerian case worked out at a maximum of £9000, payable at the optimum age of 42. As a further incentive to stay on rather than quit, compensation could now be frozen at its most favourable point for up to three years.

The complicated Nigerian negotiations did not finish with this Special List. Resignations of officers in the much-needed senior and middle seniority grades continued apace. The CO soon found Robertson on their back again. A senior CO official was despatched post-haste to Lagos. In July 1958 the CO was obliged to issue another Statement of Policy, the third Colonial Service rethink in four years.[23] This time the device was addressed to officers serving in Nigeria only. It was accepted that the Special List had failed to stem the tide of early retirement: less than 400 out of an eligible 2000 HMOCS officers in Nigeria had opted for transfer. The reasons were frankly acknowledged by HMG. 'It seems', the Statement grudgingly opened,

> that the reluctance of overseas officers to join the existing Special List is due in part to political difficulties, actual or apprehended, resulting from the transfer of power to local governments, partly to the attractions of the lump sum compensation paid to officers who decide to retire from the Nigerian services, and partly to dissatisfaction with present emoluments.[24]

The solution now put forward was to create not one but two Special Lists in Nigeria. The original scheme would remain, now re-labelled Special List A. The new Special List B would allow an officer to draw an immediate advance of 90 per cent of the lump sum compensation he would be eligible to receive on eventual retirement. To its Nigerian CAS audience, List B was the option to continue serving, if one was wanted and at the same time if one wanted, in Nigeria (and nowhere else) by transferring to one of the four Government public services (Federal, Northern, Western, Eastern). When one finally left Nigeria, that was it: from then on, it was job-hunting on the open market. Some preferred to face up to that challenge right away rather than postponing it for a few more years, when they would be that much older and the employment situation in the UK would be that much tighter. List A, on the other hand, was the option to continue serving HMG, whether overseas in what was left of the post-African empire, mostly in the Pacific, or back in Britain (the unexciting Ministry of Labour and the Inland Revenue Department not excluded). List A allowed one the leisurely option of not finding any job offer 'acceptable' and so taking five years on full salary. In the event, while official records remain unavailable, the number of officers who opted for List A and went to HMOCS jobs elsewhere in the Empire was small and likely not much more than a hundred. The majority tended to feel that for them HMOCS was Nigeria or nothing.

Two further HMOCS reforms were yet to come. In 1960, at the end of a comprehensive review in Whitehall and in the Cabinet in the context of the rapidly changing colonial scene, the future of HMOCS itself was tackled. Rather than extend the generous Nigeria-specific Special Lists A and B to other territories, HMG simply (but at last) agreed to assume responsibility for the 'expatriate' element in officers' pay and pensions.[25] The Overseas Aid Act of 1961 enabled this reform. The next year the Government revealed its future policy on recruitment for service overseas,[26] a responsibility now shed by the CO and shouldered by a new Department of Technical Co-operation (DTC). HMOCS was now no longer on general offer as a career to new entrants. By 1960 its numbers had reached approximately 20 000, ten per cent more than the Colonial Service could boast at its peak in 1957.

But the scale of that post-war Colonial Service recruitment needs to be read alongside its departmental distribution. Now it was the professional services which, following the generous Colonial Development and Welfare Act of 1949, were expanding as part of the economic and infrastructural development. The Colonial Education Service recruitment more than doubled in ten years from 139 in 1947 to 329. The Colonial Medical Service recruited 128 doctors in 1947 and 266 in 1957, and the intake into the Colonial Veterinary Service rose from 16 to 28.[27] It was the Colonial Administrative Service, the DO cadre of this study, that was declining. Posts filled in 1957 tumbled by half to 109 from the 226 of 1947. True, CAS was well up in overall terms from its early post-war peak of 1800 officers and now stood at almost 2400, but it was the notional cadet successors to those immediate pre- and post-war DOs who were no longer coming forward. After 1957, the CAS was on a downward curve; by 1967 it had become a somewhat remnant element in the new HMOCS; by 1987, it was virtually restricted to Hong Kong. However one reacts to the post-colonial (at times seemingly *post hoc*) argument that independence was inherent in the purpose of British colonial policy right from the moment of initial overlordship,[28] there is little cause to question the frank admission of a senior official in the Colonial Office that 'The Service had never been organized on the assumption that the territories in which it was employed would become independent within the life-time of its members.'[29]

SECOND CAREERS

It is against this background of attempts first to stimulate British recruitment by the device of the HMOCS and then to stem the outward flow of experienced officers opting, in the face of accelerated localization, for early retirement under the reasonably generous terms of the Special List mechanisms, that we turn to the third leg of the transfer of power tripod as it concerned overseas civil services: localization, early retirement and compensation schemes, and 'second careers'. What did the generic District Officers of Chapters 4–6 do when confronted by the premature loss of career? The diaspora of the former DO is an aspect of the post-imperial scene that has yet to attract the academic attention it deserves, both in respect of the dissolution of Britain's three overseas civil services and for the impact it had on the economic as well as the social fabric of Great Britain in the second half of the twentieth century. Here it is subsumed under the rubric of what may be termed 'Second Careers'. Once again, the process is presented on a Service-by-Service basis, leaving a territorial analysis for another occasion.

Indian Civil Service

As we saw when looking at Indianization in Chapter 8, regular recruitment to the ICS was suspended in 1940 and halted from 1942. By the end of the war in the Far East, the Government of Bengal was complaining that 'the steel frame was now more like lath and plaster, and more plaster than lath'.[30] ICS officers were left pretty much in the dark during the constitutional negotiations undertaken by the Cripps mission, though Wavell's blunt ultimatum to London that the ICS should be formally terminated unless HMG were prepared to slow down the political pace and postpone British rule for another 15–20 years[31] must have made things clear to the India Office if not welcome. The two White Papers of 1947[32] set out the options for the ICS: in brief, 'staying on'; retirement with compensation; or join the staff of the two British High Commissions. These arrangements hardened into the fundamentals of a precedent as the ICS negotiations of 1947 were followed by those for the CAS in Ceylon in 1946–8, for the SPS in 1953–5, and thereafter all the way through the colonial empire up to Hong Kong in the 1990s. In each of the three Service cases, the British Government set up a special Bureau in London to help returning officers find jobs, though in every instance there were many officers who preferred to look for a second career on their own initiative. In the case of the ICS, that responsibility was undertaken first by the Re-employment Branch of the Commonwealth Relations Office along with a special section of the London Appointments Office, and then by the India and Burma Services Re-employment Organization.

Ewing rightly makes her comment that

> much attention has been paid to the transfer of power and the constitutional issues that were raised [but] comparatively little attention has been paid to the fate of those British officers who, on 15 August 1947, suddenly found their careers abruptly brought to an end.[33]

Yet by the time even the effective ICS (Rtd.) association got round to collecting the data on relocation of its members, it was forty years since the ICS had ceased to exist. Hence the eventual privately circulated survey, invaluable as it is, relates to only 345 British officers, less than half of those in the Service in 1939. Furthermore, in the final statistical analysis, the fact that a number of officers had had more than one 'second' career means that in any total given there remains an element of double counting. In ICS summary, from a wide spectrum of employment ranging, as Ewing records,[34] from ambassadors to heads of preparatory schools and from a member of the British Board of Film Censors to a Prison Governor, a number of major directions of second career emerge.

Sixty-one officers joined the Home Civil Service. The same percentage (18 per cent) took up posts in commerce and industry. Thirty-six (over 10 per cent) gained admission to the Diplomatic Service. Thirty went into the Colonial Administrative Service, many of them then leaving early, expressing disappointment with the CAS after the greater responsibility given to them in the ICS.[35] At least one, though he seems to have slipped through this survey, is known to have gone into the SPS. Three joined the BBC. The list was too recent to have registered the four who joined the British Council back in 1948–9. Twenty officers became members of the legal profession and twenty-four went into university life, two-thirds of them as academics and the rest as administrators. Ten went into hospital administration, five qualified as doctors. Six took holy orders. Perhaps surprisingly, only five went into local government in Britain, though many more became involved in voluntary administration and politics at the local level. A mere three (1 per cent) took up national politics. Seventeen became farmers, of one scale or another. As many as fifty-nine (17.5 per cent) expressed the wish to stay on in the new civil services of the two independent states and were accepted. To list the contribution to literature by former members of the ICS over the ninety years of its life-time, whether by way of notable works of scholarship, candid autobiographies and memoirs, or the recreation of fiction, would be a Herculean task. They constitute more of a library than a bookshelf. Even in the mid-1990s, fifty years after the Service was wound up, studies and reminiscences were still being published. It would, however, be impossible and improper to fail to mention among the many, in the context of retirement occupation, Philip Mason's magisterial tributes to the ICS, *The Men Who Ruled India*, and to the Indian Army, *A Matter of Honour*.

Figures for re-employment within the first two years of the disbandment of the ICS, 1947–9, carry an importance of their own.[36] Partly they reflect an immediacy of seeking and securing a second career and partly because by the time the comprehensive survey took place, in 1987, many of the 1947–9 office-holders did not appear in it as they were no longer alive. By 1949, sixty-six officers had been accepted for a permanent post in the Home Civil Service, with a further 57 accepted on contract. In the Diplomatic Service, to the 26 who gained entry on permanent and pensionable terms another 13 were given con-tract appointments. The CAS took 40 on permanent terms and 13 others on contract. The figure for those accepted by one or other of the two new Dominion civil services on the Continent was reasonably high, 136 of the thou-sand or so on the Association's books. Twenty-eight were holding livings under Crown patronage or in other Church appointments and 23 had secured appoint-ments with Public Boards. Six had been engaged by the British Military Administration and 23 were now holding Intelligence appointments. Approximately 10 per cent reported that they were no longer looking for assist-ance in relocation.

Sudan Political Service

As with the ICS, it was not until the early 1980s that an initiative by the Director of the Oxford Development [Colonial] Records Project generated a major research project into the diaspora of the SPS that had occurred some thirty years previously. With the support of P. P. Howell and Sir Gawain Bell, both former SPS officers who had finished up in the CAS, and with the help of their Dining Club, which maintained a close and convivial link especially among those recruited before 1939, a preliminary register of second careers was com-piled, again for private circulation, in 1989.[37] More than 250 entries were con-structed, out of a Service which totalled less than 500 over its whole recruitment lifespan, 1899 to 1952. The number still serving in the SPS when the crash Sudanization programme was enforced in 1953–4 was under 120. But because the early retiring age of 48 (optional, not mandatory) had always and purposely allowed officers to take up subsequent employment, details of the second career of officers who had taken normal retirement and had not suffered the 1953–5 premature loss of career were deliberately included in the *Register*.

A Sudan Resettlement Bureau was set up in London to help prematurely retired SPS officers in their search for re-employment. One of the conspicuous second-career conclusions to emerge is the relatively high number of officers who returned to the Middle East or the arabophone Maghreb, either in busi-ness or in the Diplomatic Service. The ICS, and later CAS, option of joining the new state's civil service was not on offer to SPS personnel. At least fifteen entered the Diplomatic Service, half of them being posted at one time or another in ambassadorial rank to the Arab world. Significantly, D. C. Carden and J. F. S. Phillips returned to Khartoum as HM Ambassador, well fêted on revisiting the country where they had undergone their DC apprenticeship. A further seven were offered senior governmental positions by various Middle East states, as Minister or Development Secretary or Field Force Commander, and one ex-DC – the ebullient Hugh Boustead – as Keeper of the Horse. The oil companies were not slow to maximize this Arab-experienced and Arabic-speaking resource, employing a further dozen or so ex-DCs.

Not surprisingly, many a Sudan DC jumped at the opportunity to go on being a DC, above all in Africa: the transition did not prove as traumatic, inter-continental or inter-Service, as it had for some of the ICS transfers. More than a score were taken into the CAS. Five were assigned to Arabic-speaking Aden. The rest remained in Africa, both foreclosing West and constitutionally further-to-go East. For the first time, the SPS was about to make a numerically substantial impact on its sister-service, the CAS. Previous interservice transfer of this nature had been restricted to the gubernatorial level, with G. F. Archer and G. S. Symes coming in from the Colonial Service and H. A. MacMichael going out to it. Now, with J. W. Robertson, G. W. Bell and W. Luce all promoted to colonial governorships after the dissolution of the SPS, other SPS officers moved to Uganda and Northern Nigeria as DCs or DOs or into the Secretariat. As with the ICS, a good-sized group secured appointments in university administration, with Exeter College, Oxford, uniquely electing no fewer than four ex-SPS officers serially to its Bursarship. Others became schoolmasters and a few lecturers. The Church, which had exercised a strong influence in the Sudan from the days of Sir Reginald Wingate as Governor-General (and, of course, in the pre-Condominium context of 'Gordon of Khartoum'), attracted several DCs; six were ordained. Local government, the BBC and British Council, farming and, widely, local voluntary service became the second career of many others. Three successfully stood for Parliament: A. D. Dodds-Parker, P. Munro and M. Wheatley. Exceptionally, after 15 years as a DC, W. G. R. M. Laurie decided to qualify as a medical doctor. Another ex-DC was equally unusual in his choice of second career, Wilfred Thesiger, one of the last great British explorers. As with their ICS colleagues, an urge to write lay beneath the solar topee; once again, the pre-enforced secondary career literary output, already notable, has been vigorously reinforced by a succession of reminiscences written in retirement, the most recent Service memoir appearing forty years after the SPS came to an end.[38]

Colonial Administrative Service

If one records that the CAS has not yet experienced anything like the research into second careers that the ICS and SPS now have, for all their latter-dayness and pilot scheme nature, two viable explanations can be marshalled. One is the sheer size and spread of the CAS: nearly 2500 still serving in 1957, compared to under a third of that total in the ICS and just 5 per cent in the SPS respectively on disbandment. The second fact is that the CAS was still a going concern under the rubric HMOCS right up to 1997. Even in the mid-1970s, there were approximately 300 HMOCS officers employed on permanent and pensionable terms outside Hong Kong. Two-thirds were still in Africa, with 46 in Malawi alone. Another 40 were in the Pacific, five in the Caribbean and three on the Falkland Islands. In Hong Kong itself, there were still 1200 HMOCS officers. HMOCS, like certain milks, is characterized by the quality of long life. The UK government is in the 1990s still assailed by claims and complaints over compensation and pensions.[39] Together these factors have materially contributed to delaying any major research into the diaspora of the CAS, though some work is currently in hand.[40]

Following the model of HMG support for the relocation of the ICS and SPS, an Overseas Services Resettlement Bureau (OSRB) was set up in 1957, called at first the Malayan Services Re-employment Bureau.[41] 'Her Majesty's Government in the United Kingdom', explained a notice sent to serving officers in 1958, 'are anxious that everything possible should be done to help officers who leave HMOCS prematurely as a result of recent constitutional changes to find alternative employment.'[42] An Advisory Council was set up, and when Lord Boyd, a former Secretary of State for the Colonies, accepted the chairmanship, HMOCS took it as an earnest of its status and as a boost to the morale of job-seekers. Deliberately the Council's membership included company directors from many leading firms, for it was believed that industry was a sector where DO experience of administration, management and human relations would be at a premium. The OSRB moved its headquarters out of the old CO building in Great Smith Street to Eland House, a convenient stone's throw from Victoria Station for its steady stream of callers (the personal call was strongly urged on enquirers by the Director and his staff). The OSRB had no more than three Directors in its first twenty years, a continuity indicative of its proven success. R. L. Peel and then H. A. S. Johnston had both held senior posts in the CAS, in Malaya and Nigeria, and Sir Edwin Arrowsmith, who took over in 1965, had finished his CAS career as Governor of the Falkland Islands.

Imaginatively, OSRB opened a branch office in the industrial heartland of Birmingham. From here it sent out a catalogue to over a thousand firms, presenting the *curricula vitae* of some of those on its books who had expressed an interest in a career in business. The Ashridge College of Business Management was persuaded to offer free places on its courses. In 1963, enquiries reached a peak of 1500 new applications to the Bureau. Within less than ten years the OSRB had been able to place 5911 of the 6508 names registered on its books. Of these, 2381 had been absorbed into industry and commerce. Expectedly, those in the 45–50 and, even more, 50–55 age brackets were the hardest to place. In 1970 the Bureau registered its 10 000th client. By then it had extended its services to the Diplomatic Service, where not only was a retiring age of 60 rigidly enforced but also a recent FO review had resulted in a reduction of posts. Nor, in the context of seeking a second career, should it be forgotten that this was also a period when a reduction in the armed forces brought further competition in job-hunting by ex-HMOCS officers.

A few points can be deduced from the preliminary data in CAS re-employment so far collected and analysed. While it came as a considerable shock, sometimes interpreted as a personal snub, to many high-flying DOs in the 1960s to learn that not only was a lateral transfer to the CRO or the FO simply not on the table but that to sit the standard CSC and undergo the full rigour of the selection process was an inflexible requisite, an above-average number of DOs faced up to the challenge and started a second career in these two Crown Services with an overseas element. The CSC's Limited Competition regulations allowed HMOCS officers, together with members of HM's Forces, to deduct their length of service from their actual age and to enter for the examination even if they had not taken a degree.[43] In the event, two HMOCS officers gained admission to the FO in 1959 and three were successful in the Foreign Service Senior Branch Supplementary Competition, which had an advanced age limit of 27 to 45 and called for no written examination. The successful penetration of the Foreign Service by the Colonial Service continued. By the mid-1970s, over 125 ex-HMOCS officers were serving in the FO, distributed by territory of principal origin as 29 from the four West African territories, 50 from the three East African ones, 12 from the two Central African ones, and three from the three High Commission Territories. Outside of Africa, 14 of these ex-HMOCS new diplomats had served in Malaya, three each in Palestine, Aden and Sarawak/North Borneo, and two in Cyprus. Among them, six had by *c*.1975 already reached High Commissioner or ambassadorial rank. Several were posted back to head either the High Commission or its regional branch in the territory where they had started their first career as DO, e.g. R. Posnett to Uganda, J. R. Johnson to Kenya and W. D. Wilson to Northern Nigeria. Interestingly, a number of ex-CAS officers reached gubernatorial rank in dependent territories, not through the old CO career route but through the new FCO one. In the New Hebrides the last three Resident Commissioners appointed by the FCO had all been one-time DOs. So, too, was the Vice-Marshal of the Diplomatic Corps from 1975–82, Sir Roger du Boulay.

Of the other principal professions in which members of the CAS made their second career, the categories do not alter materially from those in which the ICS and SPS successfully engaged. However, in one respect the CAS were considerably luckier, for they came on the UK market at a time when the great expansion of higher education took place in the 1960s. This enabled a proportionately higher number to embark on a second career in university administration. In some universities in the 1960s and 1970s the Registry numbered several ex-DOs on its staff. As with the ICS, CAS officers went on to become Vice-Chancellor. A fair proportion found their first-hand experience in public administration, local government and development was of help to them in securing appointments to the teaching staffs of universities, colleges and institutes in the Third World as well as locating in the expanding tertiary education system at home. Others with a flair for developmental skills relocated successfully in the Overseas Development Administration (ODA).

Reverting to the professions which had taken on former officers from the ICS and the SPS, once again a number of CAS officers were ordained: of the 750 former DOs serving in Africa interviewed, nearly 2 per cent went into the Church.

The dissolution of two of Britain's principal overseas civil services, the ICS and the SPS, between 1947 and 1955, and the rapid rundown of the third, the CAS, from 1957 to *c*.1977 and finally in Hong Kong in 1997, has been charted both in the summary statistics on localization presented in Chapter 8 and in the mirror image, the data on premature retirement of their expatriate members and the second careers they carved out for themselves, in the present chapter. The assessment of the record of these overseas civil servants in their first career is already an integral part of imperial historiography. The evolution of their second careers and of their impact on Britain's economy and its society awaits research by social historians.[44]

10 Empowering the Imperial Administrator

This book has offered a socio-institutional history of the composition and work of Britain's three principal corps of overseas administrators during the century *c*.1860 to *c*.1960. This was the era which saw Britain's *ad hoc* appointments of imperial administrators cohere into elite cadres of professionals and the Service convert into a major career option for hundreds of British graduates in search of Crown service overseas. The same century witnessed the decline and termination of such a career, from the security of its peak of authority through the constitutional enabling of its demission of power and on to the final dissolution of the respective civil services. The focus has not been on the minutiae of imperial policy but on imperial administrators, encapsulated in the person of the generic District Officer. The DO at once represents a concept, a figure and a status instantly recognizable both *in situ* and in the literature, regardless of whether he was locally identified as the Collector of the Indian Civil Service, the Government Agent of Ceylon, the District Commissioner of the Sudan, East and Central Africa and the Pacific, the District Officer of South East Asia and West Africa, the Travelling Commissioner of the West Coast, or the Resident Magistrate of the High Commission Territories.

Part I considered the question of *who* Britain's imperial administrators were, in the context of British social history during the classic century of empire, their familial and educational provenance, and *why* they inclined – or were conditioned – towards the particular career of Crown civil service overseas. In Part II, the focus shifted to *what* that career involved, all the way from the process of selection and training in each Service to the varied yet widely shared experience of field administration and headquarters duty, and on to special assignments and sometimes supreme proconsular office. Part III looked at the period when each of the three overseas civil services was wound down, examining the localization of the successor cadres and, back home, the opportunities for re-employment of the expatriate administrators following their premature loss of career.

The concluding chapter of this study of imperial administration as a conspicuous and continuing (for the better part of a century) career opportunity for those fulfilling Lord Cromer's vision of active young men endowed with good health, character and fair abilities, addresses a fundamental question underlying the exposition of Parts I and II. *How* did the DO achieve what he was expected, and had consciously and conscientiously undertaken, to do? An integral element in this 'how' question is that of the perception of the generic DO, both his own projected image and the image received by those whom he administered: the 'what do *I* think I am doing?' reflection, not always posed, and the 'what do *we* think he is doing?' reaction, not often expressed or recorded however frequently it may have been pondered. While the matter of how 'yesterday's rulers' were looked on by the ruled as they went about their appointed task of administering the empire promises to be less and less susceptible to firsthand evidence and authoritative interpretation, its importance, arguably advanced by this comparative study of Britain's principal administrative services overseas, deserves to be emphasized when history comes to compose the final epitaph on the imperial administrator in both memory and myth.

An effective *point de départ* for analysing the 'how' factor is to go back to the principles and guidelines which motivated those in London responsible for selecting overseas administrators. Well acquainted with the nature and context of the generic DO's work, they established in their collective mind the qualities which they believed would best enable the young administrator to perform well. In the case of the ICS, even before the Old Guard was replaced by the advent of the Competition Wallahs, the need for a measure of *ad hoc* training for service in the empire had been recognized. But there was more to Service preparation than an introduction to the basics of imperial history, law and exotic languages. It could, and should, foster a sense of *esprit de corps* and promote the growth of that code and ethos which lie at the heart of every successful institution. The East India Company's Haileybury College, 1806 successor to its College of Fort William initiative of 1801, was designed to educate, psychologically as well as intellectually, its cadet intakes. Fifty years on, nobody in the ICS could fail to be unaware of the strength of the Haileyburian network, an *esprit de corps* which the building of the Indian Institute at Oxford in the 1880s aimed to replace and reinvigorate.

The routine of the annual ICS Week in provincial headquarters, culminating in the exclusivity of the ICS Dinner at Government House with the Governor himself traditionally replying to the toast to the Service, was another powerful reminder and reinforcement of a Service *esprit de corps*. Following the successful extension of the model of ICS preparation, namely from the 1870s a probationers' course at Oxford University, the CAS, when it was its turn to consolidate and professionalize in the 1920s, set about creating its own programmes of induction and – though the term would have been spurned had it ever been recognized – Service socialization at Oxford and Cambridge, and later at London. In the case of the SPS, though some of them joined with their CAS colleagues in the probationers' courses at the university, it can be argued that their Service was compact enough and its annual intake of new members small enough for its ethos to be most effectively imparted at the one-to-one personal level, all the way from recruitment feelers at the university to the palpably familial reception in Khartoum and the *ad hominem* care taken over the first posting. In each of the overseas administrative services the same ethos, of never letting the side down, lay at the heart of the matter: the DO promoted at the same time as he absorbed a vigorous sense of loyalty, tradition and standards. Finally, on leave or after retirement, he could renew it from the formal reunion dinners annually held by each Service.

Experienced Company Sergeant-Majors accept that it is possible to instil an *esprit de corps* into even the most diffuse and recalcitrant bunch of initially unresponsive rookies. How much easier this aim was to achieve when the material for moulding already possessed an innate element of uniformity and predisposition. In the case of Britain's imperial administrators, this study has argued that the overriding bonus in the promotion of a Service ethos lay in the fact that its members were predominantly drawn from the public and the 'once removed' grammar schools, conspicuously the forcing house of codes of socialization and of loyalty and the exemplar of the supreme importance of tradition. If, as social historians sometimes claim, it was the British public school which made the Empire, imperial administrators often repaid the compliment by recreating and reinforcing in their Service much of what had been ingrained in them at school about the imperative of ethos.

One more point can be made in underlining the directness and strength of the psycho-social link between, as it were, the school prefect and the putative DO. Leaving aside the preoccupation of the ICS, and of the Eastern Cadetships up to 1932, with the primacy of intellectualism as a pointer to success, the correlation between the criteria observed by the public and grammar schools for their selection of prefect or monitor, head boy or dux, and the attributes calculated by the selection boards to make the *beau idéal* imperial administrator is too close to be ignored. Prefects in a public school had considerable power, but in general they learned to exercise it with moderation, sense and sensibility. The lessons of the prefectoral system had not only been writ large; they were also written in indelible ink. Yet it was arguably not so much the influence of the literal prefectoral system as the impact of the whole boarding school system which was to be so defining in the shaping of an ethos of loyalty, discipline and *esprit de corps*.[1] As impressionistic as they might have been, as unacceptable as they would be to modern interviewing techniques, and as out of place as they might appear in the contemporary world of management, teamwork and social egalitarianism, the qualities of character, leadership, personality and self-discipline so prized in the inter-war years immediately signalled to the interviewing board something that was a positive personal attribute and would be a potential Service asset in a career in imperial administration. The fundamental creed of the selectors of imperial administrators was to change little in the period under scrutiny: pick the right man for the job and you are half way to getting that job well done. Nor did they have much doubt in their collective mind what constituted the right man: to 'have character' was a *sine qua non*. However elusive a quality 'character' might be to define, it lent itself to instant recognition among those of like mind and proved a sufficiently reliable concept to enable the selection boards successfully to deliver the goods in nine cases out of ten. 'Their eyes were steady, their mouths firm', wrote, part amusedly and part seriously, one of the last proconsuls about the photographs of his predecessors which lined the walls of London's leading tropical outfitters:

> It was abundantly clear that without exception these paragons possessed in the fullest possible manner the qualities essential to a successful colonial administrator: fortitude, fair dealing, integrity and supreme self-confidence.[2]

From that psychological intermesh of school and codes and Service, of personal attributes and attitudes, which together helped to construct an ethos, it is possible to formulate a number of more practical answers to the fundamental question of how did the generic DO manage to cope with the challenges inherent in his work as an alien administrator. The ICS, CAS and SPS may indeed have constituted examples of the administrative or service elite of modern sociological idiom. Overseas their status was acceptedly (if not always acceptably) superior, among their own countrymen as well as in the eyes of the ruled. However, that was in no way the case at home on leave or in retirement. Nor, in the event, were they as superior as the alleged 'heaven-born' or 'tin gods' they themselves sometimes liked to think. Superior, then, but not a breed of supermen. Up to the moment the DO sailed from London or Liverpool he was, in the inter-war years, pretty much on a par with hundreds of his schoolmates and fellow undergraduates, likely less brainy than some and maybe more brawny than others of his College cohort but all in all typical rather than extraordinary. So what was it that enabled him, transplanted thousands of miles away and uprooted in all senses, to take on, enjoy and generally succeed in the challenges of a career as an imperial administrator?

If what has been persuasively styled 'The Thin White Line' of imperial administration was, in numbers on the ground, truly 'exiguous to the point of disbelief',[3] where did the strength of the so-called Steel Frame lie? While each of the four resources identified below needs to be triply qualified – by geography (the milieu of imperial administrator in Sarawak or Singapore was not the same as in Sierra Leone or the Solomon Islands), by periodization (the administrative requirements of the rudimentary turn of the century were different from those of the inter-war years and again from those conditioned by the decolonization climax of the 1960s), and by the generations of manpower (the kind of DO recruited in the initial period of establishing civil administration differed from that sought in the more sophisticated middle years and again from that needed to operate a latter-day ministerial system of government) – they share enough overall relevance to justify the status of common denominators. What the generic DO required for, and what he brought to, the successful execution of his job can be mnemonically set out in the properties of collaboration, coercion, competence and confidence.

The Robinsonian thesis of collaboration has for the most part centred on political acquiescence by the ruled, especially their leaders, whether of the traditional or nationalist elite.[4] In the context of how the DO managed to operate, full play must also be given to the existence of an effective (if not always efficient) subordinate bureaucratic elite, the Native Administration (NA) of classical colonial governance. The *soi-disant* 'lone' DO did not exist outside the imagination of the novelist; in reality, the DO was seldom far away from *khansama* or *chaprassi*, clerk or interpreter, headman or local official. It was perhaps in communication, and likely in culture and companionship, but not in company, that it could be said of the DO that he was often lonely yet rarely alone. Collaboration, in the literal sense of working with people, was at the very centre of his work, just as race relations, in the primary sense of interacting with people of a different race, lay at the heart of the DO's daily contacts.

Next coercion. What is, to the historian, often surprising about the use of force in British imperial administration is how little of it was either necessary or available in the typical DO situation. The tragedies of excessive imperial force tend to obscure its absence from the other 360 days of the year: Nandi Fort in Kenya in 1905, Hadejia in 1906 and Abeokuta in 1918 in Nigeria, Amritsar in 1919, Khartoum in 1924 and Accra in 1948, and the large-scale operations – campaigns rather than days or hours of horror, such as Malaya and Kenya's Mau Mau in the 1950s and the end-game in Palestine, Cyprus and Aden. Coercion there was from time to time, including the imposition of forced labour. The continuing colonial imperative of law and order was rarely out of mind. In some areas, too, particularly in the communal tinderbox of India, sectarian – not *per se* anti-government, unless the DO interposed himself in the middle – riots were a regular feature of the season. For the most part, the police (and, outside India's substantial experience of providing aid to the civil power, the army) were conspicuously 'less a presence than an earnest'.[5] Where force was resorted to, it was often justified as a measure to avoid further force in the future.

Yet, for all the limited exercise of force, the psychological message was there. If the worst came to the very worst, say the nightmare of another 1857 as conjured up by General Dyer at Amritsar in 1919 or the spectre of a plot to murder every European in the country as sensed by the Governor of Nyasaland forty years later, then the 'lone' DO could – in theory – precipitate the intervention of the British army and navy (and, as was the experience of Somaliland, the Sudan and the North-West Frontier between the wars, of the new arm of empire, the Royal Air Force)[6] mightily to avenge him if too late to rescue him. Emotional scenario that this was, its very possibility may have played its part in converting armed resistance by the ruled into a second rather than primary reaction and in containing the ruler's recourse to heavy coercion. Omissi's judgement on the role of the army in India in providing aid to the civil power resonates for the rest of the Empire. 'The army often remained in the background', he writes of the frequent outbreaks of violence, 'but the background is an important part of the picture.'[7]

None of this is to deny the spasmodic appearance on the imperial scene of naked brutality, the occasional killer soldier like Richard Meinertzhagen[8] or the sadistic disciplinarian DO, quickly nicknamed 'Mr Twenty Lashes' and in kind satirized by Sir Evelyn Baring, Governor of Kenya, as the MFH variety of DC, 'plenty of dog biscuit and a good strong whip'.[9] Overall, however, L. H. Gann is correct in his assessment that in imperial policing Britain's authority in general rested on a minimum of force.[10] That the DO relied on personality, not the pistol, to quell trouble was a point well conveyed in Alexander Korda's direction of Edgar Wallace's *Sanders of the River*, when in reply to the panic telegram from the young DO urgently requesting the Governor to despatch a battalion of troops to help him put down an armed disturbance, HE wired back 'Am sending no troops, only Commissioner Sanders'.

Thirdly, competence. The DO was not an expert in every task that came his way; no deliberately generalist administrator was expected to excel in every one of Jack's tens of trades. What he conspicuously had, however, was competence. He was good at his job (of being a DO), which *ipso facto* called for the qualities of resourcefulness and improvization. He could be relied on to be at least adequate whatever the occasion. 'This is so', it has been claimed,

> regardless of whether he was one of the double-First masterminds of the ICS, a stereotype triple-Blue or bog baron from the Sudan, the run-of-the-mill African administrator with his modest degree in modern history at Oxford or English at Cambridge, or even the slightly scabrous, yet gentleman-to-the-last-drop 'Consul at Sunset' figure.[11]

The need for such versatility, present right from the rough-and-ready days of one-man administration when the DO was everything from judge and tax-collector to policeman and postmaster, was enhanced in the last decades of imperial rule when he was called on to, for example, establish local councils, conduct a general election, draft development plans, implement a plebiscite, direct an adult education or fertilizer campaign, or act as Clerk to the Legislature or private secretary to an elected Minister. Not only had he never – could he ever have – been trained for such a tutti-frutti of assignments; many of them, in the decolonizing decades, lay in the realm of partisan politics and 'political masters', that very milieu which he had sought to escape ten to twenty years earlier by opting for a Crown service career overseas rather than in Whitehall.[12]

In coming to the fourth of the qualities which enabled the imperial administrator to succeed in his job, the focus moves away from the demonstrable three-fold context of collaboration and coercion and competence in generalist administration, to the less tangible psychological make-up of the DO. His success, his effectiveness, his very ability to do and to be, were basically rooted in the assumption of his authority: I am the DO, *ergo quidque est*. His word was law; he was the law. To the large majority of the populace, the DO not only represented the government, he was the government. In the DO, A. P. Thornton's 'habit of authority' became the uniform of authority. Here race as well as the force of personality played a part. 'The European DO', it has been figuratively said, 'wore the bullet-proof waistcoat of a white skin. It might not stop the bullet but it nearly always deterred the other party from firing.'[13]

In the art of imperial administration, then, there was – there had to be, so thin was the 'White Line' – a generous measure of what has been called White Man's Bluff.[14] 'Whatever their motives', concedes the perceptive and popular historian of Empire, James Morris, 'they had no doubts … brisk young cadets, so fresh, so pink, so assured.'[15] Behind the face of competence lay the heart of confidence, of self-confidence. The conclusion is clear: essentially, the DC administered with the aid of a mystique of authority created by and built on his own self-confidence. It was not a sense of satrapy alone that guided him, nor force that guarded him. However misplaced or misconstrued, conscious or quite unconscious, it was a fundamental sense of one kind or another of superiority (cultural, moral, intellectual, socio-racial, technological or organizational know-how), at once unquestioned and unquestioning, which enabled the expatriate colonial administrator – be he experienced Commissioner or greenhorn cadet – to advise, to act, to accomplish, and indeed to be.[16] Two seasoned colonial administrators, fifty years, two countries and two cultures apart, expressed the same conclusion in the same way. For Robert Delavignette, the DO's secret lay in 'the personal authority of the administrator and, in the final analysis, his personal character expressed in the exercise of authority'.[17] Robert Coryndon's belief was similar:

> It is recognized that a valuable principle of Native Administration is that the desires and the measures of the Government shall be carried through as much as possible by the force of personal prestige which should be the distinguishing characteristic of Native Officials ... that, in fact, the administration of the natives should be, in a sense, by personality rather than by legislation.[18]

And if the administration of the empire may, after all, be looked on as one great confidence-trick, a huge game of White Man's bluff, it was one the generic DO played, wittingly and willingly, upon himself as well as upon the subject races. As the DC returning to London on leave said to his wife when he strode masterfully into the pell-mell traffic to cross Piccadilly Circus in the rush-hour: 'they wouldn't dare!'

In thus setting forth the problem of understanding how the imperial administrator managed to operate, it is suggested that a supplementary view of the 'how' might be gained from a twofold imagological approach. What was the DO's own image of his role and what perception did the ruled have of the ruler?

A synthesis of the literature, all the way from official documentation and unofficial record across to personal reminiscence and excursions into the short story and the novel, indicates that in the beginning, at the end and throughout the middle, a dual concern informed the concept of the DO's primary role: law and order. In the event, the two became fused into a single imperative, so that in colonial discourse 'law and order' is [*sic*] invariably followed by a singular verb. Law and order was the context in which imperial administration was – could only be – carried out. It was the precondition for any and every 'development' that followed. The primacy of law and order not only permeated the principles of general guidance issued during the colonial period to serving or would-be imperial administrators. It was being emphasized in one of the last of such publications, issued in Dar es Salaam on the eve of independence, still retaining its precedence over all other obligations:

> The DC is the focus of government authority and local administration... He is responsible for law and order... He is charged with the promotion of the economic, social and political development of the area....[19]

That the maintenance of law and order should have been the top priority when civil administration took over from military occupation is understandable. Lugard's immediate fear when news of the thunderbolt of the Satiru revolt of

1906 in Nigeria reached him was that it portended the collapse of law and order throughout the newly acquiescent emirates. Acting in aid of the civil power at Amritsar in 1919, Dyer believed he was preventing the mutinous overturn of the Indian empire. The decision to initiate Operation Jock Scott in 1952 was taken so as to pre-empt a breakdown in law and order in Nairobi rather than subsequently having laboriously to restore civil administration. Consistent with this ordering of priorities, law and order did not lose its precedence at the end of empire, either. Sir James Robertson's SOS to the Colonial Office for new measures to stem the exodus of expatriate staff was premised on the argument – the ultimate weapon in every colonial governor's armoury – that he could not guarantee the maintenance of law and order in Nigeria as it moved into its final constitutional stage unless his DOs remained in post. Wavell had the same message for the India Office when he hinted that the ICS might as well be closed down at once unless it was supported by the home government in its responsibility for law and order. His Breakdown Plan,[20] including a phased with-drawal of control and the military evacuation of Europeans, was motivated by the scenario of a total collapse in law and order. Palestine and Aden proved, Cyprus threatened to show, and Nyasaland was afraid of, what could happen to a colonial government when its administration was no longer able to maintain law and order at the moment of a nationalist forcing of the pace of decoloniza-tion. Throughout the colonial period, then, from beginning to end, administra-tors were always conscious that 'development', infrastructural or socio-economic or even constitutional, was impossible outside a framework of law and order: no peace, no progress. Such a colonial maxim has been one which post-colonial governments, too, have been quick to invoke when confronted by demonstrations, riots, strikes and activist opposition.

For the generic DO, that imperative of law and order allowed him to give expression to what may be taken as his second guiding principle in how he viewed his job. This was the application of justice. Few DOs would have dif-fered with the Dickensian contention that the law is not the same creature as justice. What, in any case, was 'law' to the DO confronted simultaneously by Islamic law (*Shari'a*), Hindu law, multifaceted customary law, native law and custom, all within the framework of a central government which observed English law? Throughout the colonial period the debate continued, sometimes in public sometimes *sotto voce*, that in the eyes of the ruled the DO acting as magistrate was in far closer touch with 'native opinion' and expectations of justice than was a professional judiciary rooted in the view from Chancery Lane. So in his search for justice, the DO sometimes found himself trying to balance his knowledge of law acquired from passing his magistrate's examination with a sense of justice, part innate, part proudly 'British', and part derived from his schoolboy code of what was fair and what was not. This is not to say he broke the law or subverted it. He may now and again, like others and betters before him, have put a metaphorical telescope to his momentarily blind eye: experi-enced seniors were wont to warn high-minded cadets puritanically committed to rooting out corruption in the Native Authority or embezzlement in the Native

Treasury with all the single-mindedness of a sniffer-dog that, if that scale of fearless justice were practised, the whole local administration would collapse because not a single accountant or ledger clerk would be left to man the Treasury nor any chief through whom to govern according to the hallowed principles of indirect rule.

Extending his likely public school-bred sense of prefectoral right and wrong to the wider scene, many a DO would have replied to the question – regrettably one which few wanted or dared to put to him – of what did he think he was there to do by declaring, 'In the first place I am here to prevent injustice.' In particular, this would mean protecting 'his' peasantry, amorphous yet real enough in his own mind, from what he perceived as the tyranny of their own rulers. 'We were concerned', records one imperial administrator with long service in the SPS and the CAS, 'with the cultivator and the herdsman ... it was to them that we believed it was our principal duty to address ourselves.'[21] This was not only despite the well-known precept that in situations of positive indirect rule not only was he expected to 'support and uphold'[22] those traditional rulers, but also in the knowledge that for a DO to acquire the local nickname of 'Friend of the Peasant' could be the kiss of promotional death if at the same time it translated into 'Scourge of the Chief'. The gradations in this self-projected role of protector are numerous, and the image is blurred by the corrective reflection that sometimes the DO's own behaviour towards the same peasantry might well have appeared to border on the petty, the tyrannical or the collaborative. Yet there is little doubt that the generic DO frequently felt, if he ever paused to ask himself why he was there, an unarticulated sense of a role (the word 'mission' would have been rejected by many of them as too goody-goody Christianizing and too arrogantly 'modernizing') of preventing injustice, defending the underdog, improving the standard of people's lives, and generally seeking to leave the District 'better' than when he came. Here was the endorsement and the realization, frequently quite unconscious, of the Lugardian vision of the DO as the idealized English gentleman, 'with an almost passionate conception of fair play, of protection of the weak, and of playing the game'.[23] As naive, starry-eyed, and possibly immature as such a mind-set may have been, it certainly had none of the evil or exploitative animus associated with the persona of the DO in the anti-imperialist demonology.

Behind that self-image of protectiveness lay the imperative of paternalism. It is often forgotten that such a stance was enshrined as a virtue by the League of Nations in its tutelary injunction that colonial powers should shelter dependent peoples from the chill winds of modern life and guide them until such time as they would be able to stand on their own feet.[24] Once again the guardian spirit of paternalism, as in the practice of indirect rule, can be discerned in the formative structures and codes of the public school authority system. Tom Brown might not have made a good DO and Flashman is unlikely to have reached the interviewing board, but both would have instantly recognized the system and likely thought of East, exuding 'transcendent coolness and self assurance',[25] as good DO material.

Arguably, and so far under-exploredly, the biggest challenge for the DO's self-image and self-confidence came not so much in the early days of acting as political officer to a punitive patrol or interposing his unarmed self between two warring factions, but in the final years of colonial rule. It was then that the generic DO may have experienced the twinge of a doubt about whether he had chosen the right career after all. District work was fun, basically that was what he had joined for. Even the so-called routine of office life in the *kacheri* or *boma* was constantly liable to the colonial unexpected. And if a spell in the urban Secretariat was held to be a necessary part of his training, to wean him away, as Douglas Newbold warned his Sudan DCs, from the delusion of Arcadianism, every month brought nearer the anticipated joy of a return to rural administration. But now, towards the end of empire, along came party politics and elected parliamentarians and all the nepotism and injustice (yesterday's NA corruption, today's Cabinet sleaze) of the ministerial way of life. It was rarely the personal dislike of serving under an Asian or African Minister but of being subordinated to any Minister at all, in Lahore, Lagos or London, that irked. Having eschewed a career in the corridors of power in Whitehall, it was ironical that the DO should now have to undergo the same experience along the verandahs of power in Assam or Accra. The new role of Your Obedient Servant was not always to the DO's taste, yet, as ever, his versatility and readiness to turn his hand to anything helped him to survive and overcome.

Despite much popular conception, the transfer of power in which the DO-turned-bureaucrat was now engaged generated little overpowering feeling of personal hostility on the part of either party, DO or nationalist politician. The DO felt anxiety about the future but little sense of bitterness or betrayal. The much-experienced Sir Gawain Bell is but one of thousands to dispute the gloomy observation in the Book of Ecclesiastes quoted by the authoritative Lord Hailey as an epitaph for the dying overseas civil services as they demitted to their local successors, 'Yea, I hated all my labour which I had taken under the sun, because I should leave it unto the man that shall be after me.'[26] The quip that the job of the ideal end-game DO in South East Asia, Africa and the Pacific was to commit occupational suicide, training up his successor and so doing himself out of a job, was one retailed with more amusement than anger.

When we turn to the other half of the imagology of the DO, not his projected self-image but that received by those whom he administered, a major evidential obstacle is encountered. While the literature by and about the DO is abundant and has in the contemporary aftermath of Empire swelled to a crescendo, the ruled have, with the obvious exception of the nationalists, only infrequently expressed their opinion of the rulers. Where they have done so, it has overwhelmingly been the view of the educated, articulate elite, rarely that of the local rulers and their officials and hardly at all that of the 'masses', rural peasantry or urban proletariat. Yet the generic DO was above all an 'up-country' animal, a creature of the bush and rarely happier than when he was among 'his' unsophisticated cultivators. One regrets the absence of a corpus of literature revealing how the traditional elite, the Kings and Maharajahs, the Sultans and

Emirs, the Princes and Paramount Chiefs, all of whom had an unusually – at times perhaps uncomfortably – close relationship with the DO, perceived and found him in real life.[27] A similar regret extends to the paucity of memoirs from the other class of officials who daily met and worked with the DO, not only the NA and local council staff but, even closer, his subordinate *khitmagars* and stewards, clerks and interpreters, orderlies and messengers, etc. It is sad, but not surprising then, that the not uncommon image of the up-country DO either frenziedly galvanizing a reluctant peasantry into digging latrines or else slavishly bound to his desk had, in the nature of things, to be constructed by caricature-led or versifying colleagues, expressing *à la* Gilbert and Sullivan what maybe the generality of the ruled thought:

> On stool in an office an Officer sat
> A-writing, a-writing, a-writing.
> I said to him, 'Officer, what are you at,
> A-writing, a-writing, a-writing?
> Do you do it for pleasure, or perhaps you are tied
> To sit on that stool and write, Sir?', I cried.
> But still he went on, and he merely replied,
> 'I'm writing, I'm writing, I'm writing'.[28]

Along with that image went another, partly self-projective but for the most part accepted by the ruled, that of the utter incorruptibility of the DO. Such a portrait was nearly always justified. Yet, as a minor Indian ruler observed, corruption can be subtle as well as blatant. Why, he argued in a revealing instance of the view from below, risk a jail sentence for attempted bribery 'when the same effect could be much more economically achieved by laying on a tiger for the Commissioner Sahib to shoot and following it up with a celebratory bottle of whisky', over which the blooded and mellowed official could be persuaded that the donor might perhaps have a point in his petition after all.[29]

Three post-imperial attempts to present the kind of history from below advocated here have more merit as pioneering studies than as adequate data. One is promisingly derived from over a hundred autobiographies by Indians, men and women, focusing on what it was like to be brought up under the Raj.[30] However, it turns out that nearly all of these are from urban, semi-elite, families, and all are written in English, the colonial language of the educated. Partially effective, too, though still consciously located at an elite level, that of 'the Western-educated middle-class whom the British fostered to serve their interests but which eventually threw them out', is Zareer Masani's stimulating response to the BBC's influential capturing of the nostalgia of British 'survivors' in its *Plain Tales* series, where the Indian voices range across the emotional spectrum, 'from fond admiration to bitter resentment'.[31] The third example is exclusively DO-focused. This is the questionnaire-based enquiry undertaken by the Sudanese scholar Francis Deng.[32] In it he develops the research finding initially discussed in his essay (and the title is significant) 'In the Eyes of the Ruled'.[33] *Bonds of Silk* sets out to provide a two-way evaluation of, to borrow its subtitle, the human factor in the British administration of the Sudan. But the limitations assume the upper hand, for the views of the Sudanese interviewed are primarily those of an elite, and a governing, British-recruited elite at that.

Overall, what is grievously lacking is, as it were, the *Mister Johnson* portrayal in reverse.[34] Indeed, the most revealing source for gaining an insight into the person and performance of the generic DO from below is frequently local post-colonial fiction, all the more valuable because it is often presented in a strongly autobiographical mode. Otherwise, it is still possible to fill in part of the histori-cal lacuna on how the rural ruled perceived their DOs by probing the rich imagery of nicknames which they consistently generated and many of which have been retained in local oral history. In such research, the linguist needs to come to the aid of the historian – and soon, too, for old men do die, even if they do not forget.

The evidence is more abundant when we come to the testimony of the edu-cated elite, in particular the nationalist leadership. Although they tended to be predominantly urban, often the early generation of political activists and Ministers-to-be had first come across the DO in their rural, home districts. Some recalled the encounter with pleasure, and when they achieved ministerial office it was not infrequently their old DO whom they wished to have as their new Permanent Secretary. Others firmly did neither. The nationalist assault on the office of DO was an early target and part of the expected agenda: the protest was against the government, and outside the capital what else was the government if not the DO? In 1930 Gandhi offered to call off his civil dis-obedience campaign in exchange for a series of Viceregal concessions which formed the core of his *purna swaraj*. Among them was the ICS, where he demanded a severe reduction in their salaries, a call renewed in the Karachi Resolution of the following year.[35] Pandit Nehru's condemnation of the ICS became part of its mythology, attacks made despite, or as some alleged because of, his disinclination to realize his father's one-time ambition of seeing him enter the Service.[36] Trevelyan has recorded Nehru's depiction of the ICS as the world's most tenacious Trade Union: 'in the land of caste they had built up a caste which was rigid and exclusive.'[37] Yet Nehru realized that in the end he would have to rely on the civil service he inherited. Setting a precedent for many another founding Prime Minister, on Independence Day he took care to assuage and encourage them 'now that the old distinctions and differences are gone'.[38] Obafemi Awolowo's tart denigration of 'the petty autocracy' of Nigeria's DOs,[39] echoing Nehru's earlier condemnation of the ICS, was quickly forgotten as on the eve of independence he set about inspiring the new Yoruba DOs and their expatriate colleagues into the creation of a model civil service. Ironically, in both cases – and, as it turned out, in most of the post-imperial states – the convenient scapegoat office of the generic DO was not only retained in the second thoughts following independence but here and there, notably in Kenya and the Sudan, was reinforced and invested with an enhanced authoritar-ianism rarely encountered in the colonial period.

Nigeria's pioneer nationalist Nnamdi Azikiwe (Zik), with Governor Richards painfully in mind, memorably dismissed the colonial fallacy of the CO's misplaced reliance on the 'man on the spot', 'whose word is law and whose maladministration often entitles him to be kicked upstairs with a GCMG or peerage as his reward'.[40] Ten years earlier, Zik the journalist had penned a vitriolic but nameless attack on 'Official Obstinacy in Nigeria', citing 'officials whose names are for ever anathematized as far as the people are concerned', along with, as he conceded, those 'whose names are engraved favourably in the minds of the people of Africa'.[41] The fiery Kwame Nkrumah was unable to discover any of the latter kind of DOs in his diatribe on how 'many of those officers were hated by the people ... their presence was harmful ... a law unto themselves', though his assessment subsequently mellowed when he got to know the incoming Governor and one-time DO Sir Charles Arden-Clarke, 'a man with a strong sense of justice and fair play, with whom I could easily be friends'.[42] Another founding Premier, Nigeria's Ahmadu Bello, was probably nearer the mark when he noted that 'DOs varied a great deal, some of them were very helpful but some thought too much of their own position to think properly of others', concluding, somewhat unexpectedly within the generality of nationalist judgement, that it was 'the earlier ones [who] were friends and teachers, the later ones – many but not all – were not'.[43] It is the Independence Day assessment of his colleague, Abubakar Tafawa Balewa, first and only Prime Minister of Nigeria, which has passed into the notional Book of Quotations on Imperialism and Independence. 'We are grateful to our British officers', he declared, 'whom we have known first as masters, and then as leaders, and finally as partners, but always as friends.'[44]

How the ruled saw the rulers is not the only under-explored question to exercise the post-colonial historian intent on the study of Britain's imperial administrators. As the age of empire recedes, already more than a hundred years beyond the defining Berlin Conference of 1885, half a century since the dissolution of the ICS and well into the second generation beyond the disbandment of the SPS and the symbolism of the closure of the Colonial Office, the social historian encounters further challenges stemming from the end of empire and the study of the role of its field agents. Fresh dimensions of the colonial encounter and of the levels of relationship between colonizer and colonized have begun to lay down rewarding markers in the post-imperial research agenda. Space allows no more than a reference to some of the strands which are already developing a substantial discourse of their own. Prominent is the whole range of socio-race relations, not only the predominantly face-to-face nature of pre-war colonial administration (far removed from the increasingly faceless screen-to-screen nature of bureaucratic and business contact everywhere sixty years on) but also in the extensive network of social inclusion and distance, among fellow expatriates as well as with local people, each group conditioned by its own gradations of status and acceptance, contact or exclusion. Was it, perhaps, not the generality of race relations which weakened imperial rule on the ground, but in particular the commonplace attitude of pre-war officialdom towards the new educated elite? In the assessment of a latter-day colonial administrator:

Overall and everywhere, the run-of-the-mill British DC is likely typically to stand revealed as having probably misjudged the character of the nationalist movement, possibly underestimated the quality of the nationalist 'minority', and generally made the mistake of concentrating his confidence and enthusiasm on the chiefly and rural classes at the cost of empathising with – or at least seeking to understand – the aspirations of the new, young, urban elite, whom he himself had helped to create and in whose hands the future was to lie.[45]

From the broad study of imperial social-cum-race relations[46] there emerged first the subset of sexuality and empire[47] and then the expanding, self-contained field of gender studies in the colonial context.[48] Still within the social parameters of race relations and empire, there is more to be discovered from, at the macro-end of the scale, exploring how colonial society reacted to and was sometimes shaped by the culture of the societies with whom it was engaged, and, maybe at the micro-end, from the perceived role and received image of the colonial Club in the minds of the rulers and the ruled.[49] Such an 'off-duty' focus could, in turn, usefully widen into an examination of the leisure pursuits of colonial officials, whether hobbies (intellectual as well as recreational) *in situ* or how they actually spent those long leaves, 'back home' and 'getting away from it all'. Taking the gubernatorial cadre alone, many a proconsul was also able to establish a leading reputation in a second 'profession': Sir Charles Eliot was an authority on marine biology and Finnish grammar, Edward Twining was an expert on the Crown jewels and Sir Cecil Clementi was a notable Sinologist. Sir Harry Johnston was a painter and Sir Alan Burns was the *Daily Telegraph*'s bridge correspondent. Sir Percy Wyn-Harris was a member of three Everest expeditions, Lord Burghley was twice an Olympic hurdles medallist, Lord Harris played cricket for England, and the Earl of Minto rode in the Grand National and won the Paris Grand Steeplechase. Nor should the view from the cantonment or the boma be allowed to obscure that from the *mofussil* or *shamba* – or, importantly, the campus. There is, too, the voice of protest in London as well as that in Lagos or Lahore, not only that of the Indian and African students studying in the metropole but also that of anti-colonial British intellectuals like those in the Movement for Colonial Freedom; or again that of the handful of colonial civil servants who, leaving the Service early in disgust, publicized their discontent with their choice of career, such as Leonard Woolf (Ceylon), Eric Blair, better known as George Orwell (Burma), Thomas Hodgkin (Palestine), A. T. Culwick (Tanganyika), W. R. Crocker (Nigeria), Norman Leys and W. MacGregor Ross (Kenya), and Leonard Barnes (Colonial Office).[50]

In all this, the reconstruction of actuality, and likely of local lore too, could make further contributions to an in-depth study of the generic DO undertaken for each separate territory (for kith-and-kin Kenya or 'settler' Palestine and the West Indies were as different from non-settler Sudan as Malaya was from Fiji or India from Hong Kong). Yet all of these research considerations and directions are equally valid for the study of the far wider total colonial society and nor merely of the Colonial Service or – the focus of the present study – of imperial administrators alone, reflecting that society (missionaries and merchants, settlers and officials) at work and at leisure, in attitude and interaction. That multi-dimensional context and subtle network of rulers and the ruled presents too vast an imperial scenario to explore here and is one where the generic DO of this book was but one actor – however conspicuous and influential – among an extensive colonial cast.

Closer to the central theme of this study of Britain's imperial administrators, one more issue relates not to how the rulers were seen by the ruled but to how the sons and grandsons of yesterday's rulers see them. While the opportunity for a Crown career in an overseas civil service is no longer on offer to Britain's undergraduates, it would be shortsighted to dismiss its one-time practitioners together with the practice as little more than one of the present's unthinkable phenomena of a past age. Britain's overseas administrative services did exist and thousands of British graduates did compete for a career in imperial administration. Imperialism has to be understood before it can be evaluated, and to understand imperialism one must first understand who its agents were – in this instance, not at the Olympian level of a Clive or a Rhodes but at the level of the generic DO. Yet the 'then' never lends itself to easy evaluation by the 'now'. George Macdonald Fraser has identified the generational trap of attitude and assessment in his discussion of the deep divide between attempts to evaluate behaviour and action in the Second World War with what he sees as the fallacy of its alleged 'unacceptable reality, rationalization and euphemisms' and the way it was viewed at the time by those who were involved:

> It is difficult for later generations to understand this; they have a tendency to envisage themselves in the 1940s, and imagine their own reactions, and make the fatal mistake of thinking that the outlook was the same then. They cannot see that they have been conditioned by the past forty years into a new philosophic tradition, requiring new explanations; they fail to realise that there is a veil between them and the 1940s. They want to see the last war in *their* terms; they want it to conform to *their* notions.[51]

His deep-felt conclusion, as one who fought at the cutting edge of the grim Burma campaign (and fought as a private soldier rather than a general, very much an example of history from below) may not be original but nevertheless needs to be repeated and recalled. It also carries a resonance for those who attempt to study the generic DO fifty years after his demise:

> [Revisionist history is] dangerous because it may be taken as true by the uninformed or thoughtless, since it fits fashionable prejudice. And that is how history is distorted. You cannot, you must not, judge the past by the present; you must try to see it in its own terms and values, if you are to have any inkling of it.[52]

Yet another contemporary, though admittedly finite, question has been opened up in Chapter 9: what has been the impact, in social and attitudinal – for the manners and mores of imperial life were, outside Kenya's Happy Valley circle, usually twenty years behind the times at home – as well as in economic and employment terms, of the thousands of one-time members of Britain's overseas civil services who, between 1947 (India) and 1997 (Hong Kong), returned to this country, often in mid-career, in search of further employment? Again, there is the need to examine the end of empire in the context of the theme that has informed this whole study, namely that for nearly a century imperial administration offered a regular, major, attractive and respectable career choice for large numbers of public and grammar (and some state) schoolboys and university graduates. What has replaced it for them? Where have all the once-upon-a-time potential DOs gone? The fact is that Britain's decolonization was far more than the transfer of power and the handing over of the seals of office. It was an integral part of the ending of a global system, economic as well as political, and pre-eminently social.

Regardless of the debate over which was the cause and which was the effect in the dual decline of the British Empire and the old-style British public school, few undergraduates of the 1960s and beyond are likely to recognize themselves in the typical public-school leaver of the 1920s who opted, unexceptionally, for a career in one of the administrative services featured in this book:

> We were very innocent of life in general. We were straight from public school, we had had no contact with adults but for the occasional schoolmaster. We had no idea at all about sex, we had no experience of English people who told lies, and we never doubted the word of a fellow Englishman.

Yet, in Charles Allen's gloss on this account, it was precisely that innocence that made them ideal officers to govern the empire, 'because they had the strictest ideas of truth, honesty, fair play and decency'.[53]

Had the life of a DO still been an option, would the undergraduate population of the 1960s and since have wanted such a career? Would they have been willing to accept a life-time of profound family and recreational restriction and health risks? The heroic work many of them have done as volunteers with NGOs in Ethiopia, Sudan, Rwanda and Bosnia suggests the answer is in a qualified affirmative: yes, as a one-off contribution, but not as a life-time career. Is the graduate of the 1990s in search of a career or just a succession of jobs? Has the whole concept of a 'career' disappeared since the employment crisis of the 1980s, exacerbated by the abolition of tenure, by the fading vision of a ladder of steady promotion, and by the advent of top management consultants, career-destructive head-hunters and bringing in outsiders? Is all that today's graduate can hope for a series of *ad hoc* 'jobs', as the notion of appointments 'for life' gives way to that of 'rolling' or 'fixed term contract' ones, as the established practice of 'full-time' employment is now threatened by the rise of the 'part-time' syndrome, and as undergraduates throng the Alternative Careers

Fair in search of some of the occupational lacunae left by the would-be careers of industry, IT, merchant banking and consultancy?

For that is the catchment area where the imperial administrator essentially came from, public school and university in search of a Crown career. If the young were not made for imperial service alone, imperial service was nevertheless overwhelmingly designed for youth. Without an empire there would still have been new public schools in the Victorian and Edwardian eras and old universities, together meeting the demands of the new professional and managerial classes for the 'proper' education of their children. Without the public schools and universities, however, there would have been no British imperial administrators displaying those qualities which were captured by the Earl of Cromer in his oft-quoted vision of 'active young men, endowed with good health, high character and fair abilities... representing the flower of those who are turned out from our schools and colleges'; were reinforced by Lord Lugard in his faith in securing 'the right class from our public schools and universities ... the best that England can give';[54] and were encapsulated in Dame Margery Perham's conviction that the generic DO represented 'one of the supreme types of the [British] nation'.[55] As the unjingoistic and unblimpish popular historian of empire has put it in her support for the project of an Empire Museum to mark the millennium:

> It [the British Empire] brought out the best and the worst in people, and it certainly brought out the most energetic... It was a colossal historical undertaking executed, for the most part, by young people ... and it had all the flair and all the failings of youth.[56]

Fifty years beyond the independence of the Indian subcontinent and the incipient decolonization of the rest of the empire, accompanied by countless periphery–centric studies of nationalism and the transfer of power, there are signs that the metropole is back at the centre of imperial history. Today's courses in imperial history attract many more students than they did in the heyday of empire, many of them from the once-imperial territories and all, to quote the historian A. J. Stockwell, 'dissociated from the guilt, nostalgia or resentments of their parents' generation, concerned less to take sides than to understand'.[57] Arguably it is also time for the imperialists to reappear in the study of imperialism; only then can the phenomenon be fully understood. As Dewey has observed in his recent study of the ICS, an Indian historiography without the ruling race is no historiography at all.[58]

For those who have at heart the history of the imperial administrator, warts and all but also dimples and all, it is possible to close this study not on some strident note of triumphalism resonant of flag-waving 'Rule Britannia', but by endorsing Sir Compton Mackenzie's requiem of fifty years ago for what Britain's post-imperial youth ultimately has lost:

> Do not let me suggest that I am under any illusion about the British Raj. It played a great part, but that part could not last for ever...

[Yet] it is sad to reflect that no young man can read Sir Arthur Lothian's book today and decide when he has turned the last page that he will enter the service of the Political Department of the Government of India and enjoy such a varied life as the author was able to enjoy. I do think that the young men of today have a right to complain of the period to which their youth has been allotted by fate. They have been born too late for the sunset of the old world and too soon for the sunrise of the new. In due course young men will be born with the prospect of adventure on other planets. To them the larger life which to us it seems Sir Arthur Lothian was able to lead may seem comparatively cribbed, cabined and confined; but those lucky young men are still many years from being born, and for an age to come books like *Kingdoms of Yesterday* will have to provide a vicarious taste of what life could be once upon a time.[59]

Notes

INTRODUCTION

1. While the Colonial Administrative Service was not established until 1932, the administration cadres of the Colonial Service were identifiable from 1895 until the closure of the Colonial Office. Hence the chosen chronology in Chapter 5, of 1895–1966.
2. Robert L. Stevenson, 'The Lamplighter', *A Child's Garden of Verses*, 1920.
3. Rumer Godden, *Black Narcissus*, 1939, 223; informal speech by Lord Wavell cited in Philip Woodruff, *The Guardians*, 1954, 360.

CHAPTER 1: ANATOMIZING THE MAKING OF THE GENERIC DISTRICT OFFICER

1. Apart from the terminology of subjective insiders' opinions, an unusual encomium is to be found in the judgement of a top 'home' civil servant on one of the overseas civil services as 'the finest body in the world' – Lord Vansittart, Foreword to H. C. Jackson, *Sudan Days and Ways*, 1954, vii.
2. Philip Mason (pseud. Woodruff), *The Guardians*, 1954, 270.
3. For example, the influential W. Guttsman, *The British Political Elite*, 1963; T. R. Bottomore, *Elites and Society*, 1964; and G. Parry, *Political Elites*, 1969.
4. E.g., P. C. Lloyd, ed., *The New Elites of Tropical Africa*, 1966; Jossleyn Hennessy, 'British Education for an Elite in India', in R. Wilkinson, ed., *Governing Elites*, 1969; INCIDI, *Problèmes des cadres dans les pays tropicaux et subtropicaux*, 1961.
5. G. M. Trevelyan, *English Social History*, 1942; F. M. L. Thompson, *The Cambridge Social History of Britain, 1750–1950*, 1990.
6. G. D. H. Cole, *Studies in Class Structure*, 1955. See also J. H. Goldthorpe et al., *The Affluent Worker in the Class Structure*, 1969.
7. Arthur Marwick, *British Society since 1945*, 1982, ch. 2. See also P. Stanworth and A. Giddens, *Elites and Power in British Society*, 1974, and A. H. Halsey, *Change in British Society*, 1986 (1978).
8. G. Mosca, *The Ruling Class*, 1939; R. H. Tawney, *The Acquisitive Society*, 1943; Hugh Thomas, *The Establishment*, 1959; C. Wright Mills, *The Power Elite*, 1956; Michael Young, *The Rise of the Meritocracy*, 1953.
9. A major text was H. Gerth and C. W. Mills, *Essays from Max Weber*, 1948.
10. For example, H. E. Dale, *The Higher Civil Service of Great Britain*, 1941; R. Kelsall, *Higher Civil Servants in Britain*, 1955; C. H. Sisson, *The Spirit of British Administration*, 1966; G. K. Fry, *Statesmen in Disguise: the Changing Role of the Administrative Class of the British Home Civil Service*, 1969, and 'The British Career Civil Service under Challenge', *Political Studies*, xxxiv, 4, 1986, 533–55.
11. Sources are cited in Chapters 4 and 6. The attack on the elitist nature of the Colonial Administrative Service came earlier, with criticism from the socialist Harold Laski in 1938 and the Fabian Colonial Bureau's reformist report of 1942, *Downing Street and the Colonial Service*. The fact that each Service had an element of stormy petrels and angry young men within its own ranks, some of whom were prepared (especially in the mid-1930s) to resign and go into print (cf. Chapter 10)

tends to reinforce the thesis that these Services were indeed *corps d'élite* and never pretended to be anything less.

12. See T. Bottomore, 'The Administrative Elite', in I. L. Horowitz, *The New Sociology: Essays in Honour of C. Wright Mills*, 1965.
13. Wilkinson, *Governing Elites*, xiii.
14. For Nehru, the ICS created another caste in the land of caste – Humphrey Trevelyan, *The India We Left*, 1942, 20.
15. It was not until after the First World War that the property qualification (an annual income of £400) was abolished for prospective diplomats.
16. These were the nine schools which formed the subject of the Clarendon Commission into the Public Schools, 1861–64. They were: Eton, Harrow, Rugby, Winchester, Shrewsbury, Charterhouse, Westminster, St Paul's, Merchant Taylors. See G. Shrosbree, *Public Schools and Private Education*, 1988.
17. Peter Parker, *The Old Lie: the Great War and the Public School Ethos*, 1987, 54.
18. Asa Briggs, *Victorian People*, 1965, 119.
19. Philip Mason, *The English Gentleman*, 1982, 61.
20. *Cradle of Empire* is the title of Meston Batchelor's history (1981) of the notable Temple Grove preparatory school.
21. J. A. Mangan, *Athleticism in the Victorian and Edwardian Public School*, 1981, 136–7.
22. P. J. Rich, *Elixir of Empire*, 1989.
23. In Elspeth Huxley's *Murder at Government House*, 1937, it is left to the Superintendent of Police to sniff out the social antecedents of the DO promoted to the Secretaryship of Native Affairs: 'Seemed a decent fellow… Matter of fact, I always had my doubts whether he was really a pukka sahib' – 220.
24. Parker, *Old Lie*, 54.
25. H. A. Vachell, *The Hill*, 1905, 58.
26. Rupert Wilkinson, *The Prefects: British Leadership and the Public School Tradition*, 1964.
27. P. J. Cain and A. G. Hopkins, *British Imperialism: I Innovation and Expansion; II Crisis and Deconstruction*, 1993
28. *Ibid.*, II, 209.
29. Mangan, *Athleticism*, 139.
30. A. H. M. Kirk-Greene, 'Imperial Administration and the Athletic Imperative: The Case of the District Officer in Africa', in W. S. Baker and J. A. Mangan, *Sport in Africa: Essays in Social History*, 1987, 81–113.
31. Clive Dewey, *Anglo-Indian Attitudes: the Mind of the Indian Civil Service*, 1993, chapter 1.
32. James Morris, *Farewell the Trumpets*, 1978, 425.
33. Kathryn Tidrick, *Empire and the English Character*, 1990, 1.
34. Ronald Hyam, *Empire and Sexuality: the British Experience*, 1990. Cf. Anton Gill's companion volume to the BBC television series of the same title, *Ruling Passions: Sex, Race and Empire*, 1995.
35. Ronald Hyam, *Britain's Imperial Century, 1815–1914: a Study of Empire and Expansion*, 1993 (1976), 272.
36. David C. Potter, *India's Political Administrators, 1919–1983*, 1986, 34.
37. *Ibid.*, 66.
38. J. Goldthorpe, 'On the Service Class, its Formation and Future', in A. Giddens and G. Mackenzie, eds, *Social Class and the Division of Labour*, 1982, 162–85.
39. Lord Cromer, *Political and Literary Essays*, 1919, 4.
40. Viscount Swinton, *I Remember*, 1948, 12.
41. Sport is one of the attributes of 'character' which have survived the end of empire, although an earlier insistence on the display of modesty in victory has not. It featured in Prime Minister John Major's 1995 list of 'lessons that other things at

school cannot teach or teach well: discipline, commitment, team spirit and good sportsmanship' – *The Times*, 14 July 1995.

42. Kenneth Bradley, *Once a District Officer*, 1965, 15. The phrase '*empire oblige*' is used by J. A. Mangan, *Athleticism*, 137.
43. James Morris, *Heaven's Command*, 1973, 8.
44. Ralph Waldo Emerson, quoted in James Morris, *Pax Britannica*, 1968, 196.
45. G. Santayana, *Soliloquies in England*, 1922. It has been revived by James Morris for the title of a chapter in *Farewell the Trumpets*, 1978.
46. Quoted, in full, in J. A. Mangan, *The Games Ethic and Imperialism*, 1986, 7.
47. A useful start is Simon Raven, *The English Gentleman*, 1961, 58–9. See also Mark Girouard, *Return to Camelot: Chivalry and the English Gentleman*, 1981, and David Castronovo, *The English Gentleman: Images and Ideals in Literature and Society*, 1987.
48. Mason, *Guardians*, 21.
49. Philip Mason, *The English Gentleman*, 1982, 170.
50. From a letter from Furse to Robert Heussler, 15 August 1960, quoted in Heussler, *Yesterday's Rulers*, 1963, 82.
51. Furse was equally enamoured of Oxbridge for its capacity to turn out the ideal product for imperial service, '… like wild blackberries. Little or no cultivation of the crop was considered necessary… Our business was to pick the ripest blackberry available and send it out by the next boat' – *Aucuparius: Reflections of a Recruiting Officer*, 1962, 18.
52. Among many, Sir Penderel Moon (ICS 1929–44) traced his Indian family connections back to 1814 and David Symington's (ICS 1926–47) great-grandfather had been on the Bombay establishment of the East India Company. Among the military, the Mayne family (of Mayne's Horse) could trace its Indian connections back to the 1760s, as could the Rivett-Carnacs. An impressive familial continuity emerges from the list of names in Charles Allen, *Plain Tales from the Raj*, 1975, 265ff.
53. From the 1920s there was a discernible Service shift by ICS fathers towards the CAS for their sons, as the prospects for a full career in the former began to dim.
54. Cf. Jeffrey Richards, ed., *Imperialism and Juvenile Literature*, 1989. See also L. D. Worgraft, *The Imperial Imagination*, 1983, 55.
55. Martin Green, *Dreams of Adventure, Deeds of Empire*, 1980. See also his analysis of the Robinson Crusoe story as a stimulus to young men to go out and join in the adventure of the British Empire in Richards, *Imperialism and Juvenile Literature*, 34–52.
56. Personal correspondence. W. L. Bell, posted as a cadet to Uganda in 1947, reveals, in his unpublished reflections on his career, a similar influence. He experienced 'a considerable degree of uncertainty as to why I was there at all. I was 27, had no degree or any other recognized qualification, knew nothing about Africa, had received no training, no Devonshire Course, no previous contact with anyone from Uganda. The fact that I was there (as opposed to why) reflected seven post-school years of active soldiering, deep uncertainty about the future, a superbly drafted Colonial Office recruitment pamphlet, and a picture compounded of *Sanders* and *She*' (personal communication).
57. Tidrick, *Empire and Character*, 4.
58. Its intellectual propagation by the American Robert Heussler in his *Yesterday's Rulers* 1963, who never quite grasped the nuances of British social class (in particular the term 'landed gentry'), is challenged in Nile Gardiner's unpublished Yale PhD thesis 'Sentinels of Empire', 1998. The thesis also takes up several other issues discussed in this chapter on the formation of the generic DO.
59. Morris, *Farewell*, 264. See also p. 513.
60. Bradley, *Once a District Officer*, 4.

61. Cain and Hopkins, *British Imperialism*, I, 117.
62. But not immediately. James Pope-Hennessy, in his biography of his grandfather with his series of colonial governorships in the 1870s and 1880s, reminds us 'that imperial outposts did not then offer desirable careers, and tended to attract civilian counterparts of Kipling's Gentlemen Troopers rather than the finer flower of Queen Victoria's island race' – *Verandah: Some Episodes in the Crown Colonies, 1867–1889*, 1964, 18.
63. Benjamin Jowett to William Gladstone, 1853, quoted in Richard Symonds, *Oxford and Empire*, 1991 (1986), 184.
64. J. A. Mangan, 'The Education of an Elite Administration: the Sudan Political Service and the British Public School System', *International Journal of African Historical Studies*, 15, 4, 1982, 680; Potter, *India's Political Administrators*, 68.
65. Cain and Hopkins, *British Imperialism*, II, 299–300.
66. Potter, *India's Political Administration*, 66ff; A. H. M. Kirk-Greene, *The Sudan Political Service: a Preliminary Profile*, 1982, 16.
67. Potter, *ibid.*, 67.
68. A. H. M. Kirk-Greene, 'On Governorship and Governors in British Africa', in L. H. Gann and Peter Duignan, eds, *African Proconsuls: European Governors in Africa*, 1978, 249. See also I. F. Nicolson and Colin A. Hughes, 'A Provenance of Proconsuls: British Colonial Governors', *Journal of Imperial and Commonwealth History*, IV, 1, 1975, 77–106.
69. The West Indian David Pitt, later Lord Pitt, became a DO in St. Vincent in 1939.
70. *The Public Schools Year-Book*, 1900, 125.
71. See P. A. Dunne, 'Education, Emigration and Empire: the Colonial College', in J. A. Mangan, ed., *'Benefits Bestowed'? Education and British Imperialism*, 1988, chapter 10.
72. Symonds, *Oxford and Empire*, 186. As late as the 1990s Oxford was still nervous at the idea of starting anything so patently vocational as a degree in Business Administration.
73. *Debates*, House of Lords, 6 May 1942.
74. See schedule in CO 877/16/21. I am grateful to Nile Gardiner for drawing my attention to this compilation.
75. J. R. de S. Honey, *Tom Brown's Universe: the Development of the Public School in the 19th Century*, 1979, 238.
76. V. Ogilvie, *The English Public School*, 1957, 198.
77. Potter, *India's Political Administrators*, 68–9.
78. Nevertheless, Potter points out that approximately half (222) of the inter-war entry came from the thirty 'popular' public schools listed in his table 5.
79. *Royal Commission on the Public Services in India* (Islington), 1915, vol. XI, 256–7.
80. Kirk-Greene, *Sudan Political Service*, Table IV. See chapter 6.
81. Pamela Kanwar, *Imperial Simla*, 1990, 74. For another Old Etonian dinner of imperial triumph, see Hyam, *Britain's Imperial Century*, 296.
82. R. J. Kerslake, *Time and the Hour*, 1997, 3. Cf. J. O'Regan, *From Empire to Commonwealth: Reflections on a Career in Britain's Overseas Service*, 1994, 11ff, and S.R. Simpson, 'Sudan Service', unpublished MS, 9.
83. See note 79.
84. See note 80. For an important non-Oxbridge recruitment contribution, see John Hargreaves, *Academe and Empire, 1860–1970*, 1994.
85. Heussler, *Yesterday's Rulers*, 50.
86. Potter, *India's Political Administrators*, 67.
87. For some of the possible reasons, see A. H. M. Kirk-Greene, 'Ours to Reason Why', *Cambridge*, 30, 1992, 75–80.
88. Bottomore, 1965; Goldthorpe, 1982; Mason, 1984; Potter, 1986; Wilkinson, 1964; Raven, 1961, all previously cited; T. O. Ranger, 'The Invention of Tradition in

Colonial Africa', in E. Hobsbawm and T. Ranger, eds, *The Invention of Tradition*, 1983, chapter 6, and 'Making Northern Rhodesia Imperial: Variations on a Royal Theme', *African Affairs*, vol. 79, no. 316, 1980, 349–73.

CHAPTER 2   AN EMPIRE TO BE ADMINISTERED: THE METROPOLITAN ORGANIZATION

1. *The Dominions Office and Colonial Office List*, 1940, ciii.
2. *The Colonial Office List*, 1966, 72.
3. Leonard Barnes, 'The Colonial Service', in *The British Civil Servant*, ed. William A. Robson, 1937, 232.
4. D. M. Young, *The Colonial Office in the Early Nineteenth Century*, 1961, 276.
5. Cf. 'Introduction' to *The Dominions and Colonial Office List*, 1932.
6. Cf. S. E. Crowe, *The Berlin West African Conference, 1884–1885*, 1942, pt II, ch. VI, 'The Third Basis'; Stig Förster, Wolfgang J. Mommsen and Ronald Robinson, eds, *Bismarck, Europe and Africa: the Berlin African Conference 1884–1885 and the Onset of Partition*, 1988, ch.14.
7. Cf. the proceedings of the sesquicentennial Durham conference held at Trent University, in *Journal of Canadian Studies*, 25, 1, 1940 (Special Issue).
8. See Anthony Clayton, *The Wars of French Decolonization*, 1994; J. Macqueen, *The Decolonization of Portuguese Africa*, 1998.
9. Latter-day writers, fascinated by the geographical relics of the British Empire, have used such titles as Simon Winchester's *Outposts*, 1985 and George Drower's 'A Fistful of Islands' in his *Britain's Dependent Territories*, 1992.
10. Cf. *The Diplomatic Service List*, 1993, 74–5.
11. Diary entry, 28 February 1671.
12. Young, *Colonial Office*, 278.
13. Ibid., 247.
14. Cf. G. V. Fiddes, *The Dominions and Colonial Offices*, 1926, ch. II; H. L. Hall, *The Colonial Office*, 1937, ch. I; C. Jeffries, *The Colonial Office*, 1956, ch. I.
15. B. L. Blakeley, *The Colonial Office, 1868–1892*, 1972, vii.
16. See J. Garner, *The Commonwealth Office, 1925–1968*, 1978, ch.I.
17. *Ibid.*, 410.
18. Cmd. 2276, 1962–3.
19. E. Blunt maintains that the use of the term 'civil servants' by the Company's non-combatant employees reaches back to at least 1765 – *The I.C.S.*, 1937, 1.
20. See Donovan Williams, *The India Office, 1858–1869*, 1983, and M. Seton, *The India Office*, 1926.
21. A. P. Kaminsky, *The India Office, 1880–1910*, 1986, 3.
22. Ibid., 5.
23. Williams, *India Office*, 455ff.
24. Quoted in Kaminsky, *India Office*, 6. Godley published his memoirs as Lord Kilbracken, *Reminiscences*, 1922.
25. Williams, *India Office*, 453.
26. Kaminsky, *India Office*, 193.
27. Such was the judgement of Lord George Hamilton, Secretary of State, 1895–1903: see his *Parliamentary Reminiscences and Reflections, 1886–1906*, 1922, II, 261. A list of all the members of the Council of India from 1858 onwards appeared in the annual *India Office List*. This paragraph draws on Kaminsky, ch.II.
28. Cf. E. Bell, *The Great Parliamentary Bore* [India], 1869.
29. *Parliamentary Debates* (House of Lords), 1914, vol. 16, ser. 5, col. 824.
30. Kaminsky, *India Office*, 194 and ff.

31. The Colonial Office's Consultative Committee on the Welfare of Colonial Students in the UK was constituted in 1951. For an early study, see A.T. Carey, *Colonial Students*, 1956, which also examines colonial students' own unions. The British Council published an annual report on the welfare of colonial students from 1951.
32. Blakeley, *Colonial Office*, 122.
33. L. S. S. O'Malley, *The Indian Civil Service, 1601–1930*, 1931; E. Blunt, *The I.C.S.*, 1937.
34. P. Woodruff, *The Men Who Ruled India*, 1953–4. His real name was Mason, which appears on the subsequent reprintings.
35. Mason, *The Guardians*, 1954, 271–2.
36. The opinion is that of Sir Henry Taylor, *Autobiography, 1800–1875*, I, 1885, 232.
37. H. L. Hall, *The Colonial Office*, 1937. His biography by C. Stephen appeared in 1906.
38. Based on the lead character in C. Buller, *Mr. Mother Country of the Colonial Office*, 1840.
39. Cabinet memorandum of 15 Dec. 1954, CAB 129/72, C(54)393. See also the memorandum of 21 June 1954 by the Minister of Works in CAB 129/69, C(54)203. There is a photograph of the No.14 Downing Street building in Hall, *Colonial Office*, and life in the CO in Downing Street is well described by Sir Cosmo Parkinson, *The Colonial Office from Within*, 1947, ch.2, and, for an earlier period, in Young, *Colonial Office*, ch. 4.
40. Notably, in terms of chronological focus, by D. M. Young (1794–1830), R. B. Pugh (1801–1925), B. L. Blakeley (1868–1892), R. V. Kubicek (1895–1903), R. Hyam (1905–8), J. A. Cross (1905–14), C. Parkinson (1909–45), G. V. Fiddes (publ. 1926), H. L. Hall (publ. 1937) and C. Jeffries (publ. 1956). For titles, see Bibliography.
41. Parkinson, *Colonial Office*, 25.
42. Fiddes, *Dominions and Colonial Offices*, 18.
43. The principal text remains A. W. Abbott, *A Short History of the Crown Agents and their Office*, 1959, for private circulation. Abbott was Chief Clerk (1948) and then Secretary of the Crown Agents (1954–8). A DPhil. thesis has been written by D. Sunderland of Wolfson College, Oxford.
44. Jeffries, *Colonial Office*, 108.
45. Sir Frederick Lugard, *The Dual Mandate in Tropical Africa*, 1922, 617.
46. Lugard reproduces this Chamberlain slogan on his title-page.
47. League of Nations Covenant, 1919, Article 22.
48. A detailed account of the names of Advisers is to be found in Parkinson, *Colonial Office*, ch. 4. Cf. D. J. Morgan, *The Official History of Colonial Development*, 1980 (five vols).
49. Parkinson, *Colonial Office*, 55.
50. Cf. table in Young, *Colonial Office*, 282, for business transacted in 1806, and Fiddes, *Dominions and Colonial Offices*, 15, for totals in 1885, 1905, 1915 and 1924.
51. The documents reproduced in R. Hyam, *The Labour Government and the End of Empire, 1945–1951*, 1992 (4 vols), indicate that the Indian precedent was kept in mind in Cabinet and had implications for Malaya. It was the Sudan which was more in the CO mind and that of colonial governors – cf. vol. I, xxvii.
52. R. B. Pugh, 'The Colonial Office, 1801–1925', in *The Cambridge History of the British Empire*, vol. 3, 1959, 717. As an amusing example, including the Secretary of State's closing minute of the operation of patronage in the earlier period, see the 1824 offer of an appointment in the CO reproduced from CO 324 in Young, *Colonial Office*, Appendix VII.
53. R. C. Snelling and I. J. Barron, 'The Colonial Office and its Permanent Officials, 1801–1914' in Gillian Sutherland, ed., *Studies in the Growth of Nineteenth-Century Government*, 1972, ch. 6; Blakeney, *Colonial Office*, 87ff.

54.   The subtitle of Ridgway F. Shinn's biography (1990) is revealing: 'The Chief Ornament of Scottish Learning'.

55.   Pugh, 'Colonial Office', 745.

56.   Cohen, with a double First from Cambridge, was assigned to the Inland Revenue in 1932, and spent the whole of his first year struggling to escape and secure a transfer to the Colonial Office – Ronald E. Robinson, 'Sir Andrew Cohen', in L. H. Gann and Peter Duignan, *African Proconsuls*, 1978, 354.

57.   W. Baillie Hamilton, 'Forty-four years at the Colonial Office', *Nineteenth Century*, lv, April 1909, 601.

58.   Parkinson, *Colonial Office*, 95.

59.   Hall, *Colonial Office*, 76.

60.   Quoted in Pugh, 'Colonial Office', 753.

61.   Curiously Parkinson, who played Cox-and-Box with Gater as PUS of the CO between 1937 and 1947, choose not to mention his colleague in the index to his very personal memoir (1947).

62.   Snelling and Barron, 'Colonial Office', 159.

63.   A. Creech Jones, 'The Colonial Service', in W. A. Robson, ed., *The Civil Service in Britain and France*, 1956, 89.

64.   Fiddes, *Dominions and Colonial Offices*, 21.

65.   Parkinson, *Colonial Office*, 101. Cf. Clyde Sanger, *Malcolm MacDonald: Bringing an End to Empire*, 1995, ch. 15.

66.   Jeffries, *Colonial Office*, Appendix V.

67.   *The Colonial Office List*, 1966, 10–11.

68.   J. Garner, *The Commonwealth Office, 1925–1968*, 1978, 27.

69.   Blakeney, *Colonial Office*, xii.

70.   Sir Robert Meade, quoted *ibid.*, 117.

71.   Quoted *ibid.*, 118. Cf. his biography by James Pope-Hennessy, *Verandah*, 1964, 22 and *passim*.

72.   Blakeney, *Colonial Office*, 90.

73.   Quoted *ibid.*, 91. See also M. Olivier, *Letters and Selected Letters with a Memoir*, 1948; Francis Lee's biography of Olivier, *Fabianism and Colonialism*, 1988; and L. Radice, *Beatrice and Sidney Webb: Fabian Socialists*, 1984.

74.   Quoted in Blakeney, *Colonial Office*, 117.

75.   Margery Pehram, *Lugard: the Years of Authority*, 1960, ch. 30.

76.   Pugh, 'Colonial Office', 768.

77.   Cf. Garner, *Commonwealth Office*, 411.

78.   See C. Jeffries, *Whitehall and the Colonial Service*, 1972.

79.   Ruth Dudley Edwards, *True Brits: Inside the Foreign Office*, 1994, 250.

80.   Cmd. 6420, 1943.

81.   See his memoir, C. H. Johnston, *The View from Steamer Point*, 1964.

82.   Cf. Raymond A. Jones, *The British Diplomatic Service, 1815–1914*, 1983, 203.

83.   A. Adu Boahen, *Britain, the Sahara and the Western Sudan*, 1964, ch. VII and Appendix II.

84.   For a discussion of the Condominium Agreement, see M. W. Daly, *Empire on the Nile: the Anglo-Egyptian Sudan, 1848–1934*, 1986, 11ff.

85.   Sir Alec Stirling, HM Ambassador to the Sudan Republic 1984–86, in his Foreword to K. D. D. Henderson, *Set in Authority*, 1987. Fortunately, Lord Vansittart had conveyed the ultimate admiration of the FO for the SPS in his fore-word to H. C. Jackson, *Sudan Days and Ways*, 1954, vii.

86.   Sir James Robertson, *Transition in Africa*, 1974, 96.

87.   Quoted in Daly, *Imperial Sudan*, 1991, 353. Cf. Graham F. Thomas, *Last of the Proconsuls: Letters of Sir James Robertson*, 1994, xiv.

88.   William Thackeray, *Vanity Fair*, 1848, chs 3 and 4.

89.   Ibid., ch. 55.

90. Sir Charles Jeffries, *The Colonial Empire and its Civil Service*, 1938, 5.
91. Jones, *British Diplomatic Service*, 186.
92. Warren Fisher Committee, Cmd. 3544.
93. Robert Heussler, *Yesterday's Rulers: the Making of the British Colonial Service*, 1963, 6.
94. Jeffries, *Colonial Empire*, 7.
95. W. B. Hamilton diary, 28 July 1896, BM Add. MSS, 48669.
96. *The Commonwealth Year Book*, 1992, 9.
97. Cf. Henry Keown-Boyd, *Soldiers of the Nile: a Biographical History of the British Officers of the Egyptian Army, 1887–1925*, 1996.
98. 'I don't think there was ever any formal official sanction; it was simply adopted and accepted' – Sir Harold MacMichael, *Sudan Political Service, 1899–1956*, n.d. 3.
99. Daly, *Imperial Sudan*, 393.
100. For example, the title of the account of India's independence by the journalists Larry Collins and Dominique Lapierre (1975).
101. MacMichael, *Sudan Political Service*, 8.
102. Quoted in Thomas, *Last of the Proconsuls*, 51.
103. G. W. Bell, *Shadows on the Sand*, 1983, 217.

CHAPTER 3   ON COMPANY AND OTHER CROWN SERVICE OVERSEAS

1. Derived from A. H. M. Kirk-Greene, *A Biographical Dictionary of the British Colonial Service, 1939–1966*, 1991, table II.
2. Derived from D. C. Potter, *India's Political Administrators, 1918–1983*, 1986, tables 8 and 9.
3. Personal communication from the Overseas Development Administration (Pensions).
4. So called because of the covenant or contract whereby the officials engaged to accept a regulated salary and subscribe to pension funds in return for giving up their right to accept presents and irregular payments. See Chapter 4 for further discussion of the ICS Covenant.
5. Quoted in Philip Mason, *The Founders*, 1953, 121.
6. These paragraphs follow L. S. S. O'Malley, *The Indian Civil Service*, 1931, ch. 1, 'A Merchant Service', and E. Blunt, *The ICS: Indian Civil Service*, 1937, ch. I.
7. Philip Mason, *The Guardians*, 1954, 363.
8. C. Chenevix Trench, *Men Who Ruled Kenya: the Kenya Administration, 1892–1963*, 1993, 2 and ch. 1.
9. G. H. Mungeam, *British Rule in Kenya, 1895–1912: the Establishment of Administration in the East Africa Protectorate*, 1966, 49.
10. Biographical sketches are to be found in T. R. H. Cashmore, 'Your Obedient Servants, 1895–1918', unpublished Ph.D. thesis, Cambridge, 1965.
11. Confidential despatch, Girouard to Crewe, CO 533/63 and especially 26 May 1910, quoted at length and with individual officers named in Mungeam, *British Rule*, 209ff.
12. L. H. Gann, *A History of Northern Rhodesia: Early Days to 1953*, 1969, 192; T. D. Carter, ed., *The Northern Rhodesian Record*, 1992, 17.
13. Gann, *Northern Rhodesia*, 95.
14. Cf. Charles Allen, ed., *Tales from the South China Seas*, 1983, 8–9.
15. *Dominions Office and Colonial Office List*, 1939, 542.
16. Obituary, *The Times*, 15 April 1994.
17. Allen, *South China Seas*, ch. 6.

18. *Colonial Office List*, 1951, 107.
19. C. 3462, *Correspondence Respecting Reorganization in Egypt*, 1883, 26. This paragraph follows M. Berger, *Bureaucracy and Society in Modern Egypt: a Story of the Higher Civil Service*, 1957, 24–33.
20. C. 4997, *Despatches from Sir E. Baring Respecting his Employment of Europeans in the Egyptian Public Service*, 1887.
21. Cd. 1131, *Report of the Special Mission to Egypt* (Milner), 1921.
22. Sarah Searight, *The British in the Middle East*, 1969, 101.
23. C. 6321, *Report on the Administration and Condition of Egypt and the Progress of Reforms*, 1891, 28.
24. C. E. Carrington, *The British Overseas: Exploits of a Nation of Shopkeepers*, 1950, 744. Cf. 'Government offices were manned by Egyptians, but behind every Egyptian stood a British official' – Penelope Lively, *Oleander, Jacaranda: a Childhood Perceived*, 1994, 21, for another angle on British life in Egypt in the 1930s.
25. L. S. S. O'Malley, *The Indian Civil Service*, 1931, 261–2; Searight, *Britain in the Middle East*, 102.
26. The subtitle of Peter Mellini's biography, *Sir Eldon Gorst*, 1977.
27. For an important study, see Mary Innes, 'In Egyptian Service: the Role of British Officials in Egypt, 1911–1936', unpublished DPhil, Oxford, 1986. The tables and appendices contain detailed personnel information. Also on British civil servants see William M. Welch, *No Country for a Gentleman: British Rule in Egypt, 1883–1907*, 1981 and P. Mansfield, The British in Egypt, 1971.
28. Sir Auckland Colvin, *The Making of Modern Egypt*, 1906.
29. Sir Ronald Storrs, *Memoirs* (New York), 1937, 17–18. The English edition was titled *Orientations*, 1943 (1939). See also A. Sattin, *Lifting the Veil: British Society in Egypt*, 1988, 162ff, and J. Marlow, *Anglo-Egyptian Relations*, 1954.
30. Clara Boyle, *A Servant of the Empire: a Memoir of Harry Boyle*, 1938, ch. VIII; D. Hopwood, *Tales of Empire: the British in the Middle East*, 1985, ch. 2.
31. Coles Pasha, *Recollections and Reflections*, n.d. (?1919), 21.
32. Obituary, *The Times*, 12 April 1954.
33. Russell Pasha, *Egyptian Service, 1902–1946*, 1949, 11.
34. Lord Edward Cecil, *The Leisure of an Egyptian Official*, 1921, 219.
35. Baron de Kusel, *An Englishman's Recollections of Egypt*, 1915.
36. Rameses [C. S. Jarvis], *Oriental Spotlight*, 1937.
37. Sattin, *Lifting the Veil*, 188ff.
38. Hopwood, *Tales of Empire*, 1989, 5. See also his 'Servants of Empire: Sidelights on the British in Egypt', in B. Bloomfield, *Middle East Studies and Libraries*, 1980.
39. Reproduced in Boyle, *Servant of Empire*, 155–8.
40. Sattin, *Lifting the Veil*, 186. A new biography by Roger Owen is in hand.
41. Berger, *Bureaucracy and Society*, 267.
42. Lord Edward Cecil, quoted in Sattin, *Lifting the Veil*, 199.
43. Coles, *Recollections*, 170.
44. T. Creagh Coen, *The Indian Political Service*, 1974, 55. Its bibliography is a good supplement to that in the *Cambridge History of India*, vol. 6, 1922.
45. C. Chenevix Trench, *Viceroy's Agent*, 1987, ix. This section is largely based on this source and that in note 44.
46. Creagh Coen, *IPS*, 37.
47. Blunt, *ICS*, 174.
48. Chenevix Trench, *Viceroy's Agent*, 11. For the unusual Magor's life, see obituary notice in *The Times*, 24 May 1995.
49. Creagh Coen, *IPS*, 35.
50. Trench, *Viceroy's Agent*, 6.
51. W. M. Hogben, 'An Imperial Dilemma: The Reluctant Indianization of the Indian Political Service', *Modern Asian Studies*, 15, 4, 1981, 769.

52. Creagh Coen, IPS, 35. He adds: 'A moderate dose of nepotism never did a cadre any harm.'
53. See Trench, *Viceroy's Agent*, 13–14, for one such viceregal luncheon.
54. Quoted in Creagh Coen, *IPS*, 37.
55. Trench, *Viceroy's Agent*, 18.
56. Mason, *Guardians*, 270.
57. Trench, *Viceroy's Agent*, 9.
58. Quoted in Blunt, *ICS*, 174.
59. Quoted in Trench, *Viceroy's Agent*, 7.
60. *Manual of Instructions to Officers of the Political Department of the Government of India*, 1924.
61. Mason, *Guardians*, 88.
62. Ibid., 270–1.
63. Paul Rich, *Biographies of the British Residents and Agents in the Arabian Gulf, 1763–1987*, 1987. For a study of the Political Service in Bahrain, see the Oxford DPhil thesis by James Onley (in process, 1998).
64. O'Malley, *ICS*, is unusually lightweight, half of his half page on the Political Department (160) consisting of a long (but highly relevant) quotation from Curzon's farewell speech delivered at Simla on 5 September 1905.
65. Creagh Coen, *ICS*, 42–3.
66. Trench, *Viceroy's Agent*, 6.
67. Quoted in Blunt, *ICS*, 174–5.
68. Trench, *Viceroy's Agent*, 340. Cf. Mason, 'They liked the Princes as a rule, they liked the states, they could not help sympathizing with the man they argued with' – *Guardians*, 231.
69. Mason, ibid., 270.
70. D. C.M. Platt, *The Cinderella Service: British Consuls since 1825*, 1971, 1–3. Parts of this section are based on this source.
71. Platt, *Cinderella Service*, 5.
72. P. D. Coates, *The China Consuls*, 1988, 433. The following paragraphs draw on this source, as well as on Platt, op. cit., ch. 5.
73. For a character sketch of this unusual career diplomat, see Coates, *China Consuls* passim, and L. Grafftey-Smith, *Bright Levant*, 1970, 238. A collection of his letters is in press.
74. Coates, *China*, 428. His ch. 14 is very strong on the social origins of the China Consuls. See also the detailed nominal roll in Appendix II.
75. Ibid., 432.
76. Charles Allen, *Tales from the South China Seas*, 1983, 17.
77. Coates, *China*, 487.
78. Platt, op. cit., 162ff.
79. R. Symonds, *Oxford and Empire: the Last Lost Cause?*, 1986, 194–5.
80. Platt, op. cit., 168.
81. Sir Reader Bullard, *The Camels Must Go*, 1961, 43.
82. Cf. Hopwood, *Tales of Empire*, 186ff.
83. Cf. *Colonial Office List*, 1925, 490.
84. Platt, op. cit., 129.
85. J. H. Longford, 'The Consular Service and its Wrongs', *Quarterly Review*, April 1903, 610.
86. Quoted in Platt, op. cit., 141.
87. *Foreign Office and Consular List*, 1936, 32B–46.
88. Platt, op. cit., 185.
89. Allen, *South China Seas*, 21.
90. Hopwood, *Tales of Empire*, 19.
91. Bullard, *Camels*, 37.

92. Philip Graves, *The Life of Sir Percy Cox*, 1941; Sir Arnold Wilson, *Loyalties: Mesopotamia, 1914–1917*, 1930.
93. Storrs, *Memoirs*, 381.
94. Ibid., 306.
95. Ibid., 382.
96. Ibid., 381.
97. Cmd. 1061, *Review of the Civil Administration of Mesopotamia*, 1920.
98. Cmd. 6589, *British Military Administration of Occupied Territories in Africa during the years 1941–1943*, 1945; Lord Rennell of Rodd, *British Military Administration of Occupied Territories in Africa, 1941–47*, 1948; K. C. Gandar Dower, *The First to be Freed: the BMA in Eritrea and Somalia, 1941–43*, 1944.
99. Richard Frost, *Enigmatic Proconsul*, 1992, ch. 10.
100. [M. Lush], *A Life of Service: the Memoirs of Maurice Lush*, 1992.
101. Cf. David Shirreff, *Bare Feet and Bandoliers*, 1995.

CHAPTER 4   THE INDIAN CIVIL SERVICE, 1858–1947

1. *Career in the Pakistan Central Superior Service*, 1954, 3.
2. Dustjacket of D. Hawley, *Sandtracks in the Sudan*, 1995.
3. For example, N. B. Bonarjee, *Under Two Masters,* 1970, 125.
4. The major collections of personal papers are those of the India Office Library and Records now moved to the British Library and at Cambridge University (see L. Carter's *Brief Guide to Original Memoirs* held in the Cambridge South Asian Archives, 1989); the sound recordings of the BBC interviews from which Charles Allen's *Plain Tales from the Raj* was distilled, deposited in the Imperial War Museum and catalogued under the same title; and the interviews behind the selected text of Roland Hunt and John Harrison, *The District Officer in India, 1930–1947*, 1980, deposited in the IOLR.
5. Ann Ewing, 'The Indian Civil Service, 1919–1924: Service Discontent and the Response in London and in Delhi', *Modern Asian Studies*, 18, 1, 1984.
6. David Potter, 'Manpower Shortage and the End of Colonialism: the Case of the Indian Civil Service', *Modern Asian Studies*, 7, 1, 1973.
7. H. M. L. Alexander, 'Discarding the "Steel Frame": Changing Images among Indian Civil Servants in the Early Twentieth Century', *South Asia*, 3, 5, 1980; W. T. Roy, 'The Steel Frame: the Legend of the Indian Civil Service', *New Zealand Journal of Public Administration*, 30, 1, 1967.
8. Bradford Spangenberg, 'The Problem of Recruitment for the Indian Civil Service during the Late Nineteenth Century', *Journal of Asian Studies*, 1970, 341–60; *British Bureaucracy in India: Status, Policy and the ICS in the Late Nineteenth Century*, 1976.
9. Simon Epstein, 'District Officers in Decline: the Erosion of British Authority in the Bombay Countryside, 1919–1947', *Modern Asian Studies*, 16, 3, 1982; Judith Brown, 'Imperial Façade: Some Constraints upon and Contradictions in the British Position in India, 1919–1935', *Transactions of the Royal Historical Society*, 5th series, 1976; D. A. Low, *Congress and the Raj*, 1977; *Eclipse of Empire*, 1991.
10. Hunt and Harrison, ch. 1.
11. Quoted by Oswyn Murray, Fellow of Balliol College, in *Oxford Today*, 1998, 10, 3, 15–16.
12. P. H. M. van den Dungen, *The Punjab Tradition: Influence and Authority in Nineteenth Century India*, 1972; L. S. S. O'Malley, *The Indian Civil Service, 1601–1930*, 1931, 56–60; E. Stokes, *The English Utilitarians and India*, 1959; Philip Mason [Woodruff], *The Founders*, 1953, Ch. XI, 'Titans of the Punjab'.

13. Philip Mason, *The Guardians*, 1954, Appendix B.
14. Spangenberg, 341, note 1.
15. Copy in Cracknell Papers, Cambridge South Asian Archive.
16. Sir Edward Blunt, *The ICS: Indian Civil Service*, 1937, 2.
17. For the pre-ICS period, see Bernard S. Cohn, 'Recruitment and Training of British Civil Servants in India, 1600–1860', in R. Braibanti, ed., *Asian Bureaucratic Systems Emergent from the British Imperial Tradition*, 1966.
18. Totals from Mason, *Guardians*, 363.
19. D. C. Potter, *India's Political Administrators, 1914–1983*, 1986, 132. Hunt and Harrison maintain that a few were appointed after 1945 – *District Officer*, 4. For a memoir from a member of the 1940 intake, see Sir Fraser Noble, *Something in India*, 1997.
20. Spangenberg, 'Problems of Recruitment', tables II and III.
21. Ibid., 349.
22. Mason, *Founders*, pt. III, ch. 8.
23. *Fourth Report of the Civil Service Commissioners*, 1859, 231.
24. Richard Symonds, *Oxford and Empire: the Last Lost Cause?*, 1986, 27–9 and ch. 10.
25. See Table in O'Malley, *ICS*, 242.
26. Ibid.
27. A key and still highly readable text is Sir George Trevelyan, *The Competition Wallah*, 1864. On the nature of the new test papers, see J. C. Collins, 'The New Scheme for the Indian Civil Service Examinations', *Contemporary Review*, 1891, 836–51.
28. R. J. Moore, 'The Abolition of Patronage in the Indian Civil Service and the Closure of Haileybury College', *Historical Journal*, VII, 2, 1969.
29. W. D. Arnold, *Short Essays on Social and Indian Subjects*, 1869, 99.
30. A. H. M. Kirk-Greene, *The Sudan Political Service: a Preliminary Profile*, 1982, table I.
31. The following paragraphs are based on an analysis of the Final Examination results for ICS probationers issued by the Civil Service Commission on 28 September 1932, copy retained in the Cracknell Papers, Cambridge South Asian Archive. I am grateful to Dr Lionel Carter for his considerable help when working in this archive. The 1938 results are taken from the list retained in the IOLR.
32. T. H. Beaglehole, 'From Rulers to Servants: the ICS and the Demission of Power in India', *Modern Asian Studies*, 11, 2, 1977, devotes much of part III to a study of the CSC examination of 1928.
33. W. H. Saumarez-Smith, *A Young Man's Country*, 1977, 12.
34. Sir Leslie Glass, *The Changing Kings*, 1985, 8.
35. H. C. Sturt took his BA at Queen's College in 1886 and became a freelance tutor.
36. Spangenberg, 'Problems of Recruitment', 346.
37. Mason, *Guardians*, 78.
38. Ibid., 236.
39. Ibid., 366.
40. *Edinburgh Review*, 39, 1874, 337.
41. Hunt and Harrison, *The District Officer*, 5.
42. Spangenberg, 'Problems of Recruitment', table II.
43. See A. H. M. Kirk-Greene, 'Ours to Reason Why', *Cambridge*, 30, 1992, for a further breakdown of the Oxford/Cambridge divide.
44. Beaglehole, 'Rulers to Servants', 246.
45. Mason, *Guardians*, 366. It is to be regretted that the tables on schools attended compiled for this study by R. V. Vernède and M. Lane were in the end not reproduced (366, note).
46. Potter, *India's Administrators*, 68ff.

47. According to Oxford lore, as Chancellor of the University Curzon once rebuked the Bursar of Balliol when he showed him the suggested menu for an important occasion with the comment 'Gentlemen do not take thick soup at luncheon'.
48. Quoted in Ann Ewing, 'The Indian Civil Service, 1919–1942', unpublished PhD thesis, Cambridge, 1980, 53.
49. Ibid., 54.
50. C. Allen, *Plain Tales from the Raj* (1976 edn), 39.
51. Summary from Spangenberg, 'Problems of Recruitment', table 1. Cf. Potter, *India's Administrators*, 58, for the calculation of 65–70 per cent from middle-class background over the period 1919–39.
52. Beaglehole, 'Rulers to Servants', 246; Ewing, 'ICS, 1919–42', 179.
53. Ewing, 'ICS, 1919–42', 35.
54. See 'A Governing-Class Pedigree', in C. E. Carrington, *The British Overseas*, 1950, appendix III.
55. Quoted in F. G. Hutchins, *The Illusion of Permanence: British Imperialism in India*, 1967, 89.
56. Wavell, *The Viceroy's Journal*, ed. Penderel Moon, 1973, 463.
57. C. Dewey, *Anglo-Indian Attitudes: the Mind of the Indian Civil Service*, 1993, 5–6. Cf. Mason, *Guardians*, 75–8, and Epilogue.
58. Potter, *India's Administrators*, 1986, 56ff.
59. Sir Percival Griffiths, in Allen, *Plain Tales*, 97.
60. A. P. Thornton, *The Habit of Authority*, 1966.
61. Trevelyan, *Competition Wallah*, 150.
62. Beaglehole, 'Rulers to Servants', 249.
63. Saumarez-Smith, *Young Man's Country*, 23. See also Hunt and Harrison, *The District Officer*, 10–16.
64. Evidence to Advisory Committee on Recruitment, 1935, IOLR.
65. In Hunt and Harrison, *The District Officer*, 17.
66. Symonds, *Oxford*, 105 and 185ff.
67. Percival Griffiths, *Vignettes of India*, 1985, 89: Hunt and Harrison, *The District Officer*, 267.
68. Hubert Evans, *Looking Back on India*, 1988, 7.
69. Blunt, *ICS*, 196.
70. Evans, *Looking Back*, 28; Sir Arthur Lothian, *Kingdoms of Yesterday*, 1951, 2, for an unpropitious Secretariat encounter in Calcutta; Hunt and Harrison, *The District Officer*, 17, for a surprising conversation with the Deputy Secretary in the Bombay Secretariat.
71. Hunt and Harrison, *The District Officer*, 86, quotes the instructions on the Collector's confidential reports on his juniors.
72. Potter, 'Shaping the Young Recruits', 889.
73. A clear insight into this, though leaving room for further research into the reasons for the choice of Province, can be gained from a scrutiny of the CSC Final Examination Lists of the order of passing and the choice of the top and bottom groups of successful candidates, retained in the IOLR.
74. 'I find I am 47th out of 53 Indian appointments ... I think if Father uses his influence they will give me UP or Bengal' – John Stewart, *Envoy of the Raj: The Career of Sir Clarmont Skrine*, 1989, 33.
75. Mason, *Guardians*, 236. *Man bap*: literally, 'mother-father'.
76. For some of the Punjab and UP 'reasons', see Allen, *Plain Tales*, 43.
77. Saumarez-Smith, *Young Man's Country*, 2.
78. Glass, *Changing of the Kings*, 10.
79. Beaglehole, 'Rulers to Servants', 248.
80. Glass, *Changing of the Kings*, 10.
81. Mason, *Guardians*, 85.

82. Cf. B. B. Misra, 'The Evolution of the Office of Collector', *Indian Journal of Public Administration*, XI, 3, 1965.

83. Dewey, *Anglo-Indian Attitudes*, 5.

84. Mason, *Guardians*, 353.

85. By the Indian Currency Act of 1927 the rupee was stabilized at 1s.6d. (7.5p).

86. Mason, *The Men Who Ruled India*. Philip Mason died in January 1999 at the age of 92. His two-volume narrative history of the men who made up the Indian Civil Service has no equal in the literature on Britain's overseas administrators.

87. *India Office List*, 1920, 395–6, from which the quotations in this paragraph are taken.

88. Mason, *Guardians*, 289. Cf. J. W. Cell, *Hailey: a Study in British Imperialism, 1872–1969*, 1992.

89. An excellent run of Bombay ICS Weeks, with illustrated and annotated Dinner Menus, is to be found among the Knight Papers, Cambridge South Asian Archive.

90. Cf. Hunt and Harrison, *The District Officer*, 128–9.

91. For a vivid description of both occasions, see Mason, *Guardians*, 284–5.

92. Hunt and Harrison, *The District Officer*, 41.

93. Beames, *Memoirs*, 81–2. The year was 1858–59.

94. Quoted in Mason, *Guardians*, 92–3, with the note that 'his description of a DO's day in the 'sixties did not need much modification seventy or eighty years later'.

95. Quoted *verbatim*, ibid., 80–4.

96. Saumarez-Smith, *Young Man's Country*, 12–13.

97. Percival Griffiths in Allen, *Plain Tales*, 164.

98. Cuthbert Bowder, ibid., 168.

99. See Hunt and Harrison, *The District Officer*, 48, and the detailed account by H. T. Lane ibid., 49–50. Cf. the description by A. Way, quoted above.

100. H. M. Kisch, *A Young Victorian in India: Letters*, 1957, 12.

101. Ibid.

102. Mason, *Guardians*, pt. I, ch. 5.

103. Ibid., 113–14.

104. Cf. Sir Francis Tuker, *While Memory Serves*, 1950, ch. XII. The stirring accounts in the press of the 'huge' scale of the riots in Bradford in the summer of 1995, with a mob of up to 700 Asian youths and 300 police 'at the height of the violence' (*The Times*, 12 June 1995) pale beside those of crowds and mob violence handled by the average DO in India before 1947.

105. Mason, *Guardians*, 257ff., from which the quotations are taken.

106. Stewart, *Envoy*, 37ff.

107. Colin Garbett, *Friend of Friend*, 1943, 163–70.

108. G. A. Haig, in Hunt and Harrison, *The District Officer*, 96.

109. Ibid., 54.

110. Clive Dewey, *Anglo-Indian Attitudes*, 1993.

111. Kisch, *Young Victorian*, 126. The pleasure of life under canvas is equally praised in David Burton, *The Raj at Table*, 1993, ch. 4, especially the quote (p.38) from G. F. Atkinson, *Curry and Rice on Forty Plates*, 1859.

112. Mason, *Guardians*, 281–2.

113. Ibid., 345.

114. Mary Bennett, *The Ilberts in India, 1882–1886*, 1995.

115. O'Malley, *ICS*, 209.

116. Quoted ibid., 224, where attention is drawn to its echo of a remark on the staffing of the ICS made by Curzon in 1904.

117. IOLR, L/S & G/7/605.

118. For example, the chosen vocabulary in the articles by Epstein (1982), Ewing (1984) and Potter (1973).

119. C. S. Venkatachar, quoted in Hunt and Harrison, *District Officer*, 186.

120. See note 53.
121. The origin of the Hunt and Harrison book.
122. Ewing, 'ICS', 53.
123. The titles of many of the post-career memoirs display a thesaurus of 'best days of my life' nostalgia and sense of service: *Land of No Regrets, Young Man's Country, Servant of India, The India We Served.* An echo of Götterdämmerung inspires others: 'Twilight', 'Sunset', 'Yesterday', 'Looking Back', 'Past', 'Vanished', 'Farewell', all feature prominently.
124. Mason, *Guardians*, 347. Some former British members of the ICS extend 'the end' of the Service to 1948, following an in-house remark by Lord Hailey that this saw its termination. Since the present study focuses on Britain's imperial civil services as a Crown career opportunity for British graduates, it can be reasonably argued that 1947, when Britain shed its responsibilities for governing India and the ICS were no longer the representatives of the King Emperor, was the end of the ICS. The convention is also accepted by Hunt and Harrison (op. cit.). A number of continuing Indian members maintained they were still in the ICS. Potter (op. cit.) projects the combined ICS/IAS into the 1980s, when the last Indian ICS officers retired.

CHAPTER 5   THE COLONIAL ADMINISTRATIVE SERVICE, 1895–1966

1. Quoted, with further sources, in Sir Austin Bertram, *The Colonial Service*, 1930, 16–17.
2. Lord Hailey, *An African Survey*, 1938, table III, 226; C. Jeffries, *Whitehall and the Colonial Service*, 1972, table I, 48.
3. A full-length history of the Colonial Service, the first to be published for sixty years, has been undertaken by A.H.M. Kirk-Greene in his *On Crown Service* (1999), commissioned to mark the ending of HMOCS at a special commemoration in Westminster Abbey in May 1999.
4. CO Misc. 123 (Selborne), 1900, CO 885/7/13843.
5. The opinion is that of Sir Charles Jeffries, *The Colonial Empire and its Civil Service*, 1938, 11.
6. For example CO 323 and CO 430, Patronage Register. See also Sir Ralph Furse, *Aucuparius: Recollections of a Recruiting Officer*, 1962, 17ff. Some of the Patronage desk diaries have been deposited in Rhodes House Library.
7. Jeffries, *Colonial Empire*, 6–7.
8. *The System of Appointment to the Colonial Office and the Colonial Service* (Warren Fisher). Cmd. 3554, 1930.
9. Quoted in Furse, *Aucuparius*, 17. On Colonial Service recruitment, see Robert Heussler, *Yesterday's Rulers: the Making of the British Colonial Service*, 1963.
10. R. E. Wraith, *Guggisberg*, 1967, 18 note.
11. William Golant, *Image of Empire: the Early History of the Imperial Institute, 1887–1925*, 1984, 14–15.
12. Furse, *Aucuparius*, 151. The quotations in this paragraph are taken from this source.
13. Col. 197, 1946, *Organization of the Colonial Service*; Col. No. 198, 1946, *Post-War Training for the Colonial Service* (Devonshire).
14. The full membership is given in Furse, *Aucuparius*, Appendix 4. Heussler's chapters VI and VII in *Yesterday's Rulers* focus on the work of the Devonshire Committee.
15. The opening paragraphs are reproduced in Furse, *Aucuparius*, 294–5.

16. Besides the fundamental Col. 198, an important linked document is the Nuffield Foundation's *Report on a Visit to Nigeria*, 1946.
17. A. H. M. Kirk-Greene, 'The Committee for Colonial Studies: the Minute Books of the First Quinquennium, 1943–48', *Oxford*, XL, 1, 1988.
18. A. H. M. Kirk-Greene, *Diplomatic Initiative: The Oxford Foreign Service Programme*, 1969–94, 1994, 5.
19. The data collected under the 'HMOCS Questionnaire' sponsored by the Oxford Development Records Project (ODRP) with the co-operation of the Overseas Service Pensioners' Association (OSPA) in the 1980s are currently being analysed by Nile Gardiner in connection with his Yale PhD thesis on CAS recruitment.
20. See the strong criticism in Sir Charles Johnston (Governor of Aden), *The View from Steamer Point*, 1964, 13. It has been further challenged in the Gardiner thesis (Note 19).
21. Kenneth Bradley, *Once a District Officer*, 1966, 4 and ch. 1. Heussler, *Yesterday's Rulers*, 122, has some interesting parental information gleaned from the Bursary files of Brasenose College, Oxford. See also the personal data gathered from files in Accra by Henrika Kuklick for her sociological study *The Imperial Bureaucrat*, 1979.
22. C. P. Snow, *The Masters*, 1951, 28.
23. Furse, *Aucuparius*, 228.
24. '"Can't Find the Staff?" It's All in the Mind', *The Times*, 15 April 1995.
25. Cf. Furse, *Aucuparius*, 220–32; Heussler, *Yesterday's Rulers*, 73–6.
26. Cmd. 2884, *Appendices to the Proceedings of the Colonial Office Conference, 1927*, 13–14.
27. Cmd. 3235, *Report of the Rt. Hon. W. G. A. Ormsby-Gore on his Visit to Malaya, Ceylon and Java in 1928*, 97.
28. Taken mostly from the Submissions to which Heussler was given privileged access and which he tellingly uses in *Yesterday's Rulers*, 75.
29. Cmd. 3554, Warren Fisher *Report*, 1930, 19.
30. Anonymous, quoted in Heussler, *Yesterday's Rulers*, 73.
31. Excerpt from Colonial Office, *Appointments Handbook* (Confidential), 13.
32. Furse, *Aucuparius*, 222.
33. A. H. M. Kirk-Greene, 'A Tale of Two Universities', *Oxford*, XLVI, 2, 1994, 73.
34. Cf. A. H. M. Kirk-Greene, Introduction to Charles Allen, *Tales from the Dark Continent*, 1976, xiv–xv.
35. Cf. W. R. Crocker, *Nigeria: a Critique of British Colonial Administration*, 1936, 200. See the *CO List* and the *Nigerian Staff List* of 1923 for the plethora of military ranks.
36. C. Jeffries, *Partners for Progress: the Men and Women of the Colonial Service*, 1949, 17.
37. P. Stigger, 'The District Commissioner as the Man in the Middle: East Africa', in A. H. M. Kirk-Greene, ed., *The Transfer of Power: the Colonial Administration in the Age of Decolonization*, 1978, 155–6.
38. Colonial Office, *Her Majesty's Oversea Civil Service: the Administrative Branch*, 1954, 3.
39. See Bertram, *Colonial Service*, ch. 3. For an important extract from an unpublished CO memorandum on financial organization and officers, see Jeffries, *Colonial Empire*, Appendix I, 243–7.
40. G. W. Bell, *Shadows on the Sand*, 1983, 16.
41. Letter home, 19 Oct. 1914, quoted in Alan Bishop, *Gentleman Rider*, 1988, 115.
42. Sir Frederick Lugard, *Political Memoranda*, 1919, Memo I, 'Duties of Political Officers', para. 4.
43. Secretary Northern Provinces [Nigeria] circular, 1 July 1928, reproduced in A. H. M. Kirk-Greene, *Principles of Native Administration in Nigeria*, 1965, 191.

308 *Notes*

44. Jeffries, *Colonial Empire*, 134.
45. Cf. M. W. Daly, *Empire on the Nile: The Anglo-Egyptian Sudan, 1898–1934*, 1986, 360 ff.
46. Sir Arthur Grimble, *A Pattern of Islands*, 1952, 40–1. Together with its earlier radio programme, this was a powerful recruitment propaganda as well as a literary triumph. June Knox-Mawer's equally evocative *A Gift of Islands*, 1965, and *Tales from Paradise*, 1986, came too late to exercise an influence on CAS recruitment.
47. A. H. M. Kirk-Greene, 'The British Colonial Service and the Dominions Selection Scheme of 1923', *Canadian Journal of African Studies*, 15, 1, 1981, 33–54; 'District Officers from Down Under: Australian Recruitment into the British Colonial Service', paper presented to the African Studies of Australia Bicentenary Conference, Melbourne, 1988 (unpublished).
48. Elizabeth Watkins, *Oscar from Africa: the Biography of O. F. Watkins*, 1995, 135, 144.
49. Cmd. 3554, 1930, 2.
50. Jeffries, *Colonial Empire*, 55. For a discussion of the reforms, see the earlier section on Recruitment.
51. *Colonial Office Conference, 1927*, Cmd. 2883.
52. Pat Holden, *Women Administrative Officers in Colonial Africa*, ODRP Report 5, Rhodes House Library, Oxford, 1985.
53. Col. 306, *Reorganization of the Colonial Service*, 1954. See also A. R. Thomas, 'The Development of the Overseas Civil Service', *Public Administration*, 35, 1958.
54. Jeffries, *Whitehall and the Colonial Service*, 71.
55. Sir Andrew Caldecott, 'Staffing the Colonies: Self-Government and After – a Central Pool', letter to *The Times*, 27 June 1947, quoted in John O'Regan, *From Empire to Commonwealth*, 1994, 184–6. See also O'Regan's chapter 10, 'Overseas Service for the New Commonwealth?'. There are extensive discussions of the proposals for a British Commonwealth Service and its variants in Jeffries, *Whitehall and the Colonial Service*, chs 5–8, and in Joe Garner, *The Commonwealth Office, 1925–1968*, 1978, part IV, ch. 5. See also PRO, CO 537 7768, 1952, File 21203/6, on proposals for a British Overseas Service.
56. Cf. K. Bradley, *Once a District Officer*, 25.
57. Quoted in the *Daily Telegraph*, 15 December 1983.
58. The antithesis was a common topic of the literature on pre-war colonial policy. For a later interpretation, see M. Crowder, *West Africa under Colonial Rule*, 1968, pt. III. See also his 'Indirect Rule – French and British style', *Africa* XXXIV, 2, 1964, 197–205, in response to H. Deschamps, 'Et maintenant, Lord Lugard?', ibid, XXXIII, 4, 1963, 293–305.
59. W. B. Cohen, 'The Lure of Empire: Why Frenchmen entered the Colonial Service', *Journal of Contemporary History*, 3, 1968, 104.
60. W. B. Cohen, *Rulers of Empire: the French Colonial Service in Africa*, 1971, ch. 1. Much of the section follows this author, the leading writer on the Service in English. See also his 'The French Colonial Service in West Africa', in P. Gifford and W. R. Louis, eds, *France and Britain in Africa: Imperial Rivalry and Colonial Rule*, 1971, ch. 14. An important contribution is the unpublished Grenoble (IEP) thesis by Véronique Dimier, 1999, on a comparative study of the training of French and British colonial administrators.
61. J. Suret-Canale, *French Colonialism in Tropical Africa, 1900–1945*, 1971, 311; R. Delavignette, *Freedom and Authority in French West Africa*, 1950, 71.
62. W. B. Cohen, *Robert Delavignette on the French Empire*, 1977, 21.
63. P. Alexandre, in M. Crowder and O. Ikime, eds, *West African Chiefs: Their Changing Status under Colonial Rule and Independence*, 1970, 5.
64. *Mondes et Cultures*, XLVI, 1, 1986, commemorative issue on ENFOM. See also Béatrice Grand, *Le 2 avenue de l'Observatoire: de l'Ecole cambodgienne à l'Institut international d'administration publique*, Paris 1996.

65. See Sir John Shuckburgh, 'Colonial Civil History of the War', n.d., vol. 4, pt. VI, 213 (unpublished).

66. Cohen, *Robert Delavignette*, 'The Colonial School', 37ff.

67. P. Messmer, 'Le métier d'administrateur', *Mondes et Cultures*, XLVI, 1, 1986.

68. Cohen, *Rulers*.

69. P. Gentil, *Ecole Nationale de la France d'Outre-Mer*, 1986, 4.

70. Cohen, 'French Colonial Service', 491. However, Amadou Hampaté Bâ's semi-biographical *L'Etrange destin de Vangrin*, 1976, suggests that aristocratic families were still sending their sons into the colonial service in the early years of this century.

71. Quoted in Cohen, *Rulers*, 22.

72. Cohen, *Rulers*, 23.

73. See Cohen, *Rulers*, Tables 7 and 10. According to H. B. Goodall in his new biography of Sir Gordon Guggisberg, the Gold Coast government at one time considered making its appointment to District Commissioner dependent on gaining a recognized legal qualification – *Beloved Imperialist*, 1998, 158 note.

74. Quoted in Cohen, 'French Colonial Service', 492.

75. Cohen, *Robert Delavignette*, 'The Commandant in Perspective', 34.

76. Cohen, *Rulers*, maps of geographic origin, Appendix IV and V.

77. G. Gorer, *Africa Dances*, 1949, 87ff.

78. This semi-legendary son of Dutch parents resident in Algeria graduated top of the 1903 cohort from the *Ecole Coloniale* with a view to being a governor within ten years. He became France's youngest governor-general ever when he was appointed to Indochina in 1914. He resigned his post to join the army and died in the trenches.

79. Cohen, *Rulers*, 147; Hailey, *African Survey (revised)*, 373.

80. See the proceedings of the centenary symposium of 18 October 1985 in the special issue of *Mondes et Cultures*, XLVI, 1, 1986.

81. B. Weinstein, *Eboué*, 1972.

82. Ministère des Colonies, *Conférence africaine-française-Brazzaville*, 1945, 37.

83. Cohen, *Rulers*, 154.

84. A. H. M. Kirk-Greene, 'From Brazzaville to Boston', *West Africa*, 31 October 1994, 1866.

85. W. S. Miles, 'Partitioned Royalty: the Evolution of Hausa Chiefs in Nigeria and Niger', *Journal of Modern African Studies*, 25, 2, 1987; Crowder and Ikime, *West African Chiefs*; A. H. M. Kirk-Greene, 'Le Roi est mort! Vive le Roi!: the Comparative Legacy of Chiefs after the Transfer of Power in British and French West Africa', in A. Kirk-Greene and D. Bach, *State and Society in Francophone Africa since Independence*, 1995, ch.2.

86. Quoted in Crowder, *West Africa*, 187–8.

87. Sir Frederick Lugard, *Political Memoranda*, 1919, Memo. IX, para. 3.

88. Ibid., para. 1.

89. On the details of such courtesies, see ibid., para. 28.

90. R. Delavignette, 'Lord Lugard et la politique africaine', *Africa*, XXI, 3, 1951.

91. A. H. M. Kirk-Greene, 'Imperial Administration and the Athletic Imperative: the Case of the District Officer in Africa', in W. J. Baker and J. D. Mangan, eds, *Sport in Africa: Essays in Social History*, 1987, 107.

92. Barot, *Guide pratique de l'Européen dans l'AOF*, quoted at length in J. D. Hargreaves, 'Colonization through the Bed', in *France and West Africa*, 1969, 206–9; R. Hyam, 'Concubinage and the Colonial Service: the Crewe Circular (1909)', *Journal of Imperial and Commonwealth History*, XIV, 3, 1986, 182–4. On *moussos*, see Cohen, *Robert Delavignette*, 'The Residency', 29–30. See also Owen White, *Children of Colonialism: Miscegenation and Colonial Society in French West Africa, 1895–1960* (1999).

93. Anton Gill, *Ruling Passions*, 1995; R. Hyam, *Empire and Sexuality: the British Experience*, 1991; F. M. Deng and M. W. Daly, *Bonds of Silk: the Human Factor in the British Administration of the Sudan*, 1989.
94. Cf. Anthony Clayton, *The Wars of French Decolonization*, 1994.
95. Cf. Cohen, *Rulers*, ch. IX.
96. Cf. T. Hayter, *French Aid*, 1966, 160ff.
97. Cohen, *Rulers*, 196.
98. For an analysis of what African experience the FCO deployed in its staff, see A. H. M. Kirk-Greene, 'Accredited to Africa: British Diplomatic Representation and African Experience', *Diplomacy and Statecraft*, Summer 1999.
99. C. Allen, *Plain Tales from the Raj*, 1975, 18–19.

CHAPTER 6   THE SUDAN POLITICAL SERVICE, 1899–1955

1. These are the figures which have, by convention, grown up with the SPS literature and were crystallized in the basic Register of its officers compiled by Sir Harold MacMichael, *Sudan Political Service*, n.d., (1958?), known externally as 'The Blue Book' and internally as 'The Book of Snobs'. D. H. Johnson, in a personal note derived from his research on the career of P. Coriat for his *Governing the Nuer*, 1993, suggests that there are so many omissions from the Register, especially among contract officers, that the total could be nearer 600.
2. MacMichael, *Sudan Political Service*, 4.
3. For a detailed breakdown of 'Blues' and Firsts, see A. H. M. Kirk-Greene, *The Sudan Political Service: A Preliminary Profile*, 1982, tables I and II.
4. J. P. S. Daniell, quoted in J. A. Mangan, 'The Education of an Elite Imperial Administration: the Sudan Political Service and the British Public School System', *International Journal of African Historical Studies*, 15, 4, 1982, 671, note 2.
5. K. D. D. Henderson, *Set Under Authority*, 1987, 9.
6. Sir James Robertson, *Transition in Africa: from Direct Rule to Independence*, 1974, 252. For the Colonial Secretary's lament on the 'tragedy' that the Sudan was the responsibility of an uninterested Foreign Office and not of the Colonial Office, see J. A. Cross, *Lord Swinton*, 1982, 130.
7. J. S. R. Duncan, *The Sudan: a Record of Achievement*, 1952, xi.
8. 'For this nomenclature I do not think there was ever any formal sanction' – MacMichael, *Sudan Political Service*, 3. MacMichael was Civil Secretary from 1926 to 1934.
9. The full text is reproduced in Duncan, *Sudan*, 134–5.
10. Lord Cromer, *Political and Literary Essays*, 1914, 4.
11. Quoted in M. W. Daly, *Empire on the Nile: the Anglo-Egyptian Sudan, 1898–1934*, 1986, 82. See also H. Keown-Boyd, *Soldiers of the Nile: a Biographical History of the British Officers of the Egyptian Army, 1882–1925*, 1996
12. Cromer, Introduction to Sir Sidney Low, *Egypt in Transition*, 1913, vii.
13. Quoted in Daly, *Empire on the Nile*, 83.
14. MacMichael, *Sudan Political Service*, 2.
15. Quoted in Kirk-Greene, *Sudan Political Service*, 4.
16. Low, *Egypt*, 89–91.
17. R. Collins, 'The Sudan Political Service: a Portrait of the "Imperialists"', *African Affairs*, 71, 284, 1972.
18. Daly, *Empire on the Nile*, 453.
19. Robertson, *Transition*, 4.

20. K. D. D. Henderson, *The Making of the Modern Sudan: the Life and Letters of Sir Douglas Newbold*, 1953, 557.

21. A subsequent cohort was known in Khartoum as 'The Seven Deadly Sins'.

22. M. W. Daly, *Imperial Sudan: the Anglo-Egyptian Condominium, 1934–1956*, 1991, 256–7.

23. Henderson, *Set Under Authority*, 1987, ch. VI; R. O. Collins, *Shadows in the Grass*, 1983, ch. 4. The former source informs the following pages. It is the outcome of a retrieval project organized by P. P. Howell among SPS officers in the 1980s and then written up by K. D. D. Henderson as 'a portrait of the life of ... [and] what it was like to work as a British District Officer in the Sudan between 1898 and 1955' (*Set Under Authority*, title page and p. 9). The original papers are deposited in the Sudan Archive, University of Durham.

24. This was the Service nickname of W. A. L. Cockburn, a DO in Eastern Nigeria: see A.F.B. Bridges, *So We Used To Do*, 1990, 152–3.

25. Adapted from Kirk-Greene, *Sudan Political Service*, 1982.

26. Cromer, *Modern Egypt*, 1908, II, 548.

27. See list in Donald Hawley, *Sandtracks in the Sudan*, 1995, 149.

28. Personal communication, Sir Gawain Bell: see Kirk-Greene, *Sudan Political Service*, 26, note 22.

29. Colonel Sir Hugh Boustead, *The Wind of Morning*, 1972; Wilfred Thesiger, *The Life of My Choice*, 1987.

30. MacMichael, *Sudan Political Service*, 4.

31. H. C. Jackson, *Sudan Days and Ways*, 1954, 15.

32. Personal communication, S. S. Richardson; cf. Mangan, 'Education', 681, n. 27.

33. MacMichael, *Sudan Political Service*, 3.

34. Robertson, *Transition*, 4.

35. E. G. Sarsfield-Hall, *From Cork to Khartoum*, 1975, 17.

36. Henderson, *Set Under Authority*, 21. The interviewee was himself.

37. Bell, *Shadows*, 15.

38. Mangan, 'Education', 699.

39. J. R. Honey, *Tom Brown's Universe: the Development of the Public School in the 19th Century*, 1977; Mangan, op. cit.

40. Mangan, ibid., 699.

41. M. A. Nigumi, *A Great Trusteeship*, 1958, 60.

42. Personal communication, K. D. D. Henderson.

43. R. Davies, *The Camel's Back*, 1957, 13, from where the following quotations are taken.

44. H. C. Jackson, *Sudan Days and Ways*, 1954. Dedication.

45. Ibid., 248–9.

46. Lord Vansittart, Foreword to Jackson, *Sudan Days*, vii–x.

47. Duncan, *Sudan*, 275.

48. Sarsfield-Hall, *Cork to Khartoum*, Appendix III, from where the following quotation is also taken.

49. The subtleties of R. Davies' 'arrangement' for funding a fourth year at Cambridge are revealing, being centred on a prowess for rowing – *Camel's Back*, 9ff.

50. Sarsfield-Hall, *Cork to Khartoum*, 18.

51. Henderson, *Set Under Authority*, 23.

52. Sarsfield-Hall, *Cork to Khartoum*, 19.

53. Bell, *Shadows*, 16.

54. Quoted in Henderson, *Set Under Authority*, 22.

55. Robertson, *Transition*, 7.

56. Bell, *Shadows*, 25.

57. Henderson, *Set Under Authority*, ch. IV.

58. Robertson, *Transition*, 19.
59. P. P. Howell, quoted in Henderson, *Set Under Authority*, 102. See also John Kenrick, in Deborah Lavin, ed., *The Condominium Remembered* (Proceedings of the Durham Sudan Historical Conference, 1982), 1991, 181.
60. Henderson, *Set Under Authority*, 30 and 59.
61. Sarsfield-Hall, *Cork to Khartoum*, Appendices, v–vii.
62. On the 'peculiar fascination in bicycling alone along the silent jungle paths', see Jackson, *Sudan Days*, 189–90.
63. Brian Kendall, quoted in Henderson, *Set Under Authority*, 75. On camels, see Davies, *The Camel's Back*, ch.VII.
64. 'The happiest hours of a DC's life', concludes Henderson at the end of his portrait of the DC in the Sudan, 'those spent on trek' – *Set Under Authority*, 66. 'A DC or ADC was expected to spend a considerable time on trek' (Hawley, *Sandtracks*, 35), often being out of his station for ten days each month. A small travel allowance was payable for each night spent out on trek. In 1926 this was 35 piastres, with 15 piastres p.d. 'climate allowance' in the South – S. R. Simpson, 'Sudan Service', unpublished (privately held), 3.
65. J. S. R. Duncan, quoted in Mangan, 'Education', 699.
66. Paul Daniell, quoted in Henderson, *Set Under Authority*, 72. See also the extract from John Kenrick's touring diary, *ibid.*, 73–4.
67. L. Grafftey-Smith, *Hands To Play*, 1975, 163. See also PRO, FO 371/113586-88, 1955, File 1017, for the activities of the Sudanization Committee.
68. British Information Service, *The Sudan, 1899–1953*, 1954, table I.
69. G. W. Bell, quoted in D. Lavin, ed., *The Making of the Sudanese State*, 1991. Part IV represents an important contribution to the study of the transfer of power. The original Conference papers have been deposited in the Sudan Archive, University of Durham.
70. While no SPS officer was retained, J. Carmichael, Permanent Secretary in the Ministry of Finance, remained as Financial and Economic Adviser till 1959. Hawley talks of 'proscription lists of British officials' being drawn up by a highly subjective Sudanization Committee – *Sandtracks*, 117.
71. J. W. Wright, in Lavin., op. cit., 175–7.
72. Lavin, op. cit., 162; Bell, *Shadows*, 217.
73. Respectively, Robertson, *Transition*, 114; K. D. D. Henderson, *Sudan Republic*, 1965, 103; Duncan, *Sudan's Path*, 184; Henderson, *Set Under Authority*, 175; G. Balfour-Paul, *The End of Empire in the Middle East*, 1991, 38.
74. J. W. Kenrick, in Lavin, op. cit., 164.
75. Durham Sudan Historical Records Conference, Durham University, 14–16 April 1982. The Proceedings appeared ten years later, in two volumes, ed. D. Lavin, *The Condominium Remembered*, 1991 and 1993.
76. K. D. D. Henderson and T. R. H. Owen, *Sudan Verse*, 1963, 66. For a preliminary inquiry into verse compiled by overseas civil servants, see A. H. M. Kirk-Greene, 'For Better or for Verse?' *Overseas Pensioner* 72, 1996, 47–50 and 75, 1998, 33–8.
77. Odette Keun, *A Foreigner Looks at the British Sudan*, 1930, 5; 49–52.
78. Pierr Crabites, *The Winning of the Sudan*, 1934, 178.
79. John Gunther, *Inside Africa*, 1954, 234–5.
80. Robert O. Collins, *Shadows in the Grass: Britain in the Southern Sudan, 1918–1956*, 1983, 460. See also the essays in R. O. Collins and F. M. Deng, eds, *The British in the Sudan, 1898–1956: the Sweetness and the Sorrow*, 1984.
81. M. W. Daly, *Empire on the Nile*, 1986, 452–3.
82. M. W. Daly, *Imperial Sudan*, 1991, 399.
83. Rameses [C. S. Jarvis], *Oriental Spotlight*, 1937, 118.
84. Margery Perham, Introduction to Henderson, *Making of the Modern Sudan*, xiii.

85. A. H. M. Kirk-Greene, *Nationalism and Arcadianism in the Sudan: the Janus Factor in the Political Service Memoirs*, 1993.
86. See Note 10.
87. Vansittart, Foreword to Jackson, *Sudan Days*, vii.
88. Robertson, *Transition*, 163, 'imposing a peace which would spare the conquered and subdue the proud'.
89. Quoted from one of Newbold's personal letters of instruction to new ADCs in Henderson, *Set Under Authority*, 43–4.
90. Balfour-Paul, *End of Empire*, ch. 6.
91. D. Sconyers, 'Servant or Saboteur?: the Sudan Political Service during the Critical Decade, 1946–1956', *Bulletin of the British Society for Middle Eastern Studies*, 14, 1, 1988, drawing on critical quotations from within the Service.
92. M. A. Nigumi, *A Great Trusteeship*, 1957, xi.
93. Francis M. Deng, 'In the Eyes of the Ruled' in Collins and Deng, ed., *The British in the Sudan*, 1984, 216ff.
94. Francis M. Deng and M. W. Daly, *Bonds of Silk*, 1989, Pt I.
95. J. Kenrick, quoted in Lavin, *Making of the Sudanese State*, 181.
96. See Note 85.
97. Duncan, *Sudan's Path*, 214; E. Atiyah, *An Arab Tells His Story*, 1946, 164. Cf. Da'ud Abd Al-Latif's comment about DCs 'who loved the camels and the nomads and didn't like the town people at all' – quoted in Collins and Deng, *British in the Sudan*, 232.
98. Quoted in Collins and Deng, *British in the Sudan*, 240.
99. Balfour-Paul, *End of Empire*, 189.
100. The judgement of the British Ambassador to Khartoum thirty years after independence, arguing that while the Sudanese are not uncritical in their view on British policy they remain consistent in this opinion – Foreword to Henderson, *Set Under Authority*, i.
101. Daly, *Imperial Sudan*, 399.

CHAPTER 7 PROCONSULS AT THE TOP

1. R. Heussler, *Yesterday's Rulers*, 1963; M. Crowder, 'The White Chiefs of Tropical Africa' in L. H. Gann and Peter Duignan, eds, *Colonialism in Africa*, vol. II, 1970, ch. 9.
2. J. W. Cell, *British Colonial Administration in the Mid-Nineteenth Century*, 1970. This is a major source for nineteenth-century data and statistics on colonial governors.
3. K. E. Robinson, *The Dilemmas of Trusteeship*, 1965, 46–7; H. L. Hall, *The Colonial Office*, 1937, 87–91. For the earlier period, see I. F. Nicolson and C. A. Hughes, 'A Provenance of Proconsuls: British Colonial Governors, 1900–1914', *Journal of Imperial and Commonwealth History*, 4, 1, 1975 On the Warren Fisher Report see Chapter 5 above.
4. J. M. Lee, *Colonial Development and Good Government*, 1967, table V, p. 138. For a fuller discussion, see A. H. M. Kirk-Greene, 'On Governorship and Governors in British Africa', in L. H. Gann and Peter Duignan, eds, *African Proconsuls*, 1978, 244–50. For collective biography of the Viceroys, see Lord Curzon, *British Government in India*, 1925, vol. 2, chs 11 and 12; Viscount Mersey, *The Viceroys and Governors-General of India*, 1949; and Mark Bence-Jones, *The Viceroys of India*, 1982. Some of the data here are derived from these three sources. Hugh Tinker's prosopographical *Viceroy*, 1997, covers only the 20th century holders of the post.
5. For an unusual portrait, see Paul Théroux, *The Happy Isles of Oceania*, 1992, 313–15 and 590.

6. J. W. Cell, *Hailey: A Study in British Imperialism*, 1992, 95, and review by D. A. Low in *Journal of Imperial and Commonwealth History*, 23, 1994, 170.
7. Curzon, *British Government*, 56.
8. Ibid., 66.
9. *The Times*, Diary, 8 February 1994.
10. Mersey, *Viceroys*, 157.
11. A. H. M. Kirk-Greene, 'The Governors-General of Canada, 1867–1952', *Journal of Canadian Studies*, 12, 4, 1977, 38.
12. Curzon, *British Administration*, 62ff. Cf. the obituary on Lord Kilbracken, *The Times*, 28 June 1932.
13. Viscount Swinton, *I Remember*, 1948, 92.
14. This and the following paragraphs are based on Kirk-Greene, 'On Governorship', 1978, table 6.
15. For insights into Cohen's tenure of Government House, see Owen Griffith's several contributions to D. and M. Brown, *Looking Back at the Protectorate: Recollections of District Officers*, 1997. Griffiths was his Private Secretary.
16. Mersey, *Viceroys*, 160.
17. Explored in detail in Peter King, *The Viceroy's Fall: How Kitchener Destroyed Curzon*, 1986.
18. Cf. G. Balfour-Paul, *The End of Empire in the Middle East*, 1991, 46 and 159.
19. Sir Ralph Williams, *How I Became a Governor*, 1913, 400.
20. Quoted in L. Mosley, *Curzon: the End of an Epoch*, 1960, 122.
21. Lord Altrincham (Sir Edward Grigg), *Kenya's Opportunities: Memories, Hopes and Ideas*, 1945, 73.
22. Quoted in Roy Lewis and Yvonne Foy, *The British in Africa*, 1971, 137.
23. 'The finest Government House in the Empire', Curzon recorded, 'designed upon the model of my own home of Kedleston in Derbyshire' – *British Administration*, vol. I, v. The whole volume is given over to the historical, architectural and social features, with many illustrations, of Government House, Calcutta. Cf. Mark Bence-Jones, *Palaces of the Raj*, 1973.
24. Bence-Jones, *Viceroys*, 250ff. Cecil Beaton found it 'pretentious' and 'of no known style' – *Indian Diary and Album*, 1945, 16.
25. Cf. Pamela Kanwar, *Imperial Simla*, 1990.
26. Quoted in Ellen Thorp, *Ladder of Bones*, 1956, 65.
27. Kirk-Greene, 'On Governorship', 219.
28. Mersey, *Viceroys*, 90.
29. Sir Alexander Grantham, *Via Ports*, 1965, 38, 66 and 122.
30. Oliver Lyttelton, *The Memoirs of Lord Chandos*, 1962, 377.
31. Sir James Robertson, *Transition in Africa*, 1974, 236.
32. The quotations which follow are taken from the 1951 edition, Col. No. 270.
33. For example, in the colonial context, T. O. Ranger, 'The Invention of Tradition in Colonial Africa', in E. Hobsbawm and Terence Ranger, eds, *The Invention of Tradition*, 1983, ch. 6; 'Making Northern Rhodesia Imperial: Variations on a Royal Theme, 1924–1938', *African Affairs*, 81, 3, 1980; and Paul Rich's trilogy (part of his 'Ritocracy Octet'), *Elixir of Empire*, 1989 (rev. 1993), *Chains of Empire*, 1991, and *Rituals of Empire* (in press).
34. Hilary Callan and Shirley Ardener, eds, *The Incorporated Wife*, 1984. See also Helen Callaway, *Gender, Culture and Empire: European Women in Nigeria*, 1987.
35 Joanna Trollope, *The Rector's Wife*, 1991.
36. Lord Tweedsmuir (John Buchan).
37. K. G. Bradley, *Once a District Officer*, 1966, 155.
38. Kirk-Greene, 'On Governorship', 255. For a collection of oral accounts, see Heather Dalton, 'The Experience of Colonial Governors' Wives', n.d. (?1989), Oxford Colonial Records Project, Rhodes House Library. For an earlier case

study, see R. D. Pearce, 'Violet Bourdillon: Colonial Governor's Wife', *African Affairs*, 1983, 82, 167–78.
39.   L. S. Amery, *My Political Life*, 3 vols, 1953, II: 370.
40.   Nigel Nicolson's biography, *Mary Curzon*, 1977, was proclaimed to the American market as 'The story of the heiress from Chicago who married Lord Curzon, Viceroy of India' (dustjacket).
41.   Personal communication.
42.   Kirk-Greene, 'On Governorship', 229–30.
43.   David Dilks, *Curzon in India: II, Frustration*, 1969, chs 49; King, op. cit.
44.   Sir Anton Bertram, *The Colonial Service*, 1930, 25.
45.   Sir Alan Burns, *Colonial Civil Servant*, 1949, 219ff; Richard Rathbone, *Murder and Politics in Colonial Ghana*, 1993.
46.   For example, in Nigeria the Clifford Minutes of 21 November 1920 and 18 March 1922, and the Cameron Memorandum of 1934, 'Principles of Native Administration'.
47.   Curzon, *British Government*, II, 129.
48.   Ibid.
49.   Robertson, *Transition*, 182ff. For the parallel onerous side of life in the capital, see Sir Edward Twining's schedule in Dar es Salaam in 1950, reproduced in D. Bates, *A Gust of Plumes*, 1972, 228–9.
50.   Sir Bryan Sharwood Smith, *But Always as Friends*, 1969, 301.
51.   Penderel Moon, *Wavell: the Viceroy's Journal*, 1973, 397.
52.   Dilks, *Curzon*, I, 198–9 and 211–13.
53.   A good start has been made in R. L. Tignor, *Capitalism and Nationalism at the End of Empire*, 1997; D. K. Fieldhouse, *Merchant Capital and Economic Decolonization*, 1994; and Sarah Stockwell's forthcoming study of business attitudes in the decolonizing Gold Coast.
54.   A. H. M. Kirk-Greene, 'Badge of Office: Sport and His Excellency in the British Empire', in J. A. Mangan, ed., *The Cultural Bond: Sport, Empire, Society*, 1992, 196.
55.   Mersey, *Viceroys*, 159.
56.   R. E. Wraith, *Guggisberg*, 1967, 329 and 336. See also H. B. Goodall, *Beloved Imperialist*, 1998, 178.
57   Sir G. William des Voeux, *My Colonial Service*, 2 vols, 1903, 1: ix.
58.   Curzon, *British Government*, II, 96ff.
59.   Rudyard Kipling, 'One Viceroy Resigns'.
60.   A. H. M. Kirk-Greene, 'The Progress of Proconsuls: Advancement and Migration among the Colonial Governors of British African Territories, 1900–1965', *Journal of Imperial and Commonwealth History*, VII, 2, 1979.
61.   Burns, *Colonial Civil Servant*, 147–8.
62.   Curzon, *British Government*, II, 57.
63.   In the Indian case, while the Provincial Governorships were traditionally filled from within the ICS, the Governorships of the Presidencies, and on occasion of Burma, were primarily political appointments.
64.   Very few colonial governors were appointed from the professional departments. A notable latter-day instance was the appoinment of Sir Selwyn Selwyn-Clarke, of the Colonial Medical Service, as Governor of the Seychelles in 1947.
65.   Personal communication.

CHAPTER 8   THE TRANSFER OF POWER AND LOCALIZATION

1.   For example, the Symposium on 'The Transfer of Power: the Colonial Administrator in the Age of Decolonization', held at St Antony's College, Oxford, March 1978; Symposium on 'Decolonization and the Colonial Office' held under

the auspices of the Institute of Contemporary British History, University of London, November 1988. Transcripts of both have been deposited in Rhodes House Library, Oxford.

2.   The liberal-minded Malcolm Macdonald's statement as Secretary of State for the Colonies on 7 December 1938: 'It may take generations, or even centuries, for the peoples in some parts of the Colonial Empire to achieve self-government.'

3.   Mary Bennett, *The Ilberts in India, 1882–1886*, 1995, 48ff.

4.   David Kimble, *A Political History of Ghana, 1850–1928*, 1963, 87ff.

5.   Sir Frederick Lugard, *Political Memoranda*, 1919, Memo No. 1, para. 4. For the Malayan system, see J. M. Gullick, *Rulers and Residents: Influence and Power in the Malay States, 1870–1920*, 1992, and S. C. Smith, *British Relations with the Malay Rulers from Decentralization to Malayan Independence, 1930–1957*, 1995.

6.   J. S. Coleman, *Nigeria: Background to Nationalism*, 1958, 123.

7.   M. Perham, *Native Administration in Nigeria*, 1937, 361. See also A. H. M. Kirk-Greene, 'Forging a Relationship with the Colonial Administrative Service', in Alison Smith and Mary Bull, eds, *Margery Perham and British Rule in Africa*, 1991, ch. 4.

8.   Kimble, *Political History*, 122ff.

9.   '... the progressive realization of responsible government in India as an integral part of the British Empire' (Montagu-Chelmsford Reforms, 1917); 'We are pledged to guide Colonial people along the road to self-government within the framework of the British Empire' (Secretary of State for the Colonies, 13 July 1943).

10.   Quoted in Richard Symonds, *The British and their Successors*, 1966, 103. The same trenchant message runs through Sir Gordon Guggisberg's gubernatorial treatise on what education must mean for the African – *The Keystone*, 1924.

11.   Quoted in Sir Edward Blunt, *The Indian Civil Service*, 1937, 49.

12.   L. S. S. O'Malley, *The Indian Civil Service*, 1931, 17.

13.   Quoted in O'Malley, *ICS*, 206. The following paragraphs owe a debt to his chapter IX pp. 357–9.

14.   Philip Mason, *The Guardians*, 1954, 156ff.

15.   O'Malley, *ICS*, 213. The phrase recalls Cromer's vision of British officers for his new Sudan Political Service, 'endowed with good health, high character and fair abilities'.

16.   S. N. Banerjea, *A Nation in the Making*, 1925, 44.

17.   Reproduced in Sir T. Raleigh, *Lord Curzon in India*, 1906, 60.

18.   R. Hunt and J. Harrison, *The District Officer in India*, 1980, xxii.

19.   Figures taken from Mason, *Guardians*, 363.

20.   See Roger Perkins, *The Punjab Mail Murder*, 1986. The officer was Lieutenant George Hext, of the 2nd/8th Punjab Regiment.

21.   Hunt and Harrison, *District Officer in India*, 4.

22.   Cf. J. W. Wright, 'A Note on ... Promotion Prospects' in D. Lavin, ed., *The Making of the Sudan State*, 1991, 175–6.

23.   G. W. Bell, *Shadows on the Sand*, 1983, 62.

24.   A. H. Marshall, *Local Government in the Sudan*, 1949. Dr Marshall was City Treasurer of Coventry.

25.   Quoted in K. D. D. Henderson, *The Making of the Modern Sudan*, 1953, 541.

26.   G. Balfour-Paul, *The End of Empire in the Middle East*, 1991, 28.

27.   Mekki Abbas, *The Sudan Question*, 1952.

28.   M. W. Daly, *Imperial Sudan*, 1991, ch.8.

29.   Bell, *Shadows*, 214; P. Woodward, *Condominium and Sudanese Nationalism*, 1979, 145.

30.   From one of the poems in K. D. D. Henderson and T. R. H. Owen, eds, *Sudan Verse*, 1963, 66–7.

31. A. L. Adu, *Civil Services in Commonwealth Africa*, 1969.
32. Kwame Arhin, *West African Colonial Civil Servants in the 19th Century*, 1985.
33. R. O. Tilman, *Bureaucratic Transition in Malaya*, 1964, ch. 5. See also J. de Vere Allen, 'Malayan Civil Service, 1874–1941: Colonial Bureaucracy/Malayan Elite', *Comparative Studies in Society and History*, 12, 2, 1970.
34. In Charles Allen, *Tales from the South China Seas*, 1983, 91.
35. Tilman, *Bureaucratic Transition*, 112.
36. This paragraph follows Symonds, *British and their Successors*, ch. V.
37. Cf. J. O'Regan, *From Empire to Commonwealth*, 1994, ch. 2.
38. R. E. Wraith, *Guggisberg*, 1967, 221ff. See also Kimble, *Political History*, ch. II.
39. Aborigines' Rights Protection Society, 1913, quoted in Kimble, *Political History*, 100.
40. Lord Hailey, *Native Administration and Political Development in British Tropical Africa, 1940–42* (Confidential), 1979, vol. I, ch. 1, section XVI.
41. Quoted in C.A. Baker, 'Africanization in the Administrative Service', in A. H. M. Kirk-Greene, ed., *The Transfer of Power: the Colonial Administrator in the Age of Decolonization*, 1979, 165.
42. A. H. M. Kirk-Greene, 'The Higher Public Service', in L. F. Blitz, ed., *The Politics and Administration of Nigerian Government*, 1965, 246–7.
43. Extensive data are to be found in Kenneth Younger, *The Public Service in New States*, 1960, and R. Symonds, *The British and their Successors*, 1966. Some of the statistics have been rounded off here.
44. The concept, now widely enough used to shed its inverted commas were it not for the consequent loss of its creators' identity, was introduced by D. A. Low and J. M. Lonsdale in their Introduction to *History of East Africa*, eds., D. A. Low and Alison Smith, vol. III, 1976, 12. It denotes the inflow of development funds in the 1950s and the concomitant increase in European civil servants at a time when their reduction and a policy of localization might have been expected to be the order of the day against approaching independence.
45. Prime Minister's letter CMC/17/65/049, dated 1 May 1961, accompanying localization statistics for the Provincial Administration, reproduced in John Lewis-Barned, *A Fanfare of Trumpets*, 1943, 113ff.
46. Younger, *Public Service*, 61ff.
47. For a complete table for the period 1958–77, see Baker, 'Africanization', 173.
48. For a description of the conference held at Chequers in 1959 to determine the likely dates of withdrawal, see C. Douglas-Home, *Evelyn Baring*, 1978, 283ff, and Michael Blundell, *So Rough a Wind*, 1964, ch.15.
49. In the Nigerian context, this basically meant that priority in filling vacancies should be given to, say in the Northern Region (*mutatis mutandis* in the other Regions), a Northern Nigerian indigene and no longer a Nigerian as under the programme of Nigerianization. At times, especially in the North, preference went to the appointment of a European rather than a non-Northern Nigerian.
50. Figures based on the statistical tables in Kirk-Greene, 'Higher Public Service', in Blitz, *Politics and Administration*, 218–35.
51. A. H. M. Kirk-Greene, 'Diplomacy and Diplomats: the Formation of Foreign Service Cadres in Black Africa', in K. Ingham, ed., *Foreign Relations of African States*, 1974, 279–322.
52. See note 45.
53. The survivor was R. Sadleir. His memoir, 'Sunset and Sunrise in Tanzania', is scheduled for publication in 1999.
54. D. Hawley, *Sandtracks in the Sudan*, 1995, 117.

CHAPTER 9   DECOLONIZATION, EARLY RETIREMENT AND SECOND CAREERS

1. Sir Charles Jeffries, *Transfer of Power: Problems of the Passage to Self-Government*, 1960, 106.
2. *Government of India, Civil Service Fundamental Rules*, 1926, Regulation 353A.
3. Ibid., 358(a).
4. *Colonial Regulations*, 1956, Regulation 16.
5. *Col. Regs.*, 17; Sir Charles Jeffries, *The Colonial Empire and its Civil Service*, 1938, 108.
6. Cf. Sir Stewart Symes, *Tour of Duty*, 1946, 164.
7. Mountbatten issued to his staff a day-to-day tear-off calendar reminding them 'X days to prepare for the Transfer of Power'– A. Campbell-Johnson, *Mission with Mountbatten*, 1951, 138.
8. From Andrew Roberts' epitaph on the last viceroyalty, in his review of Lord Blake and W. R. Louis, eds, 'Eminent Churchillians', in *The Times*, 4 August 1994, Review Section, 34.
9. See Cmd 7116 and 7189, 1947.
10. Penderel Moon, *Wavell: The Viceroy's Diary*, 1973, 406.
11 Ibid., 402.
12. Cf. R. Hunt and J. Harrison, *The District Officer in India, 1930–1947*, 1980, 244–5.
13. Cf. G. W. Bell and A. H. M. Kirk-Greene, *The Sudan Political Service, 1902–1952: a Preliminary Register of Second Careers*, 1989. For the compensation scheme in the Sudan Civil Service, see PRO, FO371, 102767–71, 1952, File 1053; 108365–72, 1954, File 1052; 113597–602, 1955, File 1052.
14. Jeffries, *Transfer of Power*, 66.
15. Sir Charles Jeffries, *Whitehall and the Colonial Service*, 1972, 42.
16. J. O'Regan, *From Empire to Commonwealth: Reflections on a Career in Britain's Overseas Service*, 1994.
17. R. O. Tilman, *Bureaucratic Transition in Malaya*, 1964, ch. 3.
18. Col. 306, *Reorganization of the Colonial Service*, 1954.
19. Based on ibid., p. 4.
20. Cmnd 1193, *Service with Overseas Governments*, 1960.
21. Cf. Jeffries, *Whitehall*, titles chosen of ch. 7 'Damp Squib' and ch. 8, 'Pyrrhic Victory'. His is the most detailed account yet published. He remained convinced that the FCO refused to take the action available to it under the 1958 Overseas Service Act to establish a central British Overseas Service – *Transfer of Power*, 112. Some of the CO and Cabinet memoranda have now been reproduced in D. Goldsworthy, *The Conservative Government and the End of Empire, 1951–1957*, 1994, vol. II, ch. 4.
22. Cmd 9768, *Her Majesty's Oversea Civil Service: Statement of Policy Regarding Reorganisation*, 1956.
23. Cmnd 497, *Her Majesty's Overseas Civil Service (Nigeria)*, 1958.
24. Ibid., p. 1.
25. Cmnd 1193, *Service in Overseas Governments*, 1960.
26. Cmnd 1740, *Recruitment for Service Overseas*, 1962.
27. Jeffries, *Whitehall*, 102.
28. For example, Sir Hilton Poynton, last PUS of the CO, in Kirk-Greene, *Transfer of Power*, 15.
29. Jeffries, *Transfer of Power*, 106.
30. Ann Ewing, *Indian Civil Service and Burma Civil Service (Class One): Post-Independence Careers*, unpublished survey, 1991, 1.
31. Quoted in ibid, 2.
32. Cmd 7116 and 7189.

33. Ewing, *ICS*, 1.
34. Ibid., 4.
35. See, for instance, J. C. Griffiths, *A Welshman Overseas: A Requiem for Colonialism*, 1993. He served in the ICS, MCS, CAS and HMOCS. It is possible to identify a small handful of officers who had experience of the ICS, SPS and CAS, e.g. D. A. Penn and C. W. North.
36. These figures, which do not reflect in the long-span Ewing survey, were kindly provided by the Secretary of the ICS (Rtd.) Association when the pilot ICS Project was initiated by the Oxford Development (Colonial) Records Project in 1983.
37. See note 13. However, a résumé was published in *Sudan Studies*, 6, 1989, 10–13 and 7, 1960, 20–3. Material associated with the Project was deposited in the Sudan Archive, Durham.
38. Donald Hawley, *Sandtracks in the Sudan*, 1995, 149, n. 9.
39. See for example correspondence in *The Overseas Pensioner* on Central Africa and Hong Kong pensions.
40. For example A. H. M. Kirk-Greene, 'The Diaspora of the District Officer', *West Africa*, 8 February 1982, 368–9; M. C. Atkinson, ed., *Careers After Nigeria*, Western Region of Nigeria Association, privately published, 1994. An analysis of the returns submitted under the HMOCS Data Project Collection (ODRP, 1983), deposited in Rhodes House Library, is currently in hand.
41. The following paragraphs are based on A. H. M. Kirk-Greene, 'Resettling the Colonial Service', *West Africa*, 1977, 652–4 and 712. See also Overseas Development Administration, *A Guide for Returning HMOCS and Aid Personnel*, 1980.
42. Overseas Service Resettlement Bureau, *Re-Employment of Ex-Officers of HMOCS*, October 1958.
43. Cmnd 1193, *Service with Overseas Governments*, 1960, Appendix C.
44. There are still some 20 000 overseas service pensioners alive (personal correspondence with ODA).

CHAPTER 10   EMPOWERING THE IMPERIAL ADMINISTRATOR

1. Cf. letter from A. Forrest, an old Wellingtonian DO in Northern Rhodesia in the 1950s, to Nile Gardiner, dated 8 May 1996, in the latter's possession.
2. Sir Gawain Bell, *Shadows on the Sand*, 1983, 18.
3. A. H. M. Kirk-Greene, 'The Thin White Line: the Size of the Colonial Service in Africa', *African Affairs*, vol. 79, no. 314, 1980, 25–44. The argument of the four resources set out below derives from this article.
4. R. E. Robinson, 'Non-European foundations of European imperialism: sketch for a theory of imperialism', in Roger Owen and Bob Sutcliffe, *Studies in the Theory of Imperialism*, 1972, 117–42. Cf. W. R. Louis and R. E. Robinson, 'The US and the End of the British Empire in Africa', in P. Gifford and W. R. Louis, eds, *The Transfer of Power in Africa: Decolonization 1940–1960*, 1982, 53–5.
5. Kirk-Greene, 'Thin White Line', 40. One recalls the comment of George Kennan, 'You have no idea how much it contributes to the general politeness and diplomacy when you have a little quiet force in the background' – quoted in F. Halliday and M. Molyneux, *The Ethiopian Revolution*, 1981, 46.
6. David E. Omissi, *Air Power and Colonial Control: The Royal Air Force, 1919–1939*, 1990. Cf. D. M. Anderson and D. Killingray, *Policing the Empire: Government, Authority and Control, 1830–1940*, 1991, and *Policing and Decolonization: Nationalism, Politics and the Police, 1917–65*, 1992.
7. D. Omissi, *The Sepoy and the Raj: the Indian Army, 1860–1940*, 1994, xx.

8.   Richard Meinertzhagen, *Kenya Diary, 1902–1906*, 1957, 224ff.
9.   Quoted in Charles Douglas-Home, *Evelyn Baring, The Last Proconsul*, 1978, 110.
10. L. H. Gann and P. Duignan, *The Rulers of British Africa, 1870–1914*, 1978, 84ff.
11. Kirk-Greene, 'Thin White Line', 43. A similar example of the generic DO's capacity for 'turning one's hand' to anything is found in D. Symington's assignment as Controller of ARP in Bombay in 1941 – James Halliday [D. Symington pseud.], *A Special India*, 1968, 204.
12. What is more, it should not be forgotten that in all his surfeit of electoral functions it was often the case that the generic DO had never cast his vote into the ballot box at home: in Britain, he remained disenfranchised as long as he was serving in HM Colonial Service.
13. Kirk-Greene, 'Thin White Line', 42.
14. Ibid., 44.
15. James Morris, *Heaven's Command*, 1973, 191; *Pax Britannica*, 1968, 53.
16. Kirk-Greene, ibid., 44.
17. R. Delavignette, *Freedom and Authority in French West Africa*, 1950, 12.
18. From the first annual report on Swaziland, 1907–8, 15–16, quoted in C. P. Youé, *Robert Thorne Corydon: Proconsular Imperialism in Southern and Eastern Africa, 1897–1925*, 1986, 61.
19. *The Administrative Officer in Tanganyika Today and Tomorrow*, Dar es Salaam, 1956, 5.
20. See Penderel Moon, *Wavell: The Viceroy's Journal*, 1973, 344.
21. Sir Gawain Bell, *An Imperial Twilight*, 1989, 237.
22. Cf. Sir Frederick Lugard, *Political Memoranda*, 1919, no. IX, 3(a).
23. Sir Frederick Lugard, *The Dual Mandate in British Tropical Africa*, 1922, 132.
24. League of Nations Covenant, 1919, Article 22.
25. Thomas Hughes, *Tom Brown's Schooldays* 1932 [1857], 66. Cf. J. R. de S. Honey, *Tom Brown's Universe*, 1977.
26. Bell, *Imperial Twilight*, 239, refuting a letter written to *The Times* by Lord Hailey in September 1963.
27. Among the few extant studies are, in part, R. M. East, *Akiga's Story*, 1939, 363ff; Margaret Plass, *The King's Day*, 1956; the Kabaka of Buganda, *Desecration of My Kingdom*, 1967; James Vaughan and Anthony Kirk-Greene, eds, *The Diary of Hamman Yaji: Chronicle of a West African Muslim Ruler*, 1995.
28. C. H. Masterman papers, Cambridge South Asian Archive, f.93.
29. W. F. Roy, '"The Steel Frame": the Legend of the Indian Civil Service', *New Zealand Journal of Public Administration*, 30, 1, 1967, 46.
30. Judith Walsh, *Growing up in British India*, 1983.
31. Zareer Masani, *Indian Tales of the Raj*, 1987, 5 and 6. Charles Allen's *Plain Tales from the Raj*, 1975, derived from the BBC programme.
32. Francis M. Deng and M. W. Daly, *Bonds of Silk*, 1989.
33. In Robert O. Collins and Francis M. Deng, *The British in the Sudan, 1898–1956: the Sweetness and the Sorrow*, 1984, 216–43.
34. Joyce Cary's novel, *Mister Johnson*, 1939, presents a telling portrait of how the generic DO of the early 1920s viewed his Nigerian clerks and NA officials.
35. M. Brecher, *Nehru: A Political Biography*, 1959, 148 and 176.
36. S. Gopal, *Jawaharlal Nehru: A Biography*, 1989 (abridged), 8.
37. H. Trevelyan, *The India We Left*, 1972, 19–20.
38. Jawaharlal Nehru, *Independence and After*, 1949, 7–9.
39. O. Awolowo, *Path to Nigerian Freedom*, 1947, 43.
40. N. Azikiwe, *Zik: A Selection of Speeches*, 1961, 155.
41. N. Azikiwe, *Renascent Africa*, 1937, 76.
42. K. Nkrumah, *Ghana: an Autobiography*, 1959, 125–6 and 113.
43. A. Bello, *My Life*, 1962, 6 and 74.

44. Independence Day Speech, 1 October 1960, quoted in full in Nigerian Ministry of Information, *Mr Prime Minister*, 1964, 47–9.
45. A. H. M. Kirk-Greene, *Nationalism and Arcadianism in the Sudan*, 1993, 29.
46. Among the pioneers of the genre are Paul Rich, *Race and Empire in British Politics*, 1986; Penelope Hetherington, *British Paternalism and Africa, 1920–1940*, 1978; and J. G. Butcher, *The British in Malaya, 1880–1941: The Social History of a European Community in Colonial South-East Asia*, 1979. A new direction of research into social communication, opening up the whole question of how far the imperial power could expect – or be expected – to govern unless it really understood the societies whom it ruled, is that explored by C. A. Bayly in his *Empire and Information: Intelligence Gathering and Social Communication, India 1780–1870*, 1997.
47. Leading texts are K. Ballhatchet, *Race, Sex and Class under the Raj*, 1980, and Ronald Hyam's *Empire and Sexuality: the British Experience*, 1990. See also Anton Gill's *Ruling Passions: Sex, Race and Empire*, 1995; N. Chaudhuri and M. Strobel, eds, *Western Women and Imperialism – Complicity and Resistance*, 1992; and Owen White, *Children of Colonialism: Miscegenation and Colonial Society in French West Africa, 1895–1960*, forthcoming 1999.
48. Important texts include Helen Callaway, *Gender, Culture and Empire: European Women in Colonial Nigeria*, 1987; Margaret Macmillan, *Women of the Raj*, 1988; Pat Barr, *The Memsahibs*, 1976, and *The Dust in the Balance*, 1989, covering British women in India from the Victorian age up to 1945; Claudia Knapman, *White Women in Fiji: The Ruin of Empire?*, 1986; and Margaret Strobel, *European Women and the Second British Empire*, 1991.
49. Cf. Anthony Kirk-Greene, 'Colonial Administration and Race Relations: some research reflections and directions', *Ethnic and Racial Studies*, 9, 3, 1986, esp. 280–283.
50. Cf. Stephen Howe, *Anticolonialism in British Politics: the Left and the End of Empire, 1918–1904*, 1993.
51. G. M. Fraser, *Quartered Safely Out Here: a Reflection of the War in Burma*, 1992, xvii and xviii.
52. Ibid., xix–xx.
53. Allen, *Plain Tales*, 42.
54. See note 23.
55. Margery Perham, Introduction to K. D. D. Henderson, *The Making of the Modern Sudan: the Life and Letters of Sir Douglas Newbold*, 1953, xiii.
56. Jan Morris, 'Now that the Sun is Setting', *The Times*, 31 December 1994.
57. A. J. Stockwell, letter to *The Times*, 9 November 1995, following on Sir Robert Rhodes James' article 'Now that the Sun has Gone Down' (3 November) in which he argued that 'despite its shortcomings the Empire had inspired generations of colonial administrators [etc.] to work in adverse climates and often vile conditions for low pay and with the threat of early death'. Interestingly, in the past few years post-post imperialist historians like Lawrence James in his *The Rise and Fall of the British Empire*, 1994, Robin Neillands in *A Fighting Retreat: the British Empire 1947–97*, 1996, and Trevor Royle, *Winds of Change: the End of Empire in Africa*, 1996, have all called for a reassessment of the record and the role of the overseas civil services.
58. Clive Dewey, *Anglo-Indian Attitudes: the Mind of the Indian Civil Service*, 1993, 8.
59. Foreword to Sir Arthur Cunningham Lothian, ICS, *Kingdoms of Yesterday*, 1951, ix–x.

A Thematic Bibliography

1 PRIVATE PAPERS IN THE UNITED KINGDOM (THE BRITISH LIBRARY)

For the Indian Civil Service, the principal repository of papers is the India Office Library and Records (IOLR) in London (now relocated in the British Library) and, especially for personal papers and unpublished memoirs, the South Asian Studies Centre at Cambridge, established in 1964. The Cambridge holdings are listed in L. Carter, *Brief Guide to Original Memoirs Held in the Cambridge South Asian Archive* (1989) and L. Carter and Dusha Bateson, *Principal Collections of Papers in the Cambridge South Asian Archive* (3rd edn, 1995), with further details in Mary Thatcher, ed., *Cambridge South Asian Archive*, vols. 1–3, 1974–83, and vol. 4, 1986 by L. Carter.

Among the extensive IOLR holdings, those most relevant to this study are the papers dealing with ICS recruitment in the Public and Judicial Home Correspondence files for the period 1880–1923 and in the Services and General Department files and collections for the years 1924–46. The individual 'Form A' completed by all candidates, critical for family data, is located in the L/P&J/ collections. Extended Histories of Service for ICS officers are located in IOR: V12, and Civil Lists in V13. Copies of the ICS examination papers and the published tables of marks are to be found in the annual *Reports of the Civil Service Commissioners* from 1858 up to 1938. Detailed career records are located in Histories of Service, arranged separately in a provincial and a departmental series covering the period 1875–1945. The annual establishment lists of the ICS appear under Civil Lists. Two IOLR publications of importance to researchers are I. A. Baxter, *A Brief Guide to Biographical Sources* (1990) and M. I. Moir, *A General Guide to the India Office Records* (1988).

The unedited interviews from which the BBC radio *Plain Tales from the Raj* (1974) was derived are deposited, both tapes and manuscripts, in the Imperial War Museum and in the School of Oriental and African Studies, University of London. The original contributions from which *The District Officer in India, 1930–1947*, edited by Roland Hunt and John Harrison (1980), was compiled are in the India Office Library holdings.

For the Colonial Administrative Service the principal collection of unpublished personal papers is housed in Rhodes House Library, Oxford. Most of these (over 10 000 items) were deposited under the retrieval and collection schemes administered by the Oxford Colonial Records Project (OCRP), 1963–72, and its lineal successor, the Oxford Development Records Project (ODRP), 1977–84: see Patricia Pugh, 'The Oxford Colonial Records Project and the Oxford Development Records Project', *Journal of the Society of Archivists*, 6, 2, 1978, and A. H. M. Kirk-Greene, 'African Source Materials from the Oxford Development Records Project', *African Research and Documentation*, 33, 1983. Personal papers continue to be deposited in Rhodes House Library under the Oxford Colonial Archives Project (OCAP). Following the earlier catalogues of *Manuscript Collections in Rhodes House Library Oxford* (L. B. Frewer, 1970, 1971; Wendy S. Byrne, 1978, containing a cumulative index to the 2561 collections), the most recent is that compiled by Clare Brown (1996), covering all the papers collected under the auspices of the ODRP. Many of the larger personal collections have an individual handlist of papers. The family data 'Form P/1' completed by all applicants has not been retained for public consultation.

Other holdings of personal papers are to be found in the Royal Commonwealth Society Library, now located in the Cambridge University Library; the National Library of Scotland; the Institute of Commonwealth Studies Library, University of London; and in the Bodleian and Cambridge University Libraries. Some personal papers, especially but not exclusively in the Private Office series, are held in the Public Record Office, Kew, and a few in the British Museum's Department of Manuscripts. A major research tool for those working on the Colonial Service in the PRO is Anne Thurston, *Sources for Colonial Studies in the Public Record Office*, vol. I: *Records of the Colonial Office, Dominions Office, Commonwealth Relations Office and Commonwealth Office*, 1995.

For the Sudan Political Service, the principal depository of private papers is the Sudan Archive at the University of Durham, established in 1957. Its *Summary Guide to the Sudan Archive* is regularly updated. The archive holds some 700 boxes of papers, 36 000 photographs and 500 maps, etc. , together with a large amount of related printed material. The ms. memoirs which provided much of the material in K. D. D. Henderson, *Set Under Authority* (1987), were deposited in the Archive. For the Middle East, notably Palestine, both Diana Grimwood-Jones, *Sources for the History of the British in the Middle East, 1800–1978* (London, 1979) and Gillian Grant, *Middle Eastern Photographic Collections in the United Kingdom* (Durham, 1989), constitute important guides to personal papers and private collections. There are also private papers in the Middle East Centre, St Antony's College, Oxford.

For the papers of the leading proconsular figures in all three Services, guidance can be found in Chris Cook, *Sources in British Political History, 1900–1951*: vol. 2, *A Guide to the Papers of Selected Public Servants* (1975) and his *The Making of Modern Africa: Guide to Archives* (1995); and, specifically, in *Private Papers of British Colonial Governors, 1782–1900* (1986), no. 5 in the Royal Commission on National Manuscripts Guide to Sources for British History series. The National Register of Archives has prepared detailed handlists of many of its recorded depositories. The Royal Commission on Historical Manuscripts regularly publishes *Accessions to Repositories and Reports* added to the National Register as well as an annual *Review*. The information on private papers occasionally found in the *Dictionary of National Biography* is substantially enhanced in the supplementary data on primary sources being collected for the *New Dictionary of National Biography*.

2 OFFICIAL PUBLICATIONS

The Administrative Officer in Tanganyika Today and To-morrow, Dar es Salaam, 1956.
British Documents on the End of Empire, London, 1992–
British Information Service, *The Sudan*, 1954.
Career in Pakistan Central Superior Service, Karachi, 1954.
The Colonial Office List, 1862–1925; 1946–66.
The Commonwealth Relations Office List, 1951–65.
The Commonwealth [Office] Yearbook, 1966–98.
The Diplomatic Service List, 1963–98.

The Dominions and Colonial Office List, 1926–40.

Federation of Malaya, *Malayanization of the Public Service: a Statement of Policy*, Kuala Lumpur, 1956.

The Foreign Office List and Diplomatic and Consular Year Book, 1936.

Government of India, *Civil Service Fundamental Rules*, New Delhi, 1926.

Hong Kong Government, *Report on the City District Officer Scheme*, 1969.

The India Office List, 1886–1936.

The India and Burma Office List, 1937–47.

List of Senior British Officers in the Egyptian Service (annual).

Malayan Information Agency, London, *Some Notes on the Government Services in British Malaya* (Harrison), 1929.

Overseas Development Administration, *A Guide for Returning HMOCS and Aid Personnel*, London, 1980.

Overseas Service Resettlement Bureau, *Re-Employment of Ex-Officers of HMOCS*, London, 1958.

The Public Schools Year-Book, London, 1900.

C. 3462, Correspondence Respecting Reorganization in Egypt, 1883.

C. 4997, Despatches from Sir E. Baring Respecting his Employment of Europeans in the Egyptian Public Service, 1887.

C. 5327,   Report of the Public Service Commission (Aitchison), 1888.

C. 6321, Report on the Administration and Condition of Egypt and the Progress of Reform, 1891.

Cd. 4360, Report of the Royal Commission upon Decentralisation in India, 1909.

Cd. 8382, Report of the Royal Commission on the Public Services in India, 1914 (Islington), 1916.

Cd. 9109, Report on Indian Constitutional Reforms (Montagu-Chelmsford), 1918.

Cmd. 1061, Review of the Civil Administration of Mesopotamia, 1920.

Cmd. 1131, Report of the Special Mission to Egypt (Milner), 1921.

Cmd. 2128, Report of the Royal Commission on the Superior Civil Services in India (Lee), 1924.

Cmd. 2883, Colonial Office Conference, 1927, Summary of Proceedings.

Cmd. 2884, Colonial Office Conference, 1927, Appendices.

Cmd. 3235, Report of the Rt. Hon. W. G. A. Ormsby-Gore on his visit to Malaya, Ceylon and Java, 1928.

Cmd. 3554, The System of Appointment to the Colonial Office and the Colonial Services (Warren Fisher), 1930.

Cmd. 3568/69, Report of the Indian Statutory Commission (Simon), 1930.

Cmd. 3628, Colonial Office Conference, 1930, Summary of Proceedings.

Cmd. 3629, Colonial Office Conference, 1930, Appendices.

Cmd. 4114, Report on the Financial and Economic Situation of Swaziland (Pim), 1932.

Cmd. 4368, Report on the Financial and Economic Position of Bechuanaland (Pim), 1933.

Cmd. 4730, Colonial Service Leave and Passage Conditions, 1934.

Cmd. 4805, Instruments of Instructions to the Governor-General and Governors [1935 Act], 1935.

Cmd. 4907, Report on the Financial and Economic Position of Basutoland (Pim), 1935.

Cmd. 6420, Proposals for Reform of the Foreign Service, 1943.

Cmd. 6589, British Military Administration of Occupied Territories in Africa during the Years 1941–1943, 1945.

Cmd. 7116, India: Compensation for the Services, 1947.

Cmd. 9768, Her Majesty's Oversea Civil Service, 1956.

Cmnd. 14, The Federation of Malaya and United Kingdom Public Offices Agreement, 1959.

Cmnd. 497, Her Majesty's Overseas Civil Service (Nigeria), 1958.

Cmnd. 1193, Service with Overseas Governments, 1960.
Cmnd. 1308, Technical Assistance from the UK for Overseas Development, 1961.
Cmnd. 1740, Recruitment for Service Overseas: Future Policy, 1962.
Cmnd. 2276, Report on Representational Services Overseas (Plowden), 1964.
Col. No. 126, An Economic Survey of the Colonial Empire, 1935.
Col. No. 147, The Colonial Administrative Service List, 1938.
Col. No. 197, Organization of the Colonial Service, 1946.
Col. No. 198, Post-War Training for the Colonial Service, 1946.
Col. No. 306, Reorganization of the Colonial Service, 1954.
Col. No. 322, Colonial Regulations, 1956.
CSR 1, Appointments to Her Majesty's Colonial Service, 1950.
OCS 1, Appointments in Her Majesty's Oversea Civil Service, 1955.
OCS 3, Appointments Overseas, 1960.

3 BIBLIOGRAPHIES

Extensive bibliographies, each carrying a number of entries on the relevant Service matters, are to be found in *The Cambridge History of the British Empire*, vol. III, *The Empire-Commonwealth*, 1959, compiled by A. Taylor Milne, and in the ongoing *Cambridge History of India*. See also L. H. Gann and P. Duignan, *History of Colonialism in Africa, 1870–1960*, of which volume 5 is *A Bibliographical Guide to Colonialism in Sub-Saharan Africa* (1973). Both volumes on the *Decolonization of Africa* edited by P. Gifford and W. R. Louis (1982, 1988) carry extensive bibliographies. *The Historiography of the British Empire-Commonwealth*, edited by R. W. Winks (1966, reprinted with a new introduction, 1995), contains an extensive and important series of historiographical chapters. Also valuable is J. P. Halstead, *Modern Imperialism: A Bibliography of Books and Articles, 1815–1972* (2 vols, 1974). The Royal Historical Society publishes an *Annual Bibliography of British and Irish History*, which includes a section on imperial and commonwealth history.

Two forthcoming publications can be expected to become major bibliographical resources: volume 5 of the *Oxford History of the British Empire*, edited by R. Winks, and the scheme directed by A. N. Porter for the Royal Historical Society *British Bibliographies*, CD Rom database (1997) project under the general editorship of J. Morrill (*History Today*, May 1994).

4 THE INDIAN CIVIL SERVICE; INDIAN POLITICAL SERVICE; VICEROYS

Alexander, H. M. L., 'Discarding the "Steel Frame": Changing Images among Indian Civil Servants in the Early Twentieth Century', *South Asia*, 5, 3, 1980.
Allen, C., ed., *Plain Tales from the Raj: Images of British India in the Twentieth Century*, London, 1975.
Arnold, W. D., *Short Essays on Social and Indian Subjects*, London, 1869.
Atkinson, G. F., *Curry and Rice on Forty Plates*, London, 1859.
Bazalgette, J., *The Captains and the Kings Depart*, Oxford, 1984.
Beaglehole, T. H., 'From Rulers to Servants: the ICS and the Demission of Power in India', *Modern Asian Studies*, 11, 2, 1977.
Beames, J., *Memoirs of a Bengal Civilian*, London, 1961.
Beaton, Cecil, *Indian Diary and Album*, Oxford, 1991.
Bell, E., *The Great Parliamentary Bore*, London, 1869.

Bence-Jones, M., *The Viceroys of India*, London, 1982.
Bennett, M., *The Ilberts in India: An Imperial Miniature*, Putney, 1995.
Blunt, E., *The I. C. S.: the Indian Civil Service*, London, 1937.
Bonerjee, N. B., *Under Two Masters*, Calcutta, 1970.
Brown, Judith, 'Imperial Façade: Some Constraints upon and Contradictions in the British Position in India, 1919–1935', *Transactions of the Royal Historical Society*, 5th ser., xxvi, 1976.
Burton, D., *The Raj at Table*, London, 1993.
Campbell Johnson, A., *Viscount Halifax* [Irwin], London 1941.
—— *Mission with Mountbatten*, London, 1951.
Caroe, Sir Olaf, *The Pathans*, Macmillan, 1958.
Carstairs, R., *The Little World of an Indian District Officer*, London, 1912.
Cell, J. W., *Hailey: a Study in British Imperialism, 1872–1969*, Cambridge, 1992.
Cohn, B. S., 'Recruitment and Training of British Civil Servants in India, 1600–1860', in R. Braibanti, ed., *Asian Bureaucratic Systems Emergent from the British Imperial Tradition*, Durham, N. C., 1966.
Collins, J. C., 'The New Scheme for the Indian Civil Service Examinations', *Contemporary Review*, 1891, 836–51.
Corfield, Sir Conrad, *The Princely India I Knew*, Madras, 1975.
Cotton, H., 'The Covenanted Civil Service of British India', *Imperial and Asiatic Quarterly Review*, viii, 1898.
Craigh Coen, T., *The Indian Political Service*, London, 1971.
Crofton, D. H., *Souvenirs of a Competition Wallah: Letters and Sketches from India, 1932–1947*, Hythe, 1994.
Lord Curzon, *British Government in India: the Story of the Viceroys and Government Houses*, 2 vols., London, 1925.
Danvers, R. L., ed., *Memoirs of Old Haileybury College*, London, 1894.
Darling, M., *Apprentice to Power: India 1904–1908*, London, 1966.
Dewey, C., 'The Education of a Ruling Caste: the Indian Civil Service in the Era of Competitive Examination', *English Historical Review*, lxxxviii, 1973.
——, *Anglo-Indian Attitudes: the Mind of the Indian Civil Service*, London, 1993.
Dilks, David, *Curzon in India*: I. *Achievement*; II. *Frustration*, New York, 1969.
Epstein, S., 'District Officers in Decline: the Erosion of British Authority in the Bombay Countryside, 1919–1947', *Modern Asian Studies*, 16, 3, 1982.
Evans, H., *Looking Back on India*, London, 1988.
Ewing, Ann, 'The Indian Civil Service, 1919–1924: Service Discontent and the Response in London and Delhi', *Modern Asian Studies*, 18, 1, 1984.
Fitze, Sir Kenneth, *Twilight of the Maharajas*, London,1956.
Garbett, C., *Friend of Friend*, Bombay, 1943.
Gilmour, D., *Curzon*, London, 1994.
Glass, L., *The Changing of Kings: Memories of Burma, 1934–1949*, London, 1985.
Goradia, Nayana, *Lord Curzon: the Last of the British Moghuls*, Delhi, 1993.
Gould, B., *The Jewel in the Lotus: Recollections of an Indian Political*, London, 1957.
Griffiths, P., *Vignettes of India*, Shaftesbury, 1985.
Halliday, J. [Symington, D.], *A Special India*, London, 1968.
Hamilton, Lord George, *Parliamentary Reminiscences and Reflections*, 2 vols, *1868–1885*; *1886–1906*, London, 1917, 1922.
Hogben, W. M., 'An Imperial Dilemma: The Reluctant Indianization of the Indian Political Service', *Modern Asian Studies*, 15, 4, 1981.
Hugh-Jones, S., 'The ICS Myth', *New Statesman*, 2 December 1966.
Hunt, R. and Harrison, J., eds, *The District Officer in India, 1930–1947*, London, 1980.
Hutchins, F. G., *The Illusion of Permanence: British Imperialism in India*, Princeton, 1967.
Iver, G. C. B., *In an Indian District*, Lahore, 1919.
Kaminsky, A. P., *The India Office, 1880–1910*, 1986.

Kanwar, P., *Imperial Simla: the Political Culture of the Raj*, Delhi, 1990.

Lord Kilbracken, *Reminiscences*, London, 1931.

King, P., *The Viceroy's Fall: How Kitchener Destroyed Curzon*, London, 1986.

Kisch, H. M., *A Young Victorian in India: Letters*, London, 1957.

Lothian, Sir Arthur, *Kingdoms of Yesterday*, London, 1951.

Low, D. A., *Congress and the Raj: Facets of the Indian Struggle, 1917–1947*.

——— , Review article of J. W. Cell, *Hailey*, in *Journal of Imperial and Commonwealth History*, 23, 1994.

Macleod, R. D., *Impressions of an Indian Civil Servant*, London, 1938.

Maconochie, E., *Life in the Indian Civil Service*, London, 1926.

Masani, Z., *Indian Tales of the Raj*, London, 1987.

Mason, P., 'The Indian Civil Service and the Last Days', *Asian Review*, 50, 1954.

——— [Woodruff]. *The Men Who Ruled India*: I. *The Founders*; II. *The Guardians*, London, 1953, 1954.

——— *A Shaft of Sunlight: Memories of a Varied Life*, London, 1978.

Viscount Mersey, *The Viceroys and Governors-General of India, 1757–1947*, London, 1949.

Milford, L. S., *Haileybury College, Past and Present*, London, 1909.

Misra, B. B., 'The Evolution of the Office of Collector', *Indian Journal of Public Administration*, XI, 3, 1965.

——— *The Bureaucracy in India: An Historical Analysis of Development up to 1947*, Delhi, 1977.

Monier-Williams, M., *Memories of Old Haileybury College*, London, 1894.

Moon, Penderel, *Wavell: the Viceroy's Journal*, London, 1973.

Moore, R. J., 'The Abolition of Patronage in the Indian Civil Service and the Closure of Haileybury College', *The Historical Journal*, vii, 2, 1969.

Mosley, L., *Curzon: the End of an Epoch*, London, 1960.

Nicolson, Nigel, *Mary Curzon*, New York, 1977.

Noble, Sir Fraser, *Something in India*, Durham, 1997.

O'Dwyer, M., *India As I Knew It*, London, 1925.

O'Malley, L. S. S., *The Indian Civil Service, 1601–1930*, London, 1931.

Panjabi, K. L., *The Civil Servant in India*, Bombay, 1965.

Perkins, R., *The Punjab Mail Murder: the Story of an Indian Army Officer*, Chippenham, 1986.

Potter, D. C., 'Manpower Shortage and the End of Colonialism: The Case of the Indian Civil Service', *Modern Asian Studies*, 7, 1, 1973.

——— 'The Shaping of Young Recruits in the Indian Civil Service', *Indian Journal of Public Administration*, xxiii, 4, 1977.

——— *India's Political Administration, 1918–1983*, Oxford, 1986.

Raleigh, Sir T., *Lord Curzon in India*, London, 1906.

Rizvi, Gowher, *Linlithgow and India*, London, 1978.

Roy, N. C., *The Civil Service in India*, Calcutta, 1960.

Roy, W. T., 'The Steel Frame: the Legend of the Indian Civil Service', *New Zealand Journal of Public Administration*, 30, 1, 1967.

Saumarez-Smith, W. H., *A Young Man's Country*, Salisbury, 1977.

Seton, M., *The India Office*, London, 1926.

Spangenberg, B., 'The Problem of Recruitment for the Indian Civil Service during the Late Nineteenth Century', *Journal of Asian Studies*, 1970, 341–60.

——— *British Bureaucracy in India: Status, Policy and the ICS in the Late Nineteenth Century*, Delhi, 1976.

Stewart, J., *Servant of the Raj: the Career of Sir Clarmont Skrine*, Maidenhead, 1989.

Stokes, E., *The English Utilitarians and India*, Oxford, 1959.

Tinker, H., *Viceroy: Curzon to Mountbatten*, Karachi, 1997.

Trench, C. Chenevix, *Viceroy's Agent*, London, 1987.

Trevaskis, H., *The End of an Era: Memories of the British Raj in India, 1905–1928*, Shoreham, 1973.

Trevelyan, G. O., *The Competition Wallah*, London, 1864.

Trevelyan, H., *The India We Left*, London, 1972.

—— *Public and Private*, London, 1980.

Tuker, Sir Francis, *While Memory Serves*, London, 1950.

van den Dungen, P. H., *The Punjab Tradition: Influence and Authority in Nineteenth Century India*, London, 1972.

Vernède, R. V., *The Collector's Bag: Traveller's Tales from India*, Gerrards Cross, 1992.

—— *British Life in India*, Delhi, 1995.

Wakefield, Sir Edward, *Past Imperative*, London, 1996.

Walsh, J., *Growing Up in British India*, New York, 1983.

Williams, Donovan, *The India Office, 1858–1869*, Hoshierpur, Punjab, 1983.

Woodruff, Philip, *see* Mason, P.

Ziegler, P., *Mountbatten: The Official Biography*, London, 1985.

5   THE COLONIAL ADMINISTRATIVE SERVICE; COLONIAL OFFICE; GOVERNORS

Abbott, A. W., *A Short History of the Crown Agents and Their Office* (privately published), 1959.

Allen, C., ed., *Tales from the Dark Continent: Images of British Colonial Africa in the Twentieth Century*, London, 1979.

—— *Tales from the South China Seas: Images of the British in South-East Asia in the Twentieth Century*, London, 1983.

Allen, J. de Vere, 'The Malayan Civil Service, 1874–1941', *Comparative Studies in Society and History*, 12, 2, 1970.

Lord Altrincham, *Kenya's Opportunity: Memories, Hopes and Ideas*, London, 1955.

Amery, L. S., *My Political Life: War and Peace, 1914–1929*, London, 1953.

Atkinson, M. C., ed., *Careers After Nigeria*, privately published, 1994.

Baker, C. A., 'Africanization in the Administrative Service', in A. H. M. Kirk-Greene, ed., *The Transfer of Power: the Colonial Administrator in the Age of Decolonization*, Oxford, 1979.

—— *Retreat from Empire: Sir Robert Armitage in Africa and Cyprus*, London, 1998.

Barnes, L., 'The Colonial Service', in William A. Robson, ed., *The British Civil Servant*, London, 1937.

Barr, P., *Taming the Jungle: The Men Who Made British Malaya*, London, 1977.

Bates, Darrell, *A Gust of Plumes: a Biography of Lord Twining of Godalming and Tanganyika*, London, 1972.

Bertram, Sir Anton, *The Colonial Service*, Cambridge, 1930.

Blakeley, B. L., *The Colonial Office, 1868–1892*, Durham, NC, 1972.

Bradley, Emily, *Dearest Priscilla: Letters to the Wife of a Colonial Civil Servant*, London, 1950.

Bradley, K. G., *A Career in the Oversea Civil Service*, London, 1955.

—— 'A Commonwealth Service', *Corona*, 10, 1958.

—— *Once a District Officer*, London, 1964.

Braine, B. R., 'Can We Create a Commonwealth Service?', *New Commonwealth*, 27 and 28, 1954.

Bridges, A. F. B., *So We Used To Do*, Edinburgh, 1990.

Brown, D. and M., *Looking Back at the Uganda Protectorate: Recollections of District Officers*, Dalkeith, Australia, 1996.

Buller, C., *Mr Mother Country of the Colonial Office*, London, 1840.

Burns, Sir Alan, *Colonial Civil Servant*, London, 1949.

—— 'The Future of the Colonial Service', *Colonial Review*, London, 5, 4, 1947.

Butcher, J. G., *The British in Malaya, 1880–1941*, London, 1979.

Callaway, Helen, *Gender, Culture and Empire: European Women in Colonial Nigeria*, St Antony's series, London, 1987.

Carnegie, D. W., *Letters from Nigeria*, London, 1902.

Carter, T. D., ed., *The Northern Rhodesia Record* (privately published), 1992.

Cary, Joyce, *Mister Johnson*, London, 1939.

Cell, J. W., *British Colonial Administration in the Mid-Nineteenth Century*, New Haven, 1970.

Clifford, Sir Hugh, *In Days That Are Dead*, New York, 1926.

—— *Bush-Whacking and Other Asiatic Tales and Memories*, London, 1929.

Cohen, W. B., 'The Lure of Empire: Why Frenchmen Entered the Colonial Service', *Journal of Contemporary History*, 3, 1968.

—— *Rulers of Empire: The French Colonial Service in Africa*, Stanford, 1971.

—— *Robert Delavignette on the French Empire: Selected Writings*, Chicago, 1977.

Creech Jones, A., 'The Colonial Office', *Political Quarterly*, 14, 1943.

—— 'The Colonial Service' in W. A. Robson, ed., *The Civil Service in Britain and France*, London, 1956.

—— ed., *New Fabian Colonial Essays*, London, 1959.

Crocker, W. R., *Nigeria: a Critique of British Colonial Administration*, London, 1936.

Cross, J. A., 'The Colonial Office and the Dominions before 1914', *Journal of Commonwealth Political Studies*, IV, 1966.

Crowder, M., 'The White Chiefs of Tropical Africa', in L. H. Gann and P. Duignan, eds., *Colonialism in Africa*, vol. II, Cambridge, 1970.

Dalton, Heather, 'The Experience of Colonial Governors' Wives', privately published, n. d., (? 1984).

Delavignette, R., *Freedom and Authority in French West Africa*, London, 1950.

des Voeux, Sir G. William, *My Colonial Service*, 2 vols, London, 1903.

Douglas-Home, C., *Evelyn Baring: the Last Proconsul*, London, 1978.

Fabian Colonial Bureau, *Downing Street and the Colonial Service*, London, 1942.

Fiddes, G. V., *The Dominions and Colonial Offices*, London, 1926.

Frost, R., *Enigmatic Proconsul: Sir Philip Mitchell and the Twilight of Empire*, London, 1992.

Furse, Sir Ralph, *Aucuparius: Recollections of a Recruiting Officer*, London, 1962.

Gann, L. H., *A History of Northern Rhodesia: Early Days to 1953*, New York, 1969.

Gann, L. H. and Duignan, P., *The British Rulers of Africa, 1870–1914*, Stanford, 1978.

—— *African Proconsuls: European Governors in Africa*, New York, 1978.

Gardner, T., *My first Eighty Years*, Durham, 1998.

Gartrell, Beverly, 'Colonial Wives: Villains or Victims?', in Hilary Callan and Shirley Ardener, eds, *The Incorporated Wife*, London, 1984.

Golant, W., *Image of Empire: the Early History of the Imperial Institute, 1887–1925*, Exeter, 1984.

Goodall, H., *Beloved Imperialist*, Durham, 1998.

Grantham, A., *Via Ports: From Hong Kong to Hong Kong*, Hong Kong, 1965.

Grimble, Sir Arthur, *A Pattern of Islands*, London, 1952.

Gullick, J. M., 'The Malay Administrator', *Merdeka Outlook*, 1, 1, 1957.

—— *Rulers and Residents: Influence and Power in the Malay States, 1870–1920*, Singapore, 1992.

Hall, H. L., *The Colonial Office: a History*, London, 1937.

Hamilton, W. B., 'Forty-four years at the Colonial Office', *Nineteenth Century*, lv, April 1909.

Heussler, R., *Yesterday's Rulers: the Making of the British Colonial Service*, Syracuse, 1963.

—— *The British in Northern Nigeria*, London, 1968.

—— *British Tanganyika: an Essay and Documents in District Administration*, Durham, NC, 1971.

—— *British Malaya: a Bibliographical and Biographical Compendium*, New York, 1981.

—— *British Rule in Malaya: the Malayan Civil Service and its Predecessors, 1867–1942*, New York, 1981.

—— *Completing a Stewardship: the Malayan Civil Service, 1942–1957*, Westport, Conn., 1983.

Hodgkin, T. L., *Letters from Palestine, 1932–1936*, London, 1986.

Holden, P., *Women Administrative Officers in Colonial Africa: Oxford Development Records Project*, Report 5, Rhodes House Library, 1985.

Hyam, R., *Elgin and Churchill at the Colonial Office, 1905–1908*, London, 1968.

—— 'Concubinage and the Colonial Service: the Crewe Circular (1909)', *Journal of Imperial and Commonwealth History*, XIV, 3, 1986.

—— *The Labour Government and the End of Empire, 1945–1951*, 1992.

Jeffries, Charles, *The Colonial Empire and its Civil Service*, Cambridge, 1938.

—— *Partners for Progress: the Men and Women of the Colonial Service*, London, 1949.

—— *The Colonial Office*, London, 1956.

—— 'The Future of the Overseas Service', *New Commonwealth*, 32, 1956.

—— *Transfer of Power: Problems of the Passage to Self-Government*, London, 1960.

—— 'The Colonial Service in Perspective', *Corona*, 14, 1962.

—— *Whitehall and the Colonial Service: an Administrative Memoir, 1939–1956*, London, 1972.

Jones, S. W., *Public Administration in Malaya*, London, 1952.

Keith-Roach, E., *Pasha of Jerusalem: Memoirs of a District Commissioner under the British Mandate*, London, 1994.

Kerslake, R. T., *Time and the Hour*, London, 1997.

Kirk-Greene, A. H. M., *The Principles of Native Administration in Nigeria: Selected Documents, 1900–1947*, London, 1965.

—— 'The Higher Public Service', in L. F. Blitz, ed., *The Politics and Administration of Nigerian Government*, London, 1965.

—— 'Resettling the Colonial Service', *West Africa*, 1977, 652–4 and 712.

—— 'On Governors and Governorship in British Africa', in L. H. Gann and P. Duignan, eds, *African Proconsuls: European Governors in Africa*, New York, 1978.

—— *The Transfer of Power: the Colonial Administrator in the Age of Decolonization*, Oxford, 1979.

—— 'The Progress of Proconsuls: Advancement and Migration Among the Colonial Governors of British African Territories, 1900–1965', *Journal of Imperial and Commonwealth History*, vii, 2, 1979.

—— *A Biographical Dictionary of the British Colonial Governor: I. Africa*, Stanford, 1980.

—— 'The Thin White Line: The Size of the Colonial Service in Africa', *African Affairs*, 79, 314, 1980.

—— 'The British Colonial Service and the Dominions Selection Scheme of 1923', *Canadian Journal of African Studies*, 15, 1, 1981.

—— 'The Diaspora of the District Officer', *West Africa*, 8 February, 1982.

—— 'Margery Perham and Colonial Administration', in F. Madden and D. K. Fieldhouse, *Oxford and the Idea of Commonwealth*, London, 1982

—— 'Imperial Administration and the Athletic Imperative: the Case of the District Officer in Africa', in W. J. Baker and J. A. Mangan, *Sport in Africa: Essays in Social History*, New York, 1987.

—— 'The Committee for Colonial Studies: the Minute Books of the First Quinquennium, 1943–1948', *Oxford*, XL, 1988.

—— 'Forging a Relationship with the Colonial Administrative Service', in Alison Smith and Mary Bull, eds, *Margery Perham and British Rule in Africa*, London, 1991.

—— *A Biographical Dictionary of the British Colonial Service, 1939–1966*, London, 1991.

—— *On Crown Service: A History of H.M. Colonial Service and HMOCS, 1837–1997*, London, 1999.

Kisch, M. S., *Letters and Sketches from Northern Nigeria*, London, 1910.

Knox-Mawer, June, *A Gift of Islands: Living in Fiji*, London, 1965.

Kubicek, R. V., *The Administration of Imperialism: Joseph Chamberlain at the Colonial Office*, Durham, NC, 1969.

Kuklick, H., *The Imperial Bureaucrat: the Colonial Administrative Service in the Gold Coast, 1920–1939*, Stanford, 1979.

Laski, H. J., 'The Colonial Civil Service', *Political Quarterly*, 4, 1938.

Lee, F., *Fabianism and Colonialism: the Life and Political Thought of Lord Sydney Olivier*, London, 1988.

Lee, J. M., *Colonial Development and Good Government: A Study of the Ideas Expressed by the British Official Classes in Planning Decolonization, 1934–1964*, Oxford, 1967.

Lee, J. M. and Petter, M., *The Colonial Office, War and Development Policy: Organization and the Planning of a Metropolitan Initiative, 1939–1945*, London, 1982.

Lethbridge, H. J., 'Hong Kong Cadets, 1862–1941', *Journal of the Hong Kong Branch of the Royal Asiatic Society*, 10, 1970.

Lewis, Roy and Foy, Yvonne, *The British in Africa*, London, 1971.

Lewis-Barned, J., *A Fanfare of Trumpets* (privately published), 1993.

Loch, J., *My First Alphabet* [Malayan Memoir], privately published, 1994.

Lugard, Sir Frederick, *Political Memoranda: Revision of Instructions to Political Officers on Subjects Chiefly Political and Administrative*, London, 1970 [Lagos 1919].

Lyttelton, Oliver, *The Memoirs of Lord Chandos*, London, 1962.

Meinertzhagen, R., *Kenya Diary, 1902–1906*, Edinburgh, 1957.

Morgan, D. J., *The Official History of Colonial Development*, 5 vols, London, 1980.

Mungeam, G.H., *British Rule in Kenya, 1895–1912: the Establishment of Administration in the East Africa Protectorate*, Oxford, 1966.

Nicolson, I. F. and Hughes, C. A., 'A Provenance of Proconsuls: British Colonial Governors, 1900–1914', *Journal of Commonwealth and Imperial History*, IV, 1, 1975.

Nuffield Foundation, *Report on a Visit to Nigeria*, London, 1946.

Olivier, M., *The Selected Letters and Writings of Sydney Olivier*, London, 1948.

O'Regan, J., *From Empire to Commonwealth: Reflections on a Career in Britain's Overseas Service*, London, 1994.

Parkinson, Sir Cosmo, *The Colonial Office from Within*, London, 1947.

Pearce, R., ed., *Then the Wind Changed: Nigerian Letters of R.. H. Wright*, London, 1992.

Perham, Margery, *Lugard: the Years of Authority, 1848–1945*, London, 1960.

Philips, H., *From Obscurity to Bright Dawn*, London, 1998.

Podmore, D., 'Localization in the Hong Kong Government Service', *Journal of Commonwealth Political Studies*, IX, 1971.

Pope-Hennessy, J., *Verandah: Some Episodes in the Crown Colonies, 1867–1889*, London, 1964.

Pugh, R. B., 'The Colonial Office, 1801–1925', in E. A. Benians, J. Butler and C. E. Carrington, *The Cambridge History of the British Empire*, vol. III, Cambridge, 1959.

Purcell, V., *Memoirs of a Malayan Officer*, London, 1965.

Radice, L., *Beatrice and Sidney Webb: Fabian Socialists*, London, 1984.

Ranger, T. O., 'Making Northern Rhodesia Imperial: Variations on a Royal Theme, 1924–1938', *African Affairs*, 81, 3, 1980.

—— 'The Invention of Tradition in Colonial Africa', in E. Hobsbawn and T. Ranger, eds, *The Invention of Tradition*, Cambridge, 1983.

Rathbone, R., *Murder and Politics in Colonial Africa*, London, 1993.

Roberts, A., *The Colonial Moment in Africa*, Cambridge, 1990

Robinson, K. E., *The Dilemmas of Trusteeship: Aspects of British Colonial Policy Between the Wars*, London, 1965.

Robinson, R. E., 'Sir Andrew Cohen: Proconsul of African Nationalism', in L. H. Gann and P. Duignan, eds, *African Proconsuls: European Governors in Africa*, New York, 1978.

Rooney, D., *Sir Charles Arden-Clarke*, London, 1982.

Sainty, J. C., *Colonial Office Officials, 1794–1870*, London, 1976.

Saunders, J. T., Turner, R. L. and Veale, D., *Report to the Nuffield Foundation on a Visit to Nigeria*, London, 1946.

Sharwood Smith, Sir Bryan, *But Always As Friends: Northern Nigeria and the Cameroons, 1921–1957*, London, 1969.

Sherman, A. J., *Mandate Days: British Lives in Palestine, 1918–1948*, London, 1997

Smith, J. H., *Colonial Cadet in Nigeria*, Durham, NC, 1968.

Smith, S. C., *British Relations with the Malay Rulers from Decentralization to Malayan Independence, 1930–1957*, Kuala Lumpur, 1995.

—— 'Rulers and Residents: British Relations with the Aden Protectorate, 1937–59', *Middle Eastern Studies*, 31, 3, 1995.

Snelling, R. C. and Barron, T. J., 'The Colonial Office and its Permanent Officials', in G. Sutherland, ed., *Studies in the Growth of Nineteenth Century Government*, London, 1972.

Snow, P., *The Years of Hope: Colonial Administration in the South Seas*, London, 1997.

—— *A Time of Renewal*, London, 1998.

Stigger, P., 'The District Commissioner as the Man in the Middle: East Africa', in A. H. M. Kirk-Greene, ed., *The Transfer of Power: the Colonial Administrator in the Age of Decolonization*, Oxford, 1979.

Viscount Swinton, *I Remember*, London, n.d. (? 1947).

Symes, Sir Stewart, *Tour of Duty*, London, 1946.

Taylor, Sir Henry, *Autobiography, 1800–1875*, London, 1885.

Temple, C. L., *Native Races and their Rulers*, Cape Town, 1918.

Thomas, A. R., 'The Development of the Overseas Civil Service', *Public Administration*, 35, 1958.

Thorp, E., *Ladder of Bones*, London, 1956.

Tilman, R.O., 'Nationalization of the Colonial Services in Malaya', *South Atlantic Quarterly*, 61, 1962.

—— *Bureaucratic Transition in Malaya*, Durham, NC, 1964.

Trench, C. Chenevix, *Men Who Ruled Kenya: the Kenya Administration, 1892–1963*, London, 1993.

Watkins, E., *Oscar from Africa: the Biography of O. F. Watkins*, London, 1995.

Williams, Sir Ralph, *How I Became a Governor*, London, 1913.

Winstedt, Sir Richard, *Start from Alif: Count from One*, Kuala Lumpur, 1969.

Woolf, L., *Growing: an Autobiography of the Years 1904–1911*, London, 1961.

Wraith, R. E., *Guggisberg*, London, 1967.

Youé, C. P., *Robert Thorne Coryndon: Proconsular Imperialism in Southern and Eastern Africa, 1897–1925*, Gerrards Cross, 1986.

Young, D. M., *The Colonial Office in the Early Nineteenth Century*, London, 1961.

Younger, K., *The Public Service in New States: a Study in Some Trained Manpower Problems*, London, 1960.

(**Note**: a comprehensive bibliography of Colonial Service titles is to be found in A. H. M. Kirk-Greene, *On Crown Service*, 1999)

6   THE SUDAN POLITICAL SERVICE; EGYPTIAN CIVIL SERVICE;GOVERNORS-GENERAL

Atiyah, E., *An Arab Tells His Story*, London, 1946.

Balfour-Paul, G., *The End of Empire in the Middle East: Britain's Relinquishment of Power in her Last Three Arab Dependencies*, Cambridge, 1991.

Bell, Sir Gawain, *Shadows on the Sand*, London, 1953.

—— *An Imperial Twilight*, London, 1989.

Bell, G. W. and Kirk-Greene, A. H. M., *The Sudan Political Service, 1902–1952: A Preliminary Register of Second Careers*, privately printed, 1989.

Berger, M., *Bureaucracy and Society in Modern Egypt: A Study of the Higher Civil Service*, Princeton, 1957.

Boustead, Sir Hugh, *The Wind of Morning*, London, 1972.

Boyle, C., *A Servant of the Empire: A Memoir of Henry Boyle*, London, 1938.

Carman, B. and McPherson, J., *Bimbashi McPherson: a Life in Egypt*, London, 1983.

Cecil, Lord Edward, *The Leisure of an Egyptian Official*, London, 1921.

Charnley, J., *Lord Lloyd and the Decline of the British Empire*, London, 1987.

Coles Pasha, *Recollections and Reflections*, London, n.d. (? 1919).

Collins, R. O., 'The Sudan Political Service: a Portrait of the "Imperialists"', *African Affairs*, 71, 284, 1972.

—— *Shadows in the Grass*, New Haven, 1983.

—— and Deng, F., eds, *The British in the Sudan, 1898–1956: the Sweetness and the Sorrow*, Stanford, 1984.

Colvin, Sir Auckland, *The Making of Modern Egypt*, New York, 1966.

Crabitès, P., *The Winning of the Sudan*, London, 1934.

Lord Cromer, *Modern Egypt*, 2 vols, London, 1908.

—— *Political and Literary Essays*, London, 1913.

Daly, M. W., *British Administration and the Northern Sudan*, Leiden, 1979.

—— 'Principal Office-Holders in the Sudan Government, 1895–1955', *International Journal of African Historical Studies*, 17, 2, 1984.

—— *Empire on the Nile: the Anglo-Egyptian Sudan, 1898–1934*, Cambridge, 1986.

—— *Imperial Sudan: the Anglo-Egyptian Condominium, 1934–56*, Cambridge, 1991.

Davies, R., *The Camel's Back*, London, 1957.

de Kusel, Baron, *An Englishman's Recollections of Egypt, 1863–87*, London, 1915.

Deng, F. M., 'In the Eyes of the Ruled', in R. O. Collins and F. M. Deng, *The British in the Sudan, 1898–1956: the Sweetness and the Sorrow*, Stanford, 1984.

Deng, F. M. and Daly, M., *Bonds of Silk: the Human Factor in the British Administration of the Sudan*, East Lansing, 1989.

Duncan, J. S. R., *The Sudan: a Record of Achievement*, Edinburgh, 1952.

Enright, D. J., *Academic Year*, Oxford, 1955.

Grafftey-Smith, L., *Bright Levant*, London, 1971.

—— *Hands to Play*, London, 1975.

Gorst, J. E., 'The Anglo-Egyptian Official', *Time*, 1899.

Graves, R., *Goodbye to All That*, London, 1957 (1929).

Gunther, J., *Inside Africa*, London, 1957.

Hawley, D., *Sandtracks in the Sudan*, Norwich, 1995.

Henderson, K. D. D., *The Making of the Modern Sudan: the Life and Letters of Sir Douglas Newbold*, London, 1953.

—— *Set Under Authority: Being a Portrait of the Life of the British District Officer in the Sudan, 1898–1955*, Castle Cary, 1987.

Henderson, K. D. D. and Owen, T. R. H., *Sudan Verse* (privately published), 1963.

Hopwood, D., 'Servants of Empire: Sidelights on the British in Egypt', in B. C. Bloomfield, ed., *Middle East Studies and Libraries*, London, 1980.

—— *Tales of Empire: the British in the Middle East*, London, 1989.

Jackson, H. C., *Sudan Days and Ways*, London, 1954.

Jarvis, C. S., *Desert and Delta*, London, 1968.

—— *Yesterday and Today in Sinai*, London, 1941.

Johnson, D. H., *Governing the Nuer: Documents of Percy Coriat on Nuer History and Ethnography, 1922–1931*, Oxford, 1993.

Kirk-Greene, A. H. M., *The Sudan Political Service: a Preliminary Profile*, Oxford, 1982.

—— 'Survey of the Sudan Political Service', *Sudan Studies*, I: 6, 1989; II: 7, 1990.

—— *Nationalism and Arcadianism in the Sudan: the Janus Factor in the Political Service Memoirs*, Oxford, 1993.
Keun, Odette, *A Foreigner Looks at the Sudan*, London, 1930.
Lavin, D., ed., *The Condominium Remembered: I, The Making of the Sudanese State*, 1991; *II, The Transformation of the Old Order in the Sudan*, Durham, 1993.
Lea, C. A. E., *On Trek in Kordofan: the Diaries of a British District Officer in the Sudan, 1931–1933*, Oxford, 1994.
Lively, P., *Oleander, Jacaranda: a Childhood Perceived*, London, 1994.
Lord Lloyd, *Egypt Since Cromer*, 2 vols, London, 1933, 1934.
Low, Sir Sidney, *Egypt in Transition*, London, 1913.
[Lush, M.], *A Life of Service: the Memoirs of Maurice Lush* (privately published), 1992.
[MacMichael, H.], *Sudan Political Service, 1899–1956* (privately published), n.d. (?1957).
Mangan, J. A., 'The Education of an Elite Imperial Administration: the Sudan Political Service and the British Public School System', *International Journal of African Historical Studies*, 15, 4, 1982.
Mansfield, P., *The British in Egypt*, London, 1971.
Marlowe, J., *Anglo-Egyptian Relations*, London, 1954.
—— *Cromer in Egypt*, London, 1970.
Marshall, A. H., *Local Government in the Sudan*, Khartoum, 1949.
Mellini, P., *Sir Eldon Gorst: the Overshadowed Proconsul*, Stanford, 1977.
Muggeridge, M., *Chronicles of Wasted Time*, London, 1972.
Newby, P., *Picnic at Sakkara*, London, 1955.
Nigumi, M. A., *A Great Trusteeship*, London, 1957.
Nightingale, E. H., *Memoirs*, privately published, n.d.
Parker, Sir Gilbert, *Donovan Pasha*, London, 1910.
Rameses [Jarvis, C. S.], *Oriental Spotlight*, London, 1937.
Robertson, Sir James, *Transition in Africa: from Direct Rule to Independence*, London, 1949.
Russell Pasha, *Egyptian Service, 1902–1946*, London, 1949.
Sanderson, G. N., *The Memoirs of Babikr Bedi* (Introduction), vol. 2, London, 1980.
Sarsfield-Hall, E. G., *From Cork to Khartoum: Memoirs of Southern Ireland and the Anglo-Egyptian Sudan*, 1886 to 1936, privately published, 1975.
Sattin, A., *Lifting the Veil: British Society in Egypt, 1768–1956*, London, 1988.
Schuster, Sir George, *Private Works and Public Causes: a Personal Record, 1881–1978*, Cambridge, 1979.
Sconyers, E., 'Servant or Saboteur? The Sudan Political Service during the Critical Decade, 1946–1956', *British Society of Middle East Studies Bulletin*, 14, 1, 1988.
Searight, S., *The British in the Middle East*, Letchworth, 1969.
Simpson, S. R., 'Sudan Service, 1926–1953', unpublished (? 1977).
Storrs, R., *Memoirs*, New York, 1937. English edition, *Orientations*, London, 1939.
Thesiger, W., *The Life of My Choice*, London, 1987.
Thomas, G. F., ed., *Last of the Proconsuls: Letters of Sir James Robertson*, London, 1994.
Warburg, G., *The Sudan Under Wingate: Administration in the Anglo-Egyptian Sudan, 1899–1915*, London, 1971.
Waterfield, G., *Professional Diplomat: Sir Percy Loraine*, London, 1973.
Welch, W. M., *No Country for a Gentleman: British Rule in Egypt, 1883–1907*, London, 1988.
Wingate, R., *Wingate of the Sudan*, London, 1955.
Woodward, P. M., *Condominium and Sudanese Nationalism*, London, 1979.

7   GENERAL

Adu, A. L., *Civil Services in Commonwealth Africa*, London, 1969.
Anderson, D. M. and Killingray, D., *Policing the Empire: Government, Authority and Control, 1830–1940*, Manchester, 1991.

—— *Policing and Decolonization: Nationalism, Politics and the Police, 1917–1965*, Manchester, 1992.

Arhin, K., *West African Colonial Civil Servants in the 19th Century*, Leiden, 1985.

Baker, W. S. and Mangan, J. A., *Sport in Africa: Essays on Social History*, New York, 1987.

Bamford, T. W., *The Rise of the Public Schools*, London, 1967.

Batchelor, M., *Cradle of Empire: A Preparatory School through Nine Reigns*, London, 1981.

Bello, Sir Ahmadu, *My Life*, Cambridge, 1962.

Beloff, Max, *Imperial Sunset*, 2 vols, London, 1987 and 1989.

Blundell, Sir Michael, *So Rough a Wind: Kenya Memoirs*, London, 1964.

Bottomore, T. R., *Elites and Society*, London, 1964.

—— 'The Administrative Elite', in I. L. Horowitz, ed., *The New Sociology*, 1965.

Briggs, Asa, *Victorian People*, Harmondsworth, 1965.

Buell, R. L., *The Native Problem in Africa*, 2 vols, New York, 1928.

Bullard, Sir Reader, *The Camels Must Go: an Autobiography*, London, 1961.

Cain, P. J. and Hopkins, A. G., *British Imperialism, I: Innovation and Expansion, II: Crisis and Deconstruction*, London, 1993.

Callan, Hilary and Ardener, Shirley, eds, *The Incorporated Wife*, London, 1954.

Carey, A. T., *Colonial Students: a Study of the Social Adaptation of Colonial Students in London*, London, 1956.

Carrington, C. E., *The British Overseas: Exploits of a Nation of Shopkeepers*, Cambridge, 1950.

Castronovo, D., *The English Gentleman: Images and Ideals in Literature and Society*, New York, 1987.

Clark, G., *The Balance Sheets of Imperialism*, New York, 1936.

Coates, P. D., *The China Consuls: British Consular Officers, 1843–1943*, Oxford, 1988.

Cole, G. D. H., *Studies in Class Structure*, London, 1955.

Collins, L. and Lapierre, D., *Freedom at Midnight: How Britain Gave Away an Empire*, London, 1975.

Cross, C., *The Fall of the British Empire*, London, 1968.

Cross, J. A., *Lord Swinton*, Oxford, 1982.

Crowder, M. and Ikime, O., eds, *West African Chiefs: Their Changing Status under Colonial Rule and Independence*, Ile-Ife, 1970.

Dale, H. E., *The Higher Civil Service of Great Britain*, London, 1941.

Drower, G., *British Dependent Territories: a Fistful of Islands*, London, 1992.

Dunne, P. A., 'Education, Emigration and Empire: the Colonial College', in J. A. Mangan, ed., *Benefits Bestowed: Education and British Imperialism*, Manchester, 1988.

Emerson, R., *Malaysia: a Study in Direct and Indirect Rule*, New York, 1937.

Fraser, G. Macdonald, *The World of the Public School*, London, 1977.

—— *Quartered Safely Out Here: a Reflection of the War in Burma*, London, 1992.

Fry, G. K., 'The British Career Civil Service under Challenge', *Political Studies*, 34, 4, 1966.

—— *Statesmen in Disguise: The Changing Role of the Administrative Class of the British Home Civil Service*, London, 1969.

Gander Dower, K. C., *The First to be Freed: the British Military Administration in Eritrea and Somalia, 1941–43*, London, 1944.

Gann, L. H. and Duignan, P., *Burden of Empire: an Appraisal of Western Colonialism in Africa South of the Sahara*, London, 1967.

Garner, Joe, *The Commonwealth Office 1925–68*, London, 1978.

Gathorne-Hardy, J., *The Public School Phenomenon*, London, 1977.

Gerth, H. and Mills, C. W., eds, *Essays from Max Weber*, London, 1948.

Giddens, A. and Mackenzie, G., *Social Class and the Division of Labour*, Cambridge, 1982.

Giddings, R., *Literature and Imperialism*, New York, 1991.

Gifford, P. and Louis, W. R., eds, *Britain and Germany in Africa: Imperial Rivalry and Colonial Rule*, New Haven, 1967.

—— *France and Britain in Africa: Imperial Rivalry and Colonial Rule*, New Haven, 1971.

—— *The Transfer of Power in Africa: Decolonization, 1940–1960*, New Haven, 1982.

—— *Decolonization and African Independence, 1960–1980*, New Haven, 1988.

Gill, A., *Ruling Passions*, London, 1995.

Girouard, Mark, *The Return to Camelot: Chivalry and the English Gentleman*, New Haven, 1981.

Goldsworthy, D., *The Conservative Government and the End of Empire, 1951–1957*, London, 1994.

Goldthorpe, J., 'On the Service Class, its Formation and Future', in A. Giddens and G. Mackenzie, eds, *Social Class and the Division of Labour*, Cambridge, 1982.

Goldthorpe, J. H. et al., *The Affluent Worker in the Class Structure*, Cambridge, 1955.

Gray, H. B., *Public Schools and Empire*, London, 1913.

Green, M., *Dreams of Adventure, Deeds of Empire*, New York, 1977.

—— 'The Robinson Crusoe Story', in J. Richards, ed., *Imperialism and Juvenile Literature*, Manchester, 1989.

Guttsman, W., *The British Political Elite*, London, 1963.

Lord Hailey, *An African Survey: A Study of Problems Arising in Africa South of the Sahara*, London, 1938.

—— ed., *Colonial Administration by European Powers*, London, 1947.

—— *An African Survey, Revised 1956*, London, 1957.

—— *Native Administration and Political Development in British Tropical Africa* (1942), Nendeln, Liechtenstein, 1979.

Halsey, A. H., *Change in British Society*, Oxford, 1986 (1978).

Hargreaves, J. D., *Academe and Empire: Some Overseas Connections of Aberdeen University, 1860–1970*, Aberdeen, 1994.

Harrison, B., *The History of the University of Oxford*: vol. VIII, *The Twentieth Century*, Oxford, 1994.

Henige, D. P., *Colonial Governors from the Fifteenth Century to the Present*, Madison, 1970.

Hennessy, J., 'British Education for an Elite in India', in R. Wilkinson, ed., *Governing Elites*, New York, 1969.

Hobsbawn, E. and Ranger, T., eds, *The Invention of Tradition*, Cambridge, 1983.

Horowitz, I. L., ed., *The New Sociology: Essays in Honour of C. Wright Mills*, New York, 1965.

Hunt, F. B. and Escritt, C. E., *Historical Notes on the Oxford University Appointments Committee, 1892–1950*, Oxford, 1951.

Hyam, R., *Empire and Sexuality: the British Experience*, Manchester, 1990.

—— *Britain's Imperial Century, 1815–1914: A Study of Empire and Expansion*, London, 1993 (1970).

James, L., *The Rise and Fall of the British Empire*, London, 1994.

Johnston, C. H., *The View from Steamer Point*, London, 1964.

Keay, J., *Last Post: The End of Empire in the Far East*, London, 1997.

Kelsall, R., *Higher Civil Servants in Britain from 1870 to the Present Time*, London, 1955.

Kimble, D., *A Political History of Ghana, 1850–1928*, Oxford, 1963.

Kirk-Greene, A. H. M., *The Principles of Native Administration in Nigeria*, London, 1965.

—— 'The Governors-General of Canada, 1867–1952', *Journal of Canadian Studies*, 12, 4, 1977.

—— 'Badge of Office: Sport and His Excellency in the British Empire', in J. A. Mangan, ed., *The Cultural Bond: Sport, Empire, Society*, London, 1992.

—— 'Ours to Reason Why?', *Cambridge*, 30, 1992.

—— 'Le Roi est mort! Vive le roi!: the Comparative Legacy of Chiefs after the Transfer of Power in British and French West Africa', in Anthony Kirk-Greene and Daniel Bach, eds, *State and Society in Francophone West Africa since Independence*, London, 1995.

Lapping, E., *End of Empire*, London, 1985.

Lee, J. M., *Colonial Development and Good Government*, Oxford, 1967.

Longford, J. H., 'The Consular Service and its Wrongs', *Quarterly Review*, April 1903.

Louis, J., 'Tom Brown's Imperialist Sons', *Victorian Studies*, 1975.

Louis, W. R. and Robinson, R. E., 'The US and the End of the British Empire in Africa', in P. Gifford and W. R. Louis, eds, *The Transfer of Power in Africa: Decolonization, 1940–1960*, New Haven, 1982.

Low, D. A., *Eclipse of Empire*, Cambridge, 1991.

Low, D. A. and Smith, A., eds, *History of East Africa*, vol. III, Oxford, 1976.

Lord Lugard, *The Dual Mandate in British Tropical Africa*, Edinburgh, 1922.

Mangan, J. A., *Athleticism in the Victorian and Edwardian Public School*, Cambridge, 1981.

—— *The Games Ethic and Imperialism*, Harmondsworth, 1986.

—— ed., *Benefits Bestowed: Education and British Imperialism*, Manchester, 1988.

—— *Making Imperial Mentalities: Socialization and British Imperialism*, Manchester, 1990.

—— 'Duty unto Death: Masculinity and Militarism in the Age of New Imperialism', *International Journal of the History of Sport*, 12, 2, 1995.

Marwick, A., *British Society since 1945*, Harmondsworth, 1982.

Marshall, P. J., ed., *The Cambridge Illustrated History of the British Empire*, Cambridge, 1996.

Mason, P., *The English Gentleman*, London, 1982.

Mills, C. Wright, *The Power Elite*, New York, 1956.

Morris, J., *Pax Britannica: the Climax of an Empire*, London, 1968.

—— *Heaven's Command: an Imperial Progress*, London, 1973.

—— *Farewell the Trumpets: an Imperial Retreat*, London, 1978.

Mosca, G., *The Ruling Class*, New York, 1939.

Neillands, R., *A Fighting Retreat: the British Empire, 1947–1997*, London, 1996.

Ogilvie, V., *The English Public School*, London, 1957.

Omissi, D., *Air Power and Colonial Control: the Royal Air Force, 1919–1939*, Manchester, 1990.

—— *The Sepoy and the Raj: the Indian Army, 1860–1940*, London, 1994.

Ormsby-Gore, W., *Comparative Methods of Colonial Administration in Native Dependencies*, London, 1930.

Owen, Roger and Sutcliffe, Bob, eds, *Studies in the Theory of Imperialism*, London, 1972.

Parker, P., *The Old Lie: the Great War and the Public School Ethos*, London, 1987

Parry, G., *Political Elites*, London, 1969.

Perham, Margery, *Native Administration in Nigeria*, London, 1937.

—— *Colonial Reckoning: the Reith Lectures, 1961*, London, 1963.

—— *Pacific Prelude: a Journey to Samoa and Australia*, London, 1988.

Perkin, H., *The Rise of Professional Society: England since 1880*, London, 1989.

Platt, D. C. M., *The Cinderella Service: British Consuls since 1825*, London, 1971.

Raven, S., *The English Gentleman*, London, 1961.

Lord Rennell of Rodd, *British Military Administration of Occupied Territories in Africa, 1941–47*, London, 1948.

Rich, P., *Biographies of the British Residents and Agents in the Arabian Gulf, 1783–1987*, Qatar, 1987.

—— *Elixir of Empire: English Public Schools, Ritualism, Freemasonry and Imperialism*, London 1989 (2nd edn, 1993).

—— *Chains of Empire: English Public Schools, Masonic Cabalism, Historical Causality and Imperial Clubdom*, London, 1991.

Richards, Jeffrey, ed., *Imperialism and Juvenile Literature*, Manchester, 1989.

Robinson, R. E., 'Non-European Foundations of European Imperialism: Sketch for a Theory of Imperialism', in Roger Owen and Bob Sutcliffe, eds, *Studies in the Theory of Imperialism*, London, 1972.

Shrosbree, C., *Public Schools and Private Education*, Manchester, 1988.
Sisson, C. H., *The Spirit of British Administration*, London, 1966.
Stanworth, P. and Giddens, A., *Elites and Power in British Society*, Cambridge, 1974.
Symonds, R., *The British and their Successors: a Study of the Development of the Government Services in the New States*, London, 1966.
—— *Oxford and Empire: the Last Lost Cause?*, Oxford, 1986.
Tawney, R. H., *The Acquisitive Society*, London, 1921.
Thomas, M., *The Establishment*, London, 1959.
Thompson, F. M. L., *The Cambridge Social History of Britain, 1750–1950*, Cambridge, 1990.
Thornton, A. P., *The Habit of Authority*, London, 1966.
Tidrick, K., *Empire and the English Character*, London, 1990.
Trevelyan, G. M., *English Social History: a Survey of Six Centuries from Chaucer to Queen Victoria*, New York, 1942.
Vance, N., 'The Ideal of Manliness', in B. Simon and I. Bradley, eds, *The Victorian Public School*, London, 1975.
Wakeford, J., *The Cloistered Elite: a Sociological Study of the English Public School*, London, 1969.
Walker, E. A., *The British Empire: its Structure and Spirit*, London, 1943.
Weber, Max, *The Theory of Social and Economic Organization* (ed., Talcott Parsons), London, 1947.
Wilkinson, R., *The Prefects: British Leadership and the Public School Tradition*, London, 1964.
—— *Governing Elites: Studies in Training and Selection*, New York, 1969.
Wilson, Sir Arnold, *Loyalties: Mesopotamia, 1914–1917*, Oxford, 1930.
Winchester, Simon, *Outposts: Journeys to the Surviving Relics of the British Empire*, London, 1985.
Wurgraft, L. D., *The Imperial Imagination*, Middleton, Conn., 1983.
Young, M., *The Rise of the Meritocracy*, Harmondsworth, 1953.

8 SELECTED UNPUBLISHED THESES

Alexander, H. M. L., 'Ruling Servants: the ICS, 1878–1923', University of Sydney, 1977.
Baldock, R., 'Colonial Governors and the Colonial Office, 1918–1925', Bristol, 1978.
Cashmore, T. R. H., 'Your Obedient Servants, 1895–1918', Cambridge, 1965.
Cross, C. W., 'Selection and Training of Candidates for the Indian Civil Service, 1870–1880', Vanderbilt, 1983.
Dimier, V., 'Construction et enjeux d'un discours scientifique et comparative sur l'administration coloniale en France et en Grande Bretagne, 1930–1950', Grenoble (IEP), 1999
Ewing, A., 'The Indian Civil Service, 1919–1942', Cambridge, 1980.
Gardiner, N., 'Sentinels of Empire: the British Colonial Administrative Service, 1919–1954', Yale University, 1998.
Hanes, W. T., 'The Rise and Fall of the Sudan Political Service', Austin, Tex., 1991.
Honda, T., 'Indian Civil Servants, 1892–1937: an age of transition', Oxford, 1996.
Innes, M., 'In Egyptian Service: the Role of British Officials in Egypt, 1911–1936', Oxford, 1986.
Sunderland, D., 'The Crown Agents for the Colonies', Oxford, 1996.
White, O., 'Miscegenation and Colonial Society in French West Africa, c.1900–1960', Oxford, 1996.

Index

Abbott, J. 76
Abell, George 220
Addiscombe College 90
Aden 26, 76, 161, 205, 281
Adu, A. L. 253
Africanization 158, 244, 254–59
Ainsworth, John 61–2, 148
Aitchison Committee 122, 248
Allen, Charles 80, 110, 289
Allenby, Viscount 68
amateur, cult of the 13
Amery, Julian 151
Amery, Leo 29, 35, 148, 151, 225
Anderson, Sir John 42, 210
appearance of candidates for appointment
    140–1
Archer, G. F. (later Sir Geoffrey) 209, 220, 235, 270
Arden-Clarke, Sir Charles 204, 286
Arkell, A. J. 192
Armbruster, C. H. 168
Arrowsmith, Sir Edwin 271
Arthur, A. V. 15
assimilation, cultural 152, 155, 158, 160, 163
athleticism *see* sport
Athlone, Earl of 225
Atiyah, Edward 200
Attlee, Clement 217
Auckland, Earl of 209
Australia 148, 208
Awolowo, Obafemi 285
Azikiwe, Nnamdi 286

Babu Nimr, Chief 201
Baddeley, G. M. 136
Bahamas 125, 231
Baily, Robin 187
Balfour, F. C. C. 193
Balfour-Paul, G. 199
Balliol College, Oxford 88, 92, 96
Banerjea, S. 246
Bannerman, W. 253
'Barbary Consuls' 49, 78
Baring, Sir Evelyn 35, 220, 237, 278; *see also* Cromer, Earl of
Barnes, Leonard 287
Barton, C. J. J. T. 44
Bathurst, Earl of 28
Battershill, Sir William 42
'beachcombing' 41–4, 46

Beaglehole, T. H. 105
Beames, John 110, 113
Beaton, A. C. 192
Bell, G. W. (later Sir Gawain) 50, 55, 174, 186, 192, 269–70, 283
Bell, Gertrude 84
Bell, K. N. 141
Bello, Ahmadu 286
Bentinck, Lord William 206, 208, 246
Berkeley, E. J. 58, 62
Bermuda 24, 26, 125, 202, 227, 237
Bernard, E. E. 167
Bertram, Anton 132
Bevin, Ernest 171, 250
Bevin-Sidky Pasha Protocol 50
Blackburne, Sir Kenneth 204
Blaikie, J. A. A. 193
Blair, Eric 199, 287
Blakeley, B. L. 29
Blunt, E. 35, 110, 132
Blunt, Wilfred Scawen 66
'Bog Barons' 166, 172, 185, 191, 194, 197
Bonham Carter, Edgar 167
Botham, Ian 181
Bottomore, T. B. 8–9, 22
Bourdillon, Bernard 35, 215, 234
Bourdillon, Imbert 136, 220
Bourges, Y. 163
Boustead, Hugh 178, 270
Bowden-Smith, H. N. 68
Bowers, Sir George 35
Boyd, Lord 271; *see also* Lennox-Boyd, Alan
Boyle, Harry 68, 70
Bradley, Kenneth 132
Brayne, F. L. 119
Brazzaville Conference (1944) 158–9
Briggs, Asa 9
British Council 41, 268
British Empire
    extent and growth of 23–5
    organization of 26–30
British Military Administration (BMA) 84, 269
British South Africa (BSA) Company 62–3, 141
Brooke family of Sarawak 63–4
Browne, E. G. 179, 184
Brunei 63–4, 205
Bullard, Sir Reader 82–3
Burdon, J. A. 61

Index